MARGARET SANGER

≫≫≫≫≫≫≫≫≫≫≫≪≪≪≪≪≪≪≪≪≪≪≪

An Autobiography

Kessinger Publishing's
Rare Mystical Reprints

THOUSANDS OF SCARCE BOOKS ON THESE AND OTHER SUBJECTS:

Freemasonry * Akashic * Alchemy * Alternative Health * Ancient Civilizations * Anthroposophy * Astrology * Astronomy * Aura * Bible Study * Cabalah * Cartomancy * Chakras * Clairvoyance * Comparative Religions * Divination * Druids * Eastern Thought * Egyptology * Esoterism * Essenes * Etheric * ESP * Gnosticism * Great White Brotherhood * Hermetics * Kabalah * Karma * Knights Templar * Kundalini * Magic * Meditation * Mediumship * Mesmerism * Metaphysics * Mithraism * Mystery Schools * Mysticism * Mythology * Numerology * Occultism * Palmistry * Pantheism * Parapsychology * Philosophy * Prosperity * Psychokinesis * Psychology * Pyramids * Qabalah * Reincarnation * Rosicrucian * Sacred Geometry * Secret Rituals * Secret Societies * Spiritism * Symbolism * Tarot * Telepathy * Theosophy * Transcendentalism * Upanishads * Vedanta * Wisdom * Yoga * *Plus Much More!*

DOWNLOAD A FREE CATALOG
AND
SEARCH OUR TITLES AT:

www.kessinger.net

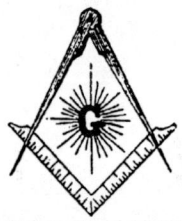

Margaret Sanger

TO ALL THE PIONEERS
OF NEW AND BETTER WORLDS TO COME

ACKNOWLEDGMENTS

My thanks are due especially to Rackham Holt for her discerning aid in organizing material and for her untiring and inspired advice during the preparation of this book; as well as to Walter S. Hayward whose able assistance has helped to make the task lighter.

In the course of preparing this narrative many books have been consulted. I trust their authors will agree with me that a bibliography in a personal history is cumbersome and accept a general but none the less grateful acknowledgment.

My admiration has always gone out to the person who can put himself in print and set down for historical purposes an exact record of his honest feelings and thoughts, even though they may seem to reflect upon many of his friends and helpers. I have not in this story hurt any one by intent. Because its thread has, of necessity, followed dramatic highlights, many people who played prominent parts have not been mentioned. These I have not forgotten, nor those numerous others who made smaller offerings. Some have pioneered in their special fields and localities; some have given generously and unfailingly of their financial help; some have volunteered in full measure their time and efforts as officers and Committee members; some have fought and labored by my side throughout the years; some have stepped in for only a brief but significant role. Although on the outskirts of the army, it is to these last as well as to those in the vanguard that the advance has been made. And particularly do I wish to thank those co-workers and members of the various staffs whose contributions can in no way be measured by their duties, and whose indefatigable, loyal devotion has been a bulwark of strength to me at all times.

It has been impossible to carry out my sincere desire to give personal and individual recognition and expression of gratitude to all. Neither a history of the birth control movement nor the part I have taken in it could be complete, however, did I not pay tribute to the integrity, valiance, courage, and clarity of vision of the men and women who, year after year, maintained their principles, and never swerved from them in a cause which belongs to all of us.

TABLE OF CONTENTS

I.	FROM WHICH I SPRING	11
II.	BLIND GERMS OF DAYS TO BE	24
III.	BOOKS ARE THE COMPASSES	33
IV.	DARKNESS THERE AND NOTHING MORE	46
V.	CORALS TO CUT LIFE UPON	58
VI.	FANATICS OF THEIR PURE IDEALS	68
VII.	THE TURBID EBB AND FLOW OF MISERY	86
VIII.	I HAVE PROMISES TO KEEP	93
IX.	THE WOMAN REBEL	106
X.	WE SPEAK THE SAME GOOD TONGUE	121
XI.	HAVELOCK ELLIS	133
XII.	STORK OVER HOLLAND	142
XIII.	THE PEASANTS ARE KINGS	153
XIV.	O, TO BE IN ENGLAND	169
XV.	HIGH HANGS THE GAUNTLET	179
XVI.	HEAR ME FOR MY CAUSE	192
XVII.	FAITH I HAVE BEEN A TRUANT IN THE LAW	210
XVIII.	LEAN HUNGER AND GREEN THIRST	224
XIX.	THIS PRISON WHERE I LIVE	238
XX.	A STOUT HEART TO A STEEP HILL	251
XXI.	THUS TO REVISIT	268
XXII.	DO YE HEAR THE CHILDREN WEEPING?	280
XXIII.	IN TIME WE CAN ONLY BEGIN	292

TABLE OF CONTENTS

XXIV.	LAWS WERE LIKE COBWEBS	306
XXV.	ALIEN STARS ARISE	316
XXVI.	THE EAST IS BLOSSOMING	327
XXVII.	ANCIENTS OF THE EARTH	337
XXVIII.	THE WORLD IS MUCH THE SAME EVERYWHERE	349
XXIX.	WHILE THE DOCTORS CONSULT	358
XXX.	NOW IS THE TIME FOR CONVERSE	369
XXXI.	GREAT HEIGHTS ARE HAZARDOUS	376
XXXII.	CHANGE IS HOPEFULLY BEGUN	392
XXXIII.	OLD FATHER ANTIC, THE LAW	398
XXXIV.	SENATORS, BE NOT AFFRIGHTED	413
XXXV.	A PAST WHICH IS GONE FOREVER	431
XXXVI.	FAITH IS A FINE INVENTION	447
XXXVII.	WHO CAN TAKE A DREAM FOR TRUTH?	461
XXXVIII.	DEPTH BUT NOT TUMULT	478
XXXIX.	SLOW GROWS THE SPLENDID PATTERN	493
	INDEX	497

MARGARET SANGER

Chapter One

FROM WHICH I SPRING

"'Where shall I begin, please your Majesty?' he asked. 'Begin at the beginning,' the King said, very gravely, 'and go on till you come to the end: then stop.'"

LEWIS CARROLL

⋙⋙⋙⋙⋙⋙⋙⋙⋙⋙⋙⋘⋘⋘⋘⋘⋘⋘⋘⋘⋘⋘⋘

THE streets of Corning, New York, where I was born, climb right up from the Chemung River, which cuts the town in two; the people who live there have floppy knees from going up and down. When I was a little girl the oaks and the pines met the stone walks at the top of the hill, and there in the woods my father built his house, hoping mother's "congestion of the lungs" would be helped if she could breathe the pure, balsam-laden air.

My mother, Anne Purcell, always had a cough, and when she braced herself against the wall the conversation, which was forever echoing from room to room, had to stop until she recovered. She was slender and straight as an arrow, with head well set on sloping shoulders, black, wavy hair, skin white and spotless, and with wide-apart eyes, gray-green, flecked with amber. Her family had been Irish as far back as she could trace; the strain of the Norman conquerors had run true throughout the generations, and may have accounted for her unfaltering courage.

Mother's sensitivity to beauty found some of its expression in flowers. We had no money with which to buy them, and she had no time to grow them, but the woods and fields were our garden. I can never remember sitting at a table not brightened with blossoms; from the first spring arbutus to the last goldenrod of autumn we had an abundance.

Although this was the Victorian Age, our home was almost free from Victorianism. Father himself had made our furniture. He had even cut and polished the slab of the big "marble-topped table," as it was always called. Only in the spare room stood a piece bought at a store—a varnished washstand. The things you made yourself were not considered quite good enough for guests. Sometimes father's visitors were doctors, teachers, or perhaps the village priest, but mostly they were the artisans of the community—cabinet makers, masons, carpenters who admired his ideas as well as shared his passion for hunting. In between tramping the woods and talking they had helped to frame and roof the house, working after hours to do this.

Father, Michael Hennessy Higgins, born in Ireland, was a nonconformist through and through. All other men had beards or mustaches—not he. His bright red mane, worn much too long according to the family, swept back from his massive brow; he would not clip it short as most fathers did. Actually it suited his finely-modeled head. He was nearly six feet tall and hard-muscled; his keen blue eyes were set off by pinkish, freckled skin. Homily and humor rippled unceasingly from his generous mouth in a brogue which he never lost. The jokes with which he punctuated every story were picked up, retold, and scattered about. When I was little they were beyond me, but I could hear my elders laughing.

The scar on father's forehead was his badge of war service. When Lincoln had called for volunteers against the rebellious South, he had taken his only possessions, a gold watch inherited from his grandfather and his own father's legacy of three hundred dollars, and had run away from his home in Canada to enlist. But he had been told he was not old enough, and was obliged to wait impatiently a year and a half until, on his fifteenth birthday, he had joined the Twelfth New York Volunteer Cavalry as a drummer boy.

One of father's adventures had been the capture of a Confederate captain on a fine mule, the latter being counted the more valuable acquisition to the regiment. We were brought up in the tradition that he had been one of three men selected by Sherman for bravery. That made us very proud of him. Better not start anything with father; he could beat anybody! But he himself had been appalled by the brutalities of war; never thereafter was he interested in fighting, unless perhaps his Irish sportsmanship cropped out when two well-matched dogs were set against each other.

Immediately upon leaving the Army father had studied anatomy, medicine, and phrenology, but these had been merely for perfecting his skill in modeling. He made his living by chiseling angels and saints out of huge blocks of white marble or gray granite for tombstones in cemeteries. He was a philosopher, a rebel, and an artist, none of which was calculated to produce wealth. Our existence was like that of any artist's family—chickens today and feathers tomorrow.

Christmases were on the poverty line. If any of us needed a new winter overcoat or pair of overshoes, these constituted our presents. I was the youngest of six, but after me others kept coming until we were eleven. Our dolls were babies—living, wriggling bodies to bathe and dress instead of lifeless faces that never cried or slept. A pine beside the door was our Christmas tree. Father liked us to use natural things and we had to rely upon ingenuity rather than the village stores, so we decorated it with white popcorn and red cranberries which we strung ourselves. Our most valuable gift was that of imagination.

We had little time for recreation. School was five miles away and we had to walk back and forth twice a day as well as perform household duties. The boys milked the cow, tended the chickens, and took care of Tom, the old white horse which pulled our sleigh up and down the hill. The girls helped put the younger children to bed, mended clothes, set the table, cleaned the vegetables, and washed the dishes. We accepted all this with no sense of deprivation or aggrievement, being, if anything, proud of sharing responsibility.

And we made the most of our vacations. There were so many of us that we did not have to depend upon outsiders, and Saturday afternoons used to put on plays by ourselves in the barn. Ordinarily we were shy about displaying emotions; we looked upon tears and temper in other homes with shocked amazement as signs of ill-breeding. Play-acting, however, was something else again. Here we could find outlet for histrionic talent and win admiration instead of lifted eyebrows. I rather fancied myself as an actress, and often mimicked some of the local characters, to the apparent pleasure of my limited audience of family and neighbors. It was not long before I slipped into declaiming. *The Lady of Lyons* was one of my specialties:

> This is thy palace, where the perfumed light
> Steals through the mist of alabaster lamps,
> And every air is heavy with the sighs
> Of orange groves, and music from the sweet lutes
> And murmurs of low fountains, that gush forth
> I' the midst of roses!

All outdoors was our playground, but I was not conscious at the time of my love for the country. Things in childhood change perspective. What was taken for granted then assumes great significance in later life. I knew how the oak tree grew and where the white and yellow violets could be found, and with a slight feeling of superiority I showed and expounded these mysteries to town children. Not until pavements were my paths did I realize how much a part of me the country was, and how I missed it.

We were all, brothers and sisters alike, healthy and strong, vigorous and active; our appetites were curtailed only through necessity. We played the same games together and shared the same sports—baseball, skating, swimming, hunting. Nevertheless, except that we all had red hair, shading from carrot to bronze, we were sharply distinct physically. The girls were small and feminine, the boys husky and brawny. When I went out into the world and observed men, otherwise admirable, who could not pound a nail or use a saw, pick, shovel, or ax, I was dumfounded. I had always taken for granted that any man could make things with his hands.

I expected this even of women. My oldest sister, Mary, possessed, more than the rest of us, an innate charm and gentleness. She could do anything along domestic lines—embroidery, dress making, tailoring, cooking; she could concoct the most delicious and unusual foods, and mix delicate pastries. But she was also an expert at upholstering, carpentry, painting, roofing with shingles or with thatch. When Mary was in the house, we never had to send for a plumber. She rode gracefully and handled the reins from the carriage seat with equal dexterity; she could milk a cow and deliver a baby; neighbors called her to tend their sick cattle, or, when death came, to lay out the body;

she tutored in mathematics and Latin, and was well-read in the classics, yet she liked most the theater, and was a dramatic critic whose judgment was often sought. In all that she did her sweetness and dearness were apparent, though she performed her many kindnesses in secret. She left the home roof while I was still a child, but she never failed to send Christmas boxes in which every member of the family shared, each gift beautifully wrapped and decorated with ribbons and cards.

My brothers were ardent sportsmen, although they might not have been outstanding scholars. They could use their fists and were as good shots as their father. For that matter, we all knew how to shoot; any normal person could manage a gun. Father was a great hunter. Our best times were when friends of his came to spend the night, talking late, starting early the next morning for the heavy woods which were full of foxes, rabbits, partridge, quail, and pheasant.

Someone was always cleaning and oiling a gun in the kitchen or carrying food to the kennels. The boys were devoted to their fox and rabbit hounds, but father lavished his affection on bird dogs. Our favorite came to us unsought, unbought, and I had a prideful part in his joining the family. One afternoon I was sitting alone by the nameless brook which ran by our house, clear and cool, deep enough in some places to take little swims on hot summer days. I was engaged in pinning together with thorns a wreath of leaves to adorn my head when a large, white dog ambled up, sniffed, wagged his tail, and seemed to want to belong. This was no ordinary cur, but a well-bred English setter which had evidently been lost. How father would love him!

Even though the dog had no collar, I was slightly uneasy as to my right of ownership. One conspicuous brown-red spot on the back of his neck simplified my problem. Unobtrusively I slipped him into the barn, tied him up, selected a brush, dipped it in one of the cans of paint always on hand, and multiplied the one spot by ten. For a day, waiting for them to dry, I fed him well with food filched from the rations of the other kennel occupants, then led him forth, his hairy dots stiffened with paint, and offered him to father as a special present.

Accepting the gift in the spirit in which it was intended, father admired the dog's points, and, with an unmistakable twinkle, lent himself to a deception which, of course, could deceive nobody. When Saturday night came, the neighborhood looked the animal over; none knew him so we named him Toss and admitted him to the house. Later he bred with an Irish setter of no importance, and one of the resultant puppies, Beauty, shared his privileges.

Toss, as well as everybody else, subscribed to the idea that the "artist" in father must be catered to. With the first sound of his clearing his throat in the morning Toss picked up the shoes which had been left out to be cleaned, and carried them one at a time to the bedroom door, then stood wagging his tail, waiting to be patted. Father's shoes were always polished, his trousers always creased. Every day, even when going to work, he put on spotless white shirts with starched collars and attachable cuffs; these were something of a luxury, because they had to be laundered at home, but they got done somehow.

Father took little or no responsibility for the minute details of the daily tasks. I can see him when he had nothing on hand, laughing and joking or reading poetry. Mother, however, was everlastingly busy sewing, cooking, doing this and that. For so ardent and courageous a woman he must have been trying, and I still wonder at her patience. She loved her children deeply, but no one ever doubted that she idolized her husband, and through the years of her wedded life to her early death never wavered in her constancy. Father's devotion to mother, though equally profound, never evidenced itself in practical ways.

The relation existing between our parents was unusual for its day; they had the idea of comradeship and not merely loved but liked and respected each other. There was no quarreling or bickering; none of us had to take sides, saying, "Father is right," or, "Mother is right." We knew that if we pleased one we pleased the other, and such an atmosphere leaves its mark; we felt secure from emotional uncertainty, and were ourselves guided towards certainty in our future. We were all friends together, though not in the modern sense of familiarity. A little dignity and formality were always maintained and we were invariably addressed by our full names. The century of the child had not yet been ushered in.

In those days young people, unless invited to speak, were seen and not heard. But as soon as father considered us old enough to have ideas or opinions, we were given full scope to express them, no matter how adolescent. He hated the slavery of pattern and following of examples and believed in the equality of the sexes; not only did he come out strongly for woman suffrage in the wake of Susan B. Anthony, but he advocated Mrs. Bloomer's bloomers as attire for women, though his wife and daughters never wore them. He fought for free libraries, free education, free books in the public schools, and freedom of the mind from dogma and cant. Sitting comfortably with his feet on the table he used to say, "You should give something back to your country because you as a child were rocked in the cradle of liberty and nursed at the breast of the goddess of truth." Father always talked like that.

Although the first Socialist in the community, father also took single tax in his stride and became the champion and friend of Henry George. *Progress and Poverty* was one of the latest additions to our meager bookshelf. He laughed and rejoiced when he came upon what to him were meaty sentences, reading them aloud to mother, who accepted them as fine because he said they were fine. The rest of us all had to plow through the book in order, as he said, to "elevate the mind." To me it still remains one of the dullest ever written.

Mother's loyalty to father was tested repeatedly. Hers were the responsibilities of feeding and clothing and managing on his income, combined with the earnings of the oldest children. But father's generosity took no cognizance of fact. Once he was asked to buy a dozen bananas for supper. Instead, he purchased a stalk of fifteen dozen, and on his way home gave every single one to schoolboys and girls playing at recess. On another occasion he showed up with eight of a neighbor's children; the ninth had been quarantined for diphtheria. They lived with us for two months, crowded into our beds, tucked in between us at the table. Mother welcomed them as she did his other guests. The house was always open. She was not so much social-minded as inherently hospitable. But with her frail body and slim pocketbook, it took courage to smile.

Once only that I can remember did mother's patience give way. That was when father invaded her realm too drastically and invited

Henry George to lecture at the leading hotel—with banquet thrown in. From the money saved for the winter coal he had taken enough to entertain fifty men whose children were well-fed and well-clothed. This was the sole time I ever knew my parents to be at odds, though even then I heard no quarreling words. Whatever happened between them I was not sure, but father spent several days wooing back the smile and light to her eyes.

After Henry George's visit we had to go without coal most of the winter.

With more pleasure than *Progress and Poverty* I recall a *History of the World, Lalla Rookh, Gulliver's Travels,* and *Aesop's Fables.* The last-named touched a sympathetic, philosophical chord in father. "Wolf! Wolf!" and "Sour Grapes" were often used to exemplify the trifling imperfections to which all human beings were subject. For his parables he drew also on the Bible, the most enormous volume you ever laid eyes on, brass bound, with heavy clasps, which was the repository of the family statistics; every birth, marriage, death was entered there. The handbooks to father's work were the physiologies, one of which was combined with a materia medica. These were especially attractive to me, perhaps because they were illustrated with vivid plates, mostly red and blue, and described the fascinating, unknown interior of the human body.

Neighbors were constantly coming to father for help. "What do you think is the matter with this child?" Even without a thermometer he could tell by feeling the skin whether you were feverish. He prescribed bismuth if the diagnosis were "summer complaint," castor oil if you had eaten something which had disagreed with you, and always sulphur and molasses in the spring "to clean the blood."

Father's cure-all was whiskey—"good whiskey," which "liberated the spirit." There was nothing from a deranged system to a depressed mind that it could not fix up. He never drank alone, but no masculine guest ever entered the door or sat down to pass the time of day without his producing the bottle. "Have a little shtimulant?"

The chief value of whiskey to father, however, was medicinal. If mumps turned into a large, ugly abscess, he put the blade of his jackknife in the fire, lanced the gland, and cleaned the wound with whiskey—good whiskey. When my face was swollen with erysipelas, he painted it morning, afternoon, and evening with tincture of iodine; the doctor had so ordered. I was held firmly in place each time this torture was inflicted, and, as soon as released, jumped and ran screaming and howling into the cellar, where I plunged my burning face into a pan of cool buttermilk until the pain subsided. This went on for several days, and I was growing exhausted from the dreaded iodine. Finally father decided to abandon the treatment and substitute good whiskey. Then I recovered.

As necessary to father as the physiologies was a book by the famous phrenologist, Orson Fowler, under whom he had studied. Father believed implicitly that the head was the sculptured expression of the soul. Straight or slanting eyes, a ridge between them, a turned-up nose, full lips, bulges in front of or behind the ears—all these traits had definite meaning for him. A research worker had to be inquisitive, a seeker with more than normal curiosity-bumps; a musician had to have order and time over the eyebrows; a pugilist could not be made but had to have the proper protuberances around the ears.

One of father's phrases was, "Nature is the perfect sculptor; she is never wrong. If you seem to have made a mistake in reading, it is because you have not read correctly." He himself seldom made a mistake, and his reputation spread far and wide. Young men in confusion of mind and the customary puzzled, pre-graduation state came from Cornell and other colleges to consult him about their careers. He examined heads and faces, told them where he thought their true vocations lay, and supplemented this advice later with voluminous interested correspondence. I could not help picking up his principles and some of his ardor, though I have never been able to analyze character so well. No amount of front or salesmanship could divert him, whereas I have often been taken in by a person's self-confidence and estimation of himself.

In the predominantly Roman Catholic community of Corning, set crosses in the cemeteries were the rule for the poor and, before they went out of style, angels in various poses for the rich. I used to watch father at work. The rough, penciled sketch indicated little; even less did the first unshaped block of stone. He played with the hard, unyielding marble as though it were clay, making a tiny chip for a mouth, which grew rounder and rounder. A face then emerged, a shoulder, a sweep of drapery, praying hands, until finally the whole stood complete with wings and halo.

Although Catholics were father's best patrons, by nature and upbringing he deplored their dogma. He joined the Knights of Labor, who were agitating against the influx of unskilled immigrants from Catholic countries, and this did not endear him to his clientele. Still less did his espousal of Colonel Robert G. Ingersoll, a man after his own heart, whose works he had eagerly studied and used as texts. Once when the challenger was sounding a ringing defiance in near-by towns, father extended an invitation to speak in Corning and enlighten it. He collected subscriptions to pay for the only hall in town, owned by Father Coghlan. A notice was inserted in the paper that the meeting would be held the following Sunday, but chiefly the news spread by word of mouth. "Better come. Tell all your friends."

Sunday afternoon arrived, and father escorted "Colonel Bob" from the hotel to the hall, I trotting by his side. We pushed through the waiting crowd, but shut doors stared silently and reprovingly—word had also reached Father Coghlan.

Some were there to hear and learn, others to denounce. Antipathies between the two suddenly exploded in action. Tomatoes, apples, and cabbage stumps began to fly. This was my first experience of rage directed against those holding views which were contrary to accepted ones. It was my first, but by no means my last. I was to encounter it many times, and always with the same bewilderment and disdain. My father apparently felt only the disdain. Resolutely he announced the meeting would take place in the woods near our home an hour later, then led Ingersoll and the "flock" through the streets. I trudged along again, my small hand clasped in his, my head held just as high.

Who cared for the dreary, dark, little hall! In the woodland was room for all. Those who had come for discussion sat spell-bound on the ground in a ring around the standing orator. For them the booing had been incidental and was ignored. I cannot remember a word of what Colonel Ingersoll said, but the scene remains. It was late in the afternoon, and the tall pines shot up against the fiery radiance of the setting sun, which lit the sky with the brilliance peculiar to the afterglows of the Chemung Valley.

Florid, gray-haired Father Coghlan, probably tall in his prime, came to call on mother. He was a kindly old gentleman, not really intolerant. Shutting the hall had been a matter of principle; he could not have an atheist within those sacred walls. But he was willing to talk about it afterwards. In fact, he rather enjoyed arguing with rebels. He was full of persuasion which he used on mother, begging her to exercise her influence with father to make him refrain from his evil ways. She had been reared in the faith, although since her marriage to a freethinker which had so distressed her parents, she had never attended church to my knowledge. The priest was troubled to see her soul damned when she might have been a good Catholic, and implored her to send her children to church and to the parochial school, to stand firm against the intrusion of godlessness. Mother must have suffered from the conflict.

None of us realized how the Ingersoll episode was to affect our well-being. Thereafter we were known as children of the devil. On our way to school names were shouted, tongues stuck out, grimaces made; the juvenile stamp of disapproval had been set upon us. But we had been so steeped in "heretic" notions that we were not particularly bothered by this and could not see ahead into the dark future when a hard childhood was to be made harder. No more marble angels were to be carved for local Catholic cemeteries, and, while father's income was diminishing, the family was increasing.

Occasionally big commissions were offered him in adjacent towns where his reputation was still high, and he was then away for days at a time, coming back with a thousand or fifteen hundred dollars in his pocket; we all had new clothes, and the house was full of plenty. Food was bought for the winter—turnips, apples, flour, potatoes. But then again a year might pass before he had another one, and meanwhile we had sunk deeply into debt.

Towards orthodox religion father's own attitude remained one of tolerance. He looked upon the New Testament as the noble story of a human being which, because of ignorance and the lack of printing presses, had become exaggerated. He maintained that religions served their purpose; some people depended on them all their lives for discipline—to keep them straight, to make them honest. Others did not need to be so held in line. But subjection to any church was a reflection on strength and character. You should be able to get from yourself what you had to go to church for.

When we asked which Sunday School we should attend, he suggested, "Try them all, but be chained to none." For a year or two I made the rounds, especially at Christmas and Easter, when you received oranges and little bags of candy. It was always cold at the Catholic church and the wooden benches were very bare and hard; some seats were upholstered in soft, red cloth but these were for the rich, who rented the pews and put dollars into the plate at collection. I never liked to see the figure of Jesus on the cross; we could not help Him because He had been crucified long ago. I much preferred the Virgin Mary; she was beautiful, smiling—the way I should like to look when I had a baby.

Saying my prayers for mother's benefit was spasmodic. Ethel, the sister nearest my own age, was more given than I to religious phases and I could get her in bed faster if I said them with her. One evening when we had finished this dutiful ritual I climbed on father's chair to kiss him good night. He asked quizzically, "What was that you were saying about bread?"

"Why, that was in the Lord's Prayer, 'Give us this day our daily bread.'"

"Who were you talking to?"

"To God."

"Is God a baker?"

I was shocked. Nevertheless, I rallied to the attack and replied as best I could, doubtless influenced by conversations I had heard. "No, of course not. It means the rain, the sunshine, and all the things to make the wheat, which makes the bread."

"Well, well," he replied, "so that's the idea. Then why don't you say so? Always say what you mean, my daughter; it is much better."

Thereafter I began to question what I had previously taken for granted and to reason for myself. It was not pleasant, but father had taught me to think. He gave none of us much peace. When we put on stout shoes he said, "Very nice. Very comfortable. Do you know who made them?"

"Why, yes, the shoemaker."

We then had to listen to graphic descriptions of factory conditions in the shoe industry, so that we might learn something of the misery and poverty the workers suffered in order to keep our feet warm and dry.

Father never talked about religion without bringing in the ballot box. In fact, he took up Socialism because he believed it Christian philosophy put into practice, and to me its ideals still come nearest to carrying out what Christianity was supposed to do. Unceasingly he tried to inculcate in us the idea that our duty lay not in considering what might happen to us after death, but in doing something here and now to make the lives of other human beings more decent. "You have no right to material comforts without giving back to society the benefit of your honest experience," was one of his maxims, and his parting words to each of his sons and daughters who had grown old enough to fend for themselves were, "Leave the world better because you, my child, have dwelt in it."

This was something to live up to.

Chapter Two

BLIND GERM OF DAYS TO BE

"I think, dearest Uncle, that you cannot really wish me to be the 'mamma d'une nombreuse famille,' for I think you will see the great inconvenience a large family would be to us all, and particularly to the country, independent of the hardship and inconvenience to myself; men never think, at least seldom think, what a hard task it is for us women to go through this very often."
QUEEN VICTORIA *to* KING LEOPOLD

OFTEN when my brothers and sisters and I meet we remind each other of funny or exciting adventures we used to have, but I never desire to live that early part of my life again. Childhood is supposed to be a happy time. Mine was difficult, though I did not then think of it as a disadvantage nor do I now.

It never occurred to me to ask my parents for pocket money, but the day came during my eighth year when I was desperately in want of ten cents. *Uncle Tom's Cabin* was coming to town. On Saturday afternoon I started out with one of my playmates, she with her dime, I with nothing but faith. We reached the Corning Opera House half an hour early. The throng at the entrance grew thicker and thicker. Curtain time had almost come, and still no miracle. Nevertheless, I simply had to get into that theater. All about me had tickets or money or both. Suddenly I felt something touch my arm—the purse of a woman who was pressed close beside me. It was open, and I could see the coveted coins within. One quick move and I could have my heart's desire. The longing was so deep and hard that it blotted out everything except my imperative need. I *had* to get into that theater.

I was about to put out my hand towards the bag when the doors were thrown wide and the crowd precipitately surged forward. Being small, I was shoved headlong under the ropes and into the safety of the nearest seat. But I could take no joy in the play.

As I lay sleepless that night, after a prayer of thanks for my many blessings, the crack of Simon Legree's whip and the off-stage hounds baying after Eliza were not occupying my mind. Their places were taken by pictures of the devil which had tempted me and the hand of God which had been stretched out to save me from theft.

Following this experience, which might have been called a spiritual awakening, I began to connect my desires with reasoning about consequences. This was difficult, because my feelings were strong and urgent. I realized I was made up of two Me's—one the thinking Me, the other, willful and emotional, which sometimes exercised too great a power; there was danger in her leadership and I set myself the task of uniting the two by putting myself through ordeals of various sorts to strengthen the head Me.

To gain greater fortitude, I began to make myself do what I feared most—go upstairs alone to bed without a light, go down cellar without singing, get up on the rafters in the barn and jump on the haystack thirty feet below. When I was able to accomplish these without flinching I felt more secure and more strong within myself.

But ahead of me still lay the hardest task of all.

Across the Chemung some friends of ours had a farm. Their orchard, heavy with delectable apples, seemed to me a veritable Eden. But to reach it by the wooden wagon bridge was three miles around; my brothers preferred the shorter route over the high, narrow, iron span of the Erie Railroad, under which the river raced deep and fast. The spaced ties held no terrors for their long legs, and they often swung them over the edge while they fished the stream beneath. When I made the trip father and brother each gave a hand to which I clung fiercely, and they half lifted me over the gaps which my shorter legs could hardly compass unaided. Held tight as I was, I became dizzy from the height, and a panic of terror seized me. In fact, the mere thought of the journey, even so well supported, made me feel queer.

The younger children were forbidden to cross the bridge unaccompanied. But I had to conquer my fear; I had to take that walk alone. I trembled as I drew near. The more I feared it, the more determined I was to make myself do it. I can recall now how stoically I put one foot on the first tie and began the venturesome and precarious passage stretching endlessly ahead of me. I dared not look down at the water; I wanted terribly to see that my feet were firmly placed, but could not trust my head.

About halfway over I heard the hum of the steel rails. My second dread had come upon me—the always possible train. I could not see it because of the curve at the end of the bridge. The singing grew louder as it came closer. I knew I could not get across in time, and turned towards the nearest girder to which I might cling. But it was six feet away. The engine with a whistling shriek burst into view—snorting, huge, menacing, rushing. I stumbled and fell.

In those days I was plump, and this plumpness saved me. Instinctively my arms went out and curled around the ties as I dropped between them. There I dangled over space. The bridge shook; the thunder swelled; the long, swift passenger cars swooped down. I was less than three feet from the outer rail, and a new terror gripped me. I had seen the sharp, sizzling steam jet out as locomotives drew near the station. I screwed my eyes shut and prayed the engineer not to turn on the steam.

After the blur of wheels had crashed by I could feel nothing. I hung there, I do not know how long, until a friend of my father, who had been fishing below, came to my rescue. He pulled up the fat, aching little body, stood me on my feet again, asked me severely whether my father knew where I was, gave me two brisk thwacks on the bottom, turned my face towards home, and went back to his rod and line.

After waiting a few moments to think matters over I realized that it would be impossible for me to retrace my course. Common sense aided me. The journey forward was no further than the journey back. I stepped ahead far more bravely, knowing if I could reach the end of the bridge I would never be so terrified again. Though bruised and sore I continued my cautious march and had as good a time at the farm as usual.

However, I returned home by the wooden bridge, the long way round, but the practical one.

When Ethel asked me that night why I was putting vaseline under my arms I merely said I had scratched myself. Foolhardiness was never highly esteemed by anyone in the family. Though resourcefulness was taken for granted, running into unnecessary danger was just nonsense, and I wanted no censure for my disobedience.

We were seldom scolded, never spanked. If an unpleasant conversation were needed, no other brother or sister was witness; neither parent ever humiliated one child in front of another. This was part of the sensitiveness of both. Mother in particular had a horror of personal vehemence or acrimonious arguments; in trying to prevent or stop them she would display amazing intrepidity— separating fighting dogs, fighting boys, even fighting men.

Peacemaker as she was, on occasion she battled valiantly for her loved ones, resenting bitterly the corporal punishment then customary in schools. Once my brother Joe came home with his hands so swollen and blistered that he could not do his evening chore of bringing in the wood. Mother looked carefully at them and asked him what had happened. He explained that the teacher had fallen asleep and several boys had started throwing spitballs. When one had hit her on the nose she had awakened with a little scream.

Most children had the trick of burying their faces behind their big geographies and appearing to be studying the page with the most innocent air in the world. But Joe had no such technique. He was doubled up with laughter. The teacher first accused him of throwing the spitball, and, when he denied it, insisted that he name the culprit. She had been embarrassed by her ridiculous situation, and had turned her emotion into what she considered righteous indignation. Joe had paid the penalty of being beaten for his unwillingness to violate the schoolboy code of honor.

This was injustice and the surest road to mother's wrath. She started at once the long trip to the school. When she found no one there, she walked more miles to the teacher's home. Reproof was called for and she administered it. But that was not enough. She then demanded that father go to the Board of Education and take Joe with him. There would have been no sleeping in the house with her had he not done so. An investigation was promised, which soon afterwards resulted in the teacher's dismissal.

The teachers at the Corning School were no worse than others of their day; many of them were much better. The brick building was quite modern for the time, with a playground around it and good principals to guide it. Its superiority was due in part to the influence of the Houghtons, the big industrialists of the town. For three generations they had been making glassware unsurpassed for texture and beauty of design, and hardly a family of means in the country did not have at least one cut-glass centerpiece from Corning. The factories had prospered during the kerosene lamp era, and now, with electricity coming into its own, they were working overtime blowing light bulbs.

Corning was not on the whole a pleasant town. Along the river flats lived the factory workers, chiefly Irish; on the heights above the rolling clouds of smoke that belched from the chimneys lived the owners and executives. The tiny yards of the former were a-sprawl with children; in the gardens on the hills only two or three played. This contrast made a track in my mind. Large families were associated with poverty, toil, unemployment, drunkenness, cruelty, fighting, jails; the small ones with cleanliness, leisure, freedom, light, space, sunshine.

The fathers of the small families owned their homes; the young-looking mothers had time to play croquet with their husbands in the evenings on the smooth lawns. Their clothes had style and charm, and the fragrance of perfume clung about them. They walked hand in hand on shopping expeditions with their children, who seemed positive in their right to live. To me the distinction between happiness and unhappiness in childhood was one of small families and of large families rather than of wealth and poverty.

In our home, too, we felt the economic pressure directly ascribable to size. I was always apprehensive that we might some day be like the families on the flats, because we always had another baby coming, another baby coming. A new litter of puppies was interesting but not out of the ordinary; so, likewise, the cry of a new infant never seemed unexpected. Neither excited any more curiosity than breakfast or dinner. No one ever told me how they were born. I just knew.

I was little more than eight when I first helped wash the fourteen-and-a-half-pound baby after one of mother's deliveries. She had had a "terrible hard time," but father had pulled her through, and, in a few weeks, tired and coughing, she was going about her work, believing as usual that her latest was the prize of perfect babies. Mother's eleven children were all ten-pounders or more, and both she and father had a eugenic pride of race. I used to hear her say that not one of hers had a mark or blemish, although she had the utmost compassion for those who might have cleft palates, crossed eyes, or be "born sick."

Late one night a woman rushed into our house, seeking protection, clutching in her shawl a scrawny, naked baby, raw with eczema. When her hysteria was calmed sufficiently we learned that her husband had reeled home drunk and had thrown the wailing infant out into the snow. Father was all for summoning the police, but mother was too wise for that. She dispatched him to talk to the man while she gave the weeping woman a warm supper and comforted her. Father returned shortly to say it was safe for her to go back to the multitude of other children because her husband had fallen asleep. Ugly and taciturn though he was I could picture him coming home after a hard day's work to a household racked with the shrieks of the suffering little thing. I could see that he too was pathetic and a victim; I had sympathy for his rage.

But mother did lose one of her beautiful babies. Henry George McGlynn Higgins had been named for two of the rebel figures father most admired. The four-year-old was playing happily in the afternoon; a few hours later he was gasping for breath. Father heated his home-made croup kettle on the stove until it boiled, and then carried it steaming to be put under the blanket which rose like a covered wagon above the bed. As soon as he realized that home remedies were failing he sent for the doctor. But events moved too swiftly for him. We had gone to bed with no suspicion that by morning we should be one less. I was shocked and surprised that something could come along and pick one of us out of the world in so few hours.

I had no time, however, to consider the bewildering verity of death. We all had to turn to consoling mother. Perhaps unconsciously she had subscribed to father's theory that the face was the mirror to the soul. She complained she had no picture of her lovely boy, and kept reminding herself of the fine shape of his head, the wide, well-set eyes, the familiar contours which had been wiped forever from her sight, and might soon be sponged from her memory as well.

Mother's grief over her lost child increased father's. Because in part he blamed himself, he was desperate to assuage her sorrow. The day after the burial he was constantly occupied in his studio, and when evening fell he took me affectionately by the hand asking me to stay up and help him on a piece of work he was about to do. I agreed willingly.

About eleven o'clock we went forth together into the pitch-black night, father pushing ahead of him a wheelbarrow full of tools and a bag of plaster of Paris. We walked on and on through the stillness for fully two miles to the cemetery where the little brother had been buried. Father knew every step, but it was scary and I clung to his hand.

Just beyond the gateway father hid the lighted lantern in the nearby bushes over a grave and told me to wait there unless I heard somebody coming. He expected me to be grown up at the age of ten. Nerves meant sickness; if any child cried out in the night it was merely considered "delicate." Consequently I obeyed and watched, shivering with cold and excitement, darting quick glances at the ghostly forms of some of father's monuments which loomed out of the darkness around me. I could hear the steady chunk, chunk, chunk of his pick and shovel, and the sharper sound when suddenly he struck the coffin.

Father had taken it as a matter of course that I should understand and had not explained what he was about to do. But I never questioned his actions. I did not know there was a law against a man's digging up his own dead child but, even had I known, I would have believed that the law was wrong.

We traveled back the long, weary way, arriving home in the early hours of the morning. Nothing was said to mother or to the others about that amazing night's adventure; I was not told to keep silent, but I knew there was mystery in the air and it was no time to talk.

For two evenings I worked with father, helping him break the death mask, mold and shape the cast. I remember the queer feeling

I had when I discovered some of the hair which had stuck in the plaster. On the third day, just after supper, father said to us all, "Will you come into the studio?" With tender eyes on mother he uncovered and presented to her the bust of the dead little boy.

She was extraordinarily comforted. Though to me the model, perfect as it was, seemed lifeless, every once in a while she entered the studio, took off the cloth which protected it from the dust, wept and was relieved, re-covered it and went on.

Not one of us dared to utter a word of criticism about mother's adored and adoring husband; nevertheless her soul was harassed at times by his philosophy of live and let live, by his principles against locked doors and private property. She was merely selfless. Often when one of her children was feverish she went to the kitchen pump for water so that it might be cooler and fresher for parched lips. Once, groping her way on such an errand, she stumbled over a tramp who had taken advantage of the unlatched door and lay sprawled on the floor. She rushed back to arouse father, telling him he must put the man out. But he only turned over on his side and muttered, "Oh, let him alone. The poor divil needs sleep like the rest of us."

Another night mother was awakened by noises outside. "Father," she called, "there's somebody at the hencoop!"

"What makes you think so?" he answered sleepily.

"I hear the chickens. They wouldn't make a noise unless somebody was in there. Get up!"

Obediently father put on his trousers and coat; not even before thieves would he appear in his nightshirt out of his bedroom. He proceeded to the kitchen door, and, holding a lamp on high, addressed the two men, one of whom was handing out chickens to the other, "Hey, you, there! What do you mean by coming to a man's house in the middle of the night and shtealing his chickens? What kind of citizens are you?"

This seemed to mother no time for a moral lecture. "Why don't you go out?" she prodded.

"It's raining."

"Give me the lamp!" she demanded, exasperated.

She started towards our nearest neighbor, splashing through the little brook, getting her feet wet, calling, "Some one's in our chicken house!"

Our neighbor armed himself and came running. A man with a gun sent the marauders scurrying up the hill. That was mother's philosophy. I think father fell in her estimation for a few days after this. She expected him to be the guardian of the home, but he was never that. His liberal views were so well known that our house was marked with the tramp's patrin of the first degree. "Always get something here. Never be turned away." If it happened to be pay day they could count on a quarter as well as a meal.

One particular evening we were expecting father home, his pockets bulging with the money from his latest commission, but by nightfall he had not yet returned. When mother heard a rap at the door she went eagerly to open it. Two ragged strangers were standing there.

"Is the boss in?"

"No, but I'm looking for him any minute."

"We want something to eat."

With no more ceremony than was customary among the knights of the open road they pushed through the door and made for the kitchen, plainly knowing their way about.

"How dare you come into this house!" exclaimed mother indignantly. "Toss! Beauty!" she cried sharply. The fear in her voice brought the dogs lunging downstairs with fangs bared and hackles bristling. They leaped at the backs of the uninvited guests.

Father came in a few hours later. The door was swinging wide, the snow was blowing in. Torn scraps of clothing, spots of blood were about, and mother was unconscious on the floor. He poured whiskey down her throat. "It was only good whiskey that brought you to," he often said afterwards, recalling his alarm. He used the same remedy to pull her through the ensuing six weeks of pneumonia. But he had been so thoroughly worried that his generosity towards tramps lessened and his largesse was curtailed.

After this illness mother coughed more than ever and it was evident the pines were not helping her. Father decided to move; the house was so obviously marked and he had to be gone so much he thought it unsafe for us to live alone so far away.

Chapter Three

BOOKS ARE THE COMPASSES

So we moved into town, still on the western hills. It marked the beginning of my adolescence, and such breaks are always disturbing. In the house in the woods we had all been children together, but now some of us were growing up.

Nevertheless, there were always smaller ones to be put to bed, to be rocked to sleep; there were feet and knees to be scrubbed and hands to be washed. Although we had more space, home study sometimes seemed to me impossible. The living room was usually occupied by the older members of the family, and the bedrooms were cold. I kept up in my lessons, but it was simply because I enjoyed them.

In most schools teachers and pupils then were natural enemies, and the one I had in the eighth grade was particularly adept at arousing antagonism. She apparently disliked her job and the youngsters under her care as much as we hated her. Sarcasm was both her defense and weapon of attack. One day in mid-June I was delayed in getting off for school. Well aware that being tardy was a heinous crime, I hurried, pulling and tugging at my first pair of kid gloves, which Mary had just given me. But the bell had rung two minutes before I walked into the room, flushed and out of breath.

The teacher had already begun the class. She looked up at the interruption. "Well, well, Miss Higgins, so your ladyship has arrived at last! Ah, a new pair of gloves! I wonder that she even deigns to come to school at all."

Giggles rippled around me as I went into the cloakroom and laid down my hat and gloves. I came back, praying the teacher would pay no more attention to me, but as I walked painfully to my seat she continued repeating with variations her mean comments. Even when I sat down she did not stop. I tried to think of something else, tried not to listen, tried to smile with the others. I endured it as long as I could, then took out my books, pyramiding arithmetic, grammar, and speller, strapped them up, rose, and left.

Mother was amazed when I burst in on her. "I will never go back to that school again!" I exclaimed dramatically. "I have finished forever! I'll go to jail, I'll work, I'll starve, I'll die! But back to that school and teacher I will never go!"

As older brothers and sisters drifted home in the evening, they were as horrified as mother. "But you have only two weeks more," they expostulated.

"I don't care if it's only an hour. I will not go back!"

When it became obvious that I would stick to my point, mother seemed glad to have me to help her. I was thorough and strong and could get through a surprising amount of work in no time. But the rest of the family was seriously alarmed. The next few months were filled with questions I could not answer. "What can you ever be without an education?" "Are you equipped to earn a living?" "Is factory life a pleasant prospect? If you don't go back to school, you'll surely end there."

"All right. I'll go to work!" I announced defiantly. Work, even in the factory, meant money, and money meant independence. I had no rebuttal to their arguments; I was acting on an impulse that transcended reason, and must have recognized that any explanation as to my momentous decision would sound foolish.

Then suddenly father, mother, my second older sister Nan, and Mary, who had been summoned to a family council, tried other tactics. I was sent for two weeks to Chautauqua, there to take courses, hear lectures from prominent speakers, listen to music. This was designed to stimulate my interest in education and dispel any idea I might have of getting a job.

My impulse had been misconstrued. I was not rebelling against education as such, but only against that particular school and that particular teacher. When fall drew near and the next session was at hand I was still reiterating that I would not go back, although I still had no answer to Nan's repeated, "What are you going to do?"

Nan was perhaps the most inspiring of all my brothers and sisters. The exact contrary to father, she wanted us all to conform and was in tears if we did not. To her, failure in this respect showed a lack of breeding. Yet even more important than conformity was knowledge, which was the basis for all true culture. She herself wanted to write, and had received prizes for stories from *St. Nicholas* and the *Youth's Companion.* But the family was too dependent upon the earnings of the older girls, and she was obliged to postpone college and her equally ardent desire to study sculpture. She became a translator of French and German until these aspirations could be fulfilled.

At the time of my mutiny Nan was especially disturbed. "You won't be able to get anywhere without an education," she stated firmly. She and Mary, joining forces, together looked for a school, reasonable enough for their purses, but good enough academically to prepare me for Cornell. Private education was not so expensive as today, and families of moderate means could afford it. My sisters selected Claverack College and Hudson River Institute, about three miles from the town of Hudson in the Catskill Mountains. Here, in one of the oldest coeducational institutions in the country, the Methodist farmers of the Dutch valley enrolled their sons and daughters; unfortunately it is now gone and with it the healthy spirit it typified. One sister paid my tuition and the other bought my books and clothes; for my board and room I was to work.

Going away to school was epochal in my life. The self-contained family group was suddenly multiplied to five hundred strangers, all living and studying under one roof. The girls' dormitory was at one end, the boys' at the other, but we shared the same dining room and sat together in classes; occasionally a boy could call on a girl in the reception hall if a teacher were present. I liked best the attitude of the teachers; they were not so much policemen as companions and friends, and their instruction was more individual and stimulating than at Corning.

I did not have money to do things the other girls did—go off for week-ends or house-parties—but waiting on table or washing dishes did not set me apart. The work was far easier than at home, and a girl was pretty well praised for doing her share. At first the students all appeared to me uninteresting and lacking in initiative. I never found the same imaginative quality I was used to in my family, but as certain ones began to stand out I discovered they had personalities of their own.

I had been at Claverack only a few days and was still feeling homesick when in the hall one morning I encountered the most beautiful creature I had ever seen. Long hair flying from her shoulders, she was so slender and wraithlike that she seemed unreal. I have never since been so moved by human loveliness as I was by Esther's. I cried at night because I sensed it was something I could not reach. Even her clothes were unlike all others. Many girls envied their taste and quality, but I knew they belonged to her of right. Of every book I had read she was the heroine come alive.

Worlds apart though we were in tradition, looks, behavior, experience, Esther and I had the same romantic outlook. Having aspirations for the theater, she remained only one year and then left to attend Charles Frohman's dramatic school. I had been too overpowered by my admiration for her to be happy in it, and it kept me from caring particularly about anyone else. Nevertheless, I am convinced that in any interchange of affection the balance is unequal; one must give and the other be able to receive. My second year I was the recipient of devotion from a younger girl similar to that I had showered upon Esther. The loyalty and praise of Amelia Stuart, my laughing friend, fed all the empty spaces in my heart. She was gay and clever, a Methodist by upbringing but not by conviction. Each Sunday afternoon, given over to the reading of the Bible, we received permission to study together in my room, and there occupied ourselves dutifully, I in mending and darning, and she reading aloud, but interspersing solemn passages with ridiculous exaggerations. What was intended to be a serious exercise of the spirit was turned into merriment.

My friendship with these two girls has been interrupted, but never broken.

Very shortly after my arrival at Claverack I had been infected by that indefinable, nebulous quality called school spirit, and before long was happily in the thick of activities. Assembly was held in the chapel every morning, during which we all in turn had to render small speeches and essays, or recite selections of poetry. I had a vivid feeling of how things should be said, putting more dramatic fervor into certain lines than my limited experience of the theater would seem to explain, and on this account the elocution teacher encouraged me to have faith in my talents.

Every girl, I suppose, at some time or other wants to be an actress. Mary had taken me to the theater now and then, once when Maude Adams was playing Juliet to John Drew's Romeo, and had gone to some pains to explain to me the difference between artistes like Mary Anderson or Julia Marlowe and mere beauty as such. She would not have been pleased at my seeing Lillian Russell, which I did during a Christmas holiday in New York; Lillian Russell was too glamorous and, furthermore, she was said to have accepted jewelry from men.

One vacation I announced to my family that I was thinking of a stage career. Disapproval was evident on all sides. Father pooh-poohed; Mary alone held out hope. She said I had ability and should go to dramatic school in New York as soon as I had finished Claverack. She would apply immediately to Charles Frohman to have me understudy Maude Adams, whom I at least was said to resemble physically—small and with the same abundant red-brown hair. Lacking good features I took pride only in my thick, long braids. I used to decorate them with ribbons and admire the effect in the mirror.

The application was made; I was photographed in various poses with and without hats. A return letter from the school management came, enclosing a form to be filled in with name, address, age, height, weight, color of hair, eyes, and skin.

But additional data were required as to the exact length of the legs, both right and left, as well as measurements of ankle, calf, knee, and thigh. I knew my proportions in a general way. Those were the days when every pack of cigarettes carried a bonus in the shape of a pictured actress, plump and well-formed. In the gymnasium the girls had compared sizes with these beauties. But to see such personal information go coldly down on paper to be sent off to strange men was unthinkable. I had expected to have to account for the quality of my voice, for my ability to sing, to play, for grace, agility, character, and morals. Since I could not see what legs had to do with being a second Maude Adams, I did not fill in the printed form nor send the photographs, but just put them all away, and turned to other fields where something beside legs was to count.

Chapel never bored me. I had come to dislike ritual in many of the churches I had visited—kneeling for prayer, sitting for instruction, standing for praise. But in a Methodist chapel anyone could get up and express a conviction. Young sprouts here were thinking and discussing the Bible, religion, and politics. Should the individual be submerged in the state? If you had a right to free thought as an individual, should you give it up to the church?

We scribbled during study periods, debated in the evenings. Without always digesting them but with great positiveness I carried over many of the opinions I had heard expounded at home. To most of the boys and girls those Saturday mornings when the more ambitious efforts were offered represented genuine torture. They stuttered and stammered painfully. I was just as nervous—more so probably. Nevertheless, I was so ardent for suffrage, for anything which would "emancipate" women and humanity, that I was eager to proclaim theories of my own.

Father was still the spring from which I drank, and I sent long letters home, getting in reply still longer ones, filled with ammunition about the historical background of the importance of women —Helen of Troy, Ruth, Cleopatra, Poppaea, famous queens, women authors and poets.

When news spread that I was to present my essay, "Women's Rights," the boys, following the male attitude which most people have forgotten but which every suffragette well remembers, jeered and drew cartoons of women wearing trousers, stiff collars, and smoking huge cigars. Undeterred, I was spurred on to think up new arguments. I studied and wrote as never before, stealing away to the cemetery and standing on the monuments over the graves. Each day in the quiet of the dead I repeated and repeated that speech out loud. What an essay it was!

"Votes for Women" banners were not yet flying, and this early faint bleating of mine aroused little enthusiasm. I turned then to an equally stern subject. The other students had automatically accepted the cause of solid money. I espoused free silver. At Chautauqua I had heard echoes of those first notes sounded by Bryan for the working classes. The spirit of humanitarianism in industry had been growing and swelling, but it was still deep buried. I believe any great concept must be present in the mass consciousness before any one figure can tap it and set it free on its irresistible way.

I had not seen the "Boy Orator of the Platte," but the country was ringing with his words, "You shall not press down upon the brow of labor this crown of thorns; you shall not crucify mankind upon a cross of gold." These rich and sonorous phrases made me realize the importance of clothing ideas in fine language. Far more, however, they struck a solemn chord within me. I, also, in an obscure and unformed way, wanted to help grasp Utopia from the skies and plant it on earth. But what to do and where to start I did not know.

Due to my "advanced ideas," for a time, at least, I am sorry to say, it was chiefly the grinds with whom I "walked in Lovers' Lane," nodding wisely and answering their earnest aspirations with profound advice. But this did not last. Soon I was going through the usual boy and girl romances; each season brought a new one. I took none of them very seriously, but adroitly combined flirtatiousness with the conviction that marriage was something towards which I must develop. Therefore I turned the vague and tentative suggestions of my juvenile beaus by saying, "I would never think of jumping into marriage without definite preparation and study of its responsibilities." Practically no women then went into professions; matrimony was the only way out. It seems ages ago.

Various pranks occurred at Claverack, such as taking walks with boys out of bounds and going forbidden places for tea. Towards the end of my last year I thought up the idea that several of us should slip out through the window and down to the village dance hall where our special admirers would meet us. About eleven-thirty, in the midst of the gayety, in walked our principal, Mr. Flack, together with the preceptress who had come for the "ladies." We were all marched back to school, uneasy but silent.

The next morning I received a special invitation to call at The Office. I entered. Mr. Flack, a small, slight, serious, student type of man, with a large head and high brow, was standing with his back to me. I sat down. He gave me no greeting but kept on at his books. To all appearances he did not know I was there. Then, without looking around, he said, "Miss Higgins, don't you feel rather ashamed of yourself for getting those girls into trouble last night, by taking them out and making them break the rules? They may even have to be sent home."

Although surprised that he should have known I was the one responsible, I could not deny it, but it flashed across my mind at first that someone must have told him. He went on with rapid flow, almost as though talking to himself, "I've watched you ever since you came and I don't need to be told that you must have been the ringleader. Again and again I've noticed your influence over others. I want to call your attention to this, because I know you're going to use it in the future. You must make your choice—whether to get yourself and others into difficulty, or else guide yourself and others into constructive activities which will do you and them credit."

I do not quite recall what else he said, but I have never forgotten going out of his room that day. This could not exactly be called a turning point in my life, but from then on I realized more strongly than before that there was a something within myself which could and should be kept under my control and direction.

Long afterwards I wrote to thank Mr. Flack for his wisdom in offering guidance instead of harsh discipline. He died a few years later, and I was glad I had been able to place a rose in his hand rather than on his grave.

I spent three happy years at Claverack. The following season I decided to try my hand at teaching, then a lady-like thing to do. A position was open to me in the first grade of a new public school in southern New Jersey. The majority of the pupils—Poles, Hungarians, Swedes—could not speak English. In they came regularly. I was beside myself to know what to do with eighty-four children who could not understand a word I said. I loved those small, black-haired and tow-headed urchins who became bored with sitting and, on their own, began stunts to entertain themselves. But I was so tired at the end of the day that I often lay down before dressing for dinner and awakened the next morning barely in time to start the routine.

In very short order I became aware of the fact that teaching was not merely a job, it was a profession, and training was necessary if you were to do it well. I was not suited by temperament, and therefore had no right to this vocation. I had been struggling for only a brief while when father summoned me home to nurse mother.

She was weak and pale and the high red spots on her cheek bones stood out startlingly against her white face. Although she was now spitting blood when she coughed we still expected her to live on forever. She had been ill so long; this was just another attack among many. Father carried her from room to room, and tried desperately to devise little comforts. We shut the doors and windows to keep out any breath of the raw March air, and in the stuffy atmosphere we toiled over her bed.

In an effort to be more efficient in caring for mother I tried to find out something about consumption by borrowing medical books from the library of the local doctor, who was a friend of the family, and in doing this became so interested in medicine that I decided definitely I would study to be an M.D. When I went back for more volumes and announced my decision the doctor gave them to me, but smiled tolerantly, "You'll probably get over it."

I had been closely confined for a long time when I was invited to Buffalo for the Easter holidays to meet again one of the boys by whom I had been beaued at Claverack. Mother insisted that I needed a vacation. Mary and Nan were both there; I could stay with them, and we planned a pleasant trip to Niagara Falls for the day.

With me out of the way mother sent off the little children one by one on some pretext or another. She had more difficulty with father. The fire bricks in the stove had split and she told him he must go to town and get new ones. Much against his will, because he was vaguely unquiet, he started for the foundry. He had left only because mother seemed to want it so much, but when he had walked a few blocks, he found he could not go on. For some Celtic mystic reason of his own he turned abruptly around and came back to the house. Mother was gasping in death. All the family hated scenes, she most of all. She had known she was to die and wanted to be alone.

It was a folk superstition that a consumptive who survived through the month of March would live until November. Mother died on the thirty-first of the month, leaving father desolate and inconsolable. I came flying home. The house was silent and he hardly spoke. Suddenly the stillness of the night was broken by a wailing and Toss was found with his paws on the coffin, mourning and howling—the most poignant and agonizing sound I had ever heard.

I had to take mother's place—manage the finances, order the meals, pay the debts. There was nothing left for my clothing nor for any outside diversions. All that could be squeezed out by making this or that do had to go for shoes or necessities for the younger brothers. Mend, patch, sew as you would, there was a limit to the endurance of trousers, and new ones had to be purchased.

To add to my woes, father seemed to me, who was sensitive to criticism, suddenly metamorphosed from a loving, gentle, benevolent parent into a most aggravating, irritating tyrant; nobody in any fairy tale I had ever read was quite so cruel. He who had given us the world in which to roam now apparently wanted to put us behind prison bars. His unreasonableness was not directed towards the boys, who were in bed as soon as lessons were done, but towards his daughters, Ethel and me. Whatever we did was wrong. He objected particularly to young men.

Ethel was receiving the concentrated attention of Jack Byrne. Father in scolding her said she should mix more. My beaus were a little older than the ones I had had at school, and more earnest in their intentions. Though not one really interested me—their conversation seemed flat, consisting of foolish questions and smart, silly replies—father scolded me also about them, "Why aren't you serious like your sister? Can't you settle yourself to one? Do you have to have somebody different every evening?"

Messages were coming to me from a young man going West, postmarked Chicago or San Francisco. These daily letters and sometimes telegrams as well, were not father's idea of wooing. What could anyone have to say every day? To his way of thinking, a decent man came to the house and did his talking straight; he sat around with the family and got acquainted. Father said, "That fellow's a scoundrel. He's too worldly. He's not even known in town."

We had to ask permission whether Tom or Jack or Henry could call. Without reason or explanation father said, "No," and that was an end to it. If we went out, we had to be back at ten and give an account of ourselves.

Then came the climax. Ethel and I had gone to an open-air concert. On the stroke of ten we were a full block away from home running with all our might. When we arrived, three minutes late, the house was in utter darkness—not a sight nor sound of a living creature anywhere. We banged and knocked. We tried the front door, the back, and the side, then again the front. It opened part way; father looked out, reached forth a hand and caught Ethel's arm, saying, "This outrageous behavior is not your fault. Come in." With that he pulled her inside, and the door slammed, leaving me in the dark, stunned and bewildered. I did not know this monster.

Hurt beyond words, I sat down on the steps, worrying not only about this night but about the next day and the next, concerned over the children left at home with this new kind of father. I was sure if I waited long enough he would come out for me, but it was a chilly evening in October. I had no wrap, and began to grow very cold.

I walked away from the house, trying to decide where I should go and what I should do. I could not linger on the streets indefinitely, with the possibility of encountering some tipsy factory hand or drummer passing through. At first there seemed no one to turn to. Finally, exhausted by stress of emotion, I went to the home of the girl who had been with us at the concert. She had not yet gone to bed, and her mother welcomed me so hospitably that I shall be eternally grateful. The next morning she lent me carfare to go to Elmira, where I had friends with whom I could stay.

Meantime father had found me gone. He had dressed and tramped up and down First Street, searching every byway, inquiring whether I had been seen. When he had returned at daybreak to find me still missing he had sent word to Mary, who received his message at almost the same time as one from me, telling her not to worry; I was all right. Both of them urged me to come back to Corning, and in a few days I did so, taking up again my responsibilities. Father and I tried to talk it over, but we could not meet on the old ground; between us a deep silence had fallen.

Father had almost stopped expounding; instead, he was reading more. Debs had come on his horizon, and the Socialist papers cropping up all over the country were appearing in the house. From the Free Library, which he had helped to establish years earlier, he was borrowing Spencer, who was modern for that time, and other books on sociology.

I had given up encouraging young men to see me, but I, too, was patronizing the library. My books were fiction. "All nonsense," father snorted at the mention of such titles as *Graustark, Prisoners of Hope,* or *Three Musketeers.* The word "novel" was still shocking to many people, and he classed them all as "love stories." "Read to cultivate and uplift your mind. Read what will benefit you in the battle of life," he admonished. But I continued my escape from the daily humdrum to revel in romances, devouring them in the evenings and hiding them under the mattress during the day.

One noon when I was waiting for the children to come in to lunch I was buried in *David Harum,* finding it very funny, and did not hear father enter. He stood ominously in the doorway. I should have felt trapped, but, instead, without warning and without reason, the old love flamed up again. I laughed and laughed. I was no longer afraid nor did I care for his scowls or his silly old notions. The long silence was broken.

"Do listen to this." And I started reading. The frown began to melt away and soon father too was chuckling. This was the first laughter that had been heard in that dreary household since mother's death. The book disappeared into his room, and soon thereafter he was caught seeking more of "that nonsense."

At last I realized why father had been so different. He had been lonely for mother, lonely for her love, and doubtless missed her ready appreciation of his own longings and misgivings. Then, too, he had always before depended on her to understand and direct us. He was probably a trifle jealous, though not consciously, because he considered jealousy an animal trait far beneath him, and refused to recognize it in himself. Nevertheless, beaus had been sidetracking the affections of his little girls. So oppressed had he been by his sense of responsibility that he had slipped in judgment and in so doing slid into the small-town rut of propriety. His belated discipline, caused by worry and anxiety, was merely an attempt to guide his children.

I, however, considered the time had passed for such guidance. I had to step forth by myself along the experimental path of adulthood. Though the immediate occasion for reading medical books had ceased with mother's death, I had never, during these months, lost my deep conviction that perhaps she might have been saved had I had sufficient knowledge of medicine. This was linked up with my latent desire to be of service in the world. The career of a physician seemed to fulfill all my requirements. I could not at the moment see how the gap in education from Claverack to medical school was to be bridged. Nevertheless, I could at least make a start with nursing.

But father, though he proclaimed his belief in perfect independence of thought and mind, could not approve nursing as a profession, even when I told him that some of the nicest girls were going into it. "Well, they won't be nice long," he growled. "It's no sort of work for girls to be doing." My argument that he himself had taught us to help other people had no effect.

Father's notions, however, were not going to divert me from my intention; no matter how peaceful the home atmosphere had become, still I had to get out and try my wings. For six months more we jogged along, then, just a year after mother had died, Esther asked me to visit her in New York. I really wanted to train in the city, but her mother knew someone on the board of the White Plains Hospital, which was just initiating a school. There I was accepted as a probationer.

Chapter Four

DARKNESS THERE AND NOTHING MORE

⋙-⋙-⋙-⋙-⋙-⋙-⋙-⋙-⋙-⋙-⋙-⋙-⋙-⋘-⋘-⋘-⋘-⋘-⋘-⋘-⋘-⋘-⋘-⋘-⋘

THE old White Plains Hospital, not at all like a modern institution, had been a three-storied manor house, long deserted because two people had once been found mysteriously dead in it and thereafter nobody would rent or buy. The hospital board, scoffing at superstition, had gladly purchased it at the low price to which it had been reduced. However, in spite of rearrangements and redecorating, many people in White Plains went all the way to the Tarrytown Hospital rather than enter the haunted portals.

Once set in spacious grounds the building was still far back from the road; a high wall immediately behind it shut off the view of the next street and nothing could be seen beyond except the roof of what had been the stable. The surrounding tall trees made it shadowy even in the daytime. To reach the office you had to cross a broad pillared veranda. Parlor and sitting room had been thrown together for the male ward, and an operating room had been tacked on to the rear. The great wide stairway of fumed oak, lighted at night by low-turned gas jets, swept up through the lofty ceiling. On the second floor were the female ward and a few private rooms. The dozen or so nurses slept in the made-over servants' quarters under the gambrel roof.

Student nurses in large modern hospitals have little idea what our life was like in a small one thirty-five years ago. The single bathroom on each floor was way at the back. We did not have a resident interne, and, consequently, had to depend mainly upon our own judgment. Since we had no electricity, we could not ring a bell and have our needs supplied, and had to use our legs for elevators. A probationer had to learn to make dressings, bandages, mix solutions, and toil over sterilizing. She put two inches of water in the washboiler, laid a board across the bricks placed in the bottom, and balanced the laundered linen and gauze on top. Then, clapping on the lid, she set the water to boiling briskly, watched the clock, and when the prescribed number of minutes had elapsed the sterilizing was over.

The great self-confidence with which I entered upon my duties soon received a slight shock. One of our cases was an old man from the County Home. He complained chiefly of pains in his leg and, since his condition was not very serious, the superintendent of nurses left him one afternoon in my care. This was my first patient. When I heard the clapper of his little nickeled bell, I hurried with a professional air to his bedside.

"Missy, will you please bandage up my sore leg? It does me so much good."

Having just had my initial lesson in bandaging, I was elated at this opportunity to try my skill. I set to work with great precision, and, when I had finished, congratulated myself on a neat job, admiring the smooth white leg. My first entry went on his record sheet.

A little later the superintendent, in making her rounds, regarded the old man perplexedly.

"Why have you got your leg bandaged?"

"I asked the nurse to do it for me."

"Why that leg? It's the other one that hurts."

"Oh, she was so kind I didn't want to stop her."

I bowed my head in embarrassment, but I was young and eager, and it did not stay bowed long.

Within a short period I considered myself thoroughly inured to what many look upon as the unpleasant aspects of nursing; the sight of blood never made me squeamish and I had watched operations, even on the brain, with none of the usual sick giddiness. Then one day the driver of a Macy delivery wagon, who had fallen off the seat, was brought in with a split nose. I was holding the basin for the young doctor who was stitching it up, when one of the other nurses said something to tease him. He dropped his work, leaving the needle and cat-gut thread sticking across the patient's nose, and chased her out of the room and down the hall. The patient, painless under a local anesthetic, gazed mildly after them; but the idea that doctor and nurse could be so callous as to play jokes horrified me.

When pursuer and pursued returned they found me in a heap on the floor, the basin tipped over beside me, instruments and sponges scattered everywhere. The patient was still sitting quietly waiting for all the foolishness to stop. I am glad to say this was the one and only time I ever fainted on duty.

The training, rigid though it was, would have been far less difficult had it not been for the truly diabolical head nurse. In the morning she was all smiles, so saintly that you could almost glimpse the halo around her head. But as the day wore on the demon in her appeared. She could always think up extra things for you to do to keep you from your regular afternoon two hours off. This was particularly hard on me because I had developed tubercular glands and was running a temperature. In my second year I was operated on, and two weeks later assigned to night duty, where I stayed for three awful months.

My worst tribulation came during this period. People then seldom went to hospitals with minor ailments; our patients were commonly the very sick, requiring a maximum of attention. There was no orderly and I could use only my left hand because my right shoulder was still bandaged. I took care of admissions, entered case histories, and, when sharp bells punctuated the waiting stillness, sometimes one coming before I had time to answer the first, I pattered hurriedly up and down the three flights, through the shadows relieved only by the faint red glow from the gas jets. I suppose adventures were inevitable.

One night an Italian was picked up on the street in a state of almost complete exhaustion, and brought to the hospital. He was so ill with suspected typhoid that he should have had a "special," but instead he was placed in the ward. An old leather couch stood across the windows, and whenever a pause came in my duties I lay down.

From there I could keep an eye on my new patient. Sick as he was he insisted on making the long trip through the ward to the bathroom. I could not explain how unwise this was, because he could not understand a word of English. He must have reeled out of his bed between thirty and forty times.

Just as the early spring dawn came creeping in the window behind me I grew drowsy. I was on the point of dozing off when some premonition warned me and I opened my eyelids enough to see the man reach under his pillow, take something out cautiously, glide from his bed. Spellbound I watched him slithering soft-footedly as he edged his way towards me. I seemed to be hypnotized with sleep and could not stir. He came nearer and nearer with eyes fixed, hands behind him. Suddenly I snapped into duty, arose quickly, ordered him back to bed, and ran ahead to straighten his sheets and pillows, not realizing my danger until he loomed over me, his knife in his hand. Before he could thrust I grabbed his arm and held it. Though I was small-boned I had good muscles, and he was very ill.

Meanwhile, another patient snatched up his bell and rang, and rang and rang. Nobody answered. The nurses were too far away to hear; the other patients in the ward were unable to help me. But the man quickly used up what little energy he had, and I was able to get the knife from him, push him back in bed, and take his temperature. I assumed he had suddenly become delirious.

About seven o'clock I answered a summons to the front door and found three policemen who wanted to know whether we had an Italian patient. "Indeed we have," I answered feelingly and called the superintendent.

When the red tape was unwound, I learned that my Italian belonged to a gang which had been hiding in a cave between Tarrytown and White Plains, holding up passers-by. Amongst them they had committed five murders. The others had all been hunted down, but this man's collapse had temporarily covered his whereabouts. The attack on me had apparently been merely incidental to his attempt at escape through the open window behind me. He was carried off to the County Hospital Jail, and I was not sorry to see him go.

After this incident an orderly was employed and, though he was allowed to sleep at night, it was reassuring to know he could be called in an emergency. The emergency soon arose. A young man of about twenty-five, of well-to-do parents, was admitted as an alcoholic. I remember that I was impressed by the softness of his handshake when I greeted him. He had the first symptoms of delirium tremens but he was now perfectly conscious and needed no more than routine attention.

Sometime in the night the new arrival asked me to get him a drink of water. When I came back into the room and offered it to him he knocked me into the corner ten feet away. As my head banged against the wall, he leaped out of bed after me and reached down for my throat. Though half-stunned and off my feet, I yet had more strength than the man whose flabby muscles refused to obey his will. The patient in the adjoining bed rang and in a few moments the orderly came to my assistance. Between us we got the poor crazed youth into a strait jacket. The doctor who was summoned could do nothing and in the morning the young man mercifully died.

To differentiate between things real and things imaginary was not always easy at nighttime. One morning about two o'clock I was writing my case histories in the reception office on the ground floor just off the veranda. Both window and curtain behind my back were up about ten inches to let in the cool, moist air. Abruptly I had a feeling that eyes were staring at me. I could not have explained why; I had heard no sound, but I was certain some human being was somewhere about. Anybody who had come on legitimate business would have spoken. Perhaps it was another patient with a knife. Should I sit still? Should I look behind me?

I turned my head to the window, and there an ugly, grinning face with a spreading, black mustache was peering in at me. It might have been disembodied; all I could see was this extraordinary face, white against the inky background. It was not a patient, not anyone in my charge. Relief was immediate and action automatic. I seized the long window pole, twice as tall as I, dashed to the outer door, and shooed him off the veranda. He ran for the outer gate while I brandished my weapon after him.

Such instantaneous responses must have been the result of having in childhood sent fears about their business before they could gather momentum. Now I could usually act without having to think very much about them or be troubled in retrospect. They were all in the day's work of the night nurse.

Probably the fact that I was low in vitality made me more susceptible to mental than physical influences. Realistic doctors and stern head nurses tried to keep tales of the old house from the probationers, but not very successfully. When the colored patients could not sleep they used to tell us weird stories, and with rolling eyes solemnly affirmed they were true. One old darky woman, hearing the hoot owls begin their mournful "too-whoo, too-whoo," would sit straight up in her bed and whisper, "Suppose dat callin' me? Hit's callin' someone in dis hospital."

Again and again after the owls' hooting either somebody in the hospital died, or was brought in to die from an accident. Reason told me this was pure coincidence, but it began to get on my nerves.

And then stranger events, for which I could find no explanation, followed. Once when I was making my rounds a little after midnight, I turned into the room occupied by the tubercular valet of a member of the Iselin family. I had expected him to be sleeping quietly because he was merely there to rest up before being sent back home to England, but he was awake and asked for ice. I started for the refrigerator, which was two flights down in the cellar. But at the top of the stairs I suddenly stopped short—"One—Two—Three!" I heard dull, distinct knocks directly under the stairway.

Not one, single, tangible thing near by could have made those sounds. In the space of a few seconds I took an inventory of the importance of my life as compared to the proper care of my patient. I had to walk deliberately down those steps, not knowing what might be lying in wait for me below. As I stepped on the first tread the same knocks came again—"One—Two—Three!"

I tried to hurry but it seemed to me that each foot had tons of iron attached to it. The little red devils of night lights blinked at me and seemed to make the shadows thicker in the corners. But nothing clutched me from the dim and ghostly hall. I got down those steps somehow and passed through the dining room into the kitchen. There I paused again. Should I take a butcher knife with me? "No, I won't do that," I answered myself resolutely, and started for the cellar stairs.

For the third time came the knocking. Glancing to right and left, my back against the dark, I crept down, reached the refrigerator, broke off some chunks of ice with trembling hands, put them in a bowl, steeled myself while I chopped them into still finer pieces, and set out on the return, my feet much lighter going up than down.

I had been away only a brief while altogether, but the patient, for no apparent cause, had had a hemorrhage, and died in a few minutes.

Many times after that I heard these nocturnal sounds, usually overhead. They began to seem more like footsteps—"tap, tap, tap, tap,"—very quick and a bit muffled. Soon I was not sleeping well in the daytime.

One morning I asked at breakfast table, "Who was walking around last night?"

"I wasn't." "Not I." "Certainly not me," came a chorus. "What makes you think someone was up?"

"I distinctly heard footsteps the full length of the third floor."

"What time?"

"Around four o'clock."

But nobody admitted to having been up. "Then one of you must have been walking in your sleep," I insisted.

The nurse who had preceded me on night duty timidly contributed, "I always heard somebody. I didn't want to say anything about it for fear you'd think I was queer."

Towards morning of the very next night when I was in the second floor ward, I heard the patter again above my head. I ran upstairs to the nurses' quarters as fast as I could and looked down the corridor. Every door was tight shut. I tore down two flights to the first floor. The noise came once more above me. Back to the second floor. All patients were in their beds. I asked the only wakeful one, "Did you get up just now?"

"No."

"Did anybody else get up?"

"No."

Some nights went by quietly. But I heard the noises often enough to become truly concerned for fear I might be imagining things. I said to one of the older nurses, "I'm going to wake you up and see whether you hear them too."

"I'll sit up with you," she offered.

"No, I'll call you. They never come until almost morning."

The next time, at the first tap, I hurried to her room, shook her awake, led her to the floor below, "There, do you hear it?"

Her expression was confirmation enough.

Leaving her I raced down another flight, and waited. In a moment the "Tap, tap, tap, tap" came again from overhead. Up I went. She said she had heard it all right but it had come from over *her* head. At least my senses were not playing me tricks. My accounts were given greater credence, and other nurses sometimes interrupted their slumbers to listen.

One of my companions told a young and intelligent doctor on the staff that I had better be taken off night duty before I had a nervous breakdown. Though he thought this was girlish nonsense, he could see I was being seriously affected, and anyhow the strain of three continuous months at such a hard task was far too much. Another nurse relieved me.

After my second glandular operation I was placed in one of the private rooms on the upper floor. I had not come through very well, and this same doctor remained in the hospital all night to be on call. Being restless, I woke up, only to hear the identical noises which had haunted me for so long. I called him and exclaimed, "There it is. Don't you hear it?"

He did, but confidently he strode upstairs to the nurses' floor. I knew he would find nothing. When he came back, I asked, "Did you see anyone?"

"No. Apparently everybody was asleep. I looked in all the rooms."

Immediately the raps came again. He moved a little faster to get downstairs. In a few minutes he put his head back in the door. "You're in bed? You haven't been up?" I assured him I had not moved, knowing well he must have heard them as always I had, from above.

Though still believing somebody was walking around the place, the doctor by this time was determined to get to the bottom of the mystery, and returned every night for a week. But the sound was a will-o'-the-wisp. He never could catch up with it. He was so eager to exhaust every possibility that he even brought the matter before the board. One of them patronizingly explained that it was probably the echo from some rat in the walls; they were in the habit of dismissing thus lightly the superstitions which clung about the old house.

The doctor continued his detective work until one day he appeared in great good humor. From the rear windows he pointed to the roof which rose beyond the high back wall. "I've found it. That stable is built on the same timbers as this house. When some horse grows restless towards morning he stamps and the vibration is carried through them underground to this building. Now do you believe in ghosts?"

Life was by no means so serious as all this sounds. Amelia had followed me into the hospital and we continued our gay times together. For that matter nursing itself often presented amusing aspects. The supply of registered nurses was very small, and in our last year of training we were sent out on private cases, thus seeing both the highlights and lowlights of life, which prepared us well in experience.

One which had romantic overtones took place immediately after Howard Willett had transferred his house-party from Aiken, South Carolina, to Gedney Farms Manor in White Plains. The indisposition of young Eugene Sugney Reynal was pronounced scarlet fever. The contagion began spreading among the guests and servants, and Dr. Julius Schmid, old and honored, a noteworthy figure in the community and also our chief of staff, detailed three of us nurses for service there, practically turning the place into a hospital for five weeks.

My special charge was Adelaide Fitzgerald, Reynal's fiancée, but as necessity arose we shifted around. Reynal's condition grew steadily worse. One morning at daybreak when the patient was almost in a coma Dr. Schmid sent for the priest to administer extreme unction, and said to me, "You'd better get Miss Fitzgerald and tell her there's very little hope."

She knelt by his bed, "Gene," she called to him, "Gene, we're going to be married—right now."

Reynal was as near death as a man could be, but her voice reached into his subconscious and summoned him back. Another nurse and I, hastily called upon to act as bridesmaids, stood in starched and rustling white beside the bed. It was extraordinary to watch; Reynal seemed to shake himself alive until he was conscious enough to respond "I do" to the priest who had arrived to perform quite a different office.

As an anti-climax to all the excitement, and to my intense disgust, I myself came down with a mild attack of scarlet fever. I was so embarrassed that I went right on working and did not take to my bed until I actually began to peel.

My usual cases offered drama of another sort. Often I was called in the middle of the night on a maternity case, perhaps ten miles away from the hospital, where I had to sterilize the water and boil the forceps over a wood fire in the kitchen stove while the doctor scrubbed up as best he could. Many times labor terminated before he could arrive and I had to perform the delivery by myself.

To see a baby born is one of the greatest experiences that a human being can have. Birth to me has always been more awe-inspiring than death. As often as I have witnessed the miracle, held the perfect creature with its tiny hands and tiny feet, each time I have felt as though I were entering a cathedral with prayer in my heart.

There is so little knowledge in the world compared with what there is to know. Always I was deeply affected by the trust patients, rich or poor, male or female, old or young, placed in their nurses. When we appeared they seemed to say, "Ah, here is someone who can tell us." Mothers asked me pathetically, plaintively, hopefully, "Miss Higgins, what should I do not to have another baby right away?" I was at a loss to answer their intimate questions, and passed them along to the doctor, who more often than not snorted, "She ought to be ashamed of herself to talk to a young girl about things like that."

All such problems were thus summarily shoved aside. We had one woman in our hospital who had had several miscarriages and six babies, each by a different father. Doctors and nurses knew every time she went out that she would soon be back again, but it was not their business or anybody's business; it was just "natural."

To be polished off neatly, the nurses in training were assigned to one of the larger city hospitals in which to work during the last three or six months of our course. Mine was the Manhattan Eye and Ear at Forty-first Street and Park Avenue, across the street from the Murray Hill Hotel, and I welcomed the chance to see up-to-date equipment and clockwork discipline. My new environment was considerably less harsh and intense, more comfortable and leisurely.

At one of the frequent informal dances held there my doctor partner received a message—not a call, but a caller. His architect wanted to go over blueprints with him. "Come along," he invited. "See whether you think my new house is going to be as fine as I do."

The architect was introduced. "This is William Sanger."

The three of us bent over the plans. The doctor was the only one unaware of the sudden electric quality of the atmosphere.

At seven-thirty the next morning when I went out for my usual "constitutional," Bill Sanger was on the doorstep. He had that type of romantic nature which appealed to me, and had been waiting there all night. We took our walk together that day and regularly for many days thereafter, learning about each other, exploring each other's minds, and discovering a community of ideas and ideals. His fineness fitted in with my whole destiny, if I can call it such, just as definitely as my hospital training.

I found Bill's mother a lovely person—artistic, musical, and highly cultured. His father had been a wealthy sheep rancher in Australia. When you travel anywhere from there, you practically have to go round the world, and on his way to San Francisco he had passed through Central Europe. In a German town he had fallen in love with the Mayor's youngest daughter, then only fourteen. When she was of marriageable age he had returned for her, and it was from this talented mother that Bill had derived his fondness for music and desire to paint.

Bill was an architect only by profession; he was pure artist by temperament. Although his heart was not in mechanical drawing, he did it well. Stanford White once told me he was one of the six best draftsmen in New York. He confided to me his dream of eventually being able to leave architecture behind and devote himself to painting, particularly murals. I had had instilled in me a feeling for the natural relationship between color and symmetry of line, and sympathized not merely with his aspirations but was intensely proud of his work. Some day we were going to be married, and as soon as we had saved enough we would go to Paris, whither the inspiration of the great French painters was summoning artists from all over the world.

These plans were nebulous and had nothing to do with my abrupt departure from New York. One afternoon, about four o'clock, I was standing under a skylight putting drops in the eyes of a convalescent patient. Unexpectedly, inexplicably, the glass began to fall apart. Almost by instinct I pulled my patient under the lintel of the door. A great blast followed and pandemonium was let loose; the ruined skylight went crashing down the stairs, plaster and radiators tumbled from the walls, doors fell out, windows cracked.

I rushed to the bed of the man who needed my first attention. He had been operated on for a cataract only a few hours previously and my orders had been not to let him move too soon lest the fluid in his eye run out and damage his sight permanently. But he with the other terrified patients was already on his feet.

Rounding up all those under my care and checking their names took several minutes, and while I was still trying to quiet them, ambulances from other hospitals came clanging up. By the time I had ushered my charges down to the ground floor, a way had been cleared through the debris of fallen brick and wood. Since mine were not stretcher cases I was able to crowd ten of them into one ambulance, and we were taken to the New York Hospital. Not until I had them all safely installed did I learn what had happened to our building. A tremendous explosion in the new Park Avenue subway had practically demolished it, and it had to be evacuated.

I returned to White Plains, where Bill came up frequently to see me. On one of our rambles he idly pulled at some vines on a stone wall, and then, with his hands, tilted my face for a kiss. The next morning, to my mortification, four telltale finger marks were outlined on my cheek by poison ivy blisters. The day after that, my face was swollen so that my eyes were tight shut, and I was sick for two months; since my training was finished, I was sent home to convalesce.

Chapter Five

CORALS TO CUT LIFE UPON

⇢⇢⇢⇢⇢⇢⇢⇢⇢⇢⇢⇢⇠⇠⇠⇠⇠⇠⇠⇠⇠⇠⇠⇠⇠

FOR a while I stayed at Corning, and then went back to New York to start nursing in earnest. On one of my free afternoons in August, Bill and I went for a drive, and he suggested we stop in at the house of a friend of his who was a minister. All had been prepared. License and rice were waiting. And so we were married.

The first year is half taken up with love and half with planning a future together which is to endure forever. These dreams feed youthful ambitions, but they seldom can come true in their entirety. In our case the obstacles arose with undue speed.

I was not well. I was paying the cost of long hours in mother's closely confined room and of continuous overwork in the hospital. Medical advice was to go West to live, but I would not go without Bill, and he had a commission which kept him in New York. Accordingly, I was packed off to a small semi-sanitarium near Saranac where the great Dr. Trudeau, specialist in pulmonary tuberculosis, was consulted.

Existence there was depressing. A man might be talking to me one day, full of life and spirit and hope, and the next morning not appear. The dead were ordinarily removed in the quiet of the night, and the doctors made no comment. In this gloomy environment I rested, preparing myself for motherhood. The flood of treatises on child psychology had not yet started, and even the books on the care and feeding of infants were few. But I read whatever I could.

Just before it was time for the baby to be born I returned to the little apartment on St. Nicholas Avenue at 149th Street, then practically suburban. Taking every precaution, we had engaged four doctors in a row. Dr. Schmid had said he would perform the ceremony unless it came at night, in which case his assistant would have to take charge. The assistant had provided that, if he were not available, his assistant would be on call, and this assistant had another assistant to assist him.

When towards three o'clock one morning I felt the first thin, fine pains of warning, Bill tried one after the other of our obstetricians —not one could be located. He had to run around the corner to the nearest general practitioner. Due almost as much to this young doctor's inexperience as to my physical state, the ordeal was unusually hard, but the baby Stuart, given Amelia's family name, was perfectly healthy, strong, and sturdy. I looked upon this as a victory, although it was only partial, because I had to go right back to the mountains. It was a wrench to leave again so soon and at such a time, but I could not believe it would be for long.

With Stuart and a nurse I took rooms in a friendly farmhouse near a small Adirondack village; I did not want the baby in the midst of sick people, and, moreover, I was not welcome at Saranac itself, since Dr. Trudeau did not like to have in residence patients whose illness had progressed beyond a certain stage. One of the most important parts of the treatment was stuffing with food. I was being filled with the then recognized remedy, creosote, and gulped capsule after capsule, which broke my appetite utterly. Still I had to pour down milk and swallow eggs, and always I had to rest and rest and rest.

At the end of eight months I was worse instead of better, and had no interest in living. Nan and Bill's mother were summoned, and two of Dr. Trudeau's associates came to see me. They advised that I should go nearer Saranac and be separated from all personal responsibilities.

"What would you yourself like to do?" they asked.

"Nothing."

"Where would you like to go?"

"Nowhere."

"Would you like to have the baby sent to your brother, or would you rather have your mother-in-law take it?"

"I don't care."

To every suggestion I was negative. I was not even interested in my baby.

The two doctors left. The younger, however, apparently not satisfied with the professional attitude, returned almost immediately, not so much in a medical capacity as one of anxious friendliness. I was still sitting in the same state of listlessness. He laid his hand on my shoulder quietly, but I had all the feeling of being violently shaken. "Don't be like this!" he exclaimed. "Don't let yourself get into such a mental condition. Do something! Want something! You'll never get well if you keep on this way."

I could not sleep that night. I had been rudely jolted from my stupor by the understanding doctor. Obviously preparations were being made for a lingering illness which would terminate in death. But if I had to die I would rather be with those I loved than disappear in the night as a part of the cold routine.

As the first glimmer of dawn appeared through the curtains I got up and stared at the steadily ticking clock. It was not yet five. I dressed quickly, then tiptoed into the bedroom where the nurse and baby were slumbering soundly. I roused her and told her to pack up; we were going back to New York. She looked up in drowsy dismay, but obeyed meekly. The farmer hitched up his horse and we jogged along all the way to the station in the early summer morning, bright with sunshine and cheery with birds.

Bill was waiting at the Grand Central Terminal, quite naturally perplexed. He had that morning received two telegrams, one saying I was to be removed to Saranac at once, pending his approval as to the care of the baby by relatives, and the other from me asking him to meet me because I was coming home. I told him as best I could the reasons for my sudden decision. Though I probably sounded incoherent he understood and, instead of scolding, soothed me tenderly and exclaimed, "You did just the right thing. I won't let you die."

"And don't make me eat! Don't even mention food to me!" He promised to let me have my own way.

At the small family hotel in Yonkers in which we settled, I lived pretty much by myself, keeping the baby and everyone else away from me; I had by now learned the dangers of contact in spreading tuberculosis. Once free from the horrors of invalidism and comforted by love and devotion I began to regain a normal interest in life, and by the end of three weeks had recovered from my hysterical rejection of food.

As soon as I was strong enough we started to explore Westchester County for a home site. We wanted something more than a mere house. We wanted space, we wanted a view, we wanted a garden. At Hastings-on-Hudson we found what we sought. There on fifty acres of hillside overlooking the river about ten families—doctors, teachers, college professors, scientists—had combined to construct the sort of dwellings they liked in the environment they considered best suited for their children. We too had in mind a family and a comfortable, serene, suburban existence, and we joined this Columbia Colony, as it was called, renting a small cottage until we could build our own.

The other wives and I spent our afternoons conferring over the momentous problems of servants, gardens, and schools. If we went to town, we took the children with us, fitting them with special shoes at Coward's, introducing them to museums, libraries, or art galleries. Life centered around them. When Stuart and his little friends began to ask questions, "Where do babies come from?" I collected them and tried to answer, using the simple phenomena of nature as illustrations—flowers, frogs, fish, and animals. I still consider this approach has its place with many children, although modern sex educationists may smile at this method, thinking it old-fashioned.

None of the colony played cards. Instead, the women formed a literary club where we read papers on George Eliot, Browning, and Shakespeare, as well as on some current authors, and we had occasional political discussions. Out of this grew the Women's Club of Hastings.

It was all very pleasant, and at first I was busy and contented. The endless details of housekeeping did not seem to me drudgery; conquering minor crises was exciting. Though I was never slavishly domestic, I was inclined to be slavishly maternal. Bill was a devoted husband. He took care of me in the little ways—starting for the train and coming back to put his head in the door and call, "It's awfully cold. Don't go out without your wrap," or, if it were hot, he offered, "Give me your list and I'll send up the groceries."

I was again leading the life of an artist's family. Bill was a hard worker; I can rarely remember one evening of just reading together. I did the reading and he drew or painted. But I was never quite sure whether we were rich or poor. He possessed the finest qualities of creative genius, and with them some of its limitations and liabilities. When he was paid for a big commission he brought me orchids and embroidered Japanese robes which I had no occasion to wear, and filled the house with luxuries. This did not go with my practical sense. If the grocery account were long unpaid, I protested, "They're beautiful. Thank you, but can we afford them?"

"Certainly," and out of his pocket came tickets for the opera or theater, his chief pleasures.

"But we shouldn't," I remonstrated as I ruffled a sheaf of bills before him.

Nevertheless, we used the tickets.

Every architect wants to embody his ideas at least once in his own home. Ours was "modern" in its square simplicity and unadorned surfaces of stuccoed hollow tile, even being called a show house; people came from afar to study it. It was designed to have a large nursery opening on a veranda overlooking the Hudson, a studio, a bath with each bedroom, fireplaces everywhere, and one especially capacious in the big library. From this room the open stairway, forking at the lower landing with a few steps leading down into the kitchen, reached up the wall to the second story.

The house took long to complete, but it was fun. The moment Bill finished his work in New York he was back at it. Theoretically he supervised at night and the builder built by day. But when an arch did not turn out to be a perfect arch, seizing an ax, he chopped out part of it, usually pounding his fingers in the process. The neighbors, careful of their pennies, held their ears at the clatter and clamor and exclaimed, "There goes another partition." When the contractor returned in the morning he found his previous day's work demolished. Some portions were entirely done over two or three times.

The color on the woodwork we applied ourselves by artificial light, plumped on our knees or stretching high overhead. If the effect were wrong, we had to match it all up again. Evening after evening we labored on the rose window which was to crown with radiance the head of the staircase. Far into the night we leaded and welded together every glowing petal. Our fingers were cut, our nerves were irritated, our eyes fatigued. But tireless love went into the composition of this rose window which symbolized the stability of our future. We were aiming at permanence and security, and our efforts seemed to be fused into indestructible unity. It was our keystone of beauty.

After the tedious worrying over details we suddenly became too impatient to wait any more, and, in spite of the raw condition of the house, late one February afternoon of half-sleet, half-rain, a moving van pulled up to our front door. Through the semi-twilight boxes, crates, and barrels were carted in.

The four-year-old Stuart was not well. We put him early to bed, and Bill stirred up a roaring fire in the furnace against the increasing cold. Then with hammer and claw we turned to our treasures, which we had not seen for such a time. It was like opening packages on Christmas morning. We had almost forgotten the tapestry Mary had sent from Persia, the rug from Egypt, Bill's paintings. "What's in this box? Oh, look here! See what I've found!" A flood of color inundated us. We tried out their warmth against our immaculate walls and floors. I was carrying my second baby and was tired hours before I wanted to stop. As I climbed up to bed I gazed down happily on the litter below.

Some time later I heard dimly through my sleep a pounding, and woke to realize it was the German maid at the door, crying, "Madam. Come! Fire in the big stove!"

We jumped out of bed. Acrid smoke was in our nostrils, and we were swept by the horror of fire by night. Bill shouted to me, "Get right out! I've got to give the alarm."

Away he rushed in his pajamas; there was no telephone within half a mile. I seized Stuart from his crib, bedclothes and all. This took only a few seconds, but the kitchen was already ablaze and flames were leaping up the staircase. I pulled the blanket over his head and started cautiously down, hugging the outer side. The blistering treads crunched as they gave under my feet, but did not collapse until I had reached the smoke-filled library.

The family across the street welcomed us in. When I had tucked Stuart into an impromptu bed I went to watch. Not merely was the fire engine trying to get up the icy hill, two steps forward and one back, but the whole village was accompanying it to help organize a bucket brigade.

The clouds had cleared and the bright moon was shining on the strange scene. The weather had turned much colder, and the rain had frozen into crystals which glittered on the branches of trees and shrubbery. It was unbelievably fantastic, and in that unreal setting the flames, as though directed by devilish intent, spurted only through our prized rose window. I stood silently regarding the result of months of work and love slowly disintegrate. Petal by petal it succumbed to the licking tongues of fire; one by one they fell into the gray-white snow. Fitting them together had taken so long; now relentlessly they were being pulled apart. A thing of beauty had perished in a few moments.

It was as though a chapter of my life had been brought to a close, and I was neither disappointed nor regretful. On the contrary, I was conscious of a certain relief, of a burden lifted. In that instant I learned the lesson of the futility of material substances. Of what great importance were they spiritually if they could go so quickly? Pains, thirsts, heartaches could be put into the creation of something external which in one sweep could be taken from you. With the destruction of the window, my scale of suburban values was consumed. I could never again pin my faith on concrete things; I must build on myself alone. I hoped I should continue to have lovely objects around me, but I could also be happy without them.

The next day was filled with neighbors coming to condole and offer help, and with insurance adjusters peering about and questioning. They found the too-heavy fire in the furnace had overheated the pipes around which the asbestos had not yet been wrapped. We lost a good deal because, although the house was covered, the insurance on the furniture had not been shifted to its new location, and, moreover, many of our possessions were irreplaceable, their worth having lain in the sentiment attached to them.

A personal catastrophe may in the end prove to be a public benefit. People in the community are brought together in sympathy, and learn by the experience of others how to protect themselves. After our mischance every householder in Columbia Colony began to look to his furnace and insure his home.

Our walls were fireproof, and much of the house could be saved, but it was really more disheartening than complete demolition would have been, for in the latter case we could have started to rebuild from the beginning. I admired Bill greatly for the resolute way he set about the painful business again. He went over every inch, here saying, "This board is all right," and there tearing out black pieces of charred wood. It was a dirty job, but he stuck to it. Nevertheless, paint and stain as we would, we could not quite get rid of the unmistakable and ineradicable odor which clings around a burned building, almost like the smell of death.

Next summer we moved in once more. But the house was never the same. Never could I recapture that first flush of joy.

Grant, my second son, was born almost immediately. I loved having a baby to tend again, and wanted at least four more as quickly as my health would permit. I could not wait another five years. I yearned especially for a daughter, and twenty months later my wish came true. After Peggy's birth, the doctor went downstairs and saw Bill sitting in the library with Grant in his arms and tears welling from his eyes.

"Why, what's the matter? There's a nice little girl upstairs."

"I'm thinking of this poor little boy. Margaret has wanted a girl so long—now she'll have no room in her heart for him."

Bill's fears were groundless. Grant was not supplanted, but Peggy was so satisfactory a baby that I was not particularly disappointed when my illness cropped up again and the doctor said my family must end at this point. I was quite content with things as they were.

Even as a little fellow, the sandy-haired, square-built Stuart was practical, loved sports, and had a reasoning, logical mind, always experimenting with life as well as with mechanical things. A thorough Higgins, he had to find out for himself and prove it. He used to stamp and scold when presented with a chore, such as mowing the lawn or bringing in wood for the fireplaces, but his rebellions were brief, and, when he realized the inevitable, he turned it into a game. "Come on over," he hailed his friends. "We've lots to do. Let's get to it! We're going to have great fun."

The other boys, taken in by his enthusiastic invitations, also believed that mowing the lawn or bringing in wood were among the best games invented.

Grant was more self-conscious than Stuart, and more inarticulate, but more affectionate. He followed the baby Peggy slavishly. They were usually hand in hand, and Grant's darkness contrasted with her bright, blond hair. From the time she could talk they referred to themselves as "we." Peggy was the most independent child I have ever seen. At three she knew what she wanted and where she was going. She was vivacious, mischievous, laughing—the embodiment of all my hopes in a daughter.

Stuart typified the scientist, Grant the artist, Peggy the doer. It was maternally gratifying to wonder whether they would carry out these propensities in their later lives.

I enjoyed my literary activities along with my children, and Bill encouraged me. "You go ahead and finish your writing. I'll get the dinner and wash the dishes." And what is more he did it, drawing the shades, however, so that nobody could see him. He thought I should make a career of it instead of limiting myself to small-town interests.

Both Bill and I were feeling what amounted to a world hunger, the pull and haul towards wider horizons. For him Paris was still over the next hill. I was not able to express my discontent with the futility of my present course, but after my experience as a nurse with fundamentals this quiet withdrawal into the tame domesticity of the pretty riverside settlement seemed to be bordering on stagnation. I felt as though we had drifted into a swamp, but we would not wait for the tide to set us free.

It was hopeless to emphasize the importance of practical necessities to an artist, and consequently I decided to resume nursing in order to earn my share. We had spent years building our home and used it only for a brief while. I was glad to leave when, in one of our financial doldrums, we plunged back into the rushing stream of New York life.

Chapter Six

FANATICS OF THEIR PURE IDEALS

WE took an apartment way uptown. It was the old-fashioned railroad type—big, high-ceilinged, with plenty of room, air, and light. The children's grandmother came to live with us and her presence gave me ease of mind when I was called on a case; my children were utterly safe in her care.

Headlong we dived into one of the most interesting phases of life the United States has ever seen. Radicalism in manners, art, industry, morals, politics was effervescing, and the lid was about to blow off in the Great War. John Spargo, an authority on Karl Marx, had translated *Das Kapital* into English, thus giving impetus to Socialism. Lincoln Steffens had published *The Shame of the Cities,* George Fitzpatrick had produced *War, What For?*, a strange and wonderful arraignment of capitalism, which sold thousands of copies.

The names of Cézanne, Matisse, and Picasso first became familiar sounds on this side of the Atlantic at the time of the notable Armory Exhibition, when outstanding examples of impressionist and cubist painting were imported from Europe. But there was so much of eccentricity—a leg on top of a head, a hat on a foot, the *Nude Descending a Staircase,* all in the name of art—that you had to close one eye to look at it. The Armory vibrated; it shook New York.

Although Bill had studied according to the old school, he could see the point of view of the radical in art, and in politics as well.

His attitude towards the underdog was much like father's. He had always been a Socialist, although not active, and held his friend Eugene V. Debs in high esteem.

A religion without a name was spreading over the country. The converts were liberals, Socialists, anarchists, revolutionists of all shades. They were as fixed in their faith in the coming revolution as ever any Primitive Christian in the immediate establishment of the Kingdom of God. Some could even predict the exact date of its advent.

At one end of the scale of rebels and scoffers were the "pink" parliamentarian socialists and theorists at whom anarchists hurled the insult "bourgeois." At the other were the Industrial Workers of the World, the "Wobblies," advocating unionization of the whole industry rather than the craft or trade. This was to be brought about, if need be, by direct action.

Almost without knowing it you became a "comrade." You could either belong to a group that believed civilization was to be saved by the vote and by protective legislation, or go further to the left and believe with the anarchists in the integrity of the individual, and that it was possible to develop human character to the point where laws and police were unnecessary.

The mental stirring was such as to make a near Renaissance. Everybody was writing on the nebulous "new liberties." Practically always people could be found to support leaders or magazines, although many of the latter lived for hardly more than a single issue.

Upton Sinclair was utilizing his gift for vivid expression and righteous wrath in trying to correct social abuses by the indirect but highly effective method of story-telling. *The Jungle* was a powerful exposé of the capitalist meat industry responsible for the "embalmed beef" which had poisoned American soldiers in '98. Courageous as he was, he was yet mistrusted by the Socialist Old Guard as being a Silk Hat Radical who retained his bourgeois philosophy. Furthermore, he had been divorced, and divorce at that time was something of a scandal. Though anarchists minded such details not a whit, Socialists were imbued with all the respectabilities; to most of these home-loving Germans, only the form of government needed change.

In the United States the party was trying to separate itself from this German influence, and the standard bearer of the American concept was the magnetic and beloved Debs. Not himself an intellectual, he did not need to be; he was intelligent. Risen as he had from the ranks of the railroad workers, he knew their hardships from experience. Though I am not sure he actually was tall, he gave the illusion of height because of his thinness and stooping shoulders. He was all flame, like a fire spirit. That was probably why the members of his coterie followed him so gladly.

Our living room became a gathering place where liberals, anarchists, Socialists, and I.W.W.'s could meet. These vehement individualists had to have an audience, preferably a small, intimate one. They really came to see Bill; I made the cocoa. I used to listen in, not at all sure my opinions would be accepted by this very superior group. When I did meekly venture something, I was quite likely to find myself on the opposite side—right in a left crowd and vice versa.

Any evening you might find visitors from the Middle West being aroused by Jack Reed, bullied by Bill Haywood, led softly towards anarchist thought by Alexander Berkman. When throats grew dry and the flood of oratory waned, someone went out for hamburger sandwiches, hot dogs, and beer, paid for by all. The luxuriousness of the midnight repast depended upon the collection of coins tossed into the middle of the table, which consisted of about what everybody had in his pocket. These considerate friends never imposed a burden either of extra work or extra expense. In the kitchen everyone sliced, buttered, opened cans. As soon as all were replenished, the conversation was resumed practically where it had left off.

Both right-wingers and left-wingers who ordinarily objected to those in between loved Jack Reed, the master reporter just out of Harvard. He refused to conform to the rule and rote of either, though his natural inclination appeared to be more in harmony with direct action.

Behind this most highly intellectual young man loomed an uncouth, stumbling, one-eyed giant with an enormous head which he tended to hold on one side. Big Bill Haywood looked like a bull about to plunge into an arena. He seemed always glancing warily this way and that with his one eye, head slightly turned as though to get the view of you. His great voice boomed; his speech was crude and so were his manners; his philosophy was that of the mining camps, where he had spent his life. But I soon found out that for gentleness and sympathy he had not his equal. He was blunt because he was simple and direct. Though he was not tailor-made, he was custom-made.

Because Big Bill's well-wishers saw so much that was fine in him, they wanted to smooth off the jagged edges. When they tried to polish his speeches, Jack Reed objected, saying, "Give him a free hand. He expresses what you and I think much more dramatically than we can. Don't try to stop him! We should encourage him."

One of Big Bill's best friends, Jessie Ashley, was, without meaning to be, a taming influence. These two were the oddest combination in the world—old Bill with his one eye, stubby, roughened fingernails, uncreased trousers, and shoddy clothes for which he refused to pay more than the minimum; Jessie with Boston accent and horn-rimmed glasses, a compromise between spectacles and lorgnette, from which dangled a black ribbon, the ultimate word in eccentric decoration.

Jessie was one of the most conspicuous of the many men and women of long pedigree who were revolting against family tradition. She was the daughter of the President of the New York School of Law, and sister of its dean. When her brother had organized the first women's law class, she had been his pupil and later had become the first woman lawyer in New York City. Her peculiarly honest mind was tolerant towards others, but uncompromising towards herself. It was said of her truly that she was always in the forefront when it took courage to be there; always in the background when there was credit to be gained. A Socialist in practice as well as theory, she spent large portions of her income in getting radicals out of jail, and her own legal experience she gave freely in their behalf. Nevertheless, her appearances at strike meetings were slightly uncomfortable; class tension rose up in waves.

Many others were trying to pull themselves out of the rut of tradition. Alexander Berkman, the gentle anarchist, understood them all. He had just been freed after fourteen years' imprisonment for his attempt to assassinate Henry Clay Frick during the Homestead Steel strike of 1892. His emergence had stirred anarchism up again, and particularly its credo of pure individualism—to stand on your own and be yourself, never to have one person dictate to another, even parent to child.

Berkman's appearance belied his reputation—blond, blue-eyed, slightly built, with thinnish hair, and sensitive, mobile face and hands. He was a thoughtful ascetic, believing sincerely that the quickest way to focus attention on social outrages was to commit some dramatic act, however violent or antipathetic it might be to his nature—and then suffer the consequences. He was not at all embittered by his sojourn in jail, and had a great sense of humor, coupled with his most extraordinary understanding of the strange congeries of people who were about to be melted down into his glowing crucible of truth.

Elizabeth Gurley Flynn had made the transition from Catholicism, Jack Reed from being a "Harvard man," Mabel Dodge from being a society matron. They all had had to get over being class conscious, and acquire instead the consciousness of the class struggle. Berkman made friends with all, and when they were faced by problems apparently insurmountable, he advised them on their spiritual journey, and supported and backed them. For this reason he was beloved by all who encountered his most gracious charm.

This was not the way of Emma Goldman, whose habit was to berate and lash with the language of scorn. She was never satisfied until people had arrived at her own doorstep and accepted the dogma she had woven for herself. Short, stocky, even stout, a true Russian peasant type, her figure indicated strength of body and strength of character, and this impression was enhanced by her firm step and reliant walk. Though I disliked both her ideas and her methods I admired her; she was really like a spring house-cleaning to the sloppy thinking of the average American. Our Government suffered in the estimation of the liberal world when she and Berkman were expelled from the country.

Of all the strange places for these diverse personalities to meet, none more strange could have been found than in Mabel Dodge's salon, which burst upon New York like a rocket. Mabel belonged to one of the old families of Buffalo, but neither in thought nor action was she orthodox. Only in the luxurious appointments of her home did she conform.

Among the sights and memories I shall never forget were her famous soirées at Ninth Street and Fifth Avenue. A certain one typical of all the others comes to mind; the whole gamut of liberalism had collected in her spacious drawing-room before an open fire. Cross-legged on the floor, in the best Bohemian tradition, were Wobblies with uncut hair, unshaven faces, leaning against valuable draperies. Their clothes may have been unkempt, but their eyes were ablaze with interest and intelligence. Each knew his own side of the subject as well as any scholar. You had to inform yourself to be in the liberal movement. Ideas were respected, but you had to back them up with facts. Expressions of mere emotion, unleashed from reason, could not be let loose to wander about.

Listener more than talker, Mabel sat near the hearth, brown bangs outlining a white face, simply gowned in velvet, beautifully arched foot beating the air. For two hours I watched fascinatedly that silken ankle never ceasing its violent agitation.

The topic of conversation turned out to be direct action. Big Bill was the figure of the evening, but everybody was looking for an opportunity to talk. Each believed he had a key to the gates of Heaven; each was trying to convert the others. It could not exactly have been called a debate, because a single person held the floor as long as he could. Then, at one of his most effective periods, somebody else half rose and interposed a "But—" The speaker hurried on; at his next telling sentence came other "But—s," until finally he was downed by the weight of interruptions. In the end, conversions were nil; all were convinced beforehand either for or against, and I never knew them to shift ground.

It is not hard to laugh about it now, but nobody could have been more serious and determined than we were in those days.

Just before the argument reached the stage of fist fights, the big doors were thrown open and the butler announced, "Madam, supper is served." Many of the boys had never heard those words, but one and all jumped up with alacrity from the floor and discussion was, for the moment at least, postponed. The wide, generous table in the dining room was burdened with beef, cold turkey, hot ham—hearty meat for hungry souls. On a side table were pitchers of lemonade, siphons, bottles of rye and Scotch.

Mabel never stirred while the banquet raged, but continued to sit, her foot still beating the air, and talked with the few who did not choose to eat.

The class contrasts encountered in a gathering there were not unique. They were to be found elsewhere, even in matrimony. When the wealthy J. G. Phelps Stokes married Rose Pastor, the Russian-Jewish cigar maker, both families felt equally outraged; he was practically sent to Coventry by his former associates and the Jews regarded her as a renegade because she wore a silver cross about her neck. William English Walling, the last word in Newport, married Anna Strunsky, the last word in the Jewish intelligentsia, and himself became a leading literary critic on the radical side.

Harvard had been turning out liberals by the dozen, and all of them were playing hob with accepted conventions in thought. One of these was Walter Lippmann, others were Norman Hapgood and his brother, Hutchins. "Hutch" was then working on the *Globe,* a paper which because of its broad editorial policy was preferred by many radicals to the *Call*. He stood by Bill Haywood and Emma Goldman, although he had much more to lose economically and socially than the out-and-out reds.

The anarchists seldom initiated anything, because they did not have the personnel or the equipment, but when something else was started which appeared to have any good in it, they came right in. This they did with the Ferrer School on Twelfth Street near Fourth Avenue, in the founding of which Hutch, with the liberal journalist, Leonard Abbott, and the author, Manuel Komroff, were moving spirits. The object was to provide a form of education more progressive than that offered by the public schools, and its name was intended to perpetuate the memory of the recently martyred Spanish libertarian, Francisco Ferrer, who had established modern free schools in Spain in which science and evolution had been taught.

Lola Ridge, intense rebel from Australia, was the organizing secretary, Robert Henri and George Bellows gave lessons in art, and a young man named Will Durant was chosen to direct the younger children, combining in his teaching Froebel, Montessori, and other new methods. Under him we enrolled Stuart.

Will Durant was of French-Canadian ancestry. His mother had worked hard to put him through a Jesuit seminary, but just before taking the vows he had abandoned the priesthood. While he had been studying he had read Krafft-Ebing and Havelock Ellis and was prepared to acquaint New York with the facts of sex psychology. Sitting nonchalantly to deliver his lectures, which evidenced scholarly background and research, he advanced to his small but serious audience practically the first public expression of this intimate subject.

The young instructor created rather a problem for the directors by unexpectedly marrying a pupil, Ida Kaufman, commonly called Puck. I remember one Saturday when she was romping with Stuart, and my laundress said to her, "Why, you're so young to be married. Do you like it?"

Puck replied, "Oh, I don't care, but I'd much rather play marbles."

Intellectuals were then flocking to enlist under the flag of humanitarianism, and as soon as anybody evinced human sympathies he was deemed a Socialist. My own personal feelings drew me towards the individualist, anarchist philosophy, and I read Kropotkin, Bakunin, and Fourier, but it seemed to me necessary to approach the ideal by way of Socialism; as long as the earning of food, clothing, and shelter was on a competitive basis, man could never develop any true independence.

Therefore, I joined the Socialist Party, Local Number Five, itself something of a rebel in the ranks, which, against the wishes of the central authority, had been responsible for bringing Bill Haywood East after his release from prison. The members—Italian, Jewish, Russian, German, Spanish, a pretty good mixture—used the rooms over a neighborhood shop as a meeting place and there they were to be found every evening reading and discussing politics.

Somebody had donated a sum of money to be spent to interest women in Socialism. As proof that we were not necessarily like the masculine, aggressive, bulldog, window-smashing suffragettes in England, I, an American and a mother of children, was selected to recruit new members among the clubs of working women. The Scandinavians, who had a housemaids' union, were the most satisfactory; they already leaned towards liberalism.

Grant, who was as yet too young to go to school, whole-heartedly disapproved of my political activities. Once when I was about to depart for the evening he climbed up on my lap and said, "Are you going to a meeting?"

"Yes."

"A soshist meeting?"

"Yes."

"Oh, I hate soshism!"

Everybody else was amused when the Sangers went to a Socialist meeting. If I had an idea, I leaned over and whispered it to Bill, who waved his hand and called for attention. "Margaret has something to say on that. Have you heard Margaret?" Many men might have labeled my opinions silly, and, indeed, I was not at all sure of them myself, but Bill thought if I had one, it was worth hearing.

John Block and his wife, Anita, were ardent workers for the cause. She was a grand person, a Barnard graduate and editor of the woman's page of the *Call*. She telephoned me one evening, "Will you help me out? We have a lecture scheduled for tonight and our speaker is unable to come. Won't you take her place?"

"But I can't speak. I've never made a speech in my life."

"You'll simply have to do it. There isn't anybody I can get, and I'm depending on you."

"How many will be there?" I asked.

"Only about ten. You've nothing to be frightened of."

But I was frightened—thoroughly so. I could not eat my supper. Shaking and quaking I faced the little handful of women who had come after their long working hours for enlightenment. Since I did not consider myself qualified to speak on labor, I switched the subject to health, with which I was more familiar. This, it appeared, was something new. They were pleased and said to Anita, "Let's have more health talks." The second time we met the audience had swelled to seventy-five and arrangements were made to continue the lectures, if such they could be called, which I prepared while my patients slept.

The young mothers in the group asked so many questions about their intimate family life that I mentioned it to Anita. "Just the thing," she said. "Write up your answers and we'll try them out in the *Call.*" The result was the first composition I had ever done for publication, a series under the general title, *What Every Mother Should Know.* I attempted, as I had with the Hastings children, to introduce the impersonality of nature in order to break through the rigid consciousness of sex on the part of parents, who were inclined to be too intensely personal about it.

Then Anita requested a second series to be called *What Every Girl Should Know.* The motif was, "If the mother can impress the child with the beauty and wonder and sacredness of the sex function, she has taught it the first lesson."

These articles ran along for three or four weeks until one Sunday morning I turned to the *Call* to see my precious little effort, and, instead, encountered a newspaper box two columns wide in which was printed in black letters,

WHAT EVERY GIRL SHOULD KNOW

NOTHING!

BY ORDER OF

THE POST-OFFICE DEPARTMENT

The words gonorrhea and syphilis had occurred in that article and Anthony Comstock, head of the New York Society for the Suppression of Vice, did not like them. By the so-called Comstock Law of 1873, which had been adroitly pushed through a busy Congress on the eve of adjournment, the Post Office had been given authority to decide what might be called lewd, lascivious, indecent, or obscene, and this extraordinary man had been granted the extraordinary power, alone of all citizens of the United States, to open any letter or package or pamphlet or book passing through the mails and, if he wished, lay his complaint before the Post Office. So powerful had his society become that anything to which he objected in its name was almost automatically barred; he had turned out to be sole censor for ninety million people. During some forty years Comstock had been damming the rising tide of new thought, thereby causing much harm, and only now was his hopeless contest against *September Morn* making him absurd and an object of ridicule.

But at this same time also John D. Rockefeller, Jr. was organizing the Bureau of Social Hygiene, in part to educate the working public regarding what were politely termed "social evils." A fine start was being made although no surveys had been completed. Lacking data, lecturers had to speak in generalities. Nevertheless, to me, who had sat through hours of highly academic exposition expressed in cultivated tones, their approach seemed timorous and their words disguised with verbiage. I saw no reason why these facts could not be given in a few minutes in language simple enough for anyone to understand.

When my series was finished it was printed in pamphlet form. I sent a copy to Dr. Prince Morrow of the Bureau, asking for his opinion and any corrections he might suggest for the next edition; to my delight he replied he would like to see it spread by the million. The Bureau had names and backing but was not proceeding very fast towards educating working people regarding venereal disease; the articles in the *Call,* on the other hand, were reaching this same class by the thousand—yet the one which mentioned syphilis was suppressed.

I continued assiduously to write pieces for the *Call.* One of these reported the laundry strike in New York City in the winter of 1912, unauthorized by Samuel Gompers and his American Federation of Labor, which claimed it alone had the right to declare strikes. To get the details I went into the houses of the Irish Amazons, who with their husbands had walked out without being called out, simply because they could not stand it any longer. They were the hardest worked, the poorest paid, had the most protracted and irregular hours of any union members. One man described his typical day: he rose at five, had ten minutes for lunch, less for supper, and dragged himself home at eleven at night. I was glad they had the courage to rebel, and it took courage to be a picket—getting up so early on bitterly cold mornings and waiting and waiting to waylay the strikebreakers and argue with them. The police were ready to pounce when the boss pointed out the ringleaders.

This was the only time I came in contact with men and women on strike together. I could see the men had two things in their minds: one economic—the two-dollar extra wage and the shorter hours they might win; the other political—the coming of the social revolution. The women really cared for neither of these. Dominating each was the relationship between her husband, her children, and herself. She might complain of being tired and not having enough money, but always she connected both with too many offspring.

Some of the strikers thought I might help them out, but I was not at all sure I believed either in direct action or legislation as a remedy for their difficulties. This lack of conviction prevented me from having the necessary force to aid them organize themselves, and in such an emergency a forceful leader was called for. The night of their rally I was amazed at the complete confusion. Anybody could speak—and was doing so.

I felt helpless in the midst of this chaos, and distressed at their helplessness. But I knew the person who could manage the situation effectively, and so I sent for Elizabeth Gurley Flynn, a direct actionist identified with the I.W.W. Her father, Tom Flynn, a labor organizer, was the same type of philosophical rebel as my father, long on conversation but short on work. Elizabeth had been out in the logging camps of the West, where she had won the complete adoration of the lumberjacks. At her tongue's end were the words and phrases they understood, and she knew exactly the right note to stir them.

Elizabeth stood on the platform, dramatically beautiful with her black hair and deep blue eyes, her cream-white complexion set off by the flaming scarf she always wore about her throat. Nothing if not outspoken, she started by saying it was folly for the strikers to give up their bread and butter by walking out. They could achieve their ends more quickly if they threw hypothetical *sabots* into the machinery. "If a shirt comes in from a man who wears size fifteen, send him back an eighteen. Replace a dress shirt with a blue denim. That's what the laundry workers of France did, and brought the employers to their knees."

The audience was being held spellbound by this instruction in the fine art of sabotage when some of Gompers' strong-arm men appeared, and the battle was on. They tramped up on the stage, moved furniture and chairs about, made so much noise Elizabeth's voice could not be heard, and finally ejected some of her sympathizers.

It was probably better in the end that the American Federation of Labor eventually took the laundry workers under its wing, because the I.W.W. was not an organized body, but merely an agitational force which scarcely had the necessary strength to lead a successful strike in New York City. Its influence in Lawrence, Massachusetts, was far more potent. Joe Ettor, once bootblack in California, with Arturo Giovanitti, scholar, idealist, poet, and editor of *Il Proletario,* had been stirring up the unorganized textile strikers with impassioned eloquence. So compelling were the words of these two that workers of seven nationalities, chiefly Italian, had walked out spontaneously.

The accidental shooting of a girl picket provided an excuse, far-fetched as it may seem, to jail the firebrands, Ettor and Giovanitti, who were charged with being "accessories *before* the fact," which meant they were accused of having known beforehand she was going to be shot by the police and were, therefore, responsible. Now, the strikers had martyrs, and the I.W.W. heroes of the West poured in to help. Bill Haywood, William E. Trautman of the United Brewery Workers, Carlo Tresca, editor and owner of an Italian paper in New York, contributed to put on the biggest show the East had ever seen—parades, banners, songs, speeches.

The entire Italian population of America was aroused. These were then a people unto themselves. For much longer than the two generations customary among other immigrant races they retained their habits, traditions, and language, ate their own type of food and read their own newspapers.

Italians in New York who were in accord with the strikers decided on a step, novel in this country although it had been tried in Italy and Belgium. The primary reason for the failure of all labor rebellions was the hunger cries of the babies; if they were only fed the strikers could usually last out. It was determined to bring the children of the textile workers to New York, where they could be taken care of until the issue was settled. This resolution was made without knowing how many there might be; provision would be forthcoming somehow.

Again because I was an American, a nurse, and reputed to be sympathetic to their cause and the cause of children, the committee asked me with John Di Gregorio and Carrie Giovanitti to fetch the youngsters. As soon as I agreed, telephone calls were put through to Lawrence, and a delegate took the midnight train to make the preliminary arrangements.

We found the boys and girls gathered in a Lawrence public hall and, before we started, I insisted on physical examinations for contagious diseases. One, though ill with diphtheria, had been working up to the time of the strike. Almost all had adenoids and enlarged tonsils. Each, without exception, was incredibly emaciated.

Our hundred and nineteen charges were of every age, from babies of two or three to older ones of twelve to thirteen. Although the latter had been employed in the textile mills, their garments were simply worn to shreds. Not a child had on any woolen clothing whatsoever, and only four wore overcoats. Never in all my nursing in the slums had I seen children in so ragged and deplorable a condition. The February weather was bitter, and we had to run them to the station. There the parents, with tears in their eyes and gratitude in their hearts, relinquished their shivering offspring.

The wind was even icier when we reached Boston, and money was scarce. I had only enough for railroad fares and none for chartering buses or hiring taxis. Consequently, again we had to scurry on foot from the North to the South Station. But, once more on the train, great was the enthusiasm of the boys and girls, who entertained themselves by singing the *Marseillaise* and the *Internationale*. All knew the words as well as the tunes, though the former might be in Polish, Hungarian, French, German, Italian, and even English. The children who sang those songs are now grown up. I wonder how they regard the present state of the world.

As we neared New York I began to worry about our arrival. We were all weary. Would preparations have been made to feed this hungry mob and house it for the night? But I should have trusted the deep feeling and the dramatic instinct of the Italians. Thousands of men and women were waiting. As my assistants and I left the train, looking like three Pied Pipers followed by our ragged cohorts, the crowd pushed through the police lines, leaped the ropes, caught up the children as they came, and hoisted them to their shoulders. I was seized by both arms and I, too, had the illusion of being swept from the ground.

The committee had secured permission to parade to Webster Hall near Union Square. Our tired feet fell into the rhythm of the band. As we swung along singing, laughing, crying, big banners bellying and torches flaring, sidewalk throngs shouted and whistled and applauded.

At Webster Hall supper was ready in plentiful quantity. Many of our small guests were so unused to sitting at table that they did not know how to behave. Like shy animals they tried to take cover, carrying their plates to a chair, a box, anything handy. Almost all snatched at their food with both fists and stuffed it down, they were so hungry.

Socialists had not initiated this fight but they were in it. Many had come to offer shelter for the duration of the strike—perhaps six weeks, perhaps six months, perhaps a year—with visions in their minds of beautiful, starry-eyed, helpless little ones. Instead they were presented with bedraggled urchins, many of whom had never seen a toothbrush. But they rallied round magnificently; I cannot speak too highly of them.

It was a responsibility to apportion the children properly, but I had willing and intelligent help. The Poles had sent a Polish delegate, the French had sent a French delegate, and so on, in order that all might be placed in homes where they could be understood.

Luckily several families were willing to take more than one child so that we were usually able to keep brother and sister together. Each, before it was handed over, was given a medical examination. The temporary foster-parents had to promise to write the real parents, and also to send a weekly report to the committee of how their charges were getting on. The tabulation was thorough, and not until four in the morning did the last of us go to bed.

The next week, ninety-two more children were brought down, but I had no part in this, because I was on a case. Hysteria had now risen to such a height that some of the parents at the Lawrence Station were beaten and arrested by the police. Victor Berger of Wisconsin, the only Socialist member of Congress, asked for an investigation of circumstances leading up to the walkout. Although I had not been identified with it, he requested me to be present at the hearings.

When Gompers testified, he literally shook with rage, and it seemed to me he was about to have apoplexy. The mill owners charged that the whole affair had been staged solely for notoriety and that the Society for the Prevention of Cruelty to Children should step in.

Unfortunately, the witnesses for the strikers were not well-documented. When it was obvious that the Congressional Committee was not receiving the correct impression, Berger asked me to take the stand and describe the condition of the children as I had seen them. Writing up statistics on hospital reports had given me the habit of classification. I was able from my brief notes to answer every question as to their nationalities, their ages, their weights, the number of those without underclothes and without overcoats. Senator Warren Gamaliel Harding led the inquiry, and I could see he was in sympathy with my vehement replies.

The publicity had been so well managed by the Italians and their leaders that popular opinion turned in favor of the strikers, and they eventually won. At the end of March the little refugees, who had endeared themselves to their foster-parents, went back to the mill district. It was hard to recognize the same children of six weeks before, plumped up and dressed in new clothes. In November Ettor and Giovanitti were acquitted.

The Paterson silk strike of the next year, in which the workers were again predominantly Italian, may have been as important as the one at Lawrence, but it was by no means so obviously dramatic. Paterson was a gloomy city, and, as a river, the Passaic was sadder than the Merrimac. Though the leadership was far more cohesive, caution was evidenced on every hand. Its chief interest to me lay in Bill Haywood's participation. At Lawrence he had only been one of the committee, whereas at Paterson he was in charge for the first time in the East. Always before he had advised strikers to "take it on the chin" and not be too gentle in hitting back. But here, before ten thousand crowding up to the rostrum, I heard him warn, "Keep your hands in your pockets, men, and nobody can say you are shooting."

An American was apt to be at a disadvantage in handling foreigners, particularly when they felt aggrieved. They objected to his manner of going about things, so different from their own, and he, on the other hand, could not fully understand their psychology, and had the added obstacle of being compelled to work through an intermediary in language.

At Paterson the Italian groups were not behind Bill. As soon as he began to temper his language and sound a more wary note of advice, his once-faithful adherents repudiated him. His clarion call of "Hands in the Pockets," which was intended to create favorable popular opinion by proving them "good boys," had actually *tied* their hands, and detectives beat and bullied them just the same. The public was not impressed and they were resentful. They claimed he did not have the old fighting spirit he had shown when directing the miners of the West, he was getting soft, he was a sick man. Although he had actually progressed tactically and left them where they were, from that time on he lost his power of leadership.

Following the method which had been so successful at Lawrence, Jack Reed endeavored to dramatize direct action in an enormous pageant at Madison Square Garden. He even had pallbearers carry an actual coffin into the hall to pictorialize the funeral of a worker who had been shot at Paterson. I could feel a tremor go through the audience, but, on the whole, conviction was lacking.

The pageant was a fitting conclusion to one period of my life.

I believe that we all had our parts to play. Some had important ones; some were there to lend support to a scene; some were merely voices off stage. Each, whatever his role, was essential. I only walked on, but it had its influence in my future.

No matter to what degree I might participate in strikes, I always came back to the idea which was beginning to obsess me—that something more was needed to assuage the condition of the very poor. It was both absurd and futile to struggle over pennies when fast-coming babies required dollars to feed them.

I was thoroughly despondent after the Paterson debacle, and had a sickening feeling that there was to be no end; it seemed to me the whole question of strikes for higher wages was based on man's economic need of supporting his family, and that this was a shallow principle upon which to found a new civilization. Furthermore, I was enough of a Feminist to resent the fact that woman and her requirements were not being taken into account in reconstructing this new world about which all were talking. They were failing to consider the quality of life itself.

Chapter Seven

THE TURBID EBB AND FLOW OF MISERY

*"Every night and every morn
Some to misery are born.
Every morn and every night
Some are born to sweet delight.
Some are born to sweet delight,
Some are born to endless night."*
                                        WILLIAM BLAKE

DURING these years in New York trained nurses were in great demand. Few people wanted to enter hospitals; they were afraid they might be "practiced" upon, and consented to go only in desperate emergencies. Sentiment was especially vehement in the matter of having babies. A woman's own bedroom, no matter how inconveniently arranged, was the usual place for her lying-in. I was not sufficiently free from domestic duties to be a general nurse, but I could ordinarily manage obstetrical cases because I was notified far enough ahead to plan my schedule. And after serving my two weeks I could get home again.

Sometimes I was summoned to small apartments occupied by young clerks, insurance salesmen, or lawyers, just starting out, most of them under thirty and whose wives were having their first or second baby. They were always eager to know the best and latest method in infant care and feeding. In particular, Jewish patients, whose lives centered around the family, welcomed advice and followed it implicitly.

But more and more my calls began to come from the Lower East Side, as though I were being magnetically drawn there by some force outside my control. I hated the wretchedness and hopelessness of the poor, and never experienced that satisfaction in working among them that so many noble women have found. My concern for my patients was now quite different from my earlier hospital attitude. I could see that much was wrong with them which did not appear in the physiological or medical diagnosis. A woman in childbirth was not merely a woman in childbirth. My expanded outlook included a view of her background, her potentialities as a human being, the kind of children she was bearing, and what was going to happen to them.

The wives of small shopkeepers were my most frequent cases, but I had carpenters, truck drivers, dishwashers, and pushcart vendors. I admired intensely the consideration most of these people had for their own. Money to pay doctor and nurse had been carefully saved months in advance—parents-in-law, grandfathers, grandmothers, all contributing.

As soon as the neighbors learned that a nurse was in the building they came in a friendly way to visit, often carrying fruit, jellies, or gefüllter fish made after a cherished recipe. It was infinitely pathetic to me that they, so poor themselves, should bring me food. Later they drifted in again with the excuse of getting the plate, and sat down for a nice talk; there was no hurry. Always back of the little gift was the question, "I am pregnant (or my daughter, or my sister is). Tell me something to keep from having another baby. We cannot afford another yet."

I tried to explain the only two methods I had ever heard of among the middle classes, both of which were invariably brushed aside as unacceptable. They were of no certain avail to the wife because they placed the burden of responsibility solely upon the husband—a burden which he seldom assumed. What she was seeking was self-protection she could herself use, and there was none.

Below this stratum of society was one in truly desperate circumstances. The men were sullen and unskilled, picking up odd jobs now and then, but more often unemployed, lounging in and out of the house at all hours of the day and night. The women seemed to slink on their way to market and were without neighborliness.

These submerged, untouched classes were beyond the scope of organized charity or religion. No labor union, no church, not even the Salvation Army reached them. They were apprehensive of everyone and rejected help of any kind, ordering all intruders to keep out; both birth and death they considered their own business. Social agents, who were just beginning to appear, were profoundly mistrusted because they pried into homes and lives, asking questions about wages, how many were in the family, had any of them ever been in jail. Often two or three had been there or were now under suspicion of prostitution, shoplifting, purse snatching, petty thievery, and, in consequence, passed furtively by the big blue uniforms on the corner.

The utmost depression came over me as I approached this surreptitious region. Below Fourteenth Street I seemed to be breathing a different air, to be in another world and country where the people had habits and customs alien to anything I had ever heard about.

There were then approximately ten thousand apartments in New York into which no sun ray penetrated directly; such windows as they had opened only on a narrow court from which rose fetid odors. It was seldom cleaned, though garbage and refuse often went down into it. All these dwellings were pervaded by the foul breath of poverty, that moldy, indefinable, indescribable smell which cannot be fumigated out, sickening to me but apparently unnoticed by those who lived there. When I set to work with antiseptics, their pungent sting, at least temporarily, obscured the stench.

I remember one confinement case to which I was called by the doctor of an insurance company. I climbed up the five flights and entered the airless rooms, but the baby had come with too great speed. A boy of ten had been the only assistant. Five flights was a long way; he had wrapped the placenta in a piece of newspaper and dropped it out the window into the court.

Many families took in "boarders," as they were termed, whose small contributions paid the rent. These derelicts, wanderers, alternately working and drinking, were crowded in with the children; a single room sometimes held as many as six sleepers. Little girls were accustomed to dressing and undressing in front of the men, and were often violated, occasionally by their own fathers or brothers, before they reached the age of puberty.

Pregnancy was a chronic condition among the women of this class. Suggestions as to what to do for a girl who was "in trouble" or a married woman who was "caught" passed from mouth to mouth —herb teas, turpentine, steaming, rolling downstairs, inserting slippery elm, knitting needles, shoe-hooks. When they had word of a new remedy they hurried to the drugstore, and if the clerk were inclined to be friendly he might say, "Oh, that won't help you, but here's something that may." The younger druggists usually refused to give advice because, if it were to be known, they would come under the law; midwives were even more fearful. The doomed women implored me to reveal the "secret" rich people had, offering to pay me extra to tell them; many really believed I was holding back information for money. They asked everybody and tried anything, but nothing did them any good. On Saturday nights I have seen groups of from fifty to one hundred with their shawls over their heads waiting outside the office of a five-dollar abortionist.

Each time I returned to this district, which was becoming a recurrent nightmare, I used to hear that Mrs. Cohen "had been carried to a hospital, but had never come back," or that Mrs. Kelly "had sent the children to a neighbor and had put her head into the gas oven." Day after day such tales were poured into my ears—a baby born dead, great relief—the death of an older child, sorrow but again relief of a sort—the story told a thousand times of death from abortion and children going into institutions. I shuddered with horror as I listened to the details and studied the reasons back of them—destitution linked with excessive childbearing. The waste of life seemed utterly senseless. One by one worried, sad, pensive, and aging faces marshaled themselves before me in my dreams, sometimes appealingly, sometimes accusingly.

These were not merely "unfortunate conditions among the poor" such as we read about. I knew the women personally. They were living, breathing, human beings, with hopes, fears, and aspirations like my own, yet their weary, misshapen bodies, "always ailing, never failing," were destined to be thrown on the scrap heap before they were thirty-five. I could not escape from the facts of their wretchedness; neither was I able to see any way out. My own cozy and comfortable family existence was becoming a reproach to me.

Then one stifling mid-July day of 1912 I was summoned to a Grand Street tenement. My patient was a small, slight Russian

Jewess, about twenty-eight years old, of the special cast of feature to which suffering lends a madonna-like expression. The cramped three-room apartment was in a sorry state of turmoil. Jake Sachs, a truck driver scarcely older than his wife, had come home to find the three children crying and her unconscious from the effects of a self-induced abortion. He had called the nearest doctor, who in turn had sent for me. Jake's earnings were trifling, and most of them had gone to keep the none-too-strong children clean and properly fed. But his wife's ingenuity had helped them to save a little, and this he was glad to spend on a nurse rather than have her go to a hospital.

The doctor and I settled ourselves to the task of fighting the septicemia. Never had I worked so fast, never so concentratedly. The sultry days and nights were melted into a torpid inferno. It did not seem possible there could be such heat, and every bit of food, ice, and drugs had to be carried up three flights of stairs.

Jake was more kind and thoughtful than many of the husbands I had encountered. He loved his children, and had always helped his wife wash and dress them. He had brought water up and carried garbage down before he left in the morning, and did as much as he could for me while he anxiously watched her progress.

After a fortnight Mrs. Sachs' recovery was in sight. Neighbors, ordinarily fatalistic as to the results of abortion, were genuinely pleased that she had survived. She smiled wanly at all who came to see her and thanked them gently, but she could not respond to their hearty congratulations. She appeared to be more despondent and anxious than she should have been, and spent too much time in meditation.

At the end of three weeks, as I was preparing to leave the fragile patient to take up her difficult life once more, she finally voiced her fears, "Another baby will finish me, I suppose?"

"It's too early to talk about that," I temporized.

But when the doctor came to make his last call, I drew him aside. "Mrs. Sachs is terribly worried about having another baby."

"She well may be," replied the doctor, and then he stood before her and said, "Any more such capers, young woman, and there'll be no need to send for me."

"I know, doctor," she replied timidly, "but," and she hesitated as though it took all her courage to say it, "what can I do to prevent it?"

The doctor was a kindly man, and he had worked hard to save her, but such incidents had become so familiar to him that he had long since lost whatever delicacy he might once have had. He laughed good-naturedly. "You want to have your cake and eat it too, do you? Well, it can't be done."

Then picking up his hat and bag to depart he said, "Tell Jake to sleep on the roof."

I glanced quickly at Mrs. Sachs. Even through my sudden tears I could see stamped on her face an expression of absolute despair. We simply looked at each other, saying no word until the door had closed behind the doctor. Then she lifted her thin, blue-veined hands and clasped them beseechingly. "He can't understand. He's only a man. But you do, don't you? Please tell me the secret, and I'll never breathe it to a soul. *Please!*"

What was I to do? I could not speak the conventionally comforting phrases which would be of no comfort. Instead, I made her as physically easy as I could and promised to come back in a few days to talk with her again. A little later, when she slept, I tiptoed away.

Night after night the wistful image of Mrs. Sachs appeared before me. I made all sorts of excuses to myself for not going back. I was busy on other cases; I really did not know what to say to her or how to convince her of my own ignorance; I was helpless to avert such monstrous atrocities. Time rolled by and I did nothing.

The telephone rang one evening three months later, and Jake Sachs' agitated voice begged me to come at once; his wife was sick again and from the same cause. For a wild moment I thought of sending someone else, but actually, of course, I hurried into my uniform, caught up my bag, and started out. All the way I longed for a subway wreck, an explosion, anything to keep me from having to enter that home again. But nothing happened, even to delay me. I turned into the dingy doorway and climbed the familiar stairs once more. The children were there, young little things.

Mrs. Sachs was in a coma and died within ten minutes. I folded her still hands across her breast, remembering how they had pleaded with me, begging so humbly for the knowledge which was her right. I drew a sheet over her pallid face. Jake was sobbing, running his hands through his hair and pulling it out like an insane person. Over and over again he wailed, "My God! My God! My God!"

I left him pacing desperately back and forth, and for hours I myself walked and walked and walked through the hushed streets. When I finally arrived home and let myself quietly in, all the household was sleeping. I looked out my window and down upon the dimly lighted city. Its pains and griefs crowded in upon me, a moving picture rolled before my eyes with photographic clearness: women writhing in travail to bring forth little babies; the babies themselves naked and hungry, wrapped in newspapers to keep them from the cold; six-year-old children with pinched, pale, wrinkled faces, old in concentrated wretchedness, pushed into gray and fetid cellars, crouching on stone floors, their small scrawny hands scuttling through rags, making lamp shades, artificial flowers; white coffins, black coffins, coffins, coffins interminably passing in never-ending succession. The scenes piled one upon another on another. I could bear it no longer.

As I stood there the darkness faded. The sun came up and threw its reflection over the house tops. It was the dawn of a new day in my life also. The doubt and questioning, the experimenting and trying, were now to be put behind me. I knew I could not go back merely to keeping people alive.

I went to bed, knowing that no matter what it might cost, I was finished with palliatives and superficial cures; I was resolved to seek out the root of evil, to do something to change the destiny of mothers whose miseries were vast as the sky.

Chapter Eight

I HAVE PROMISES TO KEEP

HOW were mothers to be saved? I went through many revolving doors, looked around, and, not finding what I was seeking, came out again. I talked incessantly to everybody who seemed to have social welfare at heart. Progressive women whom I consulted were thoroughly discouraging. "Wait until we get the vote. Then we'll take care of that," they assured me. I tried the Socialists. Here, there, and everywhere the reply came, "Wait until women have more education. Wait until we secure equal distribution of wealth." Wait for this and wait for that. Wait! Wait! Wait!

Having no idea how powerful were the laws which laid a blanket of ignorance over the medical profession as well as the laity, I asked various doctors of my acquaintance, "Why aren't physicians doing something?"

"The people you're worrying about wouldn't use contraception if they had it; they breed like rabbits. And, besides, there's a law against it."

"Information does exist, doesn't it?"

"Perhaps, but I doubt whether you can find it. Even if you do, you can't pass it on. Comstock'll get you if you don't watch out."

In order to ascertain something about this subject which was so mysterious and so unaccountably forbidden, I spent almost a year in the libraries—the Astor, the Lenox, the Academy of Medicine, the Library of Congress, and dozens of others. Hoping that psychological treatises might inform me, I read Auguste Forel and Iwan Block. At one gulp I swallowed Havelock Ellis' *Psychology of Sex,* and had psychic indigestion for months thereafter. I was not shocked, but this mountainous array of abnormalities made me spiritually ill. So many volumes were devoted to the exceptional, and so few to the maladjustments of normal married people, which were infinitely more numerous and urgent.

I read translations from the German in which women were advised to have more children because it could be proved statistically that their condition was improved by childbearing. The only article on the question I could discover in American literature was in the *Atlantic Monthly* by Edward Alsworth Ross of the University of Wisconsin, who brought to the attention of his readers the decline of the birth rate among the upper and educated classes and the increase among the unfit, the consequences of which were sure to be race suicide.

The Englishman, Thomas Robert Malthus, remained little more than a name to me, something like Plato or Henry George. Father had talked about him, but he meant mostly agriculture—wheat and food supplies in the national sense. Possibly he had a philosophy but not, to me, a live one. He had been put away on a shelf and, in my mind, had nothing to do with the everyday human problem. I was not looking for theories. What I desired was merely a simple method of contraception for the poor.

The pursuit of my quest took me away from home a good deal. The children used to come in after school and at once hunt for me. "Where's mother?" was the usual question. If they found me at my mending basket they all leaped about for joy, took hands and danced, shouting, "Mother's home, mother's home, mother's sewing." Sewing seemed to imply a measure of permanence.

I, too, wanted to drive away the foreboding barrier of separation by closer contact with them. I wanted to have them solely to myself, to feed, to bathe, to clothe them myself. I had heard of the clean, wind-swept Cape Cod dunes, which appeared to be as far from the ugliness of civilization as I could get. Socialism, anarchism, syndicalism, progressivism—I was tired of them all. At the end of the spring, thoroughly depressed and dissatisfied, I tucked the children under my arms, boarded a Fall River boat, and sailed off, a pioneer to Provincetown.

In 1913 the tip of the Cape was nothing but a fishing village with one planked walk which, I was told, had been paid for by Congress. Up and down its length the bellman, the last of the town criers, walked, proclaiming the news.

At first we lived in the upper story of a fisherman's house right on the water. After he went out in the morning, his wife and her children, and I and mine, were left alone. Then the old women recalled scenes from their early days on the whaling vessels. Their mothers had brought them forth unaided, and their own sons, in turn, had been born on the ships and apprenticed to their husbands. They fitted into life simply, but the younger Portuguese, who were taking over the fishing industry, were asking what they should do about limiting their families.

The village was rather messy and smelled of fish. I was still too close to humanity and wanted to be more alone, so we moved to the extreme end of town. Our veranda faced the Bay, and when the tide was high the water came up and lapped at the piles on which the cottage was built. Stuart, Grant, and Peggy used to sit on the steps and dabble their toes. At low tide they had two miles of beach on which to skip and run; it was a wonderful place to play, and all summer we had sunrise breakfasts, sunset picnics.

Ethel, who had married Jack Byrne, was now widowed and had also gone into nursing. She had considerable free time and stayed with me. Consequently, I was able to leave the children in her care when I made my expeditions to Boston's far-famed public library, taking the *Dorothy Bradford* at noon, and coming back the next day. Even there I found no information more reliable than that exchanged by back-fence gossips in any small town.

I spent the entire season at Provincetown, groping for knowledge, classifying all my past activities in their proper categories, weighing the pros and cons of what good there was in them and also what they lacked. It was a period of gestation. Just as you give birth to a child, so you can give birth to an idea.

Between interims of brooding and playing with the children I took part in the diversions of the minute colony of congenial people. Charles Hawthorne had a school of painting, and Mary Heaton Vorse with her husband, Joseph O'Brien, were there; so also were Hutch Hapgood and Neith Boyce. Jessie Ashley had lifted Big Bill Haywood out of the slough of the Paterson strike and brought him down to rest and recuperate.

Big Bill was one of the few who saw what I was aiming at, although fearful that my future might involve the happiness of my children. Even he did not feel that the small-family question was significant enough to be injected into the labor platform. Nevertheless, as we rambled up and down the beach he came to my aid with that cheering encouragement of which I was so sorely in need. He never wasted words in advising me to "wait." Instead, he suggested that I go to France and see for myself the conditions resulting from generations of family limitation in that country. This struck me as a splendid idea, because it would also give Bill Sanger a chance to paint instead of continuing to build suburban houses.

The trip to Europe seemed so urgent that no matter what sacrifices had to be made, we decided to make them when we came to them. In the fall we sold the house at Hastings, gave away some of our furniture and put the rest in storage. Although we did not realize it at the time, our gestures indicated a clean sweep of the past.

Anita Block proposed that we go via Scotland; she wanted me to write three or four articles on what twenty-five years of municipal ownership in Glasgow had done for women and children. Socialists were talking about how everything there belonged to the people themselves and had earned their own way—banks, schools, homes, parks, markets, art galleries, museums, laundries, bath houses, hospitals, and tramways. The city was about to pay off the last debt on the transportation system, and this was being hailed as a great victory, a perfect example of what Socialism could do. It sounded big and fine, and I, too, was impressed. Certainly in Glasgow, I thought, I should find women walking hand in hand with men, and children free and happy.

In October the Sangers sailed from Boston on a cabin boat, little and crowded, and one black night two weeks later steamed up the Clyde. The naval program of 1913 was causing every shipyard to run double shifts, and the flare and glare against the somber dark was like fairyland—giant, sparkling starlights reaching from the horizon into the sky, a beautiful introduction to Utopia.

The very next day I started out upon my investigations. To mind the children, aged nine, five, and three, I availed myself of a sort of employment bureau run by the Municipal Corporation. I had been told that anyone could call here for any imaginable type of service. In response to my summons, there promptly arrived at my door, standing straight and machine-like, a small boy in a buttons uniform, with chin strap holding his cap on the side of his head. Willie MacGuire's stipend was to be twelve cents an hour, or fifty cents for the half day. His function was to take the three out, entertain them, and return them faithfully at any time designated. Though he was no bigger than Stuart, his efficient manner reassured me, and I soon learned that he performed his duties diligently.

Religiously I made the rounds of all the social institutions, and at first everything appeared as I had been led to expect—except the weather. It had always just rained, and, when the sun did show itself, it was seldom for long enough to dry up the walks. Though the streets were clean, they were invariably wet and damp, and nobody wore rubbers. Everywhere could be seen little girls down on their knees, scrubbing the door-steps in front of the houses, or, again, carrying huge bundles or baskets of groceries to be delivered at the homes of the buyers. The people themselves seemed cold and rigid, as dismal as their climate. Only the policemen had a sense of humor.

As I proceeded, flaws in the vaunted civic enterprises began to display themselves. Glasgow had its show beauty spots, but even the model tenements were not so good as our simplest, lower-middle-class apartment buildings. One had been constructed for the accommodation of "deserving and respectable widows and widowers belonging to the working class" having one or more children with no one to care for them while the parents were away. But the building had been turned over to the exclusive use of widowers. Widows and their children had to shift for themselves.

All tenements were planned scientifically on the basis of so many cubic feet of air and so much light per so many human beings, ranging from quarters for two to those for five. No overcrowding was allowed.

"Well," I asked, "what happens when there are five or six children?"

"Oh, they can't live here," replied the superintendent. "They must go elsewhere."

"But where?"

Conversation ceased.

With particular attention I traced the adventures of one family which had expanded beyond the three-child limit. The parents had first moved over to the fringes of the city, and thereafter as more children were born had traveled from place to place, progressively more dingy, more decrepit. They now had nine and were inhabiting a hovel in the shipbuilding slums, unimaginably filthy and too far from the splendid utilities ever to enjoy them.

The further I looked, the greater grew the inconsistency. The model markets carried chiefly wholesale produce, and the really poor, who were obliged to huddle on the far side of the city, contented themselves with bread and tea and were thankful to have it. Another disappointment was the washhouses, dating from 1878 when they had been deemed a public necessity because men had protested they were being driven from their homes by washing which, on account of the incessant rain, seemed to hang there forever. A stall cost only twopence an hour, less expensive than heating water at home, and there were always women waiting in line. But the tram system, which was on the point of being liquidated in spite of its low fares, forbade laundry baskets, and, consequently, those who were not within walking distance—and they were the ones who needed it most—were deprived of its use.

Throughout the slum section I saw drunken, sodden women whose remaining, snag-like teeth stuck down like fangs and protruded from their sunken mouths. When I asked one of the executive officers of the corporation why they were so much more degraded than the men, he replied, "Oh, the women of Glasgow are all dirty and low. They're hopeless."

"But why should this be?" I persisted.

His only answer was, "It's their own fault."

Bill and I walked about late at night, overwhelmed by the unspeakable poverty. The streets were filled with fighting, shiftless beggars. Hundreds of women were abroad, the big shawls over their heads serving two purposes: one, to keep their shoulders warm; the other, to wrap around the baby which each one carried. It was apparent that their clothing consisted only of a shawl, a petticoat, a wrapper, and shoes. Older children were begging, "A ha'penny for bread, Missus, a ha'penny for bread."

It was infinitely cold, dreary, and disappointing—so much talk about more wages and better subsistence, and here the workers had it and what were they getting?—a little more light, perhaps, a few more pennies a day, the opportunity to buy food a little more cheaply, a few parks in which they could wander, a bank where their money earned a fraction more interest. But as soon as they passed beyond the border of another baby, they were in exactly the same condition as the people beyond the realm of municipal control.

Municipal ownership was one more thing to throw in the discard.

One dull, rainy day, glad to leave behind the shrill, crying voices of the beggars of Glasgow, we boarded a horrid cattle boat bound for Antwerp. The children were all seasick as we bounced and tossed over the North Sea. It was something of a job to handle the three of them with no nurse, especially when the storm threw them out of their beds on to the cabin floor. Fortunately they suffered no fractures, although twenty-six horses in the hold had to be shot because their legs had been broken.

We arrived at the Gare du Nord in Paris at the end of another dismal, bewildering day—toot-toot! steam, luggage, brusque snatching by blue-smocked, black-capped porters, all looking like villains, jam at the ticket gate, rackety taxi to a hotel on the Left Bank.

Paris seemed another Glasgow, more like a provincial village than a great metropolis. The atmosphere of petty penury destroyed my dreams of Parisian gaiety and elegance; even the French children were dressed in drab, gloomy, black aprons. Within a few days we had sub-let an apartment on the Boulevard St. Michel across from the Luxembourg Gardens where Grant and Peggy could play. It was four flights up, and the cold penetrated to the marrow of our bones. We could put tons of briquets into the little fireplaces and never get any heat. All the family went into flannel underwear, the first since my early childhood.

I presented Stuart to the superintendent of the district *lycée*. He demanded a birth certificate, and I had none.

"But without it how can I tell where he was born or how old he is?" The official seemed to imply that Stuart did not exist.

"But," I protested, "here he is. He's alive."

"No, no, Madame! The law says you must have a birth certificate."

I had to send him to a private school, which was something of a drain on the budget.

Bill found a studio on Montparnasse, just back of the Station. Again and again he came home aglow with news of meeting the great Matisse and other revolutionary painters barely emerging from obscurity. I trailed around to studios and exhibits occasionally, but I was trying to become articulate on my own subject, and paid scant attention to those who loomed up later as giants in the artistic world. The companionship of Jessie Ashley and Bill Haywood, who had just come to Paris, was more familiar to me.

I was also eager to encounter French people and discover their points of view. One of the first was Victor Dave, the last surviving leader of the French Commune of 1871. Thanksgiving Day we had a little dinner party and invited American friends to greet him. He was then over eighty, but still keen and active. As the evening wore on we started him talking about his past experiences and he held us enthralled until way into the morning, when we all had breakfast in the apartment.

The old Communard spoke English far better than any of us spoke French. He was now making three dollars a week by his linguistic abilities, because he was the sole person the Government could call upon not only for the language but the dialects of the Balkans. Just the day before he had been translating a new series of treaties which France was making with the Balkan States in a desperate attempt to tie them to the Triple Entente. Though he was a philosophical person who could be gay over his own hardships, his confidences to us were serious and sad. From the agreements then being drawn up, particularly those with Rumania, he could see nothing but war ahead, predicting definitely that within five years all nations would be at each other's throats. We newcomers to Europe could not grasp the meaning of his words, and the residents shrugged their shoulders and said, "He is getting old. He cannot see that we are now beyond war, that people are too intelligent ever to resort to it again."

As I look back it is apparent that we heard in France the whole rumblings of the World War. Unrest was in the air as it had been in the United States, but with a difference. Theaters were showing anti-German plays, *revanche* placards decorated Napoleon's tomb in the Invalides, and the rusty black draperies around the shrouded statue of Strasbourg in the Place de la Concorde pointed a macabre note. These were remembered afterwards; at the time they were merely part of the Paris scene.

I realized the disadvantage of not being better acquainted with the French language, and started in to practice what I knew and learn more. Good fortune brought me in touch with an Englishwoman, the wife of the editor of *L'Humanité,* the organ of the Confédération Générale de Travail, the famous C.G.T. To her I clung and at her home I met the Socialist leader, Jean Jaurès. His English was bad and my French worse; we had to have an interpreter. Doubtless we missed a lot, but even so we found we understood each other. I believe that his assassination on the eve of the war which he had done so much to prevent proved an irreparable loss to the cause of peace.

In my language difficulties Jessie Ashley's fluency was an everpresent help. Together we used to eat in the restaurants frequented by laborers, who came in groups, keeping their caps on, enjoying the cheap and good food accompanied by wine. Often we were the only women in the place, always excepting the inevitable cashier.

Though women were rarely seen at a C.G.T. meeting, Victor Dave took Jessie and me to a particularly impressive one which Bill Haywood was to address. His reputation as a firebrand had preceded him, and the police were making certain that no riot should ensue; they were stopping each person who crossed the bridge and demanding an account of his destination. Our passport was the venerable appearance of our escort, whose long white hair hung low about his head. His top hat, that universal badge of respectability, let us through.

The vast auditorium was filled with some three thousand French syndicalists, similar to the American I.W.W.'s, all standing, all wearing the uniform of the proletariat—black-visored caps and loose corduroys. They were being urged not to take up arms against the workers of other nations. I began to wonder whether perhaps the various tokens of disquiet which had impalpably surrounded me since coming to France had some more desperate meaning than we in America had realized. The *War, What For?* discussions in New York had seemed only a part of the evening conversations. Here again I was listening to protests against government efforts to arouse national hatred by calling it patriotism. I had heard the words so often, "Workers of the World, Unite," yet at last I was vaguely uneasy because of the difference in spirit.

As we emerged into the narrow, alley-like street we found the exits into the boulevard guarded by hundreds of gendarmes, both mounted and afoot. Had any outbreak occurred, the assembled syndicalists would literally have been trapped.

My uneasiness was increased as a result of a visit to the Hindu nationalist, Shyamaji Krishnavarma. In England he had been an agitator for Indian Home Rule and, when the London residence of the Viceroy of India had been bombed, with other Indians who might have been implicated, he had fled to France, so long the sanctuary for anyone who, because of political beliefs, got into trouble elsewhere. Krishnavarma was now editing the *Indian Sociologist*, which was being secretly spirited across the Channel.

Krishnavarma had asked whether he might be permitted to give a reception in my honor. No Hindu had ever given a reception in my honor. Trying to appear, however, as though this were a frequent occurrence, I set a time and bravely entered his salon, supported, as usual, by Jessie.

About twenty-five men were there, Indian students all, and only one other woman, Mrs. Krishnavarma, barely out of purdah and still in native dress. As a great concession she had been allowed to come in, despite the presence of men. It was evident she could listen but not speak, because, when I asked her something about her children, Krishnavarma answered for her quickly. A little later I was disputing a point with him and, to bolster up his argument, he gave her a curt command in Hindustani. She rose swiftly and soon returned with a well-thumbed and pencil-marked copy of Spencer. I had come to consider Spencer's philosophy old-fogyish. His teachings were so mild that I wondered what in the world he could ever have been hounded for. Though Krishnavarma was working towards the freedom of India he had gone no further than this pink tea which was not even pale China, let alone sturdy, black Ceylon.

I had been home scarcely more than half an hour and was dressing for dinner when Peggy ran in animatedly. "Mother, there are three soldiers at the door!" The bright uniforms of the gendarmes had taken her fancy, and she was pleased and excited. When I went out to meet them they demanded to know where we had come from, the object of our visit to France, how long we intended to stay, in what manner we had located the apartment, from whom we had rented it, where I had been that afternoon, the length of time I had known Krishnavarma, and the reason for my being at his home. Finally, they explained their presence by saying the concierge had not sent in the required information to the prefecture.

When I described the strange visitation to someone familiar with French customs, I was told that concierges were all ex officio agents of the police and were compelled to make regular reports of the activities, no matter how petty, of their tenants. These were incorporated into the dossiers of all foreigners. Actually, the police, working with the British Secret Service, were checking up on Krishnavarma's callers. Thereafter gendarmes lingered in doorways outside our apartment, and wherever I went I was conscious they were in the vicinity.

Because of the predilection of the French for quality rather than quantity, they had not only adopted the sociological definition of proletariat, "the prolific ones," a term originally applied by the Romans to the lowest class of society, but had interpreted it literally. The syndicalists in particular had made what they called conscious generation a part of their policy and principles, and had affiliated themselves with the Neo-Malthusian movement, which had its headquarters in London.

The parents of France, almost on the same wage scale as those I had seen in Glasgow, had settled the matter to their own satisfaction. Their one or two children were given all the care and advantages of French culture. I was struck with the motherly attention bestowed by our *femme de chambre* upon her only child. She came promptly to work, but nothing could persuade her to arrive before Jean had been taken to his school, and nothing could prevent her leaving promptly at noon to fetch him for his luncheon.

When Bill Haywood began taking me into the homes of the syndicalists, I found perfect acceptance of family limitation and its relation to labor. "Have you just discovered this?" I asked each woman I met.

"Oh, no, *Maman* told me."

"Well, who told her?"

"*Grandmère,* I suppose."

The *Code Napoléon* had provided that daughters should inherit equally with sons and this, to the thrifty peasant mind, had indicated the desirability of fewer offspring. Nobody would marry a girl unless she had been instructed how to regulate the numbers of her household as well as the home itself.

Some of the contraceptive formulas which had been handed down were almost as good as those of today. Although they had to make simple things, mothers prided themselves on their special recipes for suppositories as much as on those for *pot au feu* or wine.

All individual Frenchwomen considered this knowledge their individual right, and, if it failed, abortion, which was still common. I talked about the problems of my own people, but they could give me no help, merely shrugging their shoulders, apparently glad they were living in France and not in the United States. This independence of thought and action seemed wholly admirable to me at the time, and I sang the praises of the system.

Bill was happy in his studio, but I could find no peace. Each day I stayed, each person I met, made it worse. A whole year had been given over to this inactive, incoherent brooding. Family and friends had been generous in patience. I had added to my personal experience statistics from Glasgow and the little formulas I had gathered from the French peasants. With this background I had practically reached the exploding point. I could not contain my ideas, I wanted to get on with what I had to do in the world.

The last day of the year, December 31, 1913, Bill and I said good-by, unaware the parting was to be final. With the children I embarked at Cherbourg for home.

Chapter Nine

THE WOMAN REBEL

*"Oh you daughters of the West!
O you young and elder daughters! O you maidens and you
   women!
Never must you be divided, in our ranks you move united,
   Pioneers! O pioneers!"*
                                    WALT WHITMAN

THE *New York* was a nice ship and it was not too wintry to walk about on deck. After the children were safely in bed I paced round and round and absorbed into my being that quiet which comes to you at sea. That it was New Year's Eve added to the poignancy of my emotions but did not obscure the faith within.

I knew something must be done to rescue those women who were voiceless; someone had to express with white hot intensity the conviction that they must be empowered to decide for themselves when they should fulfill the supreme function of motherhood. They had to be made aware of how they were being shackled, and roused to mutiny. To this end I conceived the idea of a magazine to be called the *Woman Rebel,* dedicated to the interests of working women.

Often I had thought of Vashti as the first woman rebel in history. Once when her husband, King Ahasuerus, had been showing off to his people his fine linens, his pillars of marble, his beds of gold and silver, and all his riches, he had commanded that his beautiful Queen Vashti also be put on view. But she had declined to be exhibited as a possession or chattel. Because of her disobedience, which might set a very bad example to other wives, she had been cast aside and Ahasuerus had chosen a new bride, the meek and gentle Esther.

I wanted each woman to be a rebellious Vashti, not an Esther;

was she to be merely a washboard with only one song, one song? Surely, she should be allowed to develop all her potentialities. Feminists were trying to free her from the new economic ideology but were doing nothing to free her from her biological subservience to man, which was the true cause of her enslavement.

Before gathering friends around me for that help which I must have in stirring women to sedition, before asking them to believe, I had to chart my own course. Should I bring the cause to the attention of the people by headlines and front pages? Should I follow my own compulsion regardless of extreme consequences?

I fully recognized I must refrain from acts which I could not carry through. So many movements had been issuing defiances without any ultimate goal, shooting off a popgun here, a popgun there, and finally shooting themselves to death. They had been too greatly resembling froth—too noisy with the screech of tin horns and other cheap instruments instead of the deeper sounds of an outraged, angry, serious people.

With as crystal a view as that which had come to me after the death of Mrs. Sachs when I had renounced nursing forever, I saw the path ahead in its civic, national, and even international direction—a panorama of things to be. Fired with this vision, I went into the lounge and wrote and wrote page after page until the hours of daylight.

Having settled the principles, I left the details to work themselves out. I realized that a price must be paid for honest thinking—a price for everything. Though I did not know exactly how I was to prepare myself, what turn events might take, or what I might be called upon to do, the future in its larger aspects has actually developed as I saw it that night.

The same thoughts kept repeating themselves over and over during the remainder of the otherwise uneventful voyage. As soon as possible after reaching New York, I rented an inexpensive little flat on Post Avenue near Dyckman Street, so far out on the upper end of Manhattan that even the Broadway subway trains managed to burrow their way into sunlight and fresh air. My dining room was my office, the table my desk.

A new movement was starting, and the baby had to have a name.

It did not belong to Socialism nor was it in the labor field, and it had much more to it than just the prevention of conception. As a few companions were sitting with me one evening we debated in turn voluntary parenthood, voluntary motherhood, the new motherhood, constructive generation, and new generation. The terms already in use—Neo-Malthusianism, Family Limitation, and Conscious Generation seemed stuffy and lacked popular appeal.

The word control was good, but I did not like limitation—that was too limiting. I was not advocating a one-child or two-child system as in France, nor did I wholeheartedly agree with the English Neo-Malthusians whose concern was almost entirely with limitation for economic reasons. My idea of control was bigger and freer. I wanted family in it, yet family control did not sound right. We tried population control, race control, and birth rate control. Then someone suggested, "Drop the rate." Birth control was the answer; we knew we had it. Our work for that day was done and everybody picked up his hat and went home. The baby was named.

When I first announced that I was going to publish a magazine, "Where are you going to get the money?" was volleyed at me from all sides. I did not know, but I was certain of its coming somehow. Equally important was moral support. Those same young friends and I founded a little society, grandly titled the National Birth Control League, sought aid from enthusiasts for other causes, turning first to the Feminists because they seemed our natural allies. Armed with leaflets we went to Cooper Union to tell them that in the *Woman Rebel* they would have an opportunity to express their sentiments.

Charlotte Perkins Gilman, the Feminist leader, was trying to inspire women in this country to have a deeper meaning in their lives, which to her signified more than getting the vote. Nevertheless, at that time I struck no responsive chord from her or from such intelligent co-workers as Crystal Eastman, Marie Howe, or Henrietta Rodman. It seemed unbelievable they could be serious in occupying themselves with what I regarded as trivialities when mothers within a stone's throw of their meetings were dying shocking deaths.

Who cared whether a woman kept her Christian name—Mary Smith instead of Mrs. John Jones? Who cared whether she wore her wedding ring? Who cared about her demand for the right to work? Hundreds of thousands of laundresses, cloakmakers, scrub women, servants, telephone girls, shop workers would gladly have changed places with the Feminists in return for the right to have leisure, to be lazy a little now and then. When I suggested that the basis of Feminism might be the right to be a mother regardless of church or state, their inherited prejudices were instantly aroused. They were still subject to the age-old, masculine atmosphere compounded of protection and dominance.

Disappointed in that quarter I turned to the Socialists and trade unionists, trusting they would appreciate the importance of family limitation in the kind of civilization towards which they were stumbling. Notices were sent to *The Masses, Mother Earth, The Call, The Arm and Hammer, The Liberator,* all names echoing the spirit which had quickened them.

Shortly I had several hundred subscriptions to the *Woman Rebel,* paid up in advance at the rate of a dollar a year, the period for which I had made my plans. Proceeds were to go into a separate revolving account, scrupulously kept. Unlike so many ephemeral periodicals, mine was not to flare up and spark out before it had functioned, leaving its subscribers with only a few issues when they were entitled to more. Eventually we had a mailing list of about two thousand, but five, ten, even fifty copies often went in a bundle to be distributed without charge to some labor organization.

I was solely responsible for the magazine financially, legally, and morally; I was editor, manager, circulation department, bookkeeper, and I paid the printer's bill. But any cause that has not helpers is losing out. So many men and women secretaries, stenographers, clerks, used to come in of an evening that I could not find room for all. Some typed, some addressed envelopes, some went to libraries and looked up things for us to use, some wrote articles, though seldom signing their own names. Not one penny ever had to go for salaries, because service was given freely.

In March, 1914, appeared the first issue of the *Woman Rebel,* eight pages on cheap paper, copied from the French style, mailed first class in the city and expressed outside. My initial declaration of the right of the individual was the slogan "No Gods, No Masters." Gods, not God. I wanted that word to go beyond religion and also stop turning idols, heroes, leaders into gods.

I defined a woman's duty, "To look the world in the face with a go-to-hell look in the eyes; to have an idea; to speak and act in defiance of convention." It was a marvelous time to say what we wished. All America was a Hyde Park corner as far as criticism and challenging thought were concerned. We advocated direct action and took up the burning questions of the day. With a fine sense of irony we put anti-capitalist soapbox oratory in print. I do not know whether the financiers we denounced would have been tolerant or resentful of our onslaughts had they read them, or as full of passion for their cause as we for ours. Perhaps they too will have forgotten that emotion now.

My daily routine always started with looking over the pile of mail, and one morning my attention was caught by an unstamped official envelope from the New York Post Office. I tore it open.

Dear Madam, You are hereby notified that the Solicitor of the Post Office Department has decided that the *Woman Rebel* for March, 1914, is unmailable under Section 489, Postal Laws and Regulations.
E. M. Morgan, Postmaster.

I reread the letter. It was so unexpected that at first the significance did not sink in. I had given no contraceptive information; I had merely announced that I intended to do so. Then I began to realize that no mention was made of any special article or articles. I wrote Mr. Morgan and asked him to state what specifically had offended, thereby assisting me in my future course. His reply simply repeated that the March issue was unmailable.

I had anticipated objections from religious bodies, but believed with father, "Anything you want can be accomplished by putting a little piece of paper into the ballot box." Therefore, to have our insignificant magazine stopped by the big, strong United States Government seemed so ludicrous as almost to make us feel important.

To the newspaper world this was news, but not one of the dailies picked it out as an infringement of a free press. The *Sun* carried a headline, "'WOMAN REBEL' BARRED FROM MAILS." And underneath the comment, "Too bad. The case should be reversed. They should be barred from her and spelled differently."

Many times I studied Section 211 of the Federal Statutes, under which the Post Office was acting. This penal clause of the Comstock Law had been left hanging in Washington like the dried shell of a tortoise. Its grip had even been tightened on the moral side; in case the word obscene should prove too vague, its definition had been enlarged to include the prevention of conception and the causing of abortion under one and the same heading. To me it was outrageous that information regarding motherhood, which was so generally called sacred, should be classed with pornography.

Nevertheless, I had not broken the law, because it did not prohibit discussion of contraception—merely giving advice. I harbored a burning desire to undermine that law. But if I continued publication I was making myself liable to a Federal indictment and a possible prison term of five years plus a fine of five thousand dollars. I had to choose between abandoning the *Woman Rebel,* changing its tone, or continuing as I had begun. Though I had no wish to become a martyr, with no hesitation I followed the last-named course.

I gathered our little group together. At first we assumed Comstock had stopped the entire issue before delivery, but apparently he had not, because only the A to M's which had been mailed in the local post office had been confiscated. We took a fresh lot downtown, slipped three into one chute, four in another, walked miles around the city so that no single box contained more than a few copies.

The same procedure had to be pursued in succeeding months. Sometimes daylight caught me, with one or more assistants, still tramping from the printer's and dropping the copies, piece by piece, into various boxes and chutes. I felt the Government was absurd and tyrannical to make us do this for no good purpose. I could not get used to its methods then. I have not yet, and probably never shall.

The *Woman Rebel* produced extraordinary results, striking vibrations that brought contacts, messages, inquiries, pamphlets, books, even some money. I corresponded with the leading Feminists of Europe—Ellen Key, then at the height of her fame, Olive Schreiner,

Mrs. Pankhurst, Rosa Luxemburg, Adele Schreiber, Clara Zetkin, Roszika Schwimmer, Frau Maria Stritt. But I also heard from sources and groups I had hardly known existed—Theosophist, New Thought, Rosicrucian, Spiritualist, Mental Scientist. It was not alone from New York, but from the highways and byways of north, south, east, and west that inspiration came.

After the second number the focus had been birth control. Within six months we had received over ten thousand letters, arriving in accelerating volume. Most of them read, "Will your magazine give accurate and reliable information to prevent conception?" This I could not print. Realizing by now it was going to be a fairly big fight, I was careful not to break the law on such a trivial point. It would have been ridiculous to have a single letter reach the wrong destination; therefore, I sent no contraceptive facts through the mails.

However, I had no intention of giving up this primary purpose. I began sorting and arranging the material I had brought back from France, complete with formulas and drawings, to be issued in a pamphlet where I could treat the subject with more delicacy than in a magazine, writing it for women of extremely circumscribed vocabularies. A few hundred dollars were needed to finance publication of *Family Limitation,* as I named it, and I approached Theodore Schroeder, a lawyer of standing and an ardent advocate of free speech. He had been left a fund by a certain Dr. Foote who had produced a book on *Borning Better Babies,* and I thought my pamphlet might qualify as a beneficiary.

Dr. Abraham Brill was just then bringing out a translation of Freud, in whom Schroeder was much interested. He asked whether I had been psychoanalyzed.

"What is psychoanalysis?"

He looked at me critically as from a great height. "You ought to be analyzed as to your motives. If, after six weeks, you still wish to publish this pamphlet, I'll pay for ten thousand copies."

"Well, do you think I won't want to go on?"

"I don't only think so. I'm quite sure of it."

"Then I won't be analyzed."

I took the manuscript to a printer well known for his liberal tendencies and courage. He read the contents page by page and said, "You'll never get this set up in any shop in New York. It's a Sing Sing job."

Every one of the twenty printers whom I tried to persuade was afraid to touch it. It was impossible ever, it seemed, to get into print the contents of that pamphlet.

Meanwhile, following the March issue the May and July numbers of the *Woman Rebel* had also been banned. In reply to each of the formal notices I inquired which particular article or articles had incurred disapproval, but could obtain no answer.

At that time I visualized the birth control movement as part of the fight for freedom of speech. How much would the postal authorities suppress? What were they really after? I was determined to prod and goad until some definite knowledge was obtained as to what was "obscene, lewd, and lascivious."

Theodore Schroeder and I used to meet once in a while at the Liberal Club, and he gave much sound advice—I could not go on with the *Woman Rebel* forever. Eventually the Post Office would wear me down by stopping the issues as fast as I printed them. He warned, "They won't do so and so unless you do thus and thus. If you do such and such, then you'll have to take the consequences." He was a good lawyer and an authority on the Constitution.

When my family learned that I might be getting in deep water a council was called just as when I had been a child. A verdict of nervous breakdown was openly decreed, but back in the minds of all was the unspoken dread that I must have become mentally unbalanced. They insisted father come to New York, where he had not been for forty years, to persuade me to go to a sanitarium.

For several days father and I talked over the contents of the *Woman Rebel*. In his fine, flowing language he expressed his hatred of it. He despised talk about revolution, and despaired of anyone who could discuss sex, blaming this on my nursing training, which, he intimated, had put me in possession of all the known secrets of the human body. He was not quite sure what birth control was, and my reasoning, which retraced the pattern of our old arguments, made no impression upon him.

Father would have nothing to do with the "queer people" who

came to the house—people of whom no one had ever heard—turning up with articles on every possible subject and defying me to publish them in the name of free speech. I printed everything. For the August issue I accepted a philosophical essay on the theory of assassination, largely derived from Richard Carlile. It was vague, inane, and innocuous, and had no bearing on my policy except to taunt the Government to take action, because assassination also was included under Section 211.

Only a few weeks earlier, the war which Victor Dave had predicted had started its headlong progress. The very moment when most people were busy with geographies and atlases, trying to find out just where Sarajevo might be, the United States chose to sever diplomatic relations with me.

One morning I was startled by the peremptory, imperious, and incessant ringing of my bell. When I opened the door, I was confronted by two gentlemen.

"Will you come in?"

They followed me into my living room, scrutinized with amazement the velocipede and wagon, the woolly animals and toys stacked in the corner. One of them asked, "Are you the editor and publisher of a magazine entitled the *Woman Rebel?*"

When I confessed to it, he thrust a legal document into my hands. I tried to read it, threading my way slowly through the jungle of legal terminology. Perhaps the words became a bit blurred because of the slight trembling of my hands, but I managed to disentangle the crucial point of the message. I had been indicted—indicted on no less than nine counts—for alleged violation of the Federal Statutes. If found guilty on all, I might be liable to forty-five years in the penitentiary.

I looked at the two agents of the Department of Justice. They seemed nice and sensible. I invited them to sit down and started in to explain birth control. For three hours I presented to their imaginations some of the tragic stories of conscript motherhood. I forget now what I said, but at the end they agreed that such a law should not be on the statute books. Yet it was, and there was nothing to do about it but bring my case to court.

When the officers had gone, father came through the door of the adjoining room where he had been reading the paper. He put both arms around me and said, "Your mother would have been alive to-day if we had known all this then." He had applied my recital directly to his own life. "You will win this case. Everything is with you—logic, common sense, and progress. I never saw the truth until this instant."

Old-fashioned phraseology, but father was at last convinced. He went home quite proud, thinking I was not so crazy after all, and began sending me clippings to help prove the case for birth control —women who had drowned themselves or their children and the brutalities of parents, because even mother love might turn cruel if too hard pressed.

My faith was still childlike. I trusted that, like father, a judge representing our Government would be convinced. All I had to do was explain to those in power what I was doing and everything would come right.

August twenty-fifth I was arraigned in the old Post Office way downtown. Judge Hazel, himself a father of eight or nine children, was kindly, and I suspected the two Federal agents who had summoned me had spoken a good word on my behalf. But Assistant District Attorney Harold A. Content seemed a ferocious young fellow. When the Judge asked, "What sort of things is Mrs. Sanger doing to violate the law?" he answered, "She's printing articles advocating bomb throwing and assassination."

"Mrs. Sanger doesn't look like a bomb thrower or an assassin."

Mr. Content murmured something about not all being gold that glittered; I was doing a great deal of harm. He intimated he knew of my attempts to get *Family Limitation* in print when he said, "She is not satisfied merely to violate the law, but is planning to do it on a very large scale."

Judge Hazel, apparently believing the charges much exaggerated, put the case over until the fall term, which gave me six weeks to prepare my answer, and Mr. Content concurred, saying that if this were not enough time, I could have more.

The press also was inclined to be friendly. Reporters came up to Post Avenue, looked over the various articles. They agreed, "We think the Government absolutely wrong. We don't see how it has any case." Unfortunately, while we were talking, Peggy, who had never seen a derby before, took possession of their hats and sticks, and in the hall a little parade of children formed, marching up and down in front of the door. One of the gentlemen was so furious that I hid Peggy in the kitchen away from his wrath. As he went out he remarked, "You should have birth controlled them before they were born. Why don't you stay home and spend some thought on disciplining your own family?"

I had many things to do which could not be postponed, the most important among them being to provide for the children's future. This occupied much of my time for the next few weeks. Temporarily, I sent the younger two to the Catskills and Stuart to a camp in Maine, arranging for school in the fall on Long Island.

Defense funds were always being raised when radicals got into trouble to pay pseudo-radical lawyers to fight the cases on technicalities. I was not going to have any lawyer get me out of this. Since my indictment had not stopped my publishing the *Woman Rebel,* through the columns of the September issue I told my subscribers I did not want pennies or dollars, but appealed to them to combine forces and protest on their own behalf against government invasion of their rights. That issue and the October one were both suppressed.

During what might be called my sleepwalking stage it was as though I were heading towards a precipice and nothing could awaken me. I had no ear for the objections of family or the criticism of friends. People were around me, I knew, but I could not see them clearly; I was deaf to their warnings and blind to their signs.

When I review the situation through the eyes of those who gave me circumspect advice, I can understand their attitude. I was considered a conservative, even a bourgeoise by the radicals. I was digging into an illegal subject, was not a trained writer or speaker or experienced in the arts of the propagandist, had no money with which to start a rousing campaign, and possessed neither social position nor influence.

In the opinion of nearly all my acquaintances I would have to spend at least a year in jail, and they began to condole with me. None offered to do anything about it, just suggested how I could get through. One kind woman whom I had never seen before called late one evening and volunteered to give me dancing lessons. In a small six-by-four cabin she had developed a system which she claimed was equally applicable to a prison cell and would keep me in good health. She even wrote out careful directions for combining proper exercises with the rhythm of the dance.

But I myself had no intention of going to jail; it was not in *my* program.

One other thing I had to do before my trial. *Family Limitation* simply must be published. I had at last found the right person—Bill Shatoff, Russian-born, big and burly, at that time a linotype operator on a foreign paper. So that nobody would see him he did the job after hours when his shop was supposed to be closed.

At first I had thought only of an edition of ten thousand. However, when I learned that union leaders in the silk, woolen, and copper industries were eager to have many more copies to distribute, I enlarged my plan. I would have liked to print a million but, owing to lack of funds, could not manage more than a hundred thousand.

Addressing the envelopes took a lot of work. Night after night the faithful band labored in a storage room, wrapping, weighing, stamping. Bundles went to the mills in the East, to the mines of the West—to Chicago, San Francisco, and Pittsburgh, to Butte, Lawrence, and Paterson. All who had requested copies were to receive them simultaneously; I did not want any to be circulated until I was ready, and refused to have one in my own house. I was a tyrant about this, as firm as a general about leaving no rough edges.

In October my case came up. I had had no notice and, without a lawyer to keep me posted, did not even know it had been called until the District Attorney's office telephoned. Since Mr. Content had promised me plenty of time, I thought this was merely a formality and all I had to do was put in an appearance.

The next morning I presented myself at court. As I sat in the crowded room I felt crushed and oppressed by an intuitive sense of the tremendous, impersonal power of my opponents. Popular interest was now focused on Europe; my little defiance was no longer important. When I was brought out of my reverie by the voice of the clerk trumpeting forth in the harshly mechanical tones of a train announcer something about *The People* v. *Margaret Sanger*, there flashed into my mind a huge map of the United States, coming to life as a massive, vari-colored animal, against which I, so insignificant and small, must in some way defend myself. It was a terrific feeling.

But courage did not entirely desert me. Elsie Clapp, whose ample Grecian figure made her seem a tower of strength, marched up the aisle with me as though she, too, were to be tried. I said to Judge Hazel that I was not prepared, and asked for a month's adjournment. Mr. Content astonished me by objecting. "Mrs. Sanger's had plenty of time and I see no reason, Your Honor, why we should have a further postponement. Every day's delay means that her violations are increased. I ask that the case continue this afternoon."

A change in Judge Hazel's attitude had taken place since August. Instead of listening to my request, he advised me to get an attorney at once—my trial would go on after the noon recess.

I was so amazed that I could only believe his refusal was due to my lack of technical knowledge, and supposed that at this point I really had to have a lawyer. I knew Simon H. Pollock, who had represented labor during the Paterson strike, and I went to see him. He agreed with me that a lawyer's plea would not be rejected and that afternoon confidently asked for a month's stay. It was denied. He reduced it to two weeks. Again it was denied. At ten the following morning the case was to be tried without fail.

From the Post Office Department I received roundabout word that my conviction had already been decided upon. When I told this to Mr. Pollock he said, "There isn't a thing I can do. You'd better plead guilty and let us get you out as fast as we can. We might even be able to make some deal with the D.A. so you'd only have to pay a fine."

I indignantly refused to plead guilty under any circumstances. What was the sense of bringing about my indictment in order to test the law, and then admit that I had done wrong? I was trying to prove the law was wrong, not I. Giving Mr. Pollock no directions how to act, I merely said I would call him up.

It was now four o'clock and I sought refuge at home to think through my mental turmoil and distress. But home was crowded with too many associations and emotions pulling me this way and that. When my thoughts would not come clear and straight I packed a suitcase, went back downtown, and took a room in a hotel, the most impersonal place in the world.

There was no doubt in my mind that if I faced the hostile court the next morning, unprepared as I was, I would be convicted of publishing an obscene paper. Such a verdict would be an injustice. If I were to convince a court of the rightness of my cause, I must have my facts well marshaled, and that could not be done in eighteen hours.

Then there was the question of the children's welfare. Had I the right to leave them the heritage of a mother who had been imprisoned for some offensive literature of which no one knew the details?

What was I to do? Should I get another lawyer, one with personal influence who could secure a postponement, and should we then go into court together and fight it out? I had no money for such a luxury. Should I follow the inevitable suggestion of the "I-told-you-so's" and take my medicine? Yes, but what medicine? I would not swallow a dosage for the wrong disease.

I was not afraid of the penitentiary; I was not afraid of anything except being misunderstood. Nevertheless, in the circumstances, my going there could help nobody. I had seen so many people do foolish things valiantly, such as wave a red flag, shout inflammatory words, lead a parade, just for the excitement of doing what the crowd expected of them. Then they went to jail for six months, a year perhaps, and what happened? Something had been killed in them; they were never heard of again. I had seen braver and hardier souls than I vanquished in spirit and body by prison terms, and I was not going to be lost and broken for an issue which was not the real one, such as the entirely unimportant *Woman Rebel* articles. Had I been able to print *Family Limitation* earlier, and to swing the indictment around that, going to jail might have had some significance.

Going away was much more difficult than remaining. But if I were to sail for Europe I could prepare my case adequately and return then to win or lose in the courts. There was a train for Canada within a few hours. Could I take it? Should I take it? Could I ever make those who had advised me against this work and these activities understand? Could I ever make anyone understand? How could I separate myself from the children without seeing them once more? Peggy's leg was swollen from vaccination. This kept worrying me, made me hesitate, anxious. It was so hard to decide what to do.

Perfectly still, my watch on the table, I marked the minutes fly. There could be no retreat once I boarded that train. The torture of uncertainty, the agony of making a decision only to reverse it! The hour grew later and later. This was like both birth and death—you had to meet them alone.

About thirty minutes before train time I knew that I must go. I wrote two letters, one to Judge Hazel, one to Mr. Content, to be received at the desk the next day, informing them of my action. I had asked for a month and it had been refused. This denial of right and freedom compelled me to leave my home and my three children until I made ready my case, which dealt with society rather than an individual. I would notify them when I came back. Whether this were in a month or a year depended on what I found it necessary to do. Finally, as though to say, "Make the most of it," I enclosed to each a copy of *Family Limitation*.

Parting from all that I held dear in life, I left New York at midnight, without a passport, not knowing whether I could ever return.

Chapter Ten

WE SPEAK THE SAME GOOD TONGUE

AT Montreal I found comfort and refuge. In fact, on any road I took men and women who knew about the *Woman Rebel* came to my aid. I shall never forget the generosity of the Baineses who met me at the train and welcomed me to their home. They had been friends of Walt Whitman and still honored "his" memory. I sat at the table where "he" had sat, and in "his" chair. Among their many kindnesses they gave me an introduction to Edward Carpenter, also mentioned in awed tones, leader of the Whitman group in England and author of *Love's Coming of Age,* which was then on every modern bookshelf.

Since I was charged with felony I could be extradited. I was obliged, therefore, in buying my passage, to choose a new name. No sooner had I selected the atrociously ugly "Bertha Watson," which seemed to rob me of femininity, than I wanted to be rid of it. But once having adopted it I could not escape.

I boarded the *RMS Virginian,* laden with munitions, food, Englishmen returning home for war duty, and Canadians going over. Even before the printing of *Family Limitation* had begun in August, I had arranged a key message which would release all the pamphlets simultaneously whenever it should be received by any of four trusted lieutenants. In case one should be arrested, another ill, or a third die, still everything would go forward as provided for. Three days out of Montreal I sent a cable and shortly had one in reply that the program was being executed as planned. My soul was sick and my heart empty for those I loved; the one gleam in this dreadful night of despair was the faint hope that my efforts might, perhaps, make Peggy's future easier.

The government official examining credentials at Liverpool said sternly, "England is at war, Madam. You can't expect us to let you through. We're sending back people without passports every day, and I can't make an exception in your case."

But I had Good Luck as an ally; she comes so often to help in emergencies. A shipboard acquaintance telephoned and pulled wires, a procedure not so common in England as in the United States. On his guarantee that I would get a passport from the American Embassy immediately on reaching London I was allowed to enter.

I wound through dirty streets in a cab to the Adelphi Palace. It rained all day, the wind blew, its howling came through the windows and crept down the chimney. Homesickness swept over me worse than ever before or since. I knew it would not do to "set and think" as the Quakers say, so I wandered about in the business district, trying to adjust my mind to the prices marked in the store windows in order to have some idea of what they were in dollars and cents. I viewed church architecture and the Cathedral, which was not expected to be finished for fifty years. It did not look so splendid, but since everything about it was closed I really could not tell.

Liverpool was a quaint city. I liked its weathered brick houses, and the evenness and settled feeling, as though the people in them planned to remain where they were for time everlasting. The women of the poor were unconcernedly wearing on the streets dresses originally made for bustles, hats with feathers, caricatures which should have been stuffed away in attics forty years before.

Bertha Watson had a letter to the local Fabian Society, and at six I went to the Clarion Café, where it foregathered each Friday. I presented her letter, was welcomed heartily, and invited to the discussion. I found the English then and later polite in speech and action, tolerant in listening. One of the members helped me to locate temporary rooms while I waited for the arrival of letters and messages from the United States. These lodgings were in the home of gentle, middle-class people to whom I paid thirty shillings a week, including breakfast and dinner.

I shall always be glad I went to that meeting, because there I met Lorenzo Portet, once companion of Francisco Ferrer and now heir to his educational work, which both believed was the key to Spanish emancipation.

After the attempted assassination of Alfonso XIII and Victoria of England, the Government had arrested twenty-five hundred Spaniards having republican ideas, among them Ferrer. His school had been closed and he had been jailed. When he had been eventually released, he had still been determined to educate for universal peace by means of economic justice. Accordingly, as Portet stated it, he had reopened a school for all Spain by publishing labor texts at Barcelona. This again had earned him no reward from a grateful Government. In 1909 he had been arrested in a purge of republicans, stood up against a wall and shot, and his body thrown into a ditch.

Ferrer had left his money to Portet, who was now fulfilling his trust by feeding the country with modern scientific translations from Italy, France, and England. He was a man of middle height and weight whose alert glance summed you up with an accuracy occasionally disturbing. After our initial encounter he called on me with punctiliousness and formality, and produced an article from a New York magazine which carried the story of the indictment of Margaret Sanger. "This is you?" he questioned with the jumping of all fact which is termed intuition.

Portet, a born teacher, was then instructing youth at the University of Liverpool in Spanish. No human being I ever knew could explain with such infinite pains the details of a subject. He placed your own opposition before you, marshaled it in all its strength, and then annihilated every point, one by one. His humorous cynicism was most baffling to those who were merely emotional converts to better worlds. "Civilization?" he might say, "Mainly a question of good roads."

Sometimes in the midst of those long, drab, November weeks I escaped to Wales, where there were endless lanes, winding and hard, with very few carts, and all very quiet. Even here were Carnegie libraries, one of them turned into a restaurant. I went into the houses of the smelting workers at Green Brombo, Wexham, all lovely, minute, stone cottages of two or three rooms, huddled closely together, charming with their walks and walls and flower gardens. The folk were slow, deliberate, simple.

Liverpool was only a junction; London was my terminus. There I could study at the British Museum, and meet the Neo-Malthusians. Towards the end of the month I rolled up to London through miles of chimney-potted suburbs; it continued rainy and foggy, but still there was a friendly atmosphere in the air. I seemed to be coming to a second home.

My first quarters were on the top floor of a "bed and breakfast" on Torrington Square, just back of the British Museum. I looked out on little rows of trees, iron fences, steps going up to all the houses. There was but one bathroom and to use it cost extra. Every morning about seven came a knock, and when I opened the door I discovered a midget jug of hot water outside. I was supposed to break the ice on my large pitcher, mix the two, and pour all into my tin tub, the back of which rose behind me like a throne. After this winter I realized how the British had acquired their well-known moral courage.

I had no fireplace, but two floors below was an empty room with a grate. Occasionally I indulged myself in the luxury of renting it for the evening, and of buying wood to keep myself warm while I worked. I made up for it by not having the slatternly Cockney maid bring up tea, and also went each morning to the basement dining room for my breakfast, thereby saving a shilling a week. It was not long before I was stricken by the first digestive upset I had ever had, and was obliged to call in an American doctor. He looked me over casually and then, without further examination, asked, "Have you been drinking English coffee?"

"Why, yes."

"Well, give it up. The English can't make coffee; they only know how to make tea. Take up English tea."

I followed his advice and from that time on, instead of carrying my own eating habits with me, have tried to adjust myself to the food of the country where I happened to be. In this way I get along much better.

Sundays I attended concerts or visited art galleries, though since it was war time disappointingly few pictures were being shown. Each week day, however, found me at the British Museum, going in with the opening of the gates in the morning. In order to secure permission to work, you had to have a card, but once you obtained it, you could take a special seat and books were reserved for you. My aim was to present my case from all angles, to make the trial soundly historical so that birth control would be seriously discussed in America. Therefore, I read avidly and voluminously many weighty tomes, and turned carefully the yellowed, brittle pages of pamphlets and broadsides, finding much that was dull, much that was irrelevant, but also much that was amusing, if only for the ponderous manner of its expression. In the end I had a picture of what had gone before.

The father of family limitation was Thomas Robert Malthus, born in 1766 at the Rookery, near Dorking, Surrey. In 1798 this curate of Albury published his *Principle of Population* and in the initial chapter laid down his famous postulates: "first, that food is necessary to the existence of man; second, that the passion between the sexes is necessary, and will remain nearly in its present state. . . ." Consequently the unrestrained fertility of the human race was certain to outstrip the available fruits of the earth, and, although the natural checks of war, disease, and privation had controlled population for centuries, they had brought misery, disaster, and death in their train. His solution was voluntary and intelligent control of the birth rate by means of late marriage, which left few years for childbearing. However, human nature is such that Malthus might preach forever without anyone's heeding his advice. Not until the profound economic depression which followed the Napoleonic Wars were people worried into concern over surplus population.

To John Stuart Mill the production of large families was to be regarded in the same light as drunkenness or any other physical excess. In the very first edition of his *Political Economy* he spoke of "prudence, by which either marriages are sparingly contracted, or care is taken that children beyond a certain number shall not be the fruit," and concluded that "the grand practical problem is to find the means of limiting the number of births." But he left it merely as a grand, practical problem.

Francis Place, the master tailor of Charing Cross, was born in a private debtors' prison kept by his father in Vinegar Yard. He was the first to suggest the idea of contraception as a remedy for poverty, but was more practical in his preaching than in his performance, fathering as he did fifteen children. In 1822 he published *Illustrations and Proofs of the Principle of Population:*

If, above all, it were once clearly understood, that it was not disreputable for married persons to avail themselves of such precautionary means as would, without being injurious to health, or destructive of female delicacy, prevent conception, a sufficient check might at once be given to the increase of population beyond the means of subsistence; vice and misery, to a prodigious extent, might be removed from society, and the object of Mr. Malthus, Mr. Godwin, and of every philanthropic person, be promoted.

Place had educated himself on Adam Smith, Locke, Hume, Thomas Paine, and Burke. To his remarkable library came many notable thinkers and men of letters. Among them was Robert Owen, the textile industrialist, who, in his *Moral Physiology,* offered openly a method of contraception:

I sit down to write a little treatise, which will subject me to abuse from the self-righteous, to misrepresentation from the hypocritical, and to reproach even from the honestly prejudiced.

He spoke to young men and women who still believed in virtue and happiness. "A human being is a puppet, a slave, if his ignorance is to be the safeguard of his virtue." In reply to the accusation that coitus interruptus was unnatural, he pointed out that the thwarting of any human wish or impulse might be so termed. "If this trifling restraint is to be called unnatural, what shall be said of celibacy?"

Owen in his youth had been impressed by the sufferings of the working classes, and, in a first effort to lighten the burden of his employees, had instituted many reforms in the New Lanark Mills, himself prospering materially in so doing; he was less successful when he emigrated to the United States and at New Harmony, Indiana, established a short-lived communal colony. However, his coming to America had at least one important result. His book influenced Doctor Charles Knowlton of Boston to write a tract entitled *Fruits of Phi-*

losophy in which he recommended a chemical formula and other methods to prevent conception. I had not found a trace of this in my previous research, even in Boston where it had been published.

Knowlton's reaffirmation of the desirability both from a political and social point of view for mankind to be able to limit at will the number of offspring without sacrificing the attendant gratification of the reproductive instinct, would have been little noticed had it not been for the repercussion in England forty years later.

During the early Victorian uprush of industrialism a man's children had been breadwinners, and family limitation had naturally lapsed. But when humanitarian legislation had begun to rescue children from factories, the population specter had shown itself once more.

In 1861 was formed the Malthusian League, designed to influence public opinion and overcome the prevailing misconception of Malthusianism, and in 1876 a Bristol bookseller brought out an English edition of *Fruits of Philosophy*. He was promptly arrested on the charge of publishing an obscene book, and sentence was suspended on his plea of guilty.

The brilliant rationalist and freethinker, Charles Bradlaugh, a redoubtable personality, together with Annie Besant, later the renowned Theosophist but then a young rebel, started a printing partnership and sold the pamphlet. Although not approving it in all its details they determined to contest the right to publish it and to prove that prevention of conception was not obscene.

Extraordinary interest was aroused in their trial before Lord Chief Justice Cockburn and a special jury. The Solicitor General himself appeared as chief counsel for the prosecution. Taking a copy of *Fruits of Philosophy* in his hands he opened it solemnly and said, "It is really extremely painful to me," then hesitating, "very painful to me to have to read this." But he did so.

Bradlaugh and Besant conducted their own defense. The latter with eloquence and astonishing poise held the admiring attention of the court for two days. Nevertheless, both were convicted of defaming the morals of the public, sentenced to six months in jail and a thousand-dollar fine, and required to put up guarantees of twenty-five hundred dollars for good behavior during the next two years.

The case was immediately appealed. Fortunately the upper court dismissed it on a technicality, because specific evidence of obscenity was not included; if the words were polluting they had to appear in the record.

This decision settled for all time in England that contraception was not to be classed among the obscenities. As a result, new life was injected into the Malthusian League and its name was changed to the Neo-Malthusian Society. In the first issue of its monthly journal it set forth a modest claim: "We have the ONLY REMEDY that the disease of society can be cured by." Instead of the impractical advice of Malthus to marry late, the Neo-Malthusians advised early marriage, the use of contraceptive methods, and children born according to the earning capacity of the father; a man's station in life should determine the number of his children. Furthermore, they intended one by one to "prick the flimsy bubbles of emigration, lessened production, and home colonization, which are from time to time put forward." The emphasis was still placed on the social and economic aspects rather than the personal tragedies of women.

That was in 1876; now in 1914 the Drysdales, Dr. C. V. and his wife, Bessie, were the guiding spirits of the Society. They had a long heritage of Malthusianism behind them; the uncle of the former, Dr. George Drysdale, fresh from Edinburgh in 1854, had anonymously published his *Elements of Social Science,* which had gone into fifteen languages. He had even himself studied Chinese to ensure a reasonably accurate translation in that tongue. In the darkest days of Victorianism, this young physician had included the New Woman in his interpretation of Malthus. Both he and his brother Charles, also a physician, had been in love with Alice Vickery, who had chosen the latter and borne him a son, the present C.V.

Alice Vickery was as great in her day as Mary Wollstonecraft in hers. After a tremendous struggle, which included getting her degree in Dublin and her training in Paris, she had proved her right to enter the medical profession, and had become the first woman doctor in England.

My keenest desire was to get in touch with the Drysdales. They invited me to tea at their offices—offices in the English sense, not ours. I squelched through the inevitable rain to Queen Anne's Chambers and was astonished to find nothing on the door except Dr. C. V. Drysdale's name. The term Malthusian was not considered proper according to the landlord's ideas of propriety. In fact, throughout England the word brought up antagonism. People crossed the street to avoid it.

I entered a sitting room, gay with chintz-covered chairs and a sofa, pillows at the back, quite fitted to Queen Anne's own day. A fire was burning cheerily, yet even this was not so welcome as the open arms and excitement with which I was greeted, not only by the Drysdales but also by Dr. Binnie Dunlop, dark, Scotch, thin, and dapper, intellectually enthusiastic although not emotionally so; by Olive Johnston, the faithful secretary who had worked for many years with the Drysdales; and by F. W. Stella Browne, an ardent Feminist whose faintly florid face, hair never quite white, and indefatigable vivacity are the same a quarter of a century later. Many women in causes are like that; something in their spirit keeps them forever young.

Dr. Drysdale was then in his early forties, slender, fair, inclined to be bald. In his ebullience he was not at all British, but his pleasing, warm, and courteous personality was British at its best. Bessie Drysdale, about her husband's age, was the practical member, dispensing charming hospitality. The others were like an army meeting me, but she brought up the rear with tea and cakes and comforting things.

It seemed to me I had seen them and known them all before. I was immediately certain I had come to the right place. In the United States I had been alone, pulling against all whose broad, general principles were the same as mine but who disapproved of my actions. But these new friends saw eye to eye with me. Instead of heaping criticism and fears upon me, they offered all the force of an international organization as well as their encyclopedic minds to back me up.

The policy of the Neo-Malthusians had been to educate the educators. They believed that once the practice of family limitation had been established among the well-to-do and socially prominent, it would be taken up by the lower strata. They were not discouraged, although after almost forty years success seemed as far away as ever; the working classes not only evinced no desire for the benefits of family limitation, but did not even know such a thing existed.

Everybody in the room appreciated my rebellion and extended congratulations on a name having been coined which was so simple and easy to understand as birth control. When I told them how I had managed the distribution of the *Family Limitation* pamphlets Dr. Drysdale stood up impetuously and said, "Oh, would to God we had a Comstock law! There's nothing can so stir the British people as a bad law. Then they will do something to change it!"

That afternoon was one of the most encouraging and delightful of my life. The warmth of my reception strengthened me to face the future. It lessened my dreadful homesickness and curbed the ever-growing impulse to escape from war-sick London and hurry back to the children. During my stay I saw much of the Drysdales and their group, and between us all grew up a close kinship which has lasted through the stormy years.

I like to think of London at this time chiefly because of all my new friends and the laughter they brought me. Of late there had been little of it in my life, but with every friend I had in England—more than with any other people I have ever known—I laughed, and this laughter knit and welded the bonds of comradeship.

One day in the British Museum I was standing by the catalogs, which were in the form of books, waiting until a man near me finished the volume I wanted to consult. I glanced at him idly, then more closely, thinking I identified the profile from pictures I had seen. When he had put the book down I ventured tentatively, "Aren't you Edward Carpenter?"

Almost without looking at me he replied, "Yes, and aren't you Margaret Sanger?"

It was a shock for Bertha Watson to hear this name repeated out loud in a public place. However, Mr. Carpenter's recognition was readily explainable. He had been more or less prepared to see me because he had already received my letter and had that morning at my rooming house been told I never returned from the British Museum until evening. Since we could not talk in this hall of silence, we adjourned to the Egyptian Room, and then to lunch. He was human, full of wit, fun, and humor—a live person who exuded magnetism.

Edward Carpenter reassured me that what I was doing was not merely of the present but belonged even more to the future. From this fine spirit I drew confirmation of the purity of my endeavor, something essential for me to take back to America if others there were to experience the same sense of justification. We beyond the Atlantic were still uncertain of our ethics, and even of our morals. We needed the sanction of British public opinion and the approval of their great philosophers, so that we could be strong in our beliefs.

During the first weeks in England I did not feel vehemently about the War, especially as signs were displayed everywhere, "Business as usual." I supposed it would be a little flurry, soon over. War talk, of course, was universal. The German espionage system was much discussed. I wondered whether it were not the general characteristic of the German always to observe and be accurate in detail which made his information valuable. He did the same thing in the United States, where nobody thought of calling him a spy. Everywhere women were knitting socks and mitts, but I was more impressed by the fact they were smoking in hotel lobbies—a new indication of emancipation to me—and even rolling their own cigarettes. If a woman came in for tea, without a word being said, a bell hop produced her own box of tobacco. When she left, it was returned to its proper place.

As the months went on, however, to be an American became almost as unlucky as to be a German. Whoever wished to remain safely in England must agree with England, give over every vestige of independent thinking or free expression. Wherever I went I heard mention of "Traitorous America." At one dining-car table a gray-haired Englishman, unaware of my nationality, asserted, "Americans will do anything for money."

"Yes," agreed his companion. "They do not care whom their bullets kill. They get paid for them." He was a young Dutchman, apparently just returned from the East Indies, and the conversation between the two developed briskly. Americans were a "mixed breed without souls; they had none of the qualities which make a nation great—no traditions, history, art, music, absolutely nothing but their money; they had to come to Europe for everything—to England for laws, customs, and morals, to France for fashions and arts;

they were human leeches fastened on Europe without incentive, originality, or creative ability; they—"

I interrupted, "What do you want America to do? Why should she get into this? Does she owe loyalty to England or France or Russia?"

"Oh, no, but for Belgium. America signed the Hague Treaty with the rest of us, and she has not stood by it."

To this I advanced the argument, "We Americans are not like Europeans. We are a heterogeneous mixture of all the fighting forces and nations of the world. We include the Irish who hate England, and Jews who hardly can be said to love Russia. A large part of our population—industrious, civil, reliable, and prosperous—are Germans, with whom our Scandinavians are sympathetic. Who then have we to ally against Germany? And why?—a very small far-back mention of gratitude to France for her help in our Revolution against British rule—and the Statue of Liberty."

On the whole I came more nearly being a nationalist when I left England than when I went there. I had to do such battle to explain the United States that, almost involuntarily, I felt myself becoming less of an internationalist. It was a strange feeling, as though somebody you knew and loved were being criticized, and you took up the cudgels in defense.

Chapter Eleven

HAVELOCK ELLIS

*"He who ascends to mountain-tops shall find
Their loftiest peaks most wrapt in clouds and snow;
Round him are icy rocks, and loudly blow
Contending tempests on his naked head."*
LORD BYRON

AS Christmas approached, my loneliness for the children increased. This was their particular time. I had messages from and about them, but these could not give the small, intimate details; the Atlantic was a broad span, seeming more vast to letter writers. I missed their voices, their caresses, even their little quarrels. I almost wondered whether solitary confinement in prison were not preferable to my present isolation.

In the midst of this stark yearning to be with them and share their tree I received a cordial note from Havelock Ellis asking me to come to tea. With kindly foresight he had given me explicit directions how to reach Fourteen Dover Mansions in Brixton across the Thames. I boarded a crowded bus at Oxford Circus. Though it was a miserable day near the dark end of 1914, the spirit of Christmas was in the air and everyone was laden with beribboned bundles and bright packages.

Looking askance at the police station which occupied the lower floor I climbed up the stairs, and, with the shyness of an adolescent, full of fears and uncertainties, lifted the huge brass knocker. The figure of Ellis himself appeared in the door. He seemed a giant in stature, a lovely, simple man in loose-fitting clothes, with powerful head and wonderful smile. He was fifty-five then, but that head will never change—the shock of white hair, the venerable beard, shaggy though well-kept, the wide, expressive mouth and deep-set eyes, sad even in spite of the humorous twinkle always latent.

I was conscious immediately that I was in the presence of a great man, yet I was startled at first by his voice as he welcomed me in. It was typically English, high and thin. I once talked to a prisoner at Sing Sing who had been in the death house for three years and could speak only in whispers thereafter. Ellis had been a hermit for twenty-five. He had lived in the Bush in Australia, and later secluded himself in his study. Nevertheless, the importance of what he had to say much more than made up for the instrument which conveyed it.

He led me to the living room through which the cheerless twilight of a winter afternoon in London barely penetrated, and seated me before a little gas fire. Some rooms impress you as ghastly cold even when hot. This one, though lacking central heating, had the warmth of many books. He lit two candles on the mantel, which flickered softly over his features, giving him the aspect of a seer.

We sat down and quiet fell. I tried a few aimless remarks but I stuttered with embarrassment. Ellis was still. Small talk was not possible with him; you had to utter only the deepest truths within you. No other human being could be so silent and remain so poised and calm in silence.

While Ellis was preparing tea in the kitchen he left me to look over his library and the most recent news from America. He had laid out and marked certain pertinent items which he thought might not have come to my attention. This, I later found, was one of his most endearing characteristics. He always entered into the life of the other person in little details, never forgetting even the kind of bread or olives, fruits or wines, you preferred. His detachment was not incompatible with sympathy.

Soon appeared a large tray, laden with tea, cakes, and bread and butter, and we sat down before the humming flame and talked and talked; and as we talked we wove into our lives an intangible web of mutual interests. I began to realize then that the men who are truly great are the easiest to meet and understand. After those first few moments I was at peace, and content as I had never been before. Entirely unaware of the reverence he aroused, Ellis pasted no labels on himself, had no poses, made no effort to impress. He was simply, quite un-selfconsciously, what he was.

When he asked me to describe the details of how I had locked horns with the law, I spoke glowingly of the heartening approval which the Drysdales had just given me. He did not show the same enthusiasm; in fact he was rather concerned, and not so ready with praise for my lack of respect for the established order, believing so strongly in my case that he wanted me to avoid mistakes. I think his influence was always more or less subduing and moderating; he tried to get me, too, to take the middle road. Though he occasionally alluded to some of the more amusing phases of the trial of his own work, he had pushed it into the back of his mind.

This monumental study intended for doctors and psychologists had been projected when Ellis was a medical student of nineteen. But his short practice of medicine, his editing of the *Mermaid Series of Old British Dramatists,* and the preparation of several sociological treatises, had intervened before, in 1898, *Sexual Inversion,* the first volume, had appeared. George Bedborough, printer, had been arrested for selling a copy, and charged with "publishing an obscene libel with the intention of corrupting the laws of Her Majesty's subjects." Ellis, the scholar, preferred to ignore controversy; the martyr's crown would not have coincided favorably with calm and dispassionate research. Judging it merely stupid of the British Government to have pushed the case to trial, he suspended the sale of the volume immediately, so disappointed that his own countrymen did not understand his motives that he stated then and there he would not have his other volumes published in England, and he never has.

He, beyond any other person, has been able to clarify the question of sex, and free it from the smudginess connected with it from the beginning of Christianity, raise it from the dark cellar, set it on a higher plane. That has been his great contribution. Like an alchemist, he transmuted the psychic disturbance which had followed my reading of his books into a spiritual essence.

We had many things to discuss, but suddenly it dawned upon me that I must have outstayed my time. Seven o'clock struck before I realized how late it was. It had seemed so short to me.

I was not excited as I went back through the heavy fog to my own dull little room. My emotion was too deep for that. I felt as though I had been exalted into a hitherto undreamed-of world.

Some of my new friends, Guy Aldred, Henry Sara, and Rose Witcop, invited me to tea with them Christmas Eve. Rose was deliberate in her movements, tall and dark, with straight black hair falling low over her forehead and caught at the nape of the neck. She and Guy were both ardent pacifists. A few days earlier I had overheard them reproving their son, aged six, for suggesting that Santa Claus bring him some lead soldiers. He had seen uniforms in every street and toy replicas in every shop window; all little boys were having them. I had not been able to send many presents to my children, and before leaving the house slipped into his room. He was sound asleep and his clothes were stretched out neatly at the foot of his bed. Outraging my own principles I tucked a box of soldiers under the blanket so that he might see this martial array the first thing in the morning.

Rose and Guy were thoroughly disgusted with me.

Much that evening combined to stir me. Carol singers paraded Torrington Square, group after group lifting plaintive voices in *Good King Wenceslas* and *We Three Kings of Orient Are*. I was headachy but I went out and strolled about the streets to see Merrie England at Yuletide. I had on so much clothing that I could scarcely walk, and still I was icy cold. It was just about a year since I had left France with the children, never to be reunited with Bill.

Since I am slow in my decisions and cannot separate myself from past emotions quickly, all breaches must come gradually. A measure of frustration is an inevitable accompaniment to endeavor. My marriage had not been unhappy; I had not let it be. It had not failed because of lack of love, romance, wealth, respect, or any of those qualities which were supposed to cause marital rifts, but because the interests of each had widened beyond those of the other. Development had proceeded so fast that our lives had diverged, due to that very growth which we had sought for each other. I could not live with a human being conscious that my necessities were thwarting or dwarfing his progress.

It had been a crowded year, encompassing the heights and depths of feeling. Christmas Eve was too much for me. I went back again and sat, wondering whether the children were well and contented. The next morning came a cable from them, flowers from Bill, and a nice note from Havelock Ellis.

Thereafter Havelock aided me immensely in my studies by guiding my reading. Tuesdays and Fridays were his days at the British Museum, and he often left little messages at my seat, listing helpful articles or offering suggestions as to books which might assist me in the particular aspect I was then engaged upon.

If when traveling about with him on the tram, going to a concert, shopping for coffee and cigarettes outside the Museum, a thought came to him, he would pull out a bit of paper and jot down notes. That was how he compiled his material for books, gathering it piecemeal and storing it away in envelopes. Anything on the dance went into the dance envelope, music into music, and so on. As soon as any one became full enough to attract his attention, he took it out and started to make something of it.

Sometimes we dined together at a Soho restaurant; occasionally I had tea at his flat. In his combined kitchen and dining room, warmed by a coal stove, he did his work, and there also he cooked meals for which he marketed himself. He was proud of being able to lay a fire with fewer sticks and less paper than an expert charwoman, and once said he would rather win praise for the creation of a salad than of an essay.

One of the four rooms was set aside for the use of his wife, Edith. She preferred the country and lived on her farm in Cornwall, whereas Havelock loved to be in the city; though he was not a part of it, he liked to hear it going on about him. Whenever she came to town she found all her books and possessions inviolate; whenever he went to Cornwall he found everything ready for him. Either of them could, on impulse, board a train without baggage and in a few hours be at home.

Edith was short and stocky, high-colored, curly-haired, with mystical blue eyes but accompanying them a strain of practicality. She could run the farm, look after the livestock, and dispose of her products. Her vitality was so great that it sought other outlets in writing fiction.

Bernard Shaw was once trying to find his way to the Ellis farm and stopped at a cottage to inquire whether he was on the right road. The goodwife could not tell him.

"But I know Mr. and Mrs. Ellis live near here."

She kept protesting nobody of that name was in the neighborhood until Shaw pointed to a house which appeared as though it might be the one. "Who lives there?"

"Two strangers."

"What do they do?"

"Oh, the man he writes out of other folks' books, but she writes out of her head."

The person who saw most of Havelock was Olive Schreiner, a long-standing friend of his and of Edith. I was delighted at the chance of meeting the author of *Woman and Labor* and of another favorite, *The Story of an African Farm*. She had just come to England for the first time in twenty-five years and been caught in the War.

Knowing Havelock to be a philosopher, I had expected him to be an elderly man, but, despite his white hair, had found him young, physically and mentally. Olive Schreiner's writings were so alive that I had visualized a young woman. Instead, although her hair was black, her square and stout Dutch body was old and spread. She had, perhaps, been partly aged by the frightful asthma from which she had suffered for so many years. The effect was enhanced by the dark surroundings of the shabby hotel in which I first saw her.

Certainly another contributing factor was her despondence over the War. Although her mother was English, her father Dutch, and she a British subject, her Germanic name was causing her the most harrowing complications. Fellow hotel guests of her own sex, when they spied her name on the register or heard her paged, insisted to the manager that either she should be removed or they were going to seek quarters elsewhere. She was literally being hounded from place to place.

Possibly Olive felt the tragedy of the War more than any other person I met in London at this time. She had never believed that "the boys would be out of the trenches by Christmas," or that business as usual could continue much longer. Already she had seen the horrors of armed conflict in South Africa; it seemed to begin lightly, but it did not end that way. She feared the whole world might be trapped in this one, that internationalism and the peace movement were practically finished, and that a whole new generation had to be born before we could recover what we had lost. She appeared to me then unduly disheartened; it was only later when her words came true that I comprehended how accurate were her prophecies.

Better than any living being Olive understood Havelock. I realized this during a conversation between herself and Edith. The latter had been in the United States lecturing on three writers: her husband, James Hinton, whom he admired tremendously, and Edward Carpenter. Her reception had convinced her the name of Ellis had gone beyond the borders of England, and she wanted him to return with her the following year to reap some of the reward of the respect thousands of Americans had for him.

Havelock was terror-stricken, first at the idea of coming to a new country, and second at the mere mention of speaking in public. He could imagine no tortures worse than these. But in order to please Edith, whom he loved dearly, and also because her persistency and determination were so great that he found it hard to oppose her, he agreed to leave it to the three of us.

Edith and I had called on Olive to talk it over. She, as usual, had just recently moved. This time she was more cheerful, and after tea we took up the momentous question of the destiny of another individual. Edith, with her customary fire and fervor, started in to persuade Olive, Havelock's lifelong friend, and me, his new friend, that going to America would be a crowning glory for him. She entreated our aid in making him decide to do so.

Olive characteristically listened with rapt attention until Edith had finished. Then she turned to me. "What do you think Havelock should do?"

I, knowing how much Americans expected of a speaker in the way of voice, personality, and gift of oratory, and also how easily they could be disappointed unless gestures and external appearance fulfilled their anticipations, concluded he would not find this crown of glory or this universal acclaim, and that he would probably return disillusioned after the first fanfare of publicity. I said, without giving my reasons, "I don't think he should go."

"Have either of you asked Havelock what he wants to do?" Olive questioned.

"I have," said Edith, "and he doesn't want to."

"Then that settles the matter entirely," replied Olive. "Nobody has the authority to make another do what he doesn't want to, no matter how good you or I or any of us think it might be for him. I myself will never take a step that my instinct or intuition tells me not to. I am guided wholly by that instinct, and if I should awaken tomorrow morning and my inner voice told me to go to the top of the Himalayas, I would pack up and go."

This brief speech determined the question for Havelock, his right to stay snugly in London, and to give up all the adventure Edith had planned for him.

Olive, in her commonly dark mood, was encouraged more by the work being done for women in birth control than by anything else. She herself, who had had but one child, which had died, realized its significance. The last time I saw her she put both arms around me and said, "We may never meet again, but your endeavor is the bright star shining through the black clouds of war."

She was not able to go back to South Africa until the War was over. One morning, not long afterwards, she was found dead in her bed. According to her instructions, her little child and beloved dog were removed from their old resting places and Kaffirs carried the three of them to the peak of a mountain outside Queenstown, where they have since reposed on their high eminence.

Ellis has been called the greatest living English gentleman. But England alone cannot claim him; he belongs to all mankind. I define him as one who radiates truth, energy, and beauty. I see him in a realm above and beyond the shouting and the tumult. Captains and kings come and go. Lilliputian warriors strut their hour, and boundary lines between nations are made and unmade. Although he takes no active share in this external trafficking, he does not dwell apart in an ivory tower of his own construction.

This Olympian seems to be aloof from the pain of the world, yet he has penetrated profoundly into the persistent problems of the race. Nothing human is alien to his sympathy. His knowledge is broad and deep; his wisdom even deeper. He makes no strident, blatant effort to cry aloud his message, but gradually and in ever-increasing numbers, men and women pause to listen to his serene voice.

Here is a phenomenon more amazing than the achievements of radio-activity. Despite all the obstacles and obstructions that have hindered his expression, his truth has filtered through to minds ready to receive it. His philosophy, if it can be reduced to an essence, is that of life more abundant—attained through a more complete understanding of ourselves and an unruffled charity to all.

To Havelock Ellis we owe our concept of that Kingdom of God within us, that inner world which hides all our inherent potentialities for joy as well as suffering. Thanks to him we realize that happiness must be the fruit of an attitude towards life, that it is in no way dependent upon the rewards or the gifts of fortune. Like St. Francis of Assisi, he teaches the beauty of nature, of his brother the sun and his sister the moon, of birds and fish and animals, and all the pageantry of the passing seasons.

I have never felt about any other person as I do about Havelock Ellis. To know him has been a bounteous privilege; to claim him friend my greatest honor.

Chapter Twelve

STORK OVER HOLLAND

DAY after day the attendants at the British Museum piled books and pamphlets on the table before my seat. As I pored over the vital statistics of Europe it seemed to me that chiefly in the Netherlands was there a force operating towards constructive race building. The Dutch had long since adopted a common-sense attitude on the subject, looking upon having a baby as an economic luxury—something like a piano or an automobile that had to be taken care of afterwards.

The Drysdales often mentioned the great work done by Dr. Aletta Jacobs of Amsterdam and Dr. Johannes Rutgers of the Hague. The story of Dr. Jacobs' conquest of nearly insuperable obstacles to a medical career was particularly appealing. Born in 1854 in the Province of Groningen, she was the eighth child of a physician who, on eight hundred dollars a year, had to support his wife and eleven children. Even before adolescence she had asked defiantly, "What's the use of brains if you're born a girl?" She was determined to become a doctor like her father, though no woman had ever been admitted to Groningen University. Her spirit was so indomitable that when at seventeen she had passed the examinations and demanded entrance, she had been permitted to listen for a year, and then allowed to register as a permanent student.

In 1878 Dr. Jacobs had finished her studies in medicine at Amsterdam University and gone to London, where she had attended the Besant and Bradlaugh trial, met the Fabians, met the Malthusians, become an ardent suffragist. This first woman physician in the Netherlands had returned to Amsterdam and there had braved the disapproval of her father's friends by practicing her profession and by opening a free clinic for poor women and children, where she gave contraceptive advice and information, the first time this had ever been done in the world.

Within a few years and within a radius of five miles the proportion of stillbirths and abortions as well as venereal disease had started to decline, children were filling the schools, people were leaving their canal boats to go into agriculture.

The Netherlands being such a small country, where one person's business was everybody's business, such changes could not escape notice. Just about this time Dr. Charles R. Drysdale, then President of the English League, had been invited to address an International Medical Congress held in Amsterdam. The results of Dr. Jacobs' clinic were so apparent that immediately thereafter the Dutch Neo-Malthusian League had been formed and thirty-four physicians had joined it. When other centers were established, purely for consultation, the word clinic was applied to them also. In 1883 Dr. Mensinga, a gynecologist of Flensburg, Germany, had published a description of a contraceptive device called a diaphragm pessary, which he and Dr. Jacobs had perfected. Dr. and Madame Hoitsema Rutgers had taken charge of the League in 1899 with such success that the work had spread through that well-ordered kingdom. In recognition of its extensive and valuable accomplishment, Queen Wilhelmina had presented it with a medal of honor and a charter, and counted it one of the great public utilities.

In my statistical investigations I paid special attention to the birth and mortality rates of the Netherlands to see how they had been affected over this period of thirty-five years. They showed the lowest maternal mortality, whereas the United States was at the top of the list; three times more mothers' lives were being saved in the little dike country than in my native land. Furthermore, the infant death rate of Rotterdam, Amsterdam, and the Hague, the three cities in which the League was most active, were the lowest of all those in the world.

During the same period the death rate had been cut in half, but, surprisingly, I found that the birth rate had been reduced only a third. In other words, the death rate had fallen faster than the birth rate, which meant that the population of the Netherlands was increasing more rapidly than that of any other country in Europe.

I had much difficulty in reconciling these figures with my preconceived idea that birth control would automatically bring about a decrease in population. Since it was increasing, then perhaps birth control was not, after all, the answer to the economic international problem. If this were true all my calculations were going to be upset.

Impatient to go to the Netherlands and dig out the real facts, not only from Dutch records but from personal observation, I decided quietly—most of my decisions in those days were quiet ones—to cross the Channel. This implied possible unwelcome encounters with inquisitive officials, floating bombs, submarines, and every type of inconvenience and delay, but my eagerness made me discount the hindrances.

I applied to the Dutch Consul for a visa to Bertha Watson's passport.

"Eighty cents, please," and no questions asked.

So that I should not have to return to London before going on to Paris I presented myself at the French Consulate also. I waited two hours. "Two dollars, please," and still no queries.

I attached myself to the end of the long line waiting at Victoria Station to have passports inspected, and was soon safely on the train for Folkestone. We were late when we reached the Channel. Again we lined up for inspection. Many Belgian women with four or five children were going back to their people; the sleepy little ones and the tired women settled on the platform to rest until some had gone through. Two detectives glanced casually at my passport, and then allowed me to enter the official chamber. Inspections had been growing steadily more strict; this was the ultimate test. There sat in a row three officers in mufti, well-fed and brusque with authority. I handed my passport to the first, who looked me up and down as though I were a treacherous enemy, then pushed it over to the next. This man too viewed me with suspicion and mistrust, and pulled out a notebook, scanning the names to see whether mine were on the proscribed list. The last of the three, who was to make the final decision—crisp, trim, and hard as nails in voice and manner—demanded, "What are you going to the Continent for, Madam? Another joy ride? You Americans must think that's all this War amounts to. Can you produce any good reason for letting you through?"

Fortunately I was prepared for such a contingency. I took out of my purse a letter from Bernarr MacFadden asking me to answer certain questions in the form of articles for *Physical Culture* such as the relation between the unfit and population growth. I offered this document while those in line behind me waited restively. He read it meticulously, taking longer than necessary as it seemed to me in my nervousness. At last he folded it neatly and said, "A good work, this. Too bad someone hasn't done it before."

Then he put his last official stamp on my various papers and I passed through for the gangplank.

No complications presented themselves at the Hague, and early on a January morning in 1915 I registered at an inexpensive hotel. It was comforting to hear a radiator sizzling once more. I joined the other guests who were cheerfully breakfasting together *en famille* at a single table, and, since I spoke neither Dutch nor German, silently munched my black bread and cheese, downed the excellent coffee, and watched interestedly. Though stolid in appearance like all the Dutch, they were friendly.

I did not try to telephone Dr. Rutgers. Instead, though it was not yet nine o'clock, I hailed a taxi and held out to the driver a slip of paper on which I had written the street and number. In response to my ring at the door to which I was delivered, a tiny square window in the upper part opened mysteriously and a face—wizened, aged, and inquisitive—was framed in the aperture. It remained while I explained my mission. Apparently trust was inspired because, my story finished, the door swung wide and the face, materialized into Dr. Rutgers, ushered me into the library, where I waited until he came back in his street clothing. Then we went out to a second breakfast in a nearby café.

The doctor turned out to be a kindly little man, whose wife was now an invalid. It was hard for him to talk English. Most of the Dutch had four languages, but only those who had lived in England spoke English well. The difficulties, however, lessened as we nibbled brioches and sipped coffee after coffee until noon. Warming to my narrative of the battle in the United States, he shook his head when he thought of what I might have to face in the future, and expressed more concern over my predicament and more heartfelt sympathy with my having had to leave the children behind than anybody I had yet met. He was the first person to whom I had been able to overflow about my personal sadness.

On his part Dr. Rutgers described his hardships in keeping the clinics open and, through the League, preventing adverse legislation. Neo-Malthusianism had never been popular anywhere, no matter what the proof in the lessening of human misery and suffering. Dr. Rutgers had borne alone the brunt of all the criticism directed at his society.

The Rutgers method for establishing new clinics had resulted in a sound system for dealing with the birth rate. The men and women who acted as his councilors understood that a rising birth rate, no matter where in the country, would soon be followed by a high infant mortality rate. Accordingly, they reported this quickly to the society, which sent a midwife or practical nurse, trained in the technique standardized by Dr. Rutgers, into the congested sector to set up a demonstration clinic. She usually took an apartment with two extra rooms, one for waiting, the other a modestly equipped office like that of any country midwife.

Her duty was to go into the home where a child had died, inquire into the cause, and give friendly advice regarding the mother's own health. She also encouraged her not to have another baby until the condition of ignorance, poverty, or disease, whichever it might be, had either been bettered or eliminated. Whenever four had been born into such a family this advice was made more emphatic.

As soon as Dr. Rutgers had explained his policy to me I had that most important answer to the puzzling and bothersome problem of the increasing population in the Netherlands brought about by birth control. It was proper spacing. The numbers in a family or the numbers in a nation might be increased just as long as the arrival of children was not too rapid to permit those already born to be assured of livelihood and to become assimilated in the community.

Dr. Rutgers suggested I come to his clinic the next day and learn his technique. He was at the moment training two midwives preparatory to starting a new center in the outskirts of the Hague. Under his tutelage I began to realize the necessity for individual instruction to patients if the method of contraception prescribed was to fulfill its function. I wondered at the ease with which this could be done. Very soon even I myself, unable to talk to these women in their own tongue, instructed seventy-five.

I used to bombard the little man with questions concerning each case. I took issue with him over his autocratic system of dictating without explanation. Merely saying, "This is what you do. Do this always," had to my mind no educational value.

"Don't you think it would be a good idea to tell your patients what you're aiming at and why?" I asked.

"No, can't take time. They must do what they're told."

His was the doctor's point of view with which I was familiar, but with which I could not agree.

It also seemed to me a mistake to regard the women merely as units in a sociological scheme for bettering the human race. On the file cards were inscribed only names and addresses; no case histories. I wanted to know so much more about them. How many children had they already had? How many had they lost? What were their husbands' wages? What was the spacing in each family, and what were the effects? How successful had been the method of contraception?

If this information had then been recorded, the birth control movement could later have cited chapter and verse in its own support.

After my morning's work with Dr. Rutgers I usually repaired to the Central Bureau of Statistics with my three-in-one translator, interpreter, and guide. My findings were that in all cities and districts where clinics had been established the figures showed improvement—labor conditions were better and children were going to schools, which had raised their educational standards. Professional prostitutes were few, and even these were German, French, Belgian, or English, because Dutch women were encouraged to marry early. It made a difference. From the eugenic standpoint there had been a rapid increase in the stature of the Dutch conscript as shown by army records. The data proved conclusively that a controlled birth rate was as beneficial as I had imagined it might be, growing out of the first clinic initiated by the enterprise of Dr. Aletta Jacobs.

I was, of course, looking forward to meeting Dr. Jacobs, and sent her a note asking for the privilege of an interview. A reply came, curt and blunt; she would not see me. She was not concerned with my studies or with me, because it was a doctor's subject and one in which laymen should not interfere. Already I had come to the same conclusion in principle, but was dismayed at this first rebuff I had encountered. I was also hurt as much as I could be hurt during that period when I seemed to be one mass of aches, physically and mentally. Not until much later did I learn that to be a nurse was no recommendation in Europe, where she was more like an upper servant, a household drudge who took care of the sick instead of the kitchen.

For two months I wandered about the Netherlands, visiting clinics and independent nurses in the Hague, Rotterdam, and Amsterdam. In spite of the League propaganda against commercialization I found many shops in which a woman, if she so desired, could purchase contraceptive supplies as casually as you might buy a toothbrush. Unfortunately in some of them she could be examined and fitted by saleswomen who had but little training in technique and scant knowledge of anatomy. Although the Dutch League had several thousand members—each one active, writing to papers, talking to friends, attending meetings—and although fifty-four clinics were in operation, many well-informed people did not know anything about them. More surprising still, the medical profession as a whole appeared to be utterly ignorant of the directed birth control work that was going on. It did not, therefore, seem extraordinary that no inkling of all this—either clinics or contraceptive methods—had ever reached the United States, and practically no attempt to copy it been made in England.

Even in this neutral country signs of war were everywhere. Along the way were soldiers in uniform, armed and keeping guard, and at the stations Red Cross wagons were in readiness. Feeling among the Dutch was greatly mixed: Queen Wilhelmina's husband was a German; the army and the aristocracy were for the Triple Alliance; the poorer classes were more influenced by the sufferings of the thousands and thousands of Belgians who had flocked to Dutch firesides for food and shelter.

Nowhere else was I so impressed with the tragedies of war. Often about four o'clock I had *kaffee klatch* at the home of some Dutch lady who sat, very proper, while the maid served coffee, the best in Europe, from the big, white, porcelain pot. I suspected most of the morning had been spent in supervising preparations for the delicious food.

At one of these afternoons I was introduced to five German delegates who had come to attend the Women's Peace Conference. They found it difficult to forgive the stories of German atrocities which England had allowed to circulate. I ventured to inquire how they could disprove them, especially in view of the report of the Bryce Commission. "Was not war cruel and savage, and might not these things have happened?"

"Yes, yes," one said, "but hundreds of our German boys are brought back to us, dead and alive, whose noses and ears have been cut off, put in packages, and taken to headquarters for reward. However, we would not dream of accusing the French or the English soldiers of such barbarisms. We know that because their code forbids them to do these things themselves they have called in the Moors and the Gurkhas and the savages from Africa."

Unable to comprehend how those towards whom they felt such friendliness could return this sentiment with hatred, the women said to me in bewilderment, "Tell us really why people who do not know us hate us as they do." The dignity of their sorrow, the heavy burden of grief under which they labored, the very calmness and fairness with which they bore it, had a quieting effect.

The Netherlands was the place to regain a certain sense of balance, especially if you had passed through England, where feeling was so embittered. I overheard in Amsterdam a most illuminating conversation between two Englishmen and a German. After going over the pros and cons, they shook hands all around, agreeing that six months after the War was settled German and English trade would be hand in glove, trials and grievances forgotten.

To go directly to France from the Netherlands was next to impossible; nor did I find it easy to travel roundabout by way of England, owing to the recently instituted German submarine blockade. Then at last I heard that a freighter was to be sent to London to test it. Day after day I went to the docks for news, and employed the interval with pleasant social contacts.

Rather than have a cocktail before lunch or dinner the Dutch assembled at their favorite restaurants for apéritifs. The glass, with winged rim spreading out about half an inch from the top, was filled to overflowing with Bols. You were not supposed to touch it at first; instead you leaned over and sort of scooped a little with your mouth before picking it up and enjoying it. The French apéritifs were pleasant and mild, but Holland gin was so strong and raw that I marveled at the way they could take it with a smile. I was definitely unequal to the art.

One evening I was invited to play billiards with a Dutchman, an Englishman, and a German. I accepted as naturally as for a game of whist. Afterwards the Dutchman said that, though no respectable Dutch wife could have played billiards in that room without later being approached or insulted, an American woman could do anything and still not lose caste. She minded her own affairs, paid her own bills, and even if she were seen on the streets late at night without an escort everyone knew she must be on legitimate business.

Then the Englishman spoke to the same effect. He said you found the American woman in all sorts of out-of-the-way and often questionable places, but you needed only to look into her candid face to find an answer to what she was doing there. European women owed her a great deal for her pioneering on the Continent. In England it was a common sight to see the most estimable women smoking cigarettes in all fashionable restaurants and hotels just as in America.

"Just as in America!" I gasped, remembering my astonishment at having seen women smoke publicly in London. "I'm sure there must be some mistake. Ladies are not supposed to smoke in America. As an example to Europe they're a failure, because they haven't even won that liberty for themselves."

This was a surprise to them all. But the Dutchman rallied to the defense, shifting the subject. "Nevertheless, she is the best-dressed woman in the world."

"What about the Parisian?" I exclaimed.

"I except none. I have been over half the globe. I have paid particular attention to foreigners, their customs, their education, their tastes, and I have been convinced that today the Parisian woman has had to yield to the American in respect to clothes and fashion. Paris designs are intended for the United States, not for France or England. The Frenchwoman may be trim and neat and jaunty, but it takes a woman of wealth in France to be in the fashion, while in New York, every shopgirl wears cheap editions of the latest styles."

The German was deep in thought during these speeches, resting his chin in his hand. Aroused by the striking of the clock he suddenly interpolated, "Why, you can always tell an American couple in Europe. The woman is too bossy, she leads the way, she does all the talking and ordering, while the man trails on behind her and silently pays the bills."

"Well, you must have seen him when he was on his good behavior," I suggested, "for at home he is not so silent about paying the bills."

Unabashed, the German continued, "My brother who has long lived in America says the woman there is the head of the house, that she manages all; her word is law. Is this true?"

He seemed greatly disturbed, and I was about to reply, but the Briton rose to speak. "Of course she is, because she's far superior. Why, American men have nothing in common with the women. They are coarse, blunt, crude, while the women are finely sensitive, exquisite, and courteous. The man has nothing to give his wife but money; he comes home at night and talks business, introduces into his home only friends who will help him out financially, and when his wife discusses music, art, or literature, he falls asleep and snores. That's why she brings her fortune into Europe for a husband. She finds her equal in the Frenchman, the Italian, the Spaniard, but particularly in the Englishman. For every Englishman is a gentleman, and every American woman is a lady!"

The German added a final convulsive note to the settlement of the woman problem by adding, "Is it true the American husband not only washes the dishes but pushes the perambulator?"

"Why, yes, he often does that."

"That is terr-r-r-rrible," he answered, the r's rolling out, and his hands clasped tight to his temples.

And at that we all departed for our rest. But a few days later one or another of the quartet was demonstrated right. News came that my boat was about to leave at once, and I sought out the Captain. At the first intimation of my errand, he waved his hands and said, "No! No! No women!"

I kept on talking until I made him admit he was interested in America, in diet, and in population. When I found he was a reader of *Physical Culture* I produced my open sesame letter and again it was more potent than a passport. I stood reasoning with him on the pier, until finally he said, "There's a rule to take no women. But you Americans are not like others. I think I can put you in." I was allowed to embark.

During the voyage we were most careful, anchoring at dusk, and when it was light keeping sharp watch for floating mines which might have broken loose from their moorings. It took us two nights and a day to make a crossing that ordinarily occupied only nine or ten hours.

I had plenty of time to sort out my impressions and conclusions regarding the birth control movement. They had been revolutionized. I could no longer look upon it as a struggle for free speech, because I now realized that it involved much more than talks, books, or pamphlets. These were not enough.

Personal instruction had been proved to be the best method, and I concluded clinics were the proper places from which to disseminate information but also, admirable as they were in the Netherlands, they ought not to be placed in the hands of unskilled midwives, social workers, or even nurses. These could, of course, instruct after a fashion, but only doctors had the requisite knowledge of anatomy and physiology and training in gynecology to examine properly and prescribe accurately.

I had a new goal, but how difficult and how distant its attainment was to be I never dreamed.

Chapter Thirteen

THE PEASANTS ARE KINGS

I STAYED but a few days in London and then went on to Paris, a gloomy, gloomy city because so many people were garbed in black. Jaurès had been shot. The capital had already been moved to Bordeaux and suspicion and hysteria were in the air. When I went within easy driving distance of Paris for lunch or dinner, I could see the barbed-wire entanglements and gaps where the trees had been taken down for better visibility.

I renewed what contacts I could. But everybody was too busy now with the War to think of such a subject as family limitation, which to the French had never been anything to get excited about because they were too used to it. Furthermore, the other side of the question was now presenting itself. They were beginning to ask, "If we had a larger population, could we not have held the Germans back?"

Again I saw Victor Dave. He was literally starving to death, supported only by friendly gifts of a few francs here or there which he always accepted with laughter; what difference did it make to him whether he lived a few days longer? I never saw greater gallantry than was manifested by his smile and the shrug of his shoulders as he sauntered to work with two pieces of dry bread in his pocket.

The libraries were shut. Paris was no place for me, but I could see something of Spain, and Portet was waiting for me there. After the customary passport argument and some surprise at the cost of the sleeping-car arrangements I left for the South. It was four o'clock in the morning as the express pulled into Cerbère, the station on the border, where the French viewed all passengers with caution and mistrust.

"Cerbère!" shouted the guard, and, "Passports!" shouted an inspector following on his heels. Mine was not quite right. The train moved out leaving me and my baggage desolate on the platform. In the course of several interviews with various officials I made out that my passport lacked a particular signature, and Perpignan was the nearest town where it could be secured.

I paced up and down the tiny station watching for the train back. As usual, peasants were asleep in the waiting room, some on the floor, others sitting on bags and parcels. We were so close under the shadow of the Pyrenees that they almost seemed to be toppling over us.

From the train window I looked out on the beauty of dawn and the rising sun, a scene of such magnificence that it repaid me in pleasure for all the trouble. To one side was the far stretch of the Mediterranean, as magic a blue as I had ever imagined it. To the other were the majestic, rugged mountains with snow-capped peaks and bases covered with pink, flowering apricots. Little villages of white houses and red-tile roofs nestled in the valleys and serpentine roads coiled up the hillsides, where thousands of acres of grape vines, trim and well cared-for, bespoke the wine country.

From Perpignan I telegraphed Portet, "Live or die, sink or swim, survive or perish, I'll be in Barcelona tomorrow," and boarded the train once more with a light heart and my papers, three of them.

Already in the minute second-class compartment were a large, middle-aged woman whose sweet face was framed in a black mantilla, a small gray-haired man, evidently her husband, and a younger one of about twenty-five. It would have been crowded enough as it was, but they had brought with them packages and bundles that filled the space to the roof. However, they squeezed out enough room for me to curl myself up and go to sleep.

I awakened with a start, hearing again the fateful word, "Passports!" and found the agent examining those of my fellow passengers. I opened the bag where I had always carried my credentials, but they were not there. The officer stood waiting. "I have my papers all signed," I said, "but I cannot find them. Go on to the others and when you come back I'll have them."

Since he could not understand English my speech had little effect; he continued to wait. I began turning things out—letters, books, pamphlets of all kinds and descriptions, groping through every bag, in and out of every package. My traveling companions gazed on the commotion sympathetically and drew their legs aside so I could look under the seat.

At this point another uniform approached and the two consulted together. Then one of them blew a whistle and at its loud and shrill summons five men came running. The biggest of them threw wide the compartment door, to indicate I must get off. They were jabbering at me in French and Spanish; I was talking English. All of us were going as fast as we could. First I jumped up and expostulated, then sat down and waved my hands saying, "Go away."

Finally there appeared a young Spanish student who could speak English. He conveyed to me that the train was already late on my account; I must get off so the other passengers could catch the Barcelona Express.

I would not be bothered any more. "So do I want to catch it," I exclaimed. "Why don't they move on? I have a passport and I'll find it in a few minutes. I've paid for my ticket to Port Bou and I'm not going back. You can stop the train here for a week if you want to—I shan't budge!"

The gendarmes were standing expectantly on the platform below. The interpreter shrugged his shoulders, "She'll do as she says. She's an American woman and she'll never come down. You might as well move on."

Nevertheless, the big fellow with the long black cape resolutely seized one bag after another and handed them out. Underneath the last one were disclosed the missing papers. Straightway everybody was wreathed in smiles. The bags were restored and the agents apologized, thanked me profusely, and departed.

The passengers shooks hands with me all around.

Just before we reached Port Bou one of them peered out the window, rippled off some words to the others in Catalan. The whole compartment was as though electrified. In a few seconds parcels were being torn apart and boxes ripped open. The Señora removed her mantilla and placed a smart new hat on her head, then crowned that with another, and another, and another, until finally she was wearing four. Yards of beautiful and exquisite lace went inside her bodice. She took off her outer skirt and swathed her hips in lengths of cloth. The men stuffed their pockets and the lining of their coats. At last there were only a few rolls of braid left. The younger one lifted his trousers, wound them round and round his legs and tucked the ends in his garters. Then through the window went crumpled paper, boxes, string. Finally, as the train was slowing up they put on light-buff, linen dusters. My eyes popped out of my head to see these simple people suddenly transformed into stylish stouts returning from Paris.

The two men nonchalantly smoked cigars as though nothing out of the way were going on while the customs officials went through their bags. Everybody concerned knew they were merchants smuggling goods, but even the authorities regarded it as legitimate for them to bring in as much as they could carry on their persons. As they left the shed where my belongings were still being scrambled over, they glanced commiseratingly at me and glowered indignation at the officials that a lady should be so served.

I had expected to find in Barcelona street-corner Carmens with hibiscus blossoms in their hair, wandering guitarists and singers. But the only music that passed my window oozed out mechanically from two-wheeled, highly-ornamented hurdy-gurdies. Nevertheless, the city was full of color. Strange little wagons with canvas covers, looking as though they were part of a caravan, rattled over the cobbles. There was something gorgeously elegant about the members of the *Guardia Civil,* grandly mounted on Arabian horses, their mustachios fiercely bristling, their uniforms ablaze with scarlet and yellow topped off with black patent leather hats. The red Phrygian caps of the porters seemed almost too realistic a reminder of revolution. The workers still wore their crimson-fringed sashes, their blue French blouses, and white rope-soled shoes. The men, as a rule, were of slight frame, but conveyed an impression of strength like steel rods; the women, invariably black-clad except for the very young, were fat and waddling.

Numberless bells were constantly ringing in numberless churches. Everywhere, like crows, were priests in long swinging robes, shovel hats, and dirty bare toes sticking through their sandals. On the corners of the central streets I saw them occupying the booths of the professional correspondents who for ten cents read and answered letters for the illiterate.

Although Barcelona, capital of the separatist province of Catalonia, was the progressive, industrial center of Spain, it was not darkened by a mêlée of belching chimneys. The hundreds of factories were kept out of sight, each one isolated in the fields, leaving the city free from traffic, smoke, and the whir of machinery. The palms in the squares and parks were lovely, but set side by side with the new was the startling antiquity of the old town, congested and melancholy.

Overlooking the sea at the end of the Rambla, decorated along its length with flower stalls and trees, loud with birds, stood a tall column bearing the statue of Columbus. Around the base were scenes portraying various incidents of the voyage to America, each represented by small images cast in bronze, all beautiful to the last detail. But the effect was greatly spoiled because nearly every one remaining had a leg, arm, foot, or even head gone. After looking at this for some time and pondering over the wherefore, I concluded that figures so strongly made and set had not easily been removed, and decided it must have something to do with the Spanish-American War. When I asked my Spanish friends whether I had guessed correctly, their only explanation was that ruffians had doubtless done it for sport.

However, after I had left the country I received verification of my supposition. The monument had been stoned in '98, but no Spaniard would ever have admitted this fact to any American; it might hurt the feelings of the visitor even to mention the unpleasantness.

I began to study Spanish with a teacher, but I was not nearly far enough advanced to be able to get anywhere in my investigations. Unfortunately also, although men thronged the cafés in droves, they kept their wives in semi-Oriental seclusion and even mentally imposed their deep-rooted ideas of the isolation of women on foreigners. I could not violate this custom by going about alone, because I was a guest. As a result Portet, who was a busy man himself, provided me with a succession of male escorts.

Towards the end of a certain afternoon, tired and footsore, I was sitting with one of these accommodating gentlemen at a sidewalk table sipping an apéritif—a delicious French vermouth supplemented by olives stuffed with anchovies. Bootblacks were making their customary rounds of the patrons, and the men were having their shoes cleaned. Since I had been walking about a great deal, mine were appearing rather scuffed, and I stretched my feet out.

My companion looked at me appealingly. "I beg of you, Señora, not here."

"Why not?"

But the boy had already brought his little shoe rest, begun spitting on my oxford and rubbing with energy and enthusiasm. Embarrassed, my escort rose and moved away, but, interested in the boy's novel methods, I kept my eyes on my shoes and was unaware of anything out of the ordinary.

As soon as he had finished I glanced up. There must have been twenty-five men gathered in front of the café, all looking fixedly and intently at this unusual spectacle. When I opened my purse to pay the boy, he doffed his cap with the most gracious gesture. "Señora, this is my pleasure."

The crowd outside applauded loudly and I felt my face growing hot. Not until they had drifted off did my protector return, wan and pale and extremely agitated. "You see what you've done, you see? It will be the joke of Spain! You are the friend of Professor Portet! It is a reflection on him and on his family! You cannot do these things!"

I realized then that I had to be more circumspect.

Portet, who after all was Ferrer's successor, was watched wherever he went by the secret service, and soon pointed out that I too had a shadow—the man who sat constantly at the little, round, marble-topped table across from my hotel. He said I should always have this individual or one of his mates with me. They were on eight-hour duty, and if I were to go in for any night life I would have three separate ones over the twenty-four hours.

These government agents were to give a regular report of whom

I was with and where I went, and, in a sense, they also looked after me, although Portet was never without a revolver in his pocket. In Spain a breath of dampness, and pop—open went the umbrellas all over the place. Once on the way to a benefit for the Belgians Portet and I were waiting for the tram when a spatter of rain came up. His spy rushed to hold an umbrella over him while mine ran after my hat which the wind had saucily blown off my head. Or, if I were taking a train alone, my daytime attendant, having already been in conference with the hotel proprietor, would appear at the ticket office and explain to the clerk where I wanted to go. Had he spoken English I would have doubtless enjoyed his conversation, but Portet warned me it was beneath my dignity even to nod good morning to such a creature.

The frequent friendly attentions of our spies could not draw a word of approval from Portet, though on one occasion they performed a real service. Stopping en route at the American Express Company to get some money, we set out to see a part of the old city new to me. Only a few blocks from the banks and modern shops were center pumps from which women were carrying the water to their homes in tall earthen jugs, in just the same primitive manner as centuries ago. The houses in the red-light district were approached by outside stairways along which were niches enclosing receptacles for holy water, and into these the patrons dipped their fingers religiously, crossed themselves, and entered.

While we were walking through one of the narrow streets, high-walled on either side, suddenly and without reason I felt alarmed, and at the same moment Portet put his hand in his pocket. I glanced behind to find our two familiar guarding shadows gone; I sensed danger ahead, but I, too, tried to act as though everything were all right, as though there were nothing to worry about. We strolled in the same leisurely way to the corner. There in a flash down another street we caught a quick glimpse of struggling figures in the distance. In a moment they disappeared.

We proceeded to our destination—a little café fronting the Mediterranean. As we sat admiring it, I was startled by the sight of our two spies approaching, one of them holding a long, jagged-edged knife. I could not understand his excited words, but his pantomime was so graphically descriptive of a life-and-death struggle that my flesh began to creep and shivers ran up and down my backbone. He paused, bowed, and held out the knife, obviously offering it to me.

Portet, looking very incensed, pulled out his revolver, showed it to the man, and ordered him off. When both had retired, abashed, Portet translated briefly, "He says he has saved your life—that robbers saw you get money at the American Express this morning, and that he knew they were going to attack you. He followed and grabbed the knife away from them. I told him this was unnecessary. The thieves would have got as good as they gave! I can take care of you."

I thought I ought at least to have given the man a reward, but not Portet, the revolutionary, who was furious at the presumption. He was always angry at them. When he came to lunch with me Palm Sunday, the hotel proprietor leaned over the table confidentially and said, "The government agent wishes to speak to you."

Portet shouted, "If he comes near, I'll shoot him! The hound, the worm, the dog! How dare he?"

"Can't we find out what he wants?" I suggested.

The proprietor returned, "Nothing, Señor, except to ask whether you and the Señora are attending the bullfight this afternoon. His time is up at four o'clock, but if you are going to the *plaza de toros,* he will be glad to stay on duty another eight hours."

We went; he came right along and saw the spectacle at government expense.

The cement-like benches of the large amphitheater were crowded to full capacity. The people were gesticulating, chattering volubly as though awaiting something unusual or something good eagerly anticipated. Overhead the monotonous, gray sky seemed like a huge tent, it was so regular and colorless, but every little while a patch of blue appeared. The disposition of the onlookers changed with the same unexpectedness from gladness and joy almost instantaneously into impatience or wrath; at one moment they clapped and praised the matador, at the next they insulted and vilified him.

Most of my Spanish friends hoped I would like a bullfight, although Portet, who thought it barbaric, told me it would probably shock me; every foreigner who saw one simply shut his eyes in horror when some poor old skeleton horse was so gored that its intestines fell out and then were pushed back for its re-entry into the arena. If I were going to be conspicuous by showing my feelings, the populace might turn upon me, and, jokingly, he suggested following the example of Alfonso XIII, who had given his English bride a pair of opera glasses with perfectly black lenses because she was so open and frank at displaying her emotions. She had stood and stared blankly at them all the time, and thus got through her first bullfight.

I promised to be careful, and watched with the naked eye.

The bull came out snorting with passion and vigor, glaring around the arena with a great noble sweep of his head. Suddenly he saw a color he did not like, something inimical. He lunged towards it, and then a medieval-looking figure danced before him with a cape to confuse him. He forgot his original enemy and rushed at the red thing. Another gyrating figure distracted his attention and angered him to wheel towards the new adversary, make another plunge, and again be met by a flash of color.

Over and over and over again this happened. The poor bull's vitality was finally worn down, not from direct combat, but because of the many bewildering forces that were there to destroy him—the fluttering capes, the kaleidoscopic shapes, the swift-thrown banderillas, and the gleaming lances of the picadors. Then, when he was bleeding and utterly spent, the hero stepped out with a sword to kill him. He was dragged out, sombreros whirled into the arena, shrieks and shouts arose, the band played, a great victory had been achieved.

Within no time, even before another bull appeared, vendors came along with baskets of hot sandwiches made from the barbecued meat of the one just killed.

Not a single word would Portet let me say until we were entirely out of hearing; you could talk freely in Spain against the Church or the priests, but this sacred institution must not be criticized. Passing through my mind was the thought that a bullfight was symbolic of the struggle of the working classes. Strikes, picketing, jails exhausted their energy until they too charged blindly this way and that, always missing the main issue.

Many of my holidays were spent more happily than this. I never tired of the wooded mountains which sheltered Barcelona, most of them having some religious significance. Portet and I went up the funicular to the top of Tibidabo, the exceeding high place where the devil tempted Jesus, showing him in a moment of time the world spread out before him.

Another glorious spring day we twisted up the thirty miles of road to Montserrat, the mountain riven in two at the Crucifixion. It was the quaintest sight to one coming from a land of subways and elevators to watch the donkeys laden with packs on their backs of vegetables, eggs, and butter, and to see their owners straggling beside up and down the hills, masters of at least themselves if not of their donkeys. The breeze blew more chill as we ascended the final slope to the huge monastery at the top. Afterwards night fell, and the moon shone over the huge boulders of towering rocks, and the whispering wind swung from mass to mass and echoed back again whence it came. It was an evening of enchantment.

On making other sorties into the country I perceived an innate intelligence in the most ignorant peasant. The average one could not tell the names of the simplest plants or flowers, but one look from the eye, one tone of the voice, was comprehended in a flash. Even the gypsy children in the outskirts of Barcelona, with their little dirty feet and tattered clothing, who danced weird dances and flattered strangers for pennies, had a natural brightness beyond belief.

But this intelligence was not being directed, and one reason was inherent in the rebellious nature of the Catalan; he would have preferred no system of government at all if that had been possible, for he was restless and tumultuous under restraint.

When I saw children leading the blind about the streets day after day, I asked, "Don't they have to be in school? Isn't education made compulsory by the Government?"

I was laughed at. "If the Government sent our children to school, we would know it was the wrong sort of school."

Parents who could afford it, however, were willing enough to have them go to Ferrer's schools. Two thirds of the Spanish people had not been able to read or write before his time. The teacher, who worked constantly all the year round, averaged about sixteen dollars a month. "He is hungrier than a schoolmaster" was a household axiom.

Since Ferrer's first school had opened fourteen years previously, some forty-six had begun to operate, and, in addition, most towns of any size had at least one rationalist school which was maintained by the workers and also used Ferrer's texts. The groundwork was then being laid for the children of yesterday to become the leaders in today's fight. The pupils I saw at near-by Sabadella, at Granada, and at Seville, were being taught the processes of life from the cell up, and their instructors were really trying to give them a scientific instead of a theological attitude.

Because of the long mental and physical isolation imposed upon them by the Church, which controlled all education, five thousand towns and villages could be reached only by trails and tracks. The Church had objected to having roads built because, once transportation were made more accessible, women could more easily leave their homes in the country and go to the city where evil awaited them—their morals were being safeguarded by cowpaths.

Most of Spain was a gaunt, denuded, tragic country with vast, desolate steppes and red, impoverished soil which gave the feeling it had been soaked in human blood for centuries. Certainly the spilling of blood had been a matter of indifference in Spanish history. In a sense the whole people were lawless, hostile to rulers. Every child knew the evils of El Caciquismo. Some Spaniard has said, "Democracy, Republicanism, or Socialism have in reality little to do in our country, for we do not willingly accept either king, president, priest, or prophet."

The worker in Catalonia had small faith in government, no matter what the brand, and kept straight to the one issue—revolution through economic action, chiefly the general strike. He did not look upon the Government as a vague, mysterious something for the deeds or blunders of which no one could be blamed; he demanded that those in authority should give accounting for the results of their authority. He never forgot a wrong, and usually those responsible paid the bill. I sometimes thought his "attempts" were carried out more from a spirit of revenge and individual hatred than as a social protest.

At the head of the Rambla was a great square, the Plaza de la Constitucion, and there each day from five to six the populace took its airing. Thousands of feet had so worn the pavement that it needed replacement. One noon the square was torn up. Nobody could walk there for twenty-four hours, the workmen were busy, ropes were placed across both ends of the promenade, and a huge sign was erected, "No trespassing allowed. By Order of the Government."

Loiterers gathered to look at the proclamation. They began talking, their gestures growing more and more vehement, until finally they pulled down the ropes and deliberately trod on the fresh concrete. They were not going to be forbidden by the Government! The entire job had to be done over again, and I noticed the next night six mounted police were guarding all four sides. But nobody seemed to give either incident the slightest attention.

Catalans were a race of individualists, each a law unto himself. Their most marked characteristics were independence and personal dignity. Even Pepet, the waiter at my hotel, knew how to use his freedom. Sometimes he calmly left the dining room and went down the street for a shave while we were having our soup. He eventually returned for the following course, happy and clean, his absence unreproved.

Whenever the conversation of the guests interested him, Pepet entered in quite as naturally as though he were sitting and being served instead of serving. In any other country this would have been resented as insolence, but here every courtesy and respect was shown to him just as he showed it to others. If you said you were going to go by a certain tram to a certain place to be there at three in the afternoon, he interrupted, "Pardon me, Señora, you do not need to be there until four-thirty, and it is much better to go by this other route."

Like the rest I said, "Right, Pepet, we shall take your advice."

With the expulsion of the Jews from Spain vanished the driving force for commercial initiative, a quality, fortunately or unfortunately, greatly lacking in the country. Pérez Galdós said:

The capital defect of the Spaniards of your time is that you live exclusively the life of words, and the language is so beautiful that the delight in the sweet sound of it woos you to sleep. You speak too much. You lavish without stint a wealth of phrases to conceal the poverty of your actions.

I did not believe this entirely true, but without doubt the Spanish had a maddening habit of procrastination. It was "Sí, Sí, Señora, assuredly, certainly," all gracious promising—and then nothing happening. To an American this was especially aggravating, because he was always in a constant hurry; he expected to see and know the whole of Spain in a month. But the Spaniard was not to be rushed. When asked what time it was, he might reply, "Perhaps four hours more of the sun."

This defiance of clocks and the absence of strain and bustle pleased me personally. A story was told of a Spaniard going to seek his fortune in South America. After finding a position to his satisfaction he worked three hours and then suddenly asked for his pay. When his employer requested the cause of his abrupt leave-taking, he exclaimed angrily, "Do you think I'm going to spend all my life working for you?"

Don Quixote truly represented the Spanish temperament. The strong enthusiasm which was shown for a project and the still stronger imagination which not only saw the matter begun but also finished, was Spanish to the last degree. The knight of La Mancha thought nothing of invading cities and fighting giants, but it ended in thinking about it. "I consider all that already done."

Spanish character, so paradoxical, so attractive, and often so difficult to understand, fascinated me. I could exhaust myself in adjectives—fickle, impetuous, rich-souled, ascetic, passionate, realistic, individualistic. Courtesy and ceremony were second nature to the Catalans of Barcelona, supposed to be the most dangerous and lawless city in Europe, where thousands of anarchists gathered and plotted and where bombs were thrown wrapped up in flowers.

I remember how on the suburban trams going high into the mountains, sellers of hot and cold omelets ran up and down the station platforms. Anybody who bought one, before eating it himself, offered it to all the passengers in the car, even though they might be carrying their own lunches.

To accept, however, was a shocking breach of good form. The offerer protested that you must take it, and you had to think fast for a plausible excuse. "My friends are waiting for me to dine with them," or "I've just had something at the last station." You must never, never, never accept.

Havelock used to tell of a grave error he had once made when traveling in Spain. When he had admired a piece of jewelry, the lady to whom it belonged had removed it promptly and thrust it upon him, saying, "I am honored to give it to you." She had been so insistent that, though thoroughly uncomfortable, he had taken it — the very worst thing he could have done. Soon it disappeared from his effects, but what was his surprise on his next encounter with the lady to find her wearing it again with no sign of discomposure. Her servants had been so indignant that one of them had immediately stolen it back.

Spanish men were not only courteous to women but also to each other, having no hesitancy at showing their regard and affection. Even the beggars addressed each other in the most high-flown phrases, "Your Highness," or "Your Grace." One might ask, "Where is Your Excellency to sleep tonight?"

"Under the bridge, My Lord."

They lacked that poverty-in-the-soul look that existed in the same class in other countries. Assuming the condition of one tattered and ragged specimen to be temporary, I questioned him, "What do you do ordinarily?"

"I saunter, I idle, I loaf."

"But what work do you do?"

He drew himself up with the utmost hauteur, and said proudly, "I do not work. I am a beggar."

Doing business with the Spaniards required a knowledge of finesse quite foreign to the average American. I, for example, saw a basket in a shop window which I felt I really must have. My escort and I went into the store. Since the proprietor did not speak English, all I could do was gaze longingly, take it in my hand, and ask my companion, "How much do you suppose this is?" He made no answer, but pointed to something else on the wall, and we left without learning the price. I thought he was a terribly stupid person.

The next day I passed the same place with Portet, and I begged, "Oh, do come in and ask how much that basket is. I want to buy it."

He smiled at me indulgently. "You know in our country we cannot just go into places and find out prices. This man is a craftsman. We will talk to him."

The proprietor and his wife shook hands with us and brought the best wine from the cellar. Then the former said, "The Señora was here yesterday. Tell us about her."

"She comes from North America," answered Portet.

"Tell us about North America."

After forty minutes of this, during which I kept one eye on the wicker container but was unable to divert the conversation to it, we said, *"Hasta la vista,"* and bowed our way out.

A week later Portet and I, following the lodestone of my particular basket, sought the shop once more. Relations had now been established, and we were entitled to ask about it. But we still could not demand outright, "How much does it cost?" We must say, "This basket must be worth so and so," making the figure higher than it should be.

"Oh, no, no, no, no!" the proprietor protested. "It is not worth that. My humble hands fashioned it. It is hardly worth anything."

He endeavored to make me accept it for nothing. I had to refuse and once more try to make him take more than its value. Never was there such a juggling before we finally arrived at the exact amount of pesetas.

On my departure from the country I had to break through a similar punctilio. I spent about seven weeks in Barcelona and was never presented with a hotel bill—none for lodging, for laundry, for meals, or for extras such as coffee. The day was coming when I must go back to France, and I did not want too much Spanish money with me—just enough to take me to the border. From there I had already purchased my tickets for England.

Each time I mentioned *cuenta* to the proprietor, bowing and turning up his palms he answered, "Sí, Sí, Señora," until finally, on my last morning, I marched resolutely up to the desk and said, "I shall miss my train if I have to go to the American Express to get more money. You really must tell me how much I owe."

He went upstairs. I waited. Finally he descended, his hair standing on end. He threw the reckoning down on the table with a most vindictive look. I glanced at it. The total was very low; it could barely have covered the cost of the food.

"I have been humiliated!" he exclaimed dramatically.

"Whatever is the matter?" I questioned.

"We are living in the most hellish country on earth!"

"Why, what's happened?"

"A lady comes all the way from North America. She visits us, she stays here, we like her, and I must present her with this sordid bill!"

Some day when the fighting is over I shall return again to Spain.

Chapter Fourteen

O, TO BE IN ENGLAND

WHEN I reached London it was spring, and beautiful as only spring in England can be. I longed to get out into the country and, through the kindness of Dr. Alice Vickery, was soon lodged in a private home in Hampstead Gardens next door to her quaint, ivy-covered, red-brick house. In the large garden in back we often had tea under the blossoming apple trees. There, dressed in gray or purple, with white collar and a wisp of lace not quite a bonnet on her head, she entertained the young and modern women of England who were working for reforms of no matter what kind. Still, at the age of eighty, she was alert upon all questions of the day, busily engaged in writing leaflets or articles pointing out the weak spots in social programs.

Dr. Vickery was so full of the living side of Neo-Malthusianism that I could ill afford to forego one possible hour with her. Often when we found ourselves alone in her drawing room I sat at her feet and heard the story of the pioneer Malthusians, what they had had to undergo, and what they had accomplished. For my benefit she brought out of her attic a veritable treasure of the early days—old circulars, pamphlets, and letters now, I am afraid, destroyed.

Almost every afternoon, taking her walking stick and with Dr. Binnie Dunlop for a companion, Dr. Vickery boarded the tram to attend some gathering. She had been one of the first to welcome the militant suffragettes, and she never missed a suffrage meeting, nor, for that matter, any other significant one on infant or maternal welfare, eugenics, or public health. She always went with the definite purpose of getting the audience down to fundamentals. In time she became a familiar figure. As soon as she entered a hall you could feel those present aligning themselves against her. They knew she was going to bring up a controversial subject that no one wanted discussed, such as birth control. It was like casting a boulder into a nice quiet lake, but, with an unruffled exterior and grim determination, she invariably rose just the same, asked the chairman to recognize her, and said her say on the Feminist side of the question. From the lips of this Victorian old lady it sounded strange to hear frank remarks about the importance of limiting offspring. Dr. Dunlop, with Scotch determination, was also bent on setting people straight; he followed her and expounded the medical aspects of population.

In June Dr. Vickery asked me to tell my story to a group of her friends. Among them was Edith How-Martyn, who had recently graduated from the London School of Economics. But already the zealous ardor of this small and slight person had landed her in jail for suffrage. She had now split from Mrs. Pankhurst, unable to subscribe to the militant policy.

The American woman is apt to say, "Anything I can do for you, let me know," and then go away, her conscience relieved. The Englishwoman states definitely that she can get up a meeting, bring you in touch with so and so, give you money, or get money for you. Edith How-Martyn in her quiet manner said to me, "I think what you have told us today should have a larger audience. Will you give a lecture if we arrange it for you? We'll do the donkey work; all you have to do is speak."

In a few days the time and place were set. I was to appear in Fabian Hall the following month under my own name.

The chairs in the auditorium were wooden and the interior was unheated—not like an American hall. The audience was quite different from the little Socialist gatherings of working women I had addressed at home. The atrocious and hideous English hats gave it an intellectual and highly respectable air. These representatives of nearly every social and civic organization in London, had the rationalist attitude and preferred to listen to principles and theories. I told them what I had been trying to do through the *Woman Rebel* and explained my private and personal conception of what Feminism should mean; that is, women should first free themselves from biological slavery, which could best be accomplished through birth control. This was, generally speaking, the introduction of the term into England.

Many came up and talked to me afterwards, among them Marie Stopes, a paleontologist who had made a reputation with work on coal. Would I come to her home and discuss the book she was writing?

Over the teacups I found her to have an open, frank manner that quite won me. She took me into her confidence at once, stating her marriage had been unconsummated, and for that reason she was securing an annulment. Her book, *Married Love,* was based largely on her own experiences and the unhappiness that came to people from ignorance and lack of understanding in wedlock, and she hoped it would help others. She was extremely interested in the correlation of marital success to birth control knowledge, although she admitted she knew nothing about the latter. Could I tell her exactly what methods were used and how? In spite of my belief that the Netherlands clinics could be improved upon, I was fired with fervor for the idea as such, and described them as I had seen them.

Later when I came back to the United States, I brought with me the manuscript of *Married Love,* and tried every established publisher in New York, receiving a rejection from each. Finally I induced Dr. William J. Robinson to publish it under the auspices of his *Critic and Guide,* a monthly magazine which took up many subjects the *Journal* of the American Medical Association would not touch. Unfortunately even here it had to be expurgated. When I cabled Dr. Stopes I had a publisher in New York, her new husband, H. V. Roe, financed an unabridged English edition which appeared simultaneously.

No one can underestimate the work Marie Stopes has done. Though her other books, *Radiant Motherhood* and *Wise Parenthood,* were limited in value because they were based on limited personal experience, she has handled sex knowledge with delicacy and wisdom, placing it in a modern, practical category. She started the first birth control clinic in England, but she was not a pioneer in the movement. Annie Besant, Dr. Vickery, the Drysdales, and many others had plowed the ground and sown the seed. It needed only a new voice, articulate and clear as hers, to push her into the front ranks of the movement, where she must have been much surprised to find herself.

Many people went out of their way to be kind to me in those days. I was often asked to the home of E. P. C. Haynes, solicitor, writer on freedom of the press, and a fine adviser. Around his table, one of the grandest set anywhere in England, could usually be found a large group of distinguished people. Among them was the American Civil War veteran, Major G. P. Putnam, a dapper, lively, alert little publisher with a white mustache and cold blue eyes. He was conservative and formal, but at the same time a firebrand in his fashion and an enthusiast for certain issues. Haynes had invited him to hear my views, and himself introduced the subject of birth control. Thus I was enabled to pave the way for having G. P. Putnam's Sons eventually take over the publication of *Married Love* in this country, although not until 1931, through the Major's efforts, was the ban lifted which prohibited the importation of the complete edition into the United States.

Harold Cox, brilliant Member of Parliament and editor of the *Edinburgh Review,* was another delightful host at Old Kennards in Buckinghamshire. In the *Review* he was constantly helping to form an enlightened public opinion on birth control, having every argument at his finger tips and never missing a chance to answer questions in the London *Times.*

Hugh and Janet de Selincourt's place at Torrington, Sussex, where Shelley was born, always was a haven of refuge. After five days' work in town I could come, tired and pent-up, for a week-end. I loved the joy and simplicity of the music there, the lighthearted conversation, and tea on the lawn. From there you saw English ivy climbing up to the thatched roof, and a pond, a small one, which had been converted into a swimming pool. The general impression was of shrubbery and old walls with fruit trees trellised against them. Beyond the velvet green grass were red tree roses, beautiful borders of pink lupins, and delphiniums, the tallest and bluest I have ever seen. From the dining-room window the effect was that of a tapestry.

I wanted some day to embody the rambling spirit of this home in one of my own.

Here again laughter bound me to these people. We laughed and we laughed and we laughed. Whole days were spent in gaiety over the most absurd things. Hugh could never quite accept me as a crusader; he went into roars of merriment whenever I mentioned the subject of population—it was too much for a woman in a yellow dress to bother about.

But many of my week-ends were spent in "bothering" about it. At Sunday afternoon labor meetings in London someone was always holding forth. "Here's a chance for you to talk birth control," Rose Witcop once urged.

It was an opportunity to reach working people and I agreed, but lunch of that day found me trembling. Henry Sara, a young man but old in the ways of the speaker, noticed I was not eating or drinking and could hardly utter a word. "I say, what's the idea of all this worry? What you must think about is that everybody there comes merely to hear somebody or anybody. They've no notion what you're going to say. Anything is all right with them. Get that in your mind and stop worrying."

His friendly encouragement gave me a little more fortitude, but on the way to the hall Rose Witcop took me severely to task for the trembling, which I seemed unable to stop. "These are just plain people you're going to speak to. It's utter nonsense to be nervous about it."

When Rose stood up to introduce me, she began, "Comrades—" There was a long pause. For the second time she tried in a less assured tone, "Comrades—" Another interval and a third time, in a voice so weak she herself could hardly hear it, she attempted, "Comrades—" Then, barely whispering, "Excuse me," she sat down. By comparison my speech was not bad.

Writing at this time was a means of expression much easier than speaking. I had not forgotten my subscribers to the *Woman Rebel*. I had to fulfill my obligations and supply something to take the place of the three issues which I had been unable to furnish them. Therefore, I wrote three pamphlets on methods of contraception in England, the Netherlands, and France respectively. Printing them cost me a considerable amount of money. My friends in Canada, knowing I was not affluent, now and then when they had a little windfall or unexpected dividend sent me small checks of from five to ten pounds, saying, "To use for your work." These had come in quite often.

On one occasion I had squeezed my pocketbook dry paying for the last pamphlet; I had not another penny to buy stamps. Ten days had gone by, and I kept wishing something might come in to help me out. That morning a letter arrived. I tore it apart and a money order dropped out. Hurrying as fast as I could to the post office I received the cash, spent it all on stamps, and hastened back in the hope of getting the whole edition off on the *Arabic;* in wartime sailings had to be considered. One batch of envelopes had already gone into the pillar box, and I was just finishing addressing and stamping the second lot when I heard the knocker on the door below clatter through the house. It had the ring of authority and sounded so ominous that I felt it must have something to do with me.

Sure enough, in a few moments a bobby and a man in plain clothes appeared at my threshold. They asked whether I were the person who had been sending quantities of mail to a foreign address.

"Yes," I admitted in a small voice, wondering what on earth was going to happen now.

The bobby came closer, showed me an unopened envelope, and demanded sternly, "Did you post this?"

"I think so."

"Madam, in England we never put His Majesty on upside down. We do not represent our King standing on his head. Will you please, in affixing your stamps, pay attention to the customs of our country?"

The care with which I stuck on the remainder right side up delayed me so that I barely made the *Arabic.* Only then did I have time to read the letter. I took it out of my bag, thinking how wonderful it was of my friends to send me the money and how much good I had been able to do with it. To my consternation and amazement it was not for my use, but to buy gifts—certain books to be sent back as soon as possible.

The money was gone and the presents could not be purchased.

After all this rush and pother the *Arabic* was torpedoed and went down with the entire two thousand pamphlets. I made another effort, this time successfully completed, and shaped an article on Emerson, Thoreau, and Humphrey Noyes and the Oneida Community, about whom the English were talking.

Meanwhile I had written to Canada apologizing and saying I expected shortly to be able to fulfill the commissions. I now had an opening ahead of me for a career abroad. Portet's publishing house in Barcelona was closely allied with others in Paris. Through him I was offered the job of choosing appropriate books in English, which could be published in both French and Spanish, especially works that would be of help to women and labor. The salary was satisfactory, the job itself interesting, and it gave promise of permanency as soon as the War should be over. I had almost decided to take it, even selecting a little house in Versailles with sunny rooms and a garden for the children.

There was only one drawback—the subtle, persistent dread that something was wrong with Peggy. Night after night her voice startled me from deep sleep and left me in a state of agitation until I received the next letter containing news that all was going well. I tried to dismiss this fear and would have it partially submerged, but always the same troubled voice rang in my ears, "Mother, Mother, are you coming back?"

One definite though inexplicable experience kept puzzling me. As I unclosed my eyes in the morning, or even before I was completely awake, I became conscious of the number 6, as though that numeral were repeating itself again and again in my drowsy mind. I often tried to fit it into some event of the day—six o'clock, sixpence, the price of tea, or anything else amusing, and as casual or silly as I could make up. This I did to protect myself against the premonition which seemed at first to come upon me with the recurrence of this number. Later, like a leaf on a wall calendar, NOV. 6 stood out.

When the publisher asked me to commit myself by signing a three-year contract to stay in Paris, I said, "Yes, I will if you'll guarantee to lock me up or send me to Africa or the North Pole until after November 6th."

"Why November 6th?"

"I don't know, but I'm certain that something important is to occur on that day, something different, and something which will affect my entire future."

He drew up our plans as of January 1st of the following year.

Edith Ellis was lecturing in America, and by letter we arranged for her to bring back Peggy and Grant, because it appeared I might be staying for some time. Then, since only Peggy seemed lonely and in need of her mother and Grant was happy in school, it was determined he should be left there. Edith was to sail with Peggy on the *Lusitania*.

When word was flashed that the liner had been torpedoed, I stood in the middle of the night in front of the Cunard office, scanning with horror the mounting ranks of missing and dead. Not until two in the morning was the list complete and could I breathe once more; neither Peggy's nor Edith's name was on it. Edith had received one of those slips warning prospective passengers that the ship might be blown up, and was one of the few who had heeded the admonition and transferred to another boat. Even so, the thought of being responsible for Peggy had been too alarming and she had decided not to bring her.

The War had sent many Americans back from Europe and Bill had returned to New York. I had had a detailed letter from him describing the stirring events of the previous December. A man introducing himself as A. Heller had called upon him at his studio and requested a copy of *Family Limitation,* pleading that he was poor, had too large a family, and was a friend of mine. Bill said he was sorry but we had agreed that I was to carry on my work independently of him, and he did not even think he had any of the pamphlets. However, the man's story was so pathetic that he rummaged around and by chance found one in the library drawer.

A few days later Bill opened the door to a gray-haired, side-whiskered six-footer who lost no time in announcing, "I am Mr. Comstock. I have a warrant for your arrest on the grounds of circulating obscene literature." Accompanying him was the so-called Heller, who turned out to be Charles J. Bamberger, an agent of the New York Society for the Suppression of Vice. The three departed but Bill soon found himself in a restaurant instead of the police station. When he protested that he wished to consult a lawyer without delay, Comstock, between mouthfuls of lunch, offered advice. "Young man, I want to act as a brother to you. Lawyers are expensive and will only aggravate your case." Here he patted Bill on the shoulder. "Plead guilty to this charge, and I'll ask for a suspended sentence."

Bill's answer was that, though he had been in Europe when the pamphlet had been written, he believed in the principles embodied in it, and that, therefore, his own principles were at stake. He would not plead guilty. "You know as well as I do, Mr. Comstock, there's nothing obscene in that pamphlet."

"Young man, I have been in this work for twenty years, and that leaflet is the worst thing I have ever seen."

This sort of conversation went on all afternoon; Comstock even tried to bribe Bill to turn states' evidence by disclosing my whereabouts. It was his custom to arrive at the police station so late that his prisoner could not communicate with a lawyer or bonding office and had to spend the night in jail. He could then make a statement to the papers that his captive had been unable to secure bail.

When Comstock and Bill at last reached the Yorkville Police Court and the clerk had asked the latter how he wished to plead, Comstock spoke for him, "He pleads guilty."

"I do not," expostulated Bill. "I plead not guilty."

He was arraigned and bail fixed at five hundred dollars, but he was obliged to spend thirty-six hours in jail before it could be procured.

In September I had word that, after several postponements, his trial had finally come up before Justices McInerney, Herbert, and Salmon. He started to read his typewritten statement. "I admit that I broke the law, and yet I claim that in every real sense it is the law and not I that is on trial here today."

Justice McInerney interrupted him. "You admit you are guilty, and all this statement of yours is just opinions. I'm not going to have a lot of rigmarole on the record. We've no time to bother. This book is not only indecent but immoral. Its circulation is a menace to society. Too many women are going around advocating woman suffrage. If they would go around advocating bearing children we should be better off.

"The statute gives you the privilege of being fined for this offense, but I do not believe this should be so. A man, guilty as you are, ought to have no alternative from a prison sentence. One hundred and fifty dollars or thirty days in jail."

"Then I want to say to the court," shouted Bill, leaning forward and raising his hand for greater emphasis, "that I would rather be in jail with my self-respect than in your place without it!"

Although he was convinced of the justice of my cause, this was the first and only copy of the pamphlet he had ever given out. It was one of life's sharpest ironies that, despite our separation, he should have been drawn into my battle, and go to prison for it.

When I received Bill's letter bearing this news, I tore across the lawn to Dr. Vickery's. Dr. Drysdale happened to be there, and in his indignation his face became red and his hands were clenched. He tramped up and down the floor in a frenzy of rage that such a thing could be done to any human being. I am still touched when I think of this mild, gentle person being moved to depths of anger over an injustice which did not affect him personally.

The question before me was, "Should I go back?" As had gone Bill's trial so would probably go my own. I did not want to sacrifice myself in a lost cause. I was young, and knew I should be used for something. Temporarily postponing my final answer to the publishing house, I decided to return to the United States, but only long enough to survey the situation, to gather up my children. I intended, if possible, to come back to that little house in Versailles.

Chapter Fifteen

HIGH HANGS THE GAUNTLET

*"Let God and man decree
Laws for themselves and not for me;
Their deeds I judge and much condemn
Yet when did I make laws for them?"*
                    A. E. HOUSMAN

THE end of September, 1915, I set sail from Bordeaux. I remember how interminable that voyage was across the dangerous, foggy Atlantic. The shadow of the *Lusitania* hung over us. The ship was absolutely dark, and tension crackled in the very air. My own thoughts were black as the night and the old nervousness, the nervousness that came with a queer gripping at the pit of the stomach, was upon me; a dread presentiment and a foreboding were with me almost incessantly.

When I succeeded in snatching a few hours' sleep I was startled out of unpleasant dreams. One of them was of attempting to struggle through a crowded street against traffic; I was pushed to the curb and had to make my way cautiously. The mechanical, automaton-like crowds were walking, walking, walking, always in the opposite direction. Then suddenly in my dream the people turned into mice—thousands and thousands of them; they even smelled like mice. I awakened and had to open the porthole to rid the room of that musty smell of mice.

At last the lights of Staten Island, winking like specters in the dim dawn, signaled our safe arrival at quarantine. As the ship sidled along the wharf at West Fourteenth Street on that gray October morning, a new exhilaration, a new hope arose in my heart.

To see American faces again after the unutterable despair of

Europe, to sense the rough democracy of the porters and of the good-hearted, hard-boiled taxi-drivers; to breathe in the crisp, electric autumn air of home—all these brought with them an irresistible gladness. Because I wanted the feeling to linger, I refused a taxi, picked up my small bag, and walked away from the pier, looking about.

At the first news stand I passed I caught sight of the words, "What Shall We Do About Birth Control?" on the cover of the *Pictorial Review*. It seemed strange to be greeted, not by friends or relatives, but by a phrase of your own carried on a magazine. I purchased it and, singing to myself, went on to a hotel where the children were brought to me. I cannot describe the joy of being reunited with them.

That evening I sat down at my desk and wrote several letters. I notified Judge Hazel and Assistant District Attorney Content that I was now back and ready for trial, and inquired whether the indictments of the previous year were still pending; I was politely informed that they were.

A note more difficult to compose went to the National Birth Control League, which had been re-organized in my absence under the leadership of Mary Ware Dennett, Clara Stillman, and Anita Block. To it had been turned over all my files, including the list of subscribers to the *Woman Rebel*. I asked them what moral support I could expect from the League, saying this would help to determine the length of my stay.

Mrs. Stillman, the secretary, invited me to call a few days later at her home, where an executive meeting was to convene. I went with keen anticipation, totally unprepared for the actual answer. The committee had met. Mrs. Dennett, Mrs. Stillman, and Anita were all there. Mrs. Dennett spoke for the group; the National Birth Control League disagreed with my methods, my tactics, with everything I had done. Such an organization as theirs, the function of which was primarily to change the laws in an orderly and proper manner, could not logically sanction anyone who had broken those laws.

After delivering this ultimatum, Mrs. Dennett walked to the door with me. Would I mind giving her the names and addresses of those socially prominent and distinguished persons I had found on my

European trip to be interested? Heartsick as I was over my reception, I was also amused at her shrewdness.

Mrs. Dennett was a good promoter and experienced campaigner, a capable office executive, an indefatigable worker for suffrage and peace, with a background that might have been invaluable. I often regretted that we could not have combined our efforts. Had we been able to do so the movement might have been pushed many years ahead.

My fourth communication was to Dr. William J. Robinson, an émigré from the land of orthodox medicine, who was possessed of a sensitivity to current moods. When he had realized that Will Durant's lectures had aroused interest in sex psychology, he had stepped in to speak to larger audiences, using a more popular approach, although, as far as I know, he had never publicly discussed the prevention of conception.

Dr. Abraham Jacoby, beloved dean of the profession, in accepting the presidency of the Academy of Medicine, had backed birth control, and through Dr. Robinson's endeavors a small committee had later been formed to look into it. From the reports that had come to me I could not discover whether any harmonious agreement that the subject lay within the province of medicine had been made. To my inquiry Dr. Robinson replied that the committee had met only once and he considered I could expect no support from them. He enclosed a check for ten dollars towards the expenses of my trial.

Here were two disappointments to face. Both these organizations had seemed so well suited to continue progress: one to change the laws, the other to take proper medical charge. Neither had fulfilled my hopes and therefore I felt I had to enter the fray again. My burning concern for the thousands of women who went unregarded could apparently find no official endorsement; birth control was back again where it had started. I was convinced I had to depend solely upon the compassionate insight of intelligent women, which I was certain was latent and could be aroused.

But these problems were suddenly swept aside by a crisis of a more intimate nature, a tragedy about which I find myself still unable to write, though so many years have passed.

A few days after my arrival Peggy was taken ill with pneumonia.

When Mr. Content telephoned to say I had better come down and talk it over, I could not go. He was extremely kind, assuring me there was no hurry and he would postpone the trial until I was free. This allowed me to devote my whole attention and time to her.

Peggy died the morning of November 6, 1915.

The joy in the fullness of life went out of it then and has never quite returned. Deep in the hidden realm of my consciousness my little girl has continued to live, and in that strange, mysterious place where reality and imagination meet, she has grown up to womanhood. There she leads an ideal existence untouched by harsh actuality and disillusion.

Men and women from all classes, from nearly every city in America, poured upon me their sympathy. Money for my trial came beyond my understanding—not large amounts, but large for the senders—from miners of West Virginia and lumbermen of the North Woods. Some had walked five miles to read *Family Limitation;* others had had it copied for them. Women wrote of children dead a quarter of a century for whom they were still secretly mourning, and sent me pictures and locks of hair of their own dead babies. I had never fully realized until then that the loss of a child remains unforgotten to every mother during her lifetime.

Public opinion had been focused on Comstock's activities by Bill's sentence, and the liberals had been aroused. Committees of two and three came to request me to take up the purely legislative task of changing the Federal law. Aid would be forthcoming—special trains to Congress, investigations, commissions, and victory in sight before the year was over! It was tempting. It seemed so feasible on the surface, so much easier than agonizing delays through the courts. Many others advised me just as before that in pleading guilty I was choosing the best field in which to make my fight.

One of those to urge me towards a middle course was Max Eastman, who possessed an unusual evenness of temper and tolerance towards all who opposed him as well as a keen mind and keen imagination which followed hypotheses to logical conclusions. This soft-voiced, lethargic poet, mentally and emotionally controlled, had too great a sense of humor and ability in visualizing events in their proper perspective to advocate direct action.

Max made an appointment for me to see Samuel Untermyer, authority on constitutional law and a person to whom liberals turned because of the fight he had put up against the trusts; he might straighten out the legal aspects. I found him enthroned in his luxurious office amid the most magnificent American Beauty roses—dozens and dozens and dozens. With his piercing eyes and head too large for his frame, he appeared a disembodied brain. Though the appointment had been made with difficulty—writing and telephoning back and forth through secretaries to be verified—time now was nothing to him. He was so smooth, so courteous, so sympathetic, so unhurried; he seemed to understand and to be ready to lift the load of legal worry from my mind.

Picking up the telephone, he said, "Get me Mr. Content." Then, "Harold, come on over to my office and bring your record on Mrs. Sanger."

When the District Attorney had arrived, Mr. Untermyer's whole voice changed. He spoke sternly to the young man. "Why, Harold, what are you trying to do—persecuting this little woman, so frail and so delicate, the mother of a family? You don't want to put her behind bars, do you? She's doing a noble work in the world and here you are behaving like this! Are you representing the Government or are you merely prejudiced in your own behalf?"

Mr. Content replied respectfully, "Well, Mr. Untermyer, we don't want to prosecute Mrs. Sanger, but we want her to promise to obey the law."

"Has she broken the law?"

"We have positive proof that she has violated it on a very large scale."

Mr. Untermyer immediately assured him, "Why, of course, she'll promise not to break any more laws. Is that all it is? You just quash that indictment and forget about it."

Mr. Content left. Mr. Untermyer turned to me genially and said, "Well, you see? We've fixed that up."

"What's going to happen? The law will be the same, won't it?"

"Why, yes."

"What was that you said about a promise?"

"Oh, yes, write me a letter saying you won't break the law again."

"I couldn't promise that, Mr. Untermyer."

"What?"

"No, I couldn't do that. The law is there. Something must happen to it."

"The law may not be what it should be, but you'll never get anywhere by violating it. It must be changed by legal methods; gather all your friends and go to Congress."

Again I stated my position. The law specified obscenity, and I had done nothing obscene. I even had the best of the Government as regarded the precise charge. I had not given contraceptive information in the *Woman Rebel,* and therefore had not violated the law either in spirit or principle. But I had done so in circulating *Family Limitation,* and that would inevitably be brought up. I really wanted this, so that birth control would be defined once and for all as either obscene or not obscene.

Mr. Untermyer took down one of his ponderous books and read over the section in question. Again he said, "The evidence is that you have violated the law. We don't separate the spirit from the letter. It is all there. It seems to me that pleading guilty would let you out of your troubles without loss of dignity. You should consider yourself fortunate at the suggested outcome. You can gain nothing by trial. You cannot even get publicity in these days when the papers are crowded with war news and the big events of history are happening."

I still could not admit his interpretation. You had to differentiate between the things mentioned in that law and actual obscenity; the courts would some day have to decide on this.

"You have no case," Mr. Untermyer persisted. "If you have broken the law, there is nothing anyone can do or say to argue that fact away. We must prevent your going to jail, however. I'll see what I can do."

"I'm not concerned with going to jail. Going in or staying out has nothing to do with it. The question at stake is whether I have or have not done something obscene. If I have done nothing obscene I cannot plead guilty."

Mr. Untermyer was upset. Instead of his former warmth I was aware of a curt and cold politeness. I went from his office feeling I had had an opportunity to make a powerful friend and had lost it by refusing to accept the legal point of view.

Max also was decidedly angry. His attitude was, "We tried to help you, and you declined help." He wrote formally:

> You could accompany your plea of guilty with a statement, both before the Court and for the press, which would make it a far more signal attack upon the law to whose violation you would be pleading guilty than a plea of not guilty. It would do a thousand times more good. At the same time it would satisfy your pride, or your feeling that you ought to be brave enough to stand up for what you think, or whatever it is that is making you refuse the advice of counsel.

I would not plead guilty on any count. They could not make me. I felt deep within me that I was right and they were wrong. I still had that naïve trust that when the facts were known, the Government would not wilfully condemn millions of women to death, misery, or abortion which left them physically damaged and spiritually crippled.

Clarence Darrow and other liberal lawyers from various cities generously offered to come to New York to present the case free of charge, but after my Untermyer interview I was convinced that the quibbles of lawyers inevitably beclouded the fundamental issues; I had to move people and persuade them emotionally. I had no practice in public speaking; mine was the valor of faith. However, I was certain that speaking from the fullness of my heart I would be guided by the greatness and profundity of my conviction. In spite of the old adage that "he who has himself for a lawyer has a fool for a client," I was confident that any jury of honest men would acquit me.

I asked Mr. Content to put my case on the calendar as soon as possible. It was called for the end of November, then set for January 18th, then January 24th. I used to go almost weekly to demand that it take place, always stressing the fact that I wanted a trial by jury. One of the judges that I came before in these various courts had previously asked me in a personal letter to send him *Family Limitation*, and I had mailed it to him with my compliments. The twinkle in his eyes was reflected in mine; we both knew that he as well as I had been technically breaking the law.

As the New York *Sun* commented, "The Sanger case presents the anomaly of a prosecutor loath to prosecute and a defendant anxious to be tried." The newspapers were taking ever-increasing notice. A photograph of myself and my two young sons circulated widely and seemed to alter the attitude of a heretofore cynical public. At that time I thought the papers were against me, but looking over these old clippings today I realize this was merely the impersonality of the news columns. Their editorial hesitancy made them appear, like all other conservative and reactionary forces, my opponents. But the rank and file of American newspaperdom, though they must always have their little jokes, have always been sympathetic.

They printed the letter to Woodrow Wilson, initiated by Marie Stopes. It "begged to call the attention" of the President to the fact that I was in danger of criminal prosecution for circulating a pamphlet on birth control, which was allowed in every civilized country except the United States; that England had passed through the phase of prohibiting this subject a generation before; and that to suppress serious and disinterested opinion on anything so important was detrimental to human progress. It respectfully urged the President to exert his powerful influence in behalf of free speech and the betterment of the race. This letter was invaluable by reason of its signatories—Lena Ashwell, William Archer, Percy Ames, Aylmer Maude, M. C. Stopes, Arnold Bennett, Edward Carpenter, Gilbert Murray, and H. G. Wells, whose name was news. If a group of such eminence in England could afford to stand by me, then the same kind of people here might be less timorous.

As public sentiment grew, telegrams and letters showered upon Judge Clayton demanding the dismissal of the charges against me. He piled them in wastebaskets and remarked in a bored tone to Mr. Content, "Take these Sanger letters away." That I was preparing to go to court undefended by counsel was making the matter harder for them.

My radical allies were, according to their habit, collecting money for my defense, but this had no effect on my private financial status. My sister, Ethel, who was living with me, thought I ought to be considering the matter. One day she said, "I've a good case for you. Wouldn't you like to take it?"

"What kind?"

"Maternity. She expects to be delivered in a day or two—probably a Caesarian. She asked for me, but I'd rather you had it."

"I'm not interested, thank you. I've given up nursing."

"Well, Mrs. Sanger," she remarked ironically, "would you mind telling me what you're going to do to earn your living?"

"I'm not interested in earning my living. I've cast myself upon the universe and it will take care of me."

She looked at me sadly and with worried apprehension.

Three days later Ethel received the anticipated summons. On her way out she picked up the mail at the door. In it was a letter from a California acquaintance of hers who did not know where I was but had her address. "Will you please give the enclosed forty-five dollars to Margaret Sanger from her sympathizers?"

Ethel handed it to me with the resigned comment, "Well, here's your check from God."

The editor of the *Woman Rebel* had struck her single match of defiance, but she could be of slight significance in the forward march towards "women's rights." In Feminist circles I was little known. With my personal sorrow, my manifold domestic duties, my social shyness, I avoided meeting new people. My attitude thus created some reluctance among those who might otherwise have hastened to my aid. Indeed, I wanted a certain type of support, but I could not take the initiative in asking for it.

This was suddenly done for me. One afternoon I was invited to a tea arranged by Henrietta Rodman, Feminist of Feminists, in her Greenwich Village apartment. Wells was particularly sanctified among her group and I must be all right if he approved. As a result of that meeting the suffrage worker, Alice Carpenter, set the wheels in motion for a dinner at the Brevoort Hotel to be held January 23rd, the evening preceding my trial. I was to be given a chance to say my say, speak my piece before a gathering of influential people. Although I did not see her until some years after, I thanked her in my heart many times for what she had done.

In the ballroom were collected several hundred people. Mary Heaton Vorse, Dr. Mary Halton, Jack Reed, Dr. Robinson, Frances Brooks Ackerman, Walter Lippmann, then of the *New Republic,* and Mrs. Thomas Hepburn, the Kathy Houghton of my Corning childhood, all were there.

As we were about to go in to dinner, Rose Pastor Stokes, the Chairman, took me aside and said, "Something very disturbing has happened. We've just been talking to Dr. Jacoby. He has a speech ready in which he intends to blast you to the skies for interfering in what should be a strictly medical matter. Remember he's greatly admired and he's speaking here tonight for the doctors. We meant to have you come at the end of the program but now we're going to put you first so that you can spike his guns."

My trepidation was increased. Nevertheless, I plunged into my carefully prepared maiden speech in behalf of birth control. Fortunately I had already planned to upbraid the doctors who daily saw the conditions which had so moved me and yet made it necessary for a person like myself, not equipped as they were, to stir up public opinion. It was like carrying coals to Newcastle; they should have been teaching me.

I said I recognized that many of those before me of diverse outlooks and temperaments would support birth control propaganda if carried out in what they regarded as a safe and sane manner, although they did not countenance the methods I had been following in my attempt to arouse working women to the fact that having a child was a supreme responsibility. There was nothing new or radical in birth control, which Aristotle and Plato as well as many modern thinkers had demonstrated. But the ideas of wise men and scientists were sterile and did not affect the tremendous facts of life among the disinherited. All the while their discussions had been proceeding, the people themselves had been and still were blindly, desperately, practicing birth control by the most barbaric methods—infanticide, abortion, and other crude ways. I might have taken up a policy of safety, sanity, and conservatism—but would I have secured a hearing? Admittedly physicians and scientists had far more technical knowledge than I, but I had found myself in the position of one who had discovered a house was on fire and it was up to me to shout out the warning. Afterwards others, more experienced in executive organization, could gather together and direct all the sympathy and interest which had been aroused. Only in this way could I be vindicated.

Since my charge had forestalled his, the venerable Dr. Jacoby either had to answer me or shift his ground. He chose the latter course and talked on the question of quality in population, which might perhaps have been construed as in my favor.

Many of the women present were comfortable examples of the manner in which birth control could enable them to lead dignified lives. Elsie Clews Parsons made the suggestion that twenty-five who had practiced it should rise in court with me and plead guilty before the law. But only one volunteered. What surprised me most was the voice of Mary Ware Dennett announcing that she represented the National Birth Control League and that that body was going to stand behind Margaret Sanger in her ordeal—subscriptions were urgently needed for the League.

The next morning when I arrived at nine o'clock at the Federal Court building more than two hundred partisans were already in the corridors. A great corps of reporters and photographers was on hand. The stage had been set for an exciting drama.

Judge Henry D. Clayton and Assistant District Attorneys Knox and Content arrived at ten-thirty, apparently feeling the effects of the publicity of the night before.

The moment Knox moved to adjourn for a week I was on my feet asking immediate trial, but Judge Clayton postponed the case. Everybody went home disappointed.

February 18th the Government finally entered a nolle prosequi. Content explained there had been many assertions that the defendant was the victim of persecution, and that had never been the intent of the Federal authorities. "The case had been laid before the grand jurors as impartially as possible and since they had voted an indictment there was nothing that the District Attorney could do but prosecute. Now, however, as it was realized that the indictment was two years old, and that Mrs. Sanger was not a disorderly person and did not make a practice of publishing such articles, the Government had considered there was reason for considerable doubt."

Well, when an army marches up the hill and then marches down again some good excuse must always be given.

All my friends regarded the quashing of the Federal indictment a great achievement. There was much rejoicing and congratulation, but they acted as though they were saying, "Now settle down in your domestic corner, take your husband back, care for your children, behave yourself, and no more of this nonsense. Your duty is to do the thing you are able to do which is mind your home and not attempt something others can do better than you."

But I was not content to have a Liberty Dinner and jubilate. I could not consider anything more than a moral victory had been attained. The law had not been tested. I agreed with the loyal *Globe*, which staunchly maintained, "If the matter Mrs. Sanger sent through the mails was obscene two years ago, it is still obscene." I knew and felt instinctively the danger of having a privilege under a law rather than a right. I could not yet afford to breathe a sigh of relief.

The Federal law concerned only printed literature. My own pamphlet had given the impression that the printed word was the best way to inform women, but the practical course of contraceptive technique I had taken in the Netherlands had shown me that one woman was so different from another in structure that each needed particular information applied to herself as an individual. Books and leaflets, therefore, should be of secondary importance. The public health way was through personal instruction in clinics.

A light had been kindled; so many invitations to address meetings in various cities and towns were sent me that I was not able to accept them all but agreed to as many as I could. It was no longer to be only a free speech movement, and I wanted also if possible to present this new idea of clinics to the country. If I could start them, other organizations and even hospitals might do the same. I had a vision of a "chain"—thousands of them in every center of America, staffed with specialists putting the subject on a modern scientific basis through research.

Many states in the West had already granted woman suffrage. Having achieved this type of freedom, I was sure they would receive clinics more readily, especially California which had no law against birth control. The same thing would follow in the East. As I told the *Tribune,* "I have the word of four prominent physicians that they will support me in the work. . . . There will be nurses in attendance at the clinic, and doctors who will instruct women in the things they need to know. All married women or women about to be married will be assisted free and without question."

A splendid promise—but difficult to fulfill, as events were to prove.

Chapter Sixteen

HEAR ME FOR MY CAUSE

*"Speak clearly if you speak at all.
Carve every word before you let it fall."*
OLIVER WENDELL HOLMES

ONCE Amos Pinchot asked me how long it had taken me to prepare that first lecture I delivered on my three months' trip across the country in 1916.

"About fourteen years," I answered.

I was thinking of all the time that had passed during which experiences, tragic and stirring, had come to me and were embodied therein.

So much depended on this speech; the women of leisure must be made to listen, the women of wealth to give, the women of influence to protest. Before starting April 1st, I tried to put myself in their places and to see how their interests and imaginations could most effectively be excited, how the pictures which had so unceasingly beset me could best be brought to their minds. I felt certain that if I could do this, they would do the rest.

But the anxiety that went into the composition of the speech was as nothing to the agonies with which I contemplated its utterance. My mother used to say a decent woman only had her name in the papers three times during her life—when she was born, when she married, and when she died. Although by nature I shrank from publicity, the kind of work I had undertaken did not allow me to shirk it—but I was frightened to death. Hoping that practice would give me greater confidence, I used to climb to the roof of the Lexington Avenue hotel where I was staying and recite, my voice going out over the house tops and echoing timidly among the chimney pots.

I repeated the lecture over and over to myself before I tried it on a small audience in New Rochelle. I did not dare cut myself adrift from my notes; I had to read it, and when I had finished, did not feel it had been very successful. By the time I reached Pittsburgh, my first large city, I had memorized every period and comma, but I was still scared that if I lost one word I would not know what the next was. I closed my eyes and spoke in fear and trembling. The laborers and social workers who crowded the big theater responded so enthusiastically that I was at least sure their attention had been held by its content.

It was interesting to watch the pencils come out at the announcement that there were specifically seven circumstances under which birth control should be practiced.

First, when either husband or wife had a transmissible disease, such as epilepsy, insanity, or syphilis.

Second, when the wife suffered from a temporary affection of the lungs, heart, or kidneys, the cure of which might be retarded through pregnancy.

Third, when parents, though normal, had subnormal children.

Fourth, when husband or wife were adolescent. Early marriage, yes, but parenthood should be postponed until after the twenty-third year of the boy and the twenty-second of the girl.

Fifth, when the earning capacity of the father was inadequate; no man had the right to have ten children if he could not provide for more than two. The standards of living desirable had to be considered; it was one thing if the parents were planning college educations for their offspring, and another if they wanted them simply for industrial exploitation.

Sixth, births should be spaced between two and three years, according to the mother's health.

All the foregoing were self-evident from the physiological and economic points of view. But I wished to introduce a final reason which seemed equally important to me, though it had not been taken into account statistically.

Seventh, every young couple should practice birth control for at least one year after marriage and two as a rule, because this period should be one of physical, mental, financial, and spiritual adjustment in which they could grow together, cement the bonds of attraction, and plan for their children.

Like other professions, motherhood should serve its apprenticeship. It was not good sense to expect fruit from buds—yet if womanhood flowered from girlhood too soon it did not have a chance to be a thing in itself. I offered a hypothetical case. Suppose two young people started out in marriage, ignorant of its implications and possibilities. The bride, utterly unprepared, returned pregnant from the honeymoon—headaches, nausea, backache, general fatigue, and depression. The romantic lover never knew that girl as a woman; she forever after appeared to him only as a mother. Under such circumstances marriage seldom had an opportunity to become as fine an instrument for development as it might have been.

I wanted the world made safe for babies. From a government survey significant conclusions had emerged as to how many babies lived to celebrate their first birthday. These were based largely on three factors: the father's wage—as it went down, more died, and as it rose, more survived; the spacing of births—when children were born one year apart, more died than if the mother were allowed a two- or three-year interval between pregnancies; the relative position in the family—of the number of second-born, thirty-two out of every hundred died annually, and so on progressively until among those who were born twelfth, the rate was sixty out of a hundred.

I claimed that sympathy and charity extended towards babies were not enough, that milk stations were not enough, that maternity centers were not enough, and that protective legislation in the form of child labor laws was not enough. With all the force I could muster I insisted that the first right of a child was to be wanted, to be desired, to be planned for with an intensity of love that gave it its title to being. It should be wanted by both parents, but especially by the mother who was to carry it, nourish it, and perhaps influence its life by her thoughts, her passions, her rebellions, her yearnings.

So that all babies born could be assured sound bodies and sound minds, I suggested in lighter vein that the Government issue passports for them, calling the attention of the audience to the fact that adults in this country would never think of going abroad without a government guarantee to ensure them safe passage and preservation against harm or ill-treatment. If this were necessary for grown persons journeying into a foreign land, how much more important it was to protect children who were to enter into this strange and insecure new world.

I reminded them also that no one would consider embarking in the medical or legal profession without due preparation. Even cooks or laundresses scarcely applied for positions without experience proving they were qualified to undertake their tasks. But anyone, no matter how ignorant, how diseased mentally or physically, how lacking in all knowledge of children, seemed to consider he or she had the right to become a parent.

In the same tone I proposed a bureau of application for the unborn. I pictured a married couple coming here for a baby as though for a chambermaid, chauffeur, or gardener. The unborn child took a look at his prospective parents and propounded a few questions such as any employee has the right to ask of his employer.

To his father the unborn child said, "Do you happen to have a health certificate?"

And to the mother, "How are your nerves? What do you know about babies? What kind of a table do you set?"

And to both of them, "What are your plans for bringing me up? Am I to spend my childhood days in factories or mills, or am I to have the opportunities offered by an intelligent, healthy, family life? I am unusually gifted," the baby might add. "Do you know how to develop my talents? What sort of society have you made for the fullest expression of my genius?"

All babies came back to the practical question, "How many children have you already?"

"Eight."

"How much are you earning?"

"Ten dollars a week."

"And living in two rooms, you say? No, thank you. Next, please."

I was trying to make people think in order that they might act. My part was to give them the facts and then, when they asked what they should do about them, suggest concrete programs for leagues and clinics. Many women had far more executive and administrative experience than I, and I still expected them to carry on where I left off so that I might be free to return to Europe.

My hopes seemed well-founded when many of the Pittsburgh audience waited afterward to request help in organizing themselves. Thus the first state birth control league was formed. This and all subsequent ones I referred to Mrs. Dennett's National Birth Control League to be under its future direction.

That meeting had been held under the sponsorship of Mrs. Enoch Raugh, a philanthropist of great courage. In the early days almost everywhere I went the subject of birth control was one likely to make conspicuous those who identified themselves with it. Average well-to-do persons hesitated except for the Jewish leaders in civic affairs, who, as soon as they were personally convinced, showed no reluctance in aligning themselves publicly.

Not so did Chicago respond. Some members of the powerful Women's City Club had privately asked me to speak, but when the matter was brought up before their board, the unofficial invitation was officially canceled. Here again were conservatives enjoying the benefits of birth control for themselves but unwilling to endorse it for the less fortunate of their sex. When they did not listen, I tried to reach the women of the stockyards directly.

So many hundreds of letters had come to me—not only in English, but also in Hungarian, Bohemian, Polish, and Yiddish—clamoring for information, that I had every reason to suppose what I had to say was going to be welcome on Halsted Street. I was incredulous when I met an unforeseen resistance.

Hull House and similar settlements had been established to help the poor to help themselves. But I found that although social agencies had originally striven to win confidence by opening milk stations and day nurseries, this aim had been somewhat obscured in the interests of sheer efficiency. Many welfare workers had come to treat individuals merely as cases to be cataloged, arrogantly proclaiming they knew "what was best for the poor"; a type had developed, and those who belonged to it were lacking in human sympathy. Instead they expanded their own egos through domination.

Their desire to build up prestige and secure a position of importance in the community had formed a civic barrier, a wall, in fact, around the stockyards district, preventing any new concepts, people, or organizations from coming in without official permission. The stockyards women were literally imprisoned in their homes from advanced ideas unless they went out into other sections of the city.

Because this ridiculous situation had arisen in Chicago, no hall could be had in the immediate neighborhood. I could have held no meeting there had it not been for Fania Mindell, one of the many idealists of that time who threw themselves into the fight for the oppressed as an aftermath of their own sufferings and repressions in Russia. She had a devoted and self-sacrificing nature which made her work, slave, toil for the love of doing it. She made all the arrangements, producing an audience of fifteen hundred from the labor and stockyards environs.

These first lectures in Chicago and elsewhere attracted women in swarms, paying their twenty-five cents to fill the auditoriums; I remember that one offered her wedding ring as the price of admission, to be redeemed on pay day. They brought their children, and more than once I had to lift my voice above the persistent cooing and gurgling of a front-row baby. There was a natural understanding between infants. If one were given a bottle, another began to cry. A third in the back joined the chorus, or a small boy on the side aisle whispered shrilly, "I wantta go home!" I just ached to see those many babies, because I knew what their mothers had come for—definite help to stop having more—and it could not be given them.

Often at these meetings I saw some woman sitting down near the platform holding a bunch of wild flowers, daisies, Queen Anne's lace, or butter-and-eggs, waiting to present me with the little bouquet, to tell me that since she had received my pamphlet, she had "kept out of trouble." No matter how phrased, the gratitude was genuine.

Over and over again someone popped up in front of me, and extended a hand, "I used to subscribe to the *Woman Rebel*. I got all your pamphlets from England."

When I asked, "What's your name?" with the answer, like a flash, came the number of children and the locality, and the story sent me years earlier. And, "Didn't you live in Des Moines?" I continued.

Seldom was it the wrong place. In this way I came across dozens of "friends" who had been among the original two thousand.

I was advised by Dr. Mabel Ullrich of Minneapolis not to go there because the Twin Cities were the most conservative in America. "You won't get six people," she prophesied.

"Do you think I'll get six?"

"Perhaps."

"Then I'll go."

I was prepared to speak wherever it was possible, regardless of attendance. Six people, properly convinced, usually made sixty people think before very long. In spite of Dr. Ullrich's warning, hundreds of chairs had to be brought in to the Minneapolis Public Library to take care of the overflow.

People were frequently surprised at the size of my audiences. I should have been surprised had it been the other way about, although I did not like too many present because the subject was too intimate for great numbers in large halls. All came because birth control touched their lives deeply and vitally; they listened so earnestly, so intently that the very atmosphere was hushed and unnaturally quiet.

Here in Minneapolis arrived a telegram from Frederick A. Blossom, Ph.D., manager of the Associated Charities of Cleveland, whom I had met there. Would I speak at the National Social Workers' Conference then being held in Indianapolis? He could not get me placed on the program, but the two subjects that were currently arousing considerable interest were the prison reforms instituted by Thomas Mott Osborne at Sing Sing, and birth control. He believed it was worth my while to come.

Since I had nearly a week before my scheduled meeting in St. Louis, the time fitted in very nicely and I seized the occasion. I did not expect definite action, but I did yearn to arouse dissatisfaction over smoothing off the top, to say to these social workers plodding along in their organizations that I thought their accomplishments were temporary, and that charity was only a feather duster flicking from the surface particles which merely settled somewhere else. They could never attain their ideal of eliminating the problems of the masses until the breeding of the unending stream of unwanted babies was stopped.

Blossom, polished, educated, and clever, had a charming and disarming personality, and an ability far above the average. Part of his work had been to cultivate the rich, and in this he had been eminently successful because he was so suave, never waving a red flag in front of anybody's nose as I did; my flaming Feminism speeches had scared some of my supporters out of their wits.

This master manager knew exactly what to do and how to go about it. Notices were posted throughout the hotel and left in every delegate's mail box, announcing the meeting for four in the afternoon, the only hour when we could have the big amphitheater. Although round-table discussions were going on at the same time, it was jammed to the doors; people were sitting on the platform and on window sills and radiators.

I was almost startled that so many of those from whom I hoped for co-operation should turn out in such numbers. Walter Lippmann said, "This will kick the football of birth control straight across to the Pacific." And, indeed, the social agents, like the plumed darts of a seeded dandelion puffed into the air, scattered to every quarter of the country; thereafter, to the West and back again, I heard echoes of the meeting.

During the previous weeks in various cities it had been hard to be alone a minute. Women with the inevitable babies kept calling on me in hotels and so did men setting out to their jobs early in the morning, carrying their lunch boxes. I was so mentally weary with strain that it seemed I must get away from humanity for a little while if I were to retain my sanity. Worst of all was the ever-present loneliness and grief—the apparition of Peggy who wanted me to recognize she had gone and was no longer here.

I slipped into St. Louis two days ahead so that I could be by myself, registering at the Hotel Jefferson and asking not to be disturbed. But the telephone rang before I even had my suitcase unpacked; a reporter had seen my name at the desk and requested an interview. I replied I could not give it; I was not in St. Louis so far as he was concerned. Saying to myself, "Good, I've escaped that,"

I went to bed. But next morning a ribbon on the front page of his paper announced I was "hiding" in the city. In my ignorance I had violated the etiquette observed by welcoming committees, and mine was highly indignant. I had little rest.

Among the group of backers was Robert Minor, an old friend, formerly an outstanding cartoonist on the New York *World,* who had been dropped because he had refused to draw the kind of pictures about Germany his employers wanted. It had been arranged that I was to have the Victoria Theater Sunday night, which had already been paid for in advance so that the meeting could be free. However, at a quarter to eight when we arrived, the building was in total darkness and the doors were locked. The proprietor's office was closed; he was not at home; there was no means of finding out anything. Actually, he had temporarily effaced himself because he did not wish to admit that he had been threatened with a Catholic boycott of his theater, and had been promised protection against a possible suit for breach of contract.

At least two thousand people had gathered and were filling the air with catcalls, hisses, hurrahs, cries of "the Catholics run the town! Break in the door!" Minor urged me to stand up in the car and give my speech, but without its proper setting I was lost; here was a type of battle needing an experienced campaigner. Although I did not feel adequate, I began, but my voice could not surmount the uproar.

I was barely under way when a police sergeant reached up and seized my arm. "Here now, you'll have to come down. You can't talk here."

"Speech! Speech!" yelled the crowd. "Go on."

But the owner of the car, to my great relief, started his engine. I sat back in the seat with a thump and off we went.

The incident had repercussions. The Men's City Club, regarding the event as a blot on the fair name of the town, asked me to speak at their luncheon the next day, and I promised to wait over. Although forty Catholics then resigned in a body, St. Louis would not be coerced, and more than a hundred new members joined immediately.

William Marion Reedy, owner and publisher of the famous

Reedy's Mirror, had been at the closed theater. He printed a cartoon showing the Capitol of the United States with a papal crown on it, stated editorially that the Pope was now dictating to America what it should hear and think, and emphasized the consequent dangers to the country if any religious group were allowed such domination. "No idea let loose in the world has ever been suppressed. Ideas cannot be jailed in *oubliettes,*" was his peroration.

After I had left the Middle West and reached the Rocky Mountains the atmosphere changed. I was struck even by the attitude of the bellboys and waiters at the Brown Palace Hotel in Denver. In New York you were served by trained foreign men and boys— Italian and French. Here they were American-born, blue-eyed, fair-complexioned, strong-jawed. Without bowing or obsequiousness they brought your food and carried your bags as if doing you a favor. You hesitated to give them a tip, though, as a matter of fact, they never refused it.

I loved Denver itself. It seemed to me the women there were the most beautiful I had seen—fresh, charming, alive. They had long had the vote and used it effectively. Because they believed in Judge Ben Lindsey's juvenile court, they had kept him in office in spite of the concerted antagonism of picturesque but corrupt politicians.

Although Judge Lindsey had bitter enemies in exalted places, he had loyal friends also. When Theodore Roosevelt had stopped there in 1912 on his Western Swing, the Judge was facing opposition. The city fathers did not want to include him as a substantial citizen on their platform committee of welcome. Roosevelt peered vainly about among all these bankers and business men. "Where's Ben Lindsey?" he asked.

"We don't talk about him around here."

"Don't we? Well, he's a friend of mine. I shan't say a word until Ben Lindsey comes and sits on this platform beside me."

Nor would he speak until Lindsey arrived; everybody had to wait.

It was a high point for me at this time, so soon after my own court appearance, to have Judge Lindsey preside at my meeting. Formerly my listeners, with the exception of Indianapolis, had been chiefly of the working class. Here they were wives of doctors, lawyers, petty officials, members of clubs.

I was more than delighted to have an audience which had the power to change public opinion. The "submerged tenth" had no need of theories nor the proof of the advantages of family limitation; they were the proof—the living example of the need. It was vitally important to have reflective hearers who not only themselves used contraceptives, but who advanced thought through literature, discussions, and papers. To them I was telling the story of those millions who could not come, and trying to relate it as I knew it to be true. Stimulating them offered the best possibility of getting something done.

Judge Lindsey invited me to sit on the bench with him the next morning, and I watched enthralled the way he handled his cases. The familiar court method was punishment, and the more punishment the better. But he operated on the new psychology. For instance, he attempted to inculcate a sense of responsibility in one boy who had disobeyed his mother and run away from school, by showing him his indebtedness to her, how he should be helping rather than causing her grief.

The same tactics were employed in the case of Joseph, charged with assault on his wife, Nelly, who stood silently in the background, shawl over her head. Lindsey read the evidence, then said, "Joseph, come over here."

Joseph stepped nearer, appearing somewhat guilty, as men of his status usually did when they came into court.

"What's this I hear about you? Why did you strike Nelly?"

"She made me mad," Joseph mumbled.

"Joseph, turn your head and look at your wife. Look at her! Look!—thin, pale, weak, and you a big strong man striking that delicate little woman. Aren't you ashamed of yourself to beat Nelly? You who promised to love, honor, and protect her?"

The reprimanding lasted fully two minutes. Finally tears began to spring from Nelly's eyes and to run down her face. She moved forward, took Joseph by the hand, and said, "Oh, he's not so bad, Judge." Joseph then embraced her. Instead of punishing him, which would in effect have also been punishing Nelly, Judge Lindsey put him on parole to report back in two months' time, and husband and wife went out arm in arm.

One of the hardest things for a judge in a lower court to combat is the prejudice of the police against those who already have records. Judge Lindsey, when a case came up before him, never took the word of the ward heelers, but had his own secretary, employed and paid by him, go to the home and investigate, and he held the case until this had been done. But I thought then that either Judge Lindsey was heading straight for trouble, or Denver had a kingdom of its own where freedom reigned.

A similar attitude of liberality prevailed on the far side of the Rockies. In many places where I had previously spoken, policemen had been stationed at the doors. Occasionally they had even come to the hotel to read my speech, as at St. Louis and Indianapolis. But in Los Angeles officials of all the city, even the representatives of the women's police division, met me at the station or called on me in a friendly way.

I was still as terrified of speaking as in the beginning; I used to wake up early in the morning, sometimes before it was light, and feel a ghastly depression coming over me. I realized it was the impending lecture which was so affecting me, and I waited in trepidation for the hour. My physical illness did not grow better until I was on my feet and well into my subject.

Though this was my first visit to the West, I had no time for scenery. Whenever possible I traveled by night and arrived during the day, and by this stage of my trip I was seemingly always tired. The dead grind went on and on, an endless succession of getting off trains, introductions, talking to committees, pouring yourself out— and nothing happening. Physically and psychically it was one of the lowest periods of my life.

Someone in San Francisco did a lovely thing for me. I never knew who she was, but at the end of one meeting she picked me up in her car and swept me away into a forest of huge, tall trees where the sun broke through. There she left me for fifteen minutes in the midst of a cathedral of great evergreens with the sky overhead and myself alone. I have never forgotten the peace and quiet.

I found the West Coast a lively place. Ideas were being constantly thrashed out. Every discourse had a challenging reception. Emma Goldman had been there year after year and had stirred people to dare express themselves. All sorts of individuals catechized you, and if you were not well grounded in your subject you were quickly made aware of your ignorance. The Wobblies spent hours in libraries, not only keeping warm, but trying to find points on which to attack the next lecturer who should come to town. Often those most eager were considered cranks—on diet, free trade, single tax, and free silver—so familiar that their rising was hailed with groans. I never minded having questions asked, though everything I knew was questioned. It was as well for me that, in addition to my Malthus, I knew my Schopenhauer and Nietzsche, my Henry George, Marx, and Kropotkin. It seems to me that today the tone of audiences has deteriorated; queries rarely have the same intellectual grasp behind them.

My welcome at Portland was delightful. The sixty-year-old poet, C. E. S. Wood, dapper and gracious, made a practice of greeting personally women speakers, dedicating poems to them on their arrival, and sending bowers of flowers to their hotel rooms. The City of Roses did much to entertain its visitors.

Here I was invited by a church to address its congregation following the evening service. I had not been very well in the afternoon, but I promised over the telephone to be there if I could. I was late and the meeting had already begun. As I slipped in at the rear I heard the chairman refer to me as a Joan of Arc. Entirely too many Joans of Arc were floating about in those days. Not wishing to be a disappointment I turned right around and walked back to the hotel. Since no one had ever seen me, both my entrance and exit went unremarked.

I admired robust, vital women; they appeared so efficient, and I regretted the fact that I did not give the same impression. I felt that way, but could not help resembling, as someone phrased it, "a hungry flower drooping in the rain." If I were in a room with ten people and somebody came in who expected me to be present, she invariably approached the biggest woman and addressed her, "How do you do, Mrs. Sanger?" For a brief while I tried to make myself seem more competent-looking by wearing severe suits, but this phase did not last; for one thing, effective simplicity cost money and I did not have enough to be really well-tailored. However, the anonymity due to my appearance was, on the whole, fortunate. I was always able to go along any street, into any restaurant or shop, and seldom be identified, and this made it possible for me to maintain a relatively private life.

A dinner was given at Portland; the chairman, who had seen Susan B. Anthony and many other women with causes come and go, made a short speech of introduction. I rarely remember what people say on such occasions, but one of her statements has remained in my mind. "I would like to see Margaret Sanger again after ten years. Most movements either break you or develop the 'public figure' type of face which has become hard and set through long and furious battling. But her cause is different from any other I have ever known. I should like to see how she comes out of it."

I have thought of this many times—how, if the cause is not great enough to lift you outside yourself, you can be driven to the point of bitterness by public apathy and, within your own circle, by the petty prides and jealousies of little egos which clamor for attention and approbation.

One of the first persons I met in the city was Dr. Marie Equi, of Italian ancestry and Latin fire. Definitely, she was an individualist and a rugged one. Her strong, large body could stand miles and miles on horseback night or day. She had been brought up in the pioneer era when medical work was genuine service. If cowboys or Indians were in fights, difficulties, jail, Dr. Equi was always on hand to speak a good word for them.

It was in Portland that I realized *Family Limitation,* which had been crudely and hurriedly written in 1914, needed revising. The working women to whom it was addressed needed the facts. It had served its purpose in its unpolished state, but the time had now come to reach the middle classes, for whom it required a slightly more professional tone. Dr. Equi gave me genuine assistance in this matter.

The wider the distribution of the pamphlet, the happier I was. Since it had not been copyrighted, anybody who wanted to could reprint as many as he wished, and I.W.W. lumberjacks, for example, transients without families who moved to California for the crop harvesting in the summer, often thus provided themselves with a little extra money as they journeyed from place to place. When they unrolled the blankets draped over their shoulders out dropped a half-dozen or so pamphlets.

An automobile mechanic of Portland had made one of these reprints and asked me whether he could sell it at my next meeting. I myself had never distributed *Family Limitation* publicly, but if any local people wanted to do so, I had no objection. Accordingly the mechanic and two of his friends sold copies and were arrested. Their trial was postponed so that I could deliver my proposed lectures in Seattle and Spokane.

When these were over I came back to serve as a witness, and at another meeting held the night preceding the trial four more of us were arrested, Dr. Equi, two Englishwomen, and myself. I was tremendously gratified by seeing women for the first time come out openly with courage; over a hundred followed us through the streets to the jail asking to be "let in too. We also have broken the law."

The city jail was nice and clean and warm. The girls, who were not locked in cells, scampered around talking over their troubles and complaints with Dr. Equi, and receiving condolence and wholesome advice in return.

The seven of us were tried together the next day. Two lawyers took upon themselves the responsibility of defending us, and they were splendid. We were all found guilty. The men were fined ten dollars, which the Judge said they need not pay; the women were not fined at all.

The papers made a great to-do about the affair but it was not a type of publicity of my choosing and did little to bring the goal nearer. The year 1916 was filled with such turmoil, some of it useful, some not. The ferment was working violently. Everybody began starting things here and there. Many radicals, some of whom I did not even know, were distributing leaflets, getting themselves arrested and jailed. Meetings were being held in New York on street corners, at Union Square, Madison Square.

You had to keep a steady head, to be about your business, to make careful decisions, to waste the least possible time on trivialities; it was always a problem to prevent emotional scatter-brains from disturbing the clear flow of the stream. The public, quite naturally, could not be expected to distinguish between purposeful activities and any others carried on in the name of the movement.

Emma Goldman and her campaign manager, Ben Reitman, belatedly advocated birth control, not to further it but strategically to utilize in their own program of anarchism the publicity value it had achieved. Earlier she had made me feel she considered it unimportant in the class struggle. Suddenly, when in 1916 it had demonstrated the fact that it was important, she delivered a lecture on the subject, was arrested, and sentenced to ten days.

Ben Reitman, who used to go up and down the aisles at meetings shouting out Emma Goldman's *Mother Earth* in a voice that never needed a megaphone, was also arrested when the police found on the table of her lecture hall in Rochester several books on birth control. One of these was by Dr. Robinson, who had hastily published a volume purporting to give contraceptive information. The unwary purchaser discovered when he came to the section supposed to give him the facts for which he had paid his money that the pages were blank and empty.

Of far greater interest to me was the decision of Jessie Ashley, Ida Rauh, who was Max Eastman's wife, and Bolton Hall, a leader in the single tax movement, to make test cases on the grounds that the denial of contraceptive information to women whose health might be endangered by pregnancy was unconstitutional since the Constitution guaranteed each individual the right to liberty. These three had themselves arrested on birth control charges. They were all three convicted and given a choice of fines or terms in prison. They paid the former, announcing that they would appeal, but, most unfortunately, as it turned out later, they did not carry through their intentions.

A sympathetic thing if not a wise one was being done by a young man in Boston named Van Kleek Allison, who started handing out leaflets to workers as they emerged from factories. Early in the summer he gave one to a police decoy, was arrested and sentenced to three years. Dear old Boston, the home of the Puritan, rose in all its strength and held a huge meeting of protest on his behalf.

This was the occasion of my first heckling. A Jewish convert to

Catholicism, named Goldstein, began belligerently to fling questions at me. It was not in the sense of trying to find out the answers, but as though he had them wrapped up in his own pocket and were merely trying to trap me, and he, in turn, had his answers ready for mine. But after my Western experiences I was not unprepared and was aided, furthermore, by other members of the audience who spoke in my defense when he became almost insulting.

I never made light of questioners and never judged any question too trivial or unworthy of an honest response. I believed that for each person who had the courage to ask there must be at least twenty-five who would like to know, and I have never assumed anyone was seeking to trick me into giving illegal information, even though his inquiry might appear as intended to confuse me or be vindictively thrust at me. I usually replied, "That's an interesting point. I'm glad you raised it," and then proceeded to discuss it as best I could.

Another heckling in Albany resulted in a joyous reunion. Somebody in the audience insisted my work was unnecessary. I would ordinarily have paid no attention, not considering the statement at all personal. But there arose a lady, wearing a high lace collar propped up with whalebones, and a hat that sat flat on her head, a ghost out of my school-girl days. "I am acquainted with Margaret Sanger," she stated. "I have slept with her, I have lived with her, I have worked with her, I have delivered her, and I have named my baby for her." Here was dear old Amelia come to champion me. Her type of dress had remained the same as fifteen years before, but so had her loyalty and wit. The lecture over, we went back together to her home in Schenectady; she hauled out from the attic scrapbooks and photographs and snapshots taken at Claverack, and we sat on the floor and rocked with laughter until three in the morning.

When I returned to New York after my long trip I took a studio apartment in what seemed like a bit of old Chelsea on Fourteenth Street way over between Seventh and Eighth Avenues. Gertrude Boyle, the sculptress, had the one below me, and my sister Ethel moved in above. Occasionally father came down from Cape Cod to spend some time with us.

Although it was never quite warm enough, because it lacked central heating, it hardened me physically, and the open fireplaces, stoked incessantly by expansive and voluble Vito Silecchia, the Italian coal vendor, kept the air fresh and clean. The lovely high ceilings, the tall windows, and the broad doors flung wide between the rooms, gave an atmosphere of space, and the marvelous carved woodwork was a joy. The windows in the rear were draped with light yellow curtains, reflecting an illusory glow of sunshine. Above one of these grew a Japanese wistaria vine; whenever I looked up I saw this little bit of spring.

Chapter Seventeen

FAITH I HAVE BEEN A TRUANT IN THE LAW

"If a woman grows weary and at last dies from childbearing, it matters not. Let her only die from bearing; she is there to do it."
MARTIN LUTHER

IN the fall of 1916 whoever walked along the corridor of the top floor of 104 Fifth Avenue could have seen the words "Birth Control" printed on the door leading to an office equipped in business-like, efficient manner with files and card catalogs. Presiding over it was Fred Blossom, the perfect representative. He had told me at Cleveland he was tired of ameliorative charity and, wanting to do something more significant, had offered six months for this work. Now indefatigably he wrote, spoke, made friends, and, most important, raised money. His meals were limited to an apple for luncheon and a sandwich for dinner; he seldom left the office until midnight.

Like a vacuum cleaner Blossom sucked in volunteers from near and far to help with the boxes and trunks of letters which had come to me from all over the country—one thousand from St. Louis alone. As long as I had had no stenographic aid I had been able only to open and read them and put them sadly away. At last with fifteen or twenty assistants the task began of sorting these out and answering them. The contents almost invariably fell into certain definite categories, and I instituted a system so that such and such a paragraph could be sent in response to such and such an appeal.

We had only one paid stenographer—little Anna Lifshiz, who soon became far more a co-worker than a secretary. If we had no money in the bank she waited for her salary until we did. When I met

Anna's mother, who graced her hospitable home with an old world dignity, I realized that her daughter's fine character had been directly inherited. Every Christmas I used to receive a present of wine and cakes of Mrs. Lifshiz' own make, and Anna always said when she brought them, "My mother prays for your health, your happiness, and that you will keep well."

I had been encouraged by the interest aroused during my Western trip, but was by no means satisfied. The practical idea of giving contraceptive information in clinics set up for that purpose had seemed to meet general approval everywhere. Boston at this time appeared a possible place to begin. Though Allison had to serve sixty days in the House of Correction at Deer Island, the sum total of his sensational trial had been good. Before his arrest there had been no league in Massachusetts, and with his arrest had come publicity, friends, workers, meetings, letters, interviews, all of widespread educational value.

More important than the enthusiasm which had been stirred up, the best legal authorities in Boston had decided that contraceptive information could be given verbally by doctors as long as it was not advertised. The interpretation to be put on advertising held up the actual opening of a clinic. The old spirit was there to wage battle but it was a question of getting leadership, and this did not come about; no women doctors were willing to take the risk. If the citizens of Massachusetts had then seized the opportunity to broaden their laws, writers and speakers might now have more freedom in expressing themselves.

Blossom soon organized the New York State Birth Control League to change the state law. Beyond introducing a bill it made little headway and soon expired. It was just one of those many groups that met and talked and talked and did nothing effective.

The legislative approach seemed to me a slow and tortuous method of making clinics legal; we stood a better and quicker chance by securing a favorable judicial interpretation through challenging the law directly. I decided to open a clinic in New York City, a far more difficult proceeding than in Boston. Section 1142 of the New York statutes was definite: *No one* could give contraceptive information to *anyone* for *any* reason. On the other hand, Section 1145 distinctly stated that physicians could give prescriptions to prevent conception for the cure or prevention of disease. Two attorneys and several doctors assured me this exception referred only to venereal disease. In that case, the intent was to protect the man, which could incidentally promote immorality and permit promiscuity. I was dealing with marriage. I wanted the interpretation to be broadened into the intent to protect women from ill health as the result of excessive childbearing and, equally important, to have the right to control their own destinies.

To change this interpretation it was necessary to have a test case. This, in turn, required my keeping strictly to the letter of the law; that is, having physicians who would give only verbal information for the prevention of disease. But the women doctors who had previously promised to do this now refused. I wrote, telephoned, asked friends to ask other friends to help find someone. None was willing to enter the cause, fearful of jeopardizing her private practice and of running the risk of being censured by her profession; she might even lose her license.

They had before them the example of Dr. Mary Halton who of all the women I have known has perhaps the best understanding of the hidden secrets of the heart. She has never reached her deserts, and doubtless never will have the honors due her, though she has an unknown audience who love her not only because she has done something directly for them but because they have heard of what she has done for others. She has what to my mind is the attitude of the real physician; that it is not enough merely to cure ailments—surroundings, heartaches, privations must also be given attention. Her office is a human welfare clinic to which women of all classes, ages, nationalities go for advice, occasionally without even return carfare. The unmarried ones, who in asking help from doctors or clinics seldom admit they are unmarried, trust so deeply in Dr. Mary that they unburden themselves freely.

Dr. Mary had previously been on the staff of the Grosvenor Hospital and had held her evening clinic there. To one of her patients who had been operated on for glandular tuberculosis she had prescribed a cervical pessary. When a few evenings later the woman had come back to be refitted, Dr. Mary had been out and her substitute, horrified and shocked, had presented the matter to the board. Dr. Mary had been called before them. She had told them in no uncertain terms that the giving of contraceptive information to patients in need of it was part of her work and that she had a right under the law to do so.

The board had disagreed with her and asked for her resignation.

I did not wish to complicate the quesion of testing the law by having a nurse give information, because a nurse did not come under the Section 1145 exception. But since I could find no doctor I had to do without. Ethel, a registered nurse, had a readiness to share in helping the movement, though she did not belong to it in the same sense as I. Then, as long as I had to violate the law anyhow, I concluded I might as well violate it on a grand scale by including poverty as a reason for giving contraceptive information. I did not see why the hardships and worries of a working man's wife might not be just as detrimental as any disease. I wanted a legal opinion on this if possible.

My next problems were where the money was to come from and where the clinic was to be. Ever since I had announced that I was going to open one within a few months I had been buried under an avalanche of queries as to the place, which for a time I could not answer. The selection of a suitable locality was of the greatest importance. I tramped through the streets of the Bronx, Brooklyn, the lower sides of Manhattan, East and West. I scrutinized the Board of Health vital statistics of all the boroughs—births and infant and maternal mortality in relation to low wages, and also the number of philanthropic institutions in the vicinity.

The two questions—where and how—were settled on one and the same day.

That afternoon five women from the Brownsville Section of Brooklyn crowded into my room seeking the "secret" of birth control. Each had four children or more, who had been left with neighbors. One had just recovered from an abortion which had nearly killed her. "Another will take me off. Then what will become of my family?"

They rocked back and forth as they related their afflictions, told so simply, each scarcely able to let her friend finish before she took up the narration of her own sufferings—the high cost of food, her husband's meager income when he worked at all, her helplessness in the struggle to make ends meet, whining, sickly children, the constant worry of another baby—and always hanging over her night and day, year after year, was fear.

All cried what a blessing and godsend a clinic would be in their neighborhood.

They talked an hour and when they had finished, it seemed as though I myself had been through their tragedies. I was reminded of the story of a Spaniard who had become so desperate over the injustice meted out to innocent prisoners that he had taken a revolver into the street and fired it at the first person he met; killing was his only way of expressing indignation. I felt like doing the same thing.

I decided then and there that the clinic should open at Brownsville, and I would look for a site the next day. How to finance it I did not know, but that did not matter.

Then suddenly the telephone rang and I heard a feminine voice saying she had just come from the West Coast bringing from Kate Crane Gartz, whom I had met in Los Angeles, a check for fifty dollars to do with as I wished. I knew what I should do with it; pay the first month's rent. I visualized two rooms on the ground floor, one for waiting and one for consultation, and a place outside to leave the baby carriages.

Fania Mindell had left Chicago to assist me in New York. It was a terribly rainy day in early October that we plodded through the dreary streets of Brownsville to find the most suitable spot at the cheapest possible terms. We stopped in one of the milk stations to inquire about vacant stores. "Don't come over here," was the reply. Many social organizations were being established to meet the demands of poverty and sickness, and we asked of them all, only to receive the same response— "We don't want any trouble. Keep out of this district." The mildest comment was, "It's a good idea, but we can't help you." Although they agreed the mothers of the community should limit their families, they seemed terrified at the prospect of a birth control clinic. It sounded also as if they were afraid we would do away with social problems and they would lose their jobs.

Brownsville was not unique; Brooklyn was and still is dotted with such dismal villages, and even Queens with its pretensions to a higher standard has its share. But Brownsville was particularly dingy and squalid. Block after block, street after street, as far as we could see in every direction stretched the same endless lines of cramped, unpainted houses that crouched together as though for warmth, bursting with excess of wretched humanity.

The inhabitants were mostly Jews and Italians, some who had come to this country as children, some of the second generation. I preferred a Jewish landlord, and Mr. Rabinowitz was the answer. He was willing to let us have Number 46 Amboy Street at fifty dollars a month, a reduction from the regular rent because he realized what we were trying to do. Here in this Jewish community I need have no misgivings over breaking of windows or hurling of epithets, but I was scarcely prepared for the friendliness offered from that day on.

I sent a letter to the District Attorney of Brooklyn, saying I expected to dispense contraceptive information from this address. Without waiting for the reply, which never came, we began the fun of fixing up our little clinic. We had to keep furnishing expenses inside the budget, but Fania knew Yiddish and also how to bargain. We bought chairs, desks, floor coverings, curtains, a stove. If I were to leave no loophole in testing the law, we could only give the principles of contraception, show a cervical pessary to the women, explain that if they had had two children they should have one size and if more a larger one. This was not at all ideal, but I had no other recourse at the time. However, we might be able to get a doctor any day and, consequently, we added an examination table to our equipment.

Mr. Rabinowitz spent hours adding touches here and there to make the two shiny and spotless rooms even more snow-white. "More hospital looking," he said.

Meanwhile we had printed about five thousand notices in English, Italian, and Yiddish:

MOTHERS!
>Can you afford to have a large family?
>Do you want any more children?
>If not, why do you have them?
>**DO NOT KILL, DO NOT TAKE LIFE, BUT PREVENT**
>Safe, Harmless Information can be obtained of trained Nurses at
>46 AMBOY STREET
>NEAR PITKIN AVE.—BROOKLYN.
>Tell Your Friends and Neighbors.   All Mothers Welcome
>A registration fee of 10 cents entitles any mother to this information.

These we poked into letter boxes, house after house, day after day, upstairs, downstairs, all over the place, viewing sadly the unkempt children who swarmed in the alleyways and over the fire escapes of the condemned tenements and played on the rubbish heaps in the vacant lots. Seldom did we see a woman who was not carrying or wheeling a baby. We stopped to talk to each and gave her a supply of leaflets to hand on to her neighbors. When we passed by a drugstore we arranged with the proprietor to prepare himself for supplying the pessaries we were going to recommend.

The morning of October 16, 1916—crisp but sunny and bright after days of rain—Ethel, Fania, and I opened the doors of the first birth control clinic in America, the first anywhere in the world except the Netherlands. I still believe this was an event of social significance.

Would the women come? Did they come? Nothing, not even the ghost of Anthony Comstock, could have kept them away. We had arrived early, but before we could get the place dusted and ourselves ready for the official reception, Fania called, "Do come outside and look." Halfway to the corner they were standing in line, at least one hundred and fifty, some shawled, some hatless, their red hands clasping the cold, chapped, smaller ones of their children.

Fania began taking names, addresses, object in coming to the clinic, histories—married or single, any miscarriages or abortions, how many children, where born, what ages. Remembering how the Netherlands clinics in recording nothing had made it almost hopeless to measure what they had accomplished from the human point of view, I had resolved that our files should be as complete as it was possible to make them. Fania had a copy of *What Every Girl*

Should Know on her desk, and, if she had a free moment, read from it. When asked, she told where it could be bought, and later kept a few copies for the convenience of those who wanted them.

Children were left with her and mothers ushered in to Ethel or me in the rear room, from seven to ten at once. To each group we explained simply what contraception was; that abortion was the wrong way—no matter how early it was performed it was taking life; that contraception was the better way, the safer way—it took a little time, a little trouble, but was well worth while in the long run, because life had not yet begun.

Some women were alone, some were in pairs, some with their neighbors, some with their married daughters. Some did not dare talk this over with their husbands, and some had been urged on by them. At seven in the evening they were still coming, and men also, occasionally bringing their timid, embarrassed wives, or once in a while by themselves to say they would stay home to take care of the children if their wives could come. A hundred women and forty men passed through the doors, but we could not begin to finish the line; the rest were told to return "tomorrow."

In the course of the next few days women appeared clutching minute scraps of paper, seldom more than an inch wide, which had crept into print. The Yiddish and Italian papers had picked up the story from the handbills which bore the clinic address, and the husbands had read them on their way from work and clipped them out for their wives. Women who had seen the brief, inconspicuous newspaper accounts came even from Massachusetts, Pennsylvania, New Jersey, and the far end of Long Island.

Newly married couples with little but love, faith, and hope to save them from charity, told of the tiny flats they had chosen, and of their determination to make a go of it together if only the children were not born too soon. A gaunt skeleton suddenly stood up one morning and made an impassioned speech. "They offer us charity when we have more babies than we can feed, and when we get sick with more babies for trying not to have them they just give us more charity talks!"

Women who were themselves already past childbearing age came just to urge us to preserve others from the sorrows of ruined health, overworked husbands, and broods of defective and wayward children growing up in the streets, filling dispensaries and hospitals, filing through the juvenile courts.

We made records of every applicant and, though the details might vary, the stories were basically identical. All were confused, groping among the ignorant sex-teachings of the poor, fumbling without guidance after truth, misled and bewildered in a tangled jungle of popular superstitions and old wives' remedies. Unconsciously they dramatized the terrible need of intelligent and scientific instruction in these matters of life—and death.

As was inevitable many were kept away by the report that the police were to raid us for performing abortions. "Clinic" was a word which to the uneducated usually signified such a place. We would not have minded particularly being raided on this charge, because we could easily disprove it. But these rumors also brought the most pitiful of all, the reluctantly expectant mothers who hoped to find some means of getting out of their dilemmas. Their desperate threats of suicide haunted you at night.

One Jewish wife, after bringing eight children to birth, had had two abortions and heaven knows how many miscarriages. Worn out, beaten down, not only by toiling in her own kitchen, but by taking in extra work from a sweatshop making hats, she was now at the end of her strength, nervous beyond words, and in a state of morbid excitement. "If you don't help me, I'm going to chop up a glass and swallow it tonight."

A woman wrought to the pitch of killing herself was sick—a community responsibility. She, most of all, required concentrated attention and devotion, and I could not let any such go out of the clinic until her mood had been altered. Building up hope for the future seemed the best deterrent. "Your husband and your children need you. One more won't make so much difference." I had to make each promise to go ahead and have this baby and myself promise in return, "You won't ever have to again. We're going to take care of you."

Day after day the waiting room was crowded with members of every race and creed; Jews and Christians, Protestants and Roman Catholics alike made their confessions to us, whatever they may have professed at home or in church. I asked one bright little Catholic what excuse she could make to the priest when he learned she had been to the clinic. She answered indignantly, "It's none of his business. My husband has a weak heart and works only four days a week. He gets twelve dollars, and we can barely live on it now. We have enough children."

Her friend, sitting by, nodded approval. "When I was married," she broke in, "the priest told us to have lots of children and we listened to him. I had fifteen. Six are living. I'm thirty-seven years old now. Look at me! I might be fifty!"

That evening I made a mental calculation of fifteen baptismal fees, nine baby funerals, masses and candles for the repose of nine baby souls, the physical agonies of the mother and the emotional torment of both parents, and I asked myself, "Is this the price of Christianity?"

But it was not altogether sad; we were often cheered by gayer visitors. The grocer's wife on the corner and the widow with six children who kept the lunch room up the street dropped in to wish us luck, and the fat old German baker whose wife gave out handbills to everybody passing the door sent regular donations of doughnuts. Whenever the pressure became so overwhelming that we could not go out for a meal we were sure to hear Mrs. Rabinowitz call downstairs, "If I bring some hot tea now, will you stop the people coming?" Two jovial policemen paused at the doorway each morning to discuss the weather. Reporters looked in speculating on how long we were going to last. The postman delivering his customary fifty to a hundred letters had his little pleasantry, "Farewell, ladies; hope I find you here tomorrow."

Although the line outside was enough to arouse police attention, nine days went by without interference. Then one afternoon when I, still undiscouraged, was out interviewing a doctor, a woman, large of build and hard of countenance, entered and said to Fania she was the mother of two children and that she had no money to support more. She did not appear overburdened or anxious and, because she was so well fed as to body and prosperous as to clothes, did not seem to belong to the community. She bought a copy of *What Every Girl Should Know* and insisted on paying two dollars instead of the usual ten-cent fee.

Fania, who had an intuition about such matters, called Ethel aside and said warningly she was certain this must be a policewoman. But Ethel, who was not of the cautious type, replied, "We have nothing to hide. Bring her in anyhow." She talked with the woman in private, gave her our literature and, when asked about our future plans, related them frankly. The sceptical Fania pinned the two-dollar bill on the wall and wrote underneath, "Received from Mrs. —— of the Police Department, as her contribution." Hourly after that we expected trouble. We had known it must occur sooner or later, but would have preferred it to come about in a different way.

The next day Ethel and Fania were both absent from the clinic. The waiting room was filled almost to suffocation when the door opened and the woman who had been described to me came in.

"Are you Mrs. Sanger?"

"Yes."

"I'm a police officer. You're under arrest."

The doors were locked and this Mrs. Margaret Whitehurst and other plain-clothes members of the vice squad—used to raiding gambling dens and houses of assignation—began to demand names and addresses of the women, seeing them with babies, broken, old, worried, harrowed, yet treating them as though they were inmates of a brothel. Always fearful in the presence of the police, some began to cry aloud and the children on their laps screamed too. For a few moments it was like a panic, until I was able to assure them that only I was under arrest; nothing was going to happen to them, and they could return home if they were quiet. After half an hour I finally persuaded the policemen to let these frightened women go.

All of our four hundred and sixty-four case histories were confiscated, and the table and demonstration supplies were carried off through the patient line outside. The more timid had left, but many had stayed. This was a region where a crowd could be collected by no more urgent gesture than a tilt of the head skyward. Newspaper men with their cameras had joined the throng and the street was packed. Masses of people spilled out over the sidewalk on to the pavement, milling excitedly.

The patrol wagon came rattling up to our door. I had a certain respect for uniformed policemen—you knew what they were about

—but none whatsoever for the vice squad. I was white hot with indignation over their unspeakable attitude towards the clinic mothers and stated I preferred to walk the mile to the court rather than sit with them. Their feelings were quite hurt. "Why, we didn't do anything to you, Mrs. Sanger," they protested. Nevertheless I marched ahead, they following behind.

A reporter from the *Brooklyn Eagle* fell into step beside me and before we had gone far suggested, "Now I'll fix it up with the police that you make a getaway, and when we reach that corner you run. I'll stop and talk to them while you skip around the block and get to the station first." It was fantastic for anyone so to misconstrue what I was doing as to imagine I would run around the block for a publicity stunt.

I stayed overnight at the Raymond Street Jail, and I shall never forget it. The mattresses were spotted and smelly, the blankets stiff with dirt and grime. The stench nauseated me. It was not a comforting thought to go without bedclothing when it was so cold, but, having in mind the diseased occupants who might have preceded me, I could not bring myself to creep under the covers. Instead I lay down on top and wrapped my coat around me. The only clean object was my towel, and this I draped over my face and head. For endless hours I struggled with roaches and horrible-looking bugs that came crawling out of the walls and across the floor. When a rat jumped up on the bed I cried out involuntarily and sent it scuttling out.

My cell was at the end of a center row, all opening front and back upon two corridors. The prisoners gathered in one of the aisles the next morning and I joined them. Most had been accused of minor offenses such as shoplifting and petty thievery. Many had weather-beaten faces, were a class by themselves, laughing and unconcerned. But I heard no coarse language. Underneath the chatter I sensed a deep and bitter resentment; some of them had been there for three or four months without having been brought to trial. The more fortunate had a little money to engage lawyers; others had to wait for the court to assign them legal defenders.

While I was talking to the girls, the matron bustled up with, "The ladies are coming!" and shooed us into our cells. The Ladies, a committee from a society for prison reform, peered at us as though we were animals in cages. A gentle voice cooed at me, "Did you come in during the night?"

"Yes," I returned, overlooking the assumption that I was a street walker.

"Can we do anything for you?"

The other inmates were sitting in their corners looking as innocent and sweet as they could, but I startled her by saying, "Yes, you can. Come in and clean up this place. It's filthy and verminous."

The Committee departed hurriedly down the corridor. One more alert member, however, came back to ask, "Is it really very dirty?"

Although I told her in some detail about the blankets, the odors, the roaches, she obviously could not picture the situation. "I'm terribly sorry, but we can't change it."

I was still exasperated over this reply when I was called to the reception room to give an interview to reporters. In addition to answering questions about the raid I said I had a message to the taxpayers of Brooklyn; they were paying money to keep their prisons run in an orderly fashion as in any civilized community and should know it was being wasted, because the conditions at Raymond Street were intolerable.

My bail was arranged by afternoon and when I emerged I saw waiting in front the woman who was going to swallow the glass; she had been there all that time.

I went straight back to the clinic, reopened it, and more mothers came in. I had hoped a court decision might allow us to continue, but now Mr. Rabinowitz came downstairs apologetically. He said he was sorry, and he really was, but the police had made him sign ejection papers, on the ground that I was "maintaining a public nuisance."

In the Netherlands a clinic had been cited as a public benefaction; in the United States it was classed as a public nuisance.

Two uniformed policemen came for me, and with them I was willing to ride in the patrol wagon to the station. As we started I heard a scream from a woman who had just come around the corner on her way to the clinic. She abandoned her baby carriage, rushed through the crowd, and cried, "Come back! Come back and save me!" For a dozen yards she ran after the van before someone caught her and led her to the sidewalk. But the last thing I heard was this poor distracted mother, shrieking and calling, "Come back! Come back!"

Chapter Eighteen

LEAN HUNGER AND GREEN THIRST

*"All that we know who lie in gaol
Is that the wall is strong;
And that each day is like a year,
A year whose days are long."*
OSCAR WILDE

LOOKING back upon this period fraught with emotional distress, I have no regrets. But, looking ahead, I am grateful that there looms no necessity for repeating those passionate, dangerous, and menacing days.

Out of the raid four separate cases resulted: Ethel was charged with violating Section 1142 of the Penal Code, designed to prevent dissemination of contraceptive information; Fania with having sold an allegedly indecent book entitled *What Every Girl Should Know;* I, first, with having conducted a clinic in violation of the same Section 1142, second, with violating Section 1530 by maintaining a public nuisance.

I claimed that Section 1142 which forbade contraceptive information to, for, and by anyone was unconstitutional, because no state was permitted to interfere with a citizen's right to life or liberty, and such denial was certainly interference. Experience had shown it did the case no good merely to defend such a stand in a lower court; it must be carried to a higher tribunal, and only a lawyer versed in whereases and whatsoevers and inasmuchases could accomplish this. But I was still hopeful of finding one who was able to see that the importance of birth control could not be properly emphasized if we bowed too deeply before the slow and ponderous majesty of the law.

The attorney who offered himself, J. J. Goldstein, had a background which made him more sympathetic than other lawyers, even the most liberal. He was one of those young Jewish men of promise who had been guided through adolescence by Mary Simkhovitch, founder of Greenwich House, and Lillian Wald, founder of the Henry Street Settlement. The seeds of social service had been planted in him; his legal training only temporarily slowed down their growth.

J.J. had placed himself in a difficult position for a youthful Tammany Democrat, some day to be a magistrate; he might have been forgiven more easily had he received a larger fee. Though he had to be convinced that we declined to have anything to do with political wire-pulling, he fought for us valiantly.

November 20th we pleaded not guilty and trial was set for November 27th. J.J. endeavored to have the three of us tried simultaneously, but the Court of Special Sessions would have none of it. Then he asked for a jury trial, which could be granted at the discretion of the Supreme Court; application was denied. An appeal to the Appellate Division was dismissed; writs of habeas corpus were dismissed; another appeal to the Appellate Division was dismissed; adjournments pending appeal were urged but not granted. Indeed I was being swiftly educated in the technicalities of criminal law.

I felt like a victim who passed into the courtroom, was made to bow before the judge, and did not know what it was all about. Every gesture had its special significance, which must not be left out if appeals were to be possible. We had to make many more appearances than would otherwise have been necessary; everything had to be correctly on the record.

Evening after evening J.J. rehearsed the arguments he was going to present and directed me to respond to questioning. I did not understand the technicalities and begged to be allowed to tell the story in my own way, fearful lest the heartaches of the mothers be lost in the labyrinthine maze of judicial verbiage. But he maintained if the case were to be appealed to a higher court, it had to be conducted according to certain formalities.

"Why should it have to be in legal language?" I demanded. "I'm a simple citizen, born in a democratic country. A court should also listen to my plea expressed in plain language for the common people. I'm sure I can make them understand and arouse their compassion."

He reiterated that I could not address a court as though I were trying to instil my views in an individual. "You can't talk to them that way. You'll have to let me talk."

"But that's the way I talk and I'm the accused."

I fully expected that if I were permitted to set forth my human version of the Brownsville tragedies, no appeal would be required. But J.J. knew the courts and had no such hopes. He was still doubtful of any success before the lower tribunal, and was still unable to see my point, counting chiefly on technicalities to win the case.

J.J. had formally objected to having our trial set during the November session because Justice McInerney was due to preside that month, and at previous trials he had expressed biased opinions. This objection was overruled.

The strictly legal method having failed, I resorted to my own and wrote Justice McInerney an open letter:

As an American pledged to the principles and spirit in which this Republic was founded, as a judge obligated by oath to fair and impartial judgment, do you in your deepest conscience consider yourself qualified to try my case?

In those birth control cases at which you have presided, you have shown to all thinking men and women an unfailing prejudice and exposed a mind steeped in the bigotry and intolerance of the Inquisition.

To come before you implies conviction.

Judge McInerney "made application to the District Attorney to be taken off this case."

Trial was marked for January 4, 1917, but the first case, that of Ethel, was reached so late in the afternoon it had to be postponed. Four days afterwards, in spite of our attempts to be tried together, she appeared alone. She freely admitted she had described birth control methods but denied the District Attorney's accusation that our ten-cent registration fee made it a "money making" affair. This and other sensational charges, such as "the clinic was intended to do away with the Jews" were often inserted in the records for reporters to pick up, make good stories of them, and in consequence influence newspaper readers against us. They were great stumbling blocks.

Our most important witness, Dr. Morris H. Kahn, physician in

Bloomingdale's Department Store who also maintained a private clinic where he gave out birth control information, was ready to testify, but his evidence was ruled out as "irrelevant, incompetent, and immaterial." To be sure the charge against Ethel was as a lay person; nevertheless, it was extraordinary that we could get no hearing for a doctor. J.J. was allowed only fifteen minutes to present his argument on the unconstitutionality of Section 1142, and the presiding Judge decided that the court was bound to hold it constitutional on precedent, regardless of argument.

Ethel was found guilty.

In the two weeks before sentence was to be pronounced we debated what she and I should do. Perhaps it could be stayed, which would settle everything, but we each had to be prepared for either a short term of imprisonment or a long one. In case of the former, submission was the wiser course, because the public would not consider it of sufficient moment to bestir itself; in the latter event, a hunger strike seemed indicated, but, again, only if sufficient attention could be called to it.

The New York *World* had the most liberal policy of all the leading morning dailies, and therefore appeared to offer the best likelihood of being favorably disposed. I approached one of its editors and asked whether he would print our entire story if I were to give him a scoop and guarantee accuracy. He agreed, and assigned us a special reporter.

Ethel was sentenced January 22nd to thirty days in the Workhouse on Blackwell's Island in the East River. In spite of our discussion over this possibility, she was utterly shocked, and exclaimed, "I'm going to go on that hunger strike."

After spending the night in the Tombs, she was returned the next morning to the Federal District Court of Brooklyn on a writ of habeas corpus as a means of suspending sentence pending appeal. Daylight had brought no change in her determination to continue with the hunger strike. "I haven't had anything to eat yet," she declared, and, remembering the tale that one hunger striker had received nourishment in her cups of water, she added, "and, if they send me back, I shan't drink anything either."

Neither J.J. nor I considered such a short sentence worth breaking your life for. Furthermore, the cause did not mean to Ethel what it did to me. "Think this over very carefully," I reminded her. "A hunger strike is not necessary, and if you once start you'll have to keep it up." She insisted that she was ready to die if need be; she had made her will and arranged for the disposition of her two children—the hunger strike was to go on. The writ was refused and she was remanded to the Workhouse. On her way there she told the women with whom she shared the patrol wagon the salient facts of birth control.

When Commissioner of Correction Burdette G. Lewis was asked to comment on Ethel's decision he scoffed. "Others have threatened hunger strikes. It means nothing." At first no food at all was brought her, but after the publicity began the authorities were in despair to make her eat. This was a case they did not know how to handle; they were mentally unprepared for prisoners who were guilty of performing a legal wrong in order to win a legal right.

Ethel had gone one hundred and three hours without eating when Commissioner Lewis established a precedent in American prison annals by ordering her forcibly fed, the first woman to be so treated in this country. He stated optimistically to the press how simple the process was, consisting of merely rolling her in a blanket so she could not struggle, and then having milk, eggs, and a stimulant forced into her stomach through a rubber tube. He stressed how healthy she continued to be, how little opposition she offered, how foolish the whole thing appeared to him anyhow; he was going to charge her for the expense incurred in calling in an expert to feed her.

As soon as I heard my sister was "passive under the feeding" I became desperately anxious about her; nothing but complete loss of strength could have lessened her resistance.

After one interview Commissioner Lewis had barred all reporters and given out a statement of his own. "I have not much patience with Mrs. Byrne's efforts to get advertising for her cause, and I won't help such a campaign along by issuing bulletins."

But bulletins were being issued, nevertheless—and printed.

From prearranged sources I was receiving messages and notes each evening, and reports on Ethel's pulse and temperature. Thus I learned her vision was becoming affected and her heart was beginning to miss beats, due to lack of liquids. "Going without water was pretty bad," she said herself. "At night the woman whose duty it was to go up and down the corridors to give the prisoners a drink if they wanted it stopped right by my cell and cried, 'Water! Water!' till it seemed as if I could not stand it. And on the other side of me was the sound of the river through the window."

Nobody was allowed to visit Ethel but J.J., who, as her lawyer, could not well be refused. But reporters have their own mysterious ways of getting what they want. The *World* man succeeded in reaching her. It was not on the whole a successful interview, because she did not know who he was, but it did have one important result— it confirmed at first hand our statements as to the seriousness of her condition.

In the midst of my anxiety over Ethel, my own trial opened January 29th in the same bare, smoky, upstairs Brooklyn court in which she had appeared. Justices John J. Freschi, Italian, Moses Hermann, Jewish, and George J. O'Keefe, Irish, sat on the bench. Judge Freschi, a rather young man, presided, and on him we pinned our hopes. We did not expect anything of old Judge Herrmann except that, because he was Jewish, he might be broad-minded. As to Judge O'Keefe we had no illusions.

No less than thirty of the mothers of Brownsville had been subpoenaed by the prosecution, but about fifty arrived—some equipped with fruit, bread, pacifiers, and extra diapers, others distressed at having had to spend carfare, timid at the thought of being in court, hungry because no kosher food could be obtained near by. Nevertheless, all smiled and nodded at me reassuringly.

Formerly, a few women of wealth but of liberal tendencies had been actively concerned in the movement, but now some who were prominent socially were coming to believe on principle that birth control should not be denied to the masses. The subject was in the process of ceasing to be tagged as radical and revolutionary, and becoming admittedly humanitarian.

In this room, side by side with the ones to be helped, sat new helpers. Among them was Mrs. Amos Pinchot, Chairman of the Women's Committee of One Hundred, formed to lend support to the defense. Her reddish hair betrayed a temper quick and easily aroused in the cause of justice. Aristocratic of bearing, autocratic by position, she was one to command and be obeyed, and was easily a leading personality in the philanthropic smart set of New York. Among her valuable services was the bringing into the fold of the mothers and aunts of the present active Junior Leaguers.

Mrs. Lewis L. Delafield's limousine stood in front of the doors at almost every trial and it meant a great deal to the defendants to have the wife of one of the most eminent members of the New York bar in the courtroom. By her very demeanor and looks—white-haired, a fragile countenance—you knew she could touch nothing that was not fine, and that she had the spiritual courage to stand by her ideas and ideals in both her public and private life. Always she opened her home and her heart and her arms to those she loved.

Fania was called first. She was a girl with a pale and delicate face, and was too worried to bear the strain. She should not be punished for co-operating, and I told J.J. to notify the court that she was not well, though I strictly forbade him to say anything about my health. Her trial was brief, narrowing itself down to whether *What Every Girl Should Know* was to be classed as indecent. A few days later she was found guilty and sentenced to fifty dollars' fine, a decision which was eventually reversed on appeal.

It surprised me that in my trial the prosecution should be carried on so vehemently, because the prosecutor had little to prove. To me there seemed to be no argument at all; the last thing in my mind was to deny having given birth control advice. Certainly I had violated the letter of the law, but that was what I was opposing.

I grew more and more puzzled by the stilted language, the circumlocutions, the respect for precedent. These legal battles, fought in a curiously unreal world, intensified my defiance to the breaking point. I longed for a discussion in the open on merit and in simple, honest terms.

I thought I might have my wish when Judge Freschi, holding up a cervical cap which the prosecuting attorney had put in evidence, said, "Who can prove this is a violation; the law states that contraception is permitted for the prevention of disease. May it not be used for medical reasons?"

This question raised my hopes high. At last the law might be interpreted according to the definition I so desired; ill health resulting from pregnancy caused by lack of its use might be construed as disease.

Then one by one the Brownsville mothers were called to the stand to answer the District Attorney. "Have you ever seen Mrs. Sanger before?"

"Yess. Yess, I know Mrs. Sanger."

"Where did you see her?"

"At the cleenic."

"Why did you go there?"

"To have her stop the babies."

The witness bowed sweet acknowledgment to me until she was peremptorily commanded to address the court.

"Did you get this information?"

"Yess. Yess, dank you, I got it. It wass gut, too."

"Enough." the District Attorney barked, and called another.

Time after time they gave answers that were like nails to seal my doom, yet each thought she was assisting me.

J.J. saw how their testimony could be turned to our advantage.

He asked, "How many miscarriages have you had? How much sickness in your family? How much does your husband earn? The answers were seven, eight, nine dollars a week."

At last one woman more miserable and more poverty-stricken than the rest was summoned. "How many children have you?"

"Eight and three that didn't live."

"What does your husband earn?"

"Ten dollars a veek—ven he vorks."

Judge Freschi finally exclaimed, "I can't stand this any longer," and the court adjourned over the week-end.

J.J. was jubilant, because he said there was nothing for him to do; the court was arguing his case for him.

I myself was feeling a little conscience-smitten. A mass meeting of sympathizers had been organized by the Committee of One Hundred for that evening in Carnegie Hall, and I went straight there from the courtroom. I had a speech ready in which I said we were being persecuted, not prosecuted; that the judges were no better than witch-burners. It was unfortunate, but copies had already been released to the press and the wording could not be changed.

Helen Todd, the Chairman, a grand person who had been trained under Jane Addams, had given the mothers of Brownsville places of honor on the platform to let everybody see what kind of women we were fighting for. She asked for twenty volunteers to follow the example of the English suffragettes who had gone on hunger strikes en masse, but no women whose names registered socially in the public mind were willing thus to join in protesting against the law; only working girls came forward.

Three days later Jessie Ashley and I took the train for Albany with Mrs. Pinchot, who was a close friend of Governor Charles S. Whitman, to ask him to appoint a commission to investigate birth control and make a report to the State Legislature. The Governor, who was fair and intelligent, quite distinctly representing a class of liberal politicians, received us cordially.

Ethel and her hunger strike had been front-page news for ten days; in the subway, on street corners, everywhere people gathered, she was being discussed. In Washington and Albany congressmen and legislators were sending out for the latest details. Governor Whitman naturally asked about her, and we seized the opportunity to try to impress on him the outrageousness of making her suffer for so just a cause. He said directly her incarceration was a disgrace to the State. He was entirely out of sympathy with the courts and judges, and offered a pardon conditional upon her ceasing to disseminate birth control information.

But I had not come to ask that favor.

"My sister wouldn't take a pardon," I replied, much to the distress of Mrs. Pinchot. However, I accepted gratefully his letter to the warden at Blackwell's Island authorizing me to see her.

The next morning I appeared again before the court. During the three-day interim the effect of the mothers' testimony had evidently been effaced from the judges' minds, and they were infuriated by my Carnegie Hall denunciation. But far more detrimental to my hope of a new interpretation was the prosecution's introduction of a Federal agent who had once confiscated a copy of *Family Limitation* in which was the picture of this same cervical cap; he read aloud my advice to women to use it as a means of preventing conception. Not even the most friendly judge could get away from the fact that I had intended a far broader definition than any permitted by the existing law.

The prosecution argued further that the constitutionality of Section 1142 could not be challenged, because the exception for physicians in Section 1145 already guaranteed "liberty" to citizens. And, since I was not a physician and consequently did not come under the exception, the court must, in any event, find me guilty. This they did.

The day had been so full that I was not able to avail myself of Governor Whitman's permit to visit Ethel until evening, when Mr. and Mrs. Pinchot took me in their car to the Workhouse. I remember how cold it was; the trip on the ferry seemed to go on forever. But when we finally arrived, at the name of Pinchot, the friend of the Governor, doors swung open; officialdom turned polite and courteous and salaamed us on our way.

The Pinchots remained below while I was sent up to Ethel's cell, where she was lying on her iron cot, dressed in readiness for her release. Her appearance shocked and horrified me. She had grown thin and emaciated, her eyes were sunken and her tongue swollen, high red spots stood out on her cheeks. She could not see me even across the narrow cell, knowing me only by my voice. Hers was muffled as she whispered me to come nearer, her mind confused. "Liberty," she kept repeating, "I want my liberty."

Her life was all that mattered to me now. I had to eat humble pie, and said to the matron I was going to telegraph Governor Whitman that she was too ill to accept the conditions of the pardon for herself, but I would promise on her behalf. I was told that he had already signed the pardon, was on his way to New York, and to wait downstairs, please.

After about half an hour we were informed Mrs. Byrne was coming down. I went along the hallway to meet her. She was being held up by two attendants, the matron following with wraps. Her head was rolling from side to side, and I could see from the pallor of her face, especially from the pinched look of her nose and mouth, that she was losing consciousness. I protested to the matron, but orders had been given and were being obeyed; Commissioner Lewis wanted the newspaper pictures to show her coming out on her feet.

Running back to the room where the Pinchots were sitting, I exclaimed, "She's fainting!" Then Mrs. Pinchot clapped her hands imperiously and directed the attendants to lay Ethel down immediately and bring a stretcher. A command from her worked like magic. She wrapped her own fur coat around the pathetic figure and, as soon as Ethel felt the softness and warmth, she knew she was safe. We carried her over to my apartment to begin the protracted period of recuperation. Only after a year's convalescence was she able to take up a normal life again.

Being the real instigator, I had every reason to expect a longer term than Ethel. Logically, her hunger strike had served its purpose; that form of strategy was closed. But personally I decided that, if I should receive a year, I should do the same. On the other hand, if I were given three months or less, I could study and make use of my time. J.J. had heard on reliable authority that if I were to change my plea to guilty, I could have a suspended sentence. To his mind freedom alone meant victory, and he urged me to accept it if it were offered.

This, it developed, was the intention of the court when on Monday I was called back for sentence. Having Ethel off the front page had brought a sigh of relief of almost national scope. But all the publicity had had its effect on public opinion, and doubtless influenced the judges also to a certain extent. Since they could not agree to change the interpretation of the law, they had been obliged to find me guilty, but they did not really want to inflict punishment.

They were, however, extremely suspicious of our assertion that we were going to carry the case higher. Jessie Ashley, Ida Rauh, and Bolton Hall had all been let off with fines on the understanding they proposed to appeal, and then they had not done so. Courts were beginning to assume this was just a trick of birth control advocates, not meant in good faith.

I sat listening to what seemed an interminable discussion between J.J. and Judge Freschi over whether the appeal were going to be prosecuted in a quick and orderly fashion, until I was nearly lulled to sleep. Suddenly my attention was caught by hearing J.J. declare that I would "promise not to violate the law."

My mind clicked. It was not in my program to bargain for freedom. J.J., knowing full well I would make no such promise, had planted himself in front of me so the court could not see my belligerent face. He was trying to act as a buffer and, at the same time, for fear of what I might say, to avoid having me summoned to the stand. I tried to peer around him, but he shifted from side to side, obscuring my view. I tugged on his coat like a badly brought up child, but he took no notice. Finally one of the judges interposed, "Your client wishes to speak to you, counselor." I could be ignored no longer, and was called. "Margaret Sanger, stand up."

History is written in retrospect, but contemporary documents must be consulted; therefore I have gone to the official records for the facts. After all, one courtroom is much like another, and the attitude of one justice not so dissimilar from that of another. I was combating a mass ideology, and the judges who were its spokesmen merged into a single voice, all saying, "Be good and we'll let you off." This is what I heard:

You have been in court during the time that your counsel made the statement that pending the prosecution of appeal neither you nor those affiliated with you in this so called movement will violate the law; that is the promise your counsel makes for you. Now, the Court is considering extreme clemency in your case. Possibly you know what extreme clemency means. Now, do you personally make that promise?
THE DEFENDANT: Pending the appeal.
THE COURT: If Mrs. Sanger will state publicly and openly that she will be a law-abiding citizen without any qualifications whatsoever, this Court is prepared to exercise the highest degree of leniency.
THE DEFENDANT: I'd like to have it understood by the gentlemen of the Court that the offer of leniency is very kind and I appreciate it very much. It is with me not a question of personal imprisonment or personal disadvantage. I am today and always have been more concerned with changing the law regardless of what I have to undergo to have it done.
THE COURT: Then I take it that you are indifferent about this matter entirely.
THE DEFENDANT: No, I am not indifferent. I am indifferent as to the personal consequences to myself, but I am not indifferent to the cause and the influence which can be attained for the cause.
THE COURT: Since you are of that mind, am I to infer that you in-

tend to go on in this matter, violating the law, irrespective of the consequences?

THE DEFENDANT: I haven't said that. I said I am perfectly willing not to violate Section 1142—pending the appeal.

JUSTICE HERRMANN: The appeal has nothing to do with it. Either you do or you don't.

THE COURT: (to Mr. Goldstein) What is the use of beating around the bush? You have communicated to me in my chambers the physical condition of your client, and you told me that this woman would respect the law. This law was not made by us. We are simply here to judge the case. We harbor no feeling against Mrs. Sanger. We have nothing to do with her beliefs, except in so far as she carries those beliefs into practice and violates the law. But in view of your statement that you intend to prosecute this appeal and make a test case out of this and in view of the fact that we are to regard her as a first offender, surely we want to temper justice with mercy and that's all we are trying to do. And we ask her, openly and above board, "Will you publicly declare that you will respect the law and not violate it?" and then we get an answer with a qualification. Now, what can the prisoner at the bar for sentence expect? I don't know that a prisoner under such circumstances is entitled to very much consideration after all."

THE COURT: (to the Defendant) We don't want you to do impossible things, Mrs. Sanger, only the reasonable thing and that is to comply with this law as long as it remains the law. It is the law for you, it is the law for me, it is the law for all of us until it is changed; and you know what means and avenues are open to you to have it changed, and they are lawful ways. You may prosecute these methods, and no one can find fault with you. If you succeed in changing the law, well and good. If you fail, then you have to bow in submission to the majority rule.

THE DEFENDANT: It is just the chance, the opportunity to test it.

THE COURT: Very good. You have had your day in court; you advocated a cause, you were brought to the bar, you wanted to be tried here, you were judged, you didn't go on the stand and commit perjury in any sense, you took the facts and accepted them as true, and you are ready for judgment, even the worst. Now, we are prepared, however, under all the circumstances of this case, to be extremely lenient with you if you will tell us that you will respect this law and not violate it again.

THE DEFENDANT: I have given you my answer.

THE COURT: We don't want any qualifications. We are not concerned with the appeal.

MR. GOLDSTEIN: Just one other statement, your Honor, one final statement on my part. Your Honor did well say that you didn't want anything unreasonable. With all due deference to your Honor, to ask a person what her frame of mind will be with so many exigencies in future, that is, if the commission did nothing or the Legislature did nothing—

THE COURT: All we are concerned about is this statute, and as long as it remains the law will this woman promise here and now unqualifiedly to respect it and obey it? Now, it is yes or no. What is your answer, Mrs. Sanger? Is it yes or no?

THE DEFENDENT: I can't respect the law as it stands today.

THE COURT: Margaret Sanger, there is evidence that you established and maintained a birth control clinic where you kept for sale and exhibition to various women articles which purported to be for the prevention of conception, and that there you made a determined effort to disseminate birth control information and advice. You have challenged the constitutionality of the law under consideration and the jurisdiction of this Court. When this is done in an orderly way no one can find fault. It is your right as a citizen. . . . Refusal to obey the law becomes an open defiance of the rule of the majority. While the law is in its present form, defiance provokes anything but reasonable consideration. The judgment of the Court is that you be confined to the Workhouse for the period of thirty days.

A single cry, "Shame!" was followed by a sharp rap of the gavel, and silence fell.

Chapter Nineteen

THIS PRISON WHERE I LIVE

⇛⇛⇛⇛⇛⇛⇛⇛⇛⇛⇛⇛⇛⇚⇚⇚⇚⇚⇚⇚⇚⇚⇚⇚⇚⇚

I SAT in the front row while the court routine continued. The room buzzed with conversation. J.J. was busy with formalities; reporters were leaning over to ask me questions. Through the near-by doorway I saw several young men awaiting their sentences like actors in the wings listening for their cues. One was propped against the wall smoking a cigarette. At the sound of his name he raised his head, signifying he had heard, and yet kept on smoking. When it was called a second time an attendant shoved him forward roughly. I could almost feel the hardening of his soul under this brutal attitude and the physical handling. He gave still another puff; then deliberately dropped the stub, stepped on it, and sauntered leisurely forward to receive his sentence.

I was led into an anteroom where other prisoners were being put through the regular fingerprinting procedure. I refused; there was a definite connection in my mind between admission of guilt and fingerprinting; both in their different ways placed me in the category of criminals. My refractoriness was reported to the court. But the judges, poor dears, had worn themselves out trying to avoid sending me to jail and were exasperated and cross; one more rebellion was too much for them. "Don't bother us with that. It's not our job. Take her away."

We were then herded through the rear of the building into an open yard where the van was standing. The careless youth who had answered the court's call with such unconcern was waving farewell to friends who loitered outside.

"How long, Alf?" asked one.

"Five years," and he laughed as he said it.

Two more boys, their arms fraternally flung across one another's shoulders, shouted, "Three!" and, "Four!" consecutively. Were they normal? Could liberty be of so little account? The muscles in my throat contracted as I pictured the maternal love once spent on their infancy, and now the reckless disregard for freedom culminating in this ride. Thirty days seemed to me the end of the world, but they made light of marking time in life for years, calling this their "sleeping time." They paid no attention to me; I was entirely out of their realm.

The women huddled beside me were more serious. An hysterical and tearful "one-monther" had been obliged to leave her small four-year-old son sitting on the veranda watching for her return. She had not even been allowed to go back to see him and arrange for his care during her absence.

Some experiences, though unexpected, are nevertheless partially anticipated in the subconscious. I had believed fully and firmly that some miracle would occur to keep me from going to jail. There had been no miracle. The doors banged shut, two blue uniforms stared stolidly at each other, the automobile jerked forward.

The trip to Raymond Street was short. We were ushered into a waiting room. A thin-lipped attendant of huge size callously pushed one weeping girl through the door.

"Get ready there, you!" she tossed over her shoulder at me.

"For what?"

"For the doctor." I sat still. She repeated, "Do you hear me? Go in and get your examination!"

I resented this attitude with every fiber of my being and replied, "I'm not being examined."

"Ho, you're not? You're one of the fighting kind, are you? Well, we'll soon fix you, young lady!"

She swung her heavy, massive frame out the door, leaving me wondering, but quivering with excited determination. I was not sure what would happen to me. Within five minutes, however, she came back with an entirely different manner and tone. "Oh, you're Mrs. Sanger. It's all right. Come this way, please."

The next morning I was given a cup of bitter, turbid, lukewarm coffee, and then placed inside the van, which set off for the Workhouse. There all my possessions were taken from me. A long wait. The men were sent somewhere and the women somewhere else, I did not know where. I just sat. After what seemed hours my belongings were returned and a woman in coat and hat told me to follow her. I did. A man added himself to our party, and the three of us climbed into another van. We were driven some distance down the Island, then put into a boat and ferried over to New York. I had no idea where we were going. I asked but could elicit no answer.

We took a street car and after various transfers I caught sight of a Loose-Wiles biscuit sign. But it did not help me because I had not seen it before; the section was unfamiliar to me. In early afternoon we reached the Queens County Penitentiary, Long Island City. Evidently the Workhouse authorities had had enough of the Higgins family and wanted no more responsibility of this nature.

Warden Joseph McCann, who met me, was a jovial young Irishman who had risen from the police ranks. "Have you had any lunch?" he asked. The cause of his solicitude emerged when he inquired anxiously whether I intended to go on a hunger strike. Remembering my morning cup of coffee, I replied, "Not unless your food is too bad." He introduced Mrs. Sullivan, the motherly matron.

I answered the usual interrogatory about where I was born, how old I was, etc., etc. When the clerk came to "What religion?" I replied, "Humanity." He had never heard of this form of belief, and rephrased the question. "Well, what church do you go to?"

"None."

He looked at me in sharp surprise. All inmates of the penitentiary went to church; ninety-eight percent in my corridor had been reared as Catholics.

The prison clothing which I was handed was much like a nurse's uniform and did not disturb me. But when I was recalled to the warden's office to be fingerprinted, I said flatly I would not submit. He sent me back to my cell.

The floor was arranged rather on the order of a hospital ward, with little alcoves of ten or fifteen cells running off the gallery. Mine, Number 210, was small but clean. I had a bed, toilet, and washstand. There was no chair; I sat on my bunk.

All the prisoners were at work except Josephine, a German Catholic who had lost her husband and three children within a short period. She was eager to tell me her story. A few days after they had died, she had gone to their graves and covered those of the children with blankets to keep them warm. Someone saw her, decided she was insane, and had her committed to jail. It was a spring day when she was let out on parole. She was pleased and happy. A hurdy-gurdy was playing her favorite tune, *Just As the Sun Went Down*. She paid the man a nickel to play it over, then another, and another, and another. The policeman at the corner, hearing it, looked her over and arrested her again. During her next ten days in prison she nursed a grievance against this injustice and, as soon as she came out, had several drinks, went after the policeman, scratched his face, and tore his buttons off.

Thereafter, Josephine drank whenever she could, and each time she drank she fought, and, since she had developed a complex against policemen, she landed back in jail in short order; she had been in some seventy times.

I found Josephine a kind, big-hearted person, and, though erratic, fairly intelligent. She had a terrible tongue and a terrible temper, and undoubtedly had periods when she was of unsound mind. Most people were frightened of her.

She was supposed to put curses on her enemies, and they came true. Once a person who had treated her badly and been cursed in consequence had promptly contracted pneumonia and died. At another time the matron of a certain jail had kept her three weeks in a dark cell on bread and water. After the fifth day, when bread was handed into the hole, she said it tasted like cake it was so sweet. From the two or three cups of water daily, she had to assuage her thirst, wash her face, and clean her teeth. When she came out of this Stygian place she could scarcely see, but she managed to distinguish the matron sufficiently to put the curse of God upon her. The next night someone forgot to close the door of the elevator shaft, and the matron walked through the open gate, fell to the bottom, and was instantly killed. Now, Josephine was let alone.

In spite of my depression I was intensely interested in Josephine; she begged me to help her, and I said I would try. The rest of that afternoon was consumed in this tale of woe until at five o'clock I began my initiation into the prison routine of hours and meals. The dining room was filled with long tables and wooden benches. No one had a knife or fork—only a tablespoon, edge blunted so as to be unserviceable as a weapon. Supper consisted of tea and molasses, stewed dried peaches, and two slices of bread which tasted queer; it was said to have saltpeter in it. We were locked in an hour later; lights were out at nine. Bells began ringing at six the next morning, and the cells were opened at seven. For breakfast we had oatmeal with salt and milk, again two slices of the same bread, and coffee without sugar. Dinner was more bread, a boiled potato with the skin half on, and a sorry hunk of meat.

Because of my active tuberculosis the prison doctor soon put me on what was called a diet. This meant I could have crackers and milk and tea in my cell instead of going to the supper table. Due probably to the influence of the Osborne innovations at Sing Sing the men at the Queens Penitentiary were better treated than the women. Their food was of higher quality and they could buy tobacco and even newspapers. The sole reading matter available to women were two Catholic weeklies and the *Christian Science Monitor*. Our only other news came from the two visitors a month allowed. So fine a mesh screen was placed in the reception room that inmates could with difficulty distinguish, as through a veil, the features of those to whom they were talking. This was a hardship not even imposed at Sing Sing.

After morning cell-cleaning we took a fifteen-minute walk in the yard with our hooded capes over our heads. During this cold tramp the women scanned the ground avidly for butts of cigarettes tossed away by the men. It was tragic to see human beings forced to such a low level as to dig with their fingers in the frozen earth to retrieve these mangled stubs. Each used to grab her little bit and hide it.

When the matron went to her lunch we were locked in our corridors but not in our cells. Ordinarily she took a nap afterwards, and the girls could usually count on her not being back until three or perhaps four o'clock. This gave them an opportunity to dry their shreds of tobacco under the radiator, then wrap them in toilet paper ready for smoking. At night when we were all locked in they struck the steel ribs from their corsets against the stone floor, and thus ignited pieces of cotton to give them lights. I could see tiny glowing points in the darkness as they puffed away greedily.

Somehow, with the ingenuity born of necessity, these women also managed to have smuggled in to them occasional small news items. The first day one of the girls approached me and in a stage whisper demanded, "Cross your heart and hope to die you won't tell."

I crossed my heart and hoped to die.

She slipped into my hand a short clipping about my trial. Apparently others had been keeping up with events, because a few minutes later Lisa, a little colored girl, called out, "You'se eats, don't yer?"

A third asked me to explain to them what "sex hygiene" was all about. Accordingly I sought permission of Mrs. Sullivan to be allowed in their corridor during her dinner hour.

"What for?"

"The girls want me to tell them about sex hygiene."

"Ah, gwan wid ye," she laughed. "They know bad enough already."

Some of the most lovely-looking girls were drug addicts. It seemed monstrous that the State could take such liberties with human lives as to convict them as criminals and sentence them to as much as three years for something which should have been considered disease.

Other women were pickpockets, embezzlers, prostitutes, keepers of brothels, "Tiffany," or high-class thieves, accomplices of safe blowers, and a few "transatlantic flyers," who assisted in big hauls from Paris or London.

The class snobbishness among the offenders interested me beyond words. No one cared how or where another had been reared, what kind of family background or education she had; the nature of her offense was the key to her social position. The one who picked pockets was scorned by the girl who helped herself to pearl or diamond necklaces; the shoplifter did not "sell her body."

The prisoners sometimes slid their arms in mine as we paced along in the yard. One took me to task. "I saw you walking with Gracie. You mustn't associate with her."

"Why not?"

"Do you know what she's in here for? She's a petty thief. Whenever she gets out she rides in street cars and steals money from the pocketbooks of poor people going to pay their rent, or women coming home with their husbands' wages."

"And what are you here for?"

"Oh, I steal from the rich; I take only from people who have jewelry and bank accounts."

I never did the regular work of cleaning, not even my own cell. Nor was I sent into the workshop to sew or to operate the machines with the others. When I asked Mrs. Sullivan why, she replied jollily, "Oh, you look better over there with a pen in your hand."

She had fixed up a table to serve as a desk, and there I sat the entire day with my papers and books, planning ahead and reading countless letters; the tenor of all was much like this from Sarah Goldstein:

The women here in Brownsville need help very bad. Mrs. Sanger has got put away in the penitentiary for being friends with us, but she said we was to use her place while she was gone. If we can have a meeting over here in the clinic, I will put a fire in the stove and ask the women to come Saturday.

We women here want to find out what the President, the Mayor, and the Judges and everybody is trying to do. First they put Mrs. Sanger in jail for telling us women how not to have any more children, and then they get busy for the starve of the ones we've got. First they take the meat and the egg, then the potato, the onion, and the milk, and now the lentils and the butter, and the children are living on bread and tea off the tea leaves that is kept cooking on the back of the stove.

Honest to God, we ought to call a meeting and do something about it.

Part of my time also was devoted to helping some of the girls to read or to write the two letters a month permitted them. I had not believed that any American-born of sixteen to eighteen years of age could be illiterate, but there were at least ten.

I had been in the penitentiary for several days before I noticed a tall, erect woman with white hair and a face which obviously did not belong there; I had never seen her in the yard or at table. Although she had been over nine months sharing the other prisoners' food and working beside them she had not become one of them. Because of her aloofness I found it hard to make her acquaintance, but ultimately "the Duchess," as she was called, told me her story.

After having been a teacher for fifteen years, she had married a minister who lived on a pension. They stayed in hotels, always spending more than their income, while he steadily drew on his insurance money. His sudden death left her practically penniless. Due to her age and the fact she had not taught for so long her application for a teacher's job was refused. She continued in the hotel until she had used up everything and was forced to move. Thereafter, she went from hotel to hotel, fleeing each time angry looks and bills; finally she was arrested and given an indeterminate sentence of from one to three years.

Her constant brooding over her past was not preparing her for any future. I suggested she might keep her hand in by instructing the illiterate girls, and asked J.J., my only visitor, to have his friend William Spinney send some primers and lower grade text-books from Henry Holt and Company where he worked; this was done free of charge. The Duchess was contentedly happy from the day she began teaching again.

In the desire to learn whether the girls' background might not be related to the causes of their imprisonment, I asked Warden McCann whether I could see the records, especially as to the size of the families from which they came. He said it was against the rules, but he was willing to give me such facts separately, assuring me I was going to be surprised and disappointed. I was.

When I inquired, "How many brothers and sisters does Rosie have?" the answer was, "None."

"And Marie?"

"She had a brother, but he's dead."

It appeared from the entries that all these women had been single children or, if a brother or sister had been born, he or she no longer survived. This was difficult to believe, but I had to accept it at first.

However, when I became better acquainted with the old-timers they told me quite a different history. The registers were merely evidence of the unwritten rule among them to keep their families out of it.

The madam of a house of assignation was putting her daughter of seventeen through a fashionable boarding school. To prevent the child from knowing anything about her occupation she wrote letters, sent them West, where she was supposed to be traveling, and had them redirected to the school. Many other prisoners were mothers also, and the scheming and planning to hide the painful knowledge of their whereabouts was worthy of the deepest admiration.

One after another admitted she had given false statements to save her relatives from disgrace or constant annoyance by the police. The result of a poll of the thirty-one in our corridor showed an average of seven children to each girl's family.

I was always interested to know why the pretty ones were there. Frances, one of the loveliest, had a radiant color, rosebud mouth, and the most innocent eyes; she even managed to wear her apron with a Gallic chic. It did not seem possible she could have committed a crime, but she turned out to be one of the rogues who made a practice of frequenting gatherings where careless people offered opportunities to pickpockets. She told me how she, with two other girls, had once gone to an up-State fair. After making a grand haul of watches and purses and anything they could lay their hands upon, her two companions said, "We've got enough. We're clearing out."

But Frances had spotted an easy-looking wallet. It was not quite easy enough. Unfortunately for her the owner shouted, "Somebody's stolen my money!"

A bystander pointed, "She did it. I've been in three places today where things have been lost, and she's been there every time."

Other people gathered round. Frances began to cry. Because the friends of the man who had been robbed and he himself insisted she must be arrested the police were called.

Frances continued to weep until several lusty young farmers were ready to defy her accusers. How could they say such things about such a sweet girl! It looked as though a fight were imminent, and she hoped to slip away during the excitement. But the police arrived too soon and took her to the station. They found nothing on her; somehow she had rid herself of the wallet.

Frances' new-found allies were ready to go her bail, but it so happened that a police chief from a neighboring town who had come to the fair for the express purpose of identifying possible petty criminals recognized her from his sheaf of photographs of habitual offenders. He said to her supporters, "Boys, you're crazy. This girl's as crooked as a snake. Here's her picture!"

"Why, you're crazy yourself! Your girl's a blonde, and this one's dark."

The chief snatched at Frances' hair, and off came her wig. As she told me this great joke on herself she shook with merriment.

But this was not the end of the story. The station captain had been influenced by her attractiveness and, since the wallet had not actually been discovered on her, wanted to let her off. He made a compromise. "I'm going to give you a ticket to Montreal. You either go to jail or take it and get out."

She accepted the ticket, but left the train at a near-by point and rejoined her friends at another fair. There, wearing a different costume, she continued her trade. Although to look at her ingenuous face I could hardly believe it, pitting her wits against the police was to her a type of game.

Gertrude had been equally clever. She was of German origin, very stylish, moving in good circles when not in prison. She had learned that the officers of the submarine, *Deutschland,* which had just crossed the ocean, were to be entertained at a party. Having secured an invitation, she devoted herself to a lieutenant who, she had discovered, was carrying seven hundred dollars in his pocket. When the gathering broke up she took him back to his hotel in her car, suggesting they stop at a night club en route. There she put a drug in his glass. It took a bit of time to work, but after they had started on again he fell asleep. She gave five dollars to the doorman to take him to his room, saying he had drunk a bit too much, and then went home.

At seven the following morning, while Gertrude and her little girl were still in bed, the police raided her apartment. They could unearth nothing except what she could honestly account for. Her effects were turned upside down, and still no money was to be found.

"Then how could they send you to jail?" I queried. "You didn't take it, did you?"

"Of course I did," she asserted, looking at me as if I were dull-witted. "They couldn't pin it on me, that's all."

Even though Gertrude had been brighter than the police, she, like many of the others, had been convicted on her past record and the present suspicious circumstances.

Josephine was another case in point. After I myself had been released I had her paroled under her own recognizance and secured a place for her as chambermaid in a hotel. Fate so arranged that in the very first room she entered on her first morning's work she was confronted with the corpse of a man who had died in his bed during the night. She rushed out immediately, got drunk, and went directly back to jail again.

The resentment thus engendered in these caged women was like a strong, glowing flame, of a depth that I scarcely had believed possible. The shivers ran up and down my back when I heard the details of their unguided and loveless childhoods, which explained in large part the curious manner in which their minds worked. They thought only in terms of getting away with their crimes, of beating the system —although their presence here was proof that it could not be beaten. Three of the younger girls, too old for Bedford Reformatory but almost too young for the penitentiary, definitely shocked me with their plans for wrong-doing without being apprehended. They asked me about my case. "Was it true the judge gave you a chance not to go to jail if you'd promise not to break the law?"

"Yes."

"Well, why didn't you do it?"

"I couldn't promise that."

"But you didn't have to keep your promise!"

The ever-present bitterness arose, not from being caught in the act, but from being convicted without having been, according to their own belief, proved guilty. It was the woeful mental attitude rather than the actual physical condition of their imprisonment which so appalled me. Not one of them intended to go straight. They hated the police who were drawing good salaries from the State and getting credit for putting them in jail; yet all the time they had been smarter. This sounds inconsistent, but it was their peculiar psychological twist.

I talked it over later with several judges to whom it was rather a new point of view. Among other cases I cited that of a brothel keeper who conducted her house as a club and did it so carefully that no evidence could be obtained against her. Therefore, a detective had put opium in the plumbing and she had been sentenced on a narcotic charge, although it was well known this was not her offense.

"The prisoners were guilty, weren't they?" said one of the judges. "You know that, don't you?"

"Yes," I rejoined, "but to my mind that doesn't end the State's responsibility. It seems to me your detectives should be more intelligent than the criminals they are set to catch."

The girls at Queens Penitentiary were unaware they were entitled to bring a far more serious charge against society than clumsy and inept police methods. I have never since visited an institution for juvenile offenders without thinking how stupid people are not to recognize that most adolescents are subjected to temptation on some occasion or other; that anyone, in an emotional fragment of time, when young and when the consequences are not clear, may do some forbidden thing. More often than not it is merely incidental, and in no way warrants a life of penance.

The only brutal treatment I received was during the last two hours. Since my fingerprints had not been taken on arrival, Warden McCann first tried to talk me into compliance. His argument that all prisoners' prints must be on file, that not having them was unheard of, got us nowhere. I refused to submit, even though it postponed my release. He then turned me over to two keepers. One held me, the other struggled with my arms, trying to force my fingers down on the inkpad. I do not know from what source I drew my physical strength, but I managed to prevent my hands from touching it. My arms were bruised and I was weak and exhausted when an officer at headquarters, where J.J. was protesting against the delay, telephoned an order to discharge me without the usual ceremony.

March 6, 1917, dawned a bitter, stinging morning. Through the metal doors I stepped, and the tingling air beat against my face. No other experience in my life has been like that. Gathered in front were my old friends who had frozen through the two hours waiting to celebrate "Margaret's coming out party." They lifted their voices in the *Marseillaise*. Behind them at the upper windows were my new friends, the women with whom I had spent the month, and they too were singing. Something choked me. Something still chokes me whenever I hear that triumphant music and ringing words, "Ye sons of freedom wake to glory!"

I plunged down the stairs and into the car which stood ready for me, and we swept out of the yard towards my apartment. At the entrance were Vito, the coal man, and his wife, beaming and proudly pointing to the blazing fire they had made on the hearth to welcome me home.

Chapter Twenty

A STOUT HEART TO A STEEP HILL

"When a thing ceases to be a subject of controversy, it ceases to be a subject of interest."
                                                    WILLIAM HAZLITT

THE noisy clamor of the world could not reach me through thick stone walls; prison had been a quiet interim for reflection, for assembling past experiences and preparing for the future. The tempestuous season of agitation—courts and jails and shrieking and thumbing-the-nose—should now end. Heretofore there had been much notoriety and but little understanding. The next three steps were to be: first, education; then, organization; and, finally, legislation. All were clearly differentiated, though they necessarily overlapped to a certain extent.

I based my program on the existence in the country of a forceful sentiment which, if co-ordinated, could become powerful enough to change laws. Horses wildly careering around a pasture have as much strength as when harnessed to a plow, but only in the latter case can the strength be measured and turned to some useful purpose. The public had to be educated before it could be organized and before the laws could be changed as a result of that organization. I set myself to the task. It was to be a long one, because the press did not want articles stating the facts of birth control; they wanted news, and to them news still consisted of fights, police, arrests, controversy.

One of the early essays in education was a moving picture dramatizing the grim and woeful life of the East Side. Both Blossom and I believed it would have value, and I continue to be of the same mind. He had not approved of the clinic and had declined to have anything to do with it, but was eager to join me in capitalizing on the ensuing publicity. Together we wrote a scenario of sorts, concluding with the trial. Although I had long since lost faith in my abilities as an actress, I played the part of the nurse, and an associate of Blossom's financed its production. But before it could appear Commissioner of Licenses George H. Bell ordered it suppressed.

To prove the film mirrored conditions which called for birth control, we gave a private showing at a theater, inviting some two hundred people concerned with social welfare. All agreed the public should see it, and signed a letter to that effect. Justice Nathan Bijur issued an injunction against interfering with its presentation. The moving picture theaters, however, fearful lest the breath of censure wither their profits, were too timid to take advantage of this.

Of infinitely greater and more lasting significance than this venture was the *Birth Control Review,* which, from 1917 to 1921, was the spearhead in the educational stage. It could introduce a quieter and more scientific tone, and also enable me to keep in touch with people everywhere whose interest had already been evoked. Emotion was not enough; ideas were not enough; facts were what we needed so that leaders of opinion who were articulate and willing to speak out might have authoritative data to back them up.

The first issue of the *Review,* prepared beforehand, had come out in February, 1917, while I was in the penitentiary. It was not a very good magazine then; it had few contributors and no editorial policy. Anyone—sculptor, spiritualist, cartoonist, poet, free lance—could express himself here; the pages were open to all. In some ways it was reminiscent of the old days of the *Woman Rebel,* when everybody used to lend a hand—always with this vital difference, that we held strictly to education instead of agitation. I had learned a little editorial knowledge from my previous magazine efforts and now obtained a more professional touch from the newspaper men and women who gradually came in, among them William E. Williams, formerly of the Kansas City *Star,* Walter A. Roberts, who later published the few issues of the *American Parade,* and Rob Parker, editor and make-up man. Among the associates were Jessie Ashley, Mary Knoblauch, and Agnes Smedley.

That extraordinarily shy and mysterious woman, Agnes Smedley, had been born in a covered wagon of squatter parents, and, though she had become a teacher in the California public schools, her early habits of thought remained with her; she was consistently for the under dog. The British Government had suspected her of connection with the seditious activities of a group of Hindu students and persuaded the Federal authorities to investigate. All they had been able to find on which to charge her were a few copies of *Family Limitation*. This brought her within our province, and when she was arraigned in New York John Haynes Holmes procured her ten-thousand-dollar bail. After her acquittal she worked with us at various times until she left for post-War Germany.

On this and other occasions John Haynes Holmes, a speaker second to none, brought the convincing force of his arguments and mind to our aid. By the shape of his head and the honesty of his eyes you could recognize the practical idealist in this Unitarian minister. He never straddled issues. During the War he said if one flag were to be hung out his church windows, then those of all nations should be flown; no peoples were enemies of his.

Two numbers of the *Review* had appeared when the United States entered the War and Blossom and I fell out. He was an ardent Francophile and, like most masculine members of the intelligentsia, threw in his lot with the Allies. I wrote a pacifist editorial; he refused to run it and resigned.

To Blossom, as to so many others, pacifism was automatically labeled pro-Germanism, on the old theory that "he who is not for me is against me." I had already seen in Europe what propaganda could do to build up a war spirit, and prayed every morning when I awoke that I could keep my head clear and cool. I had heard the plaintive pleas of French mothers, but had talked also with German mothers. In the hearts of none had there been hatred or desire for their sons to kill other sons.

I knew what I thought about the War; it was so outrageous I would not be mixed up in it. I still believe it was not only a dreadful thing in itself—a slaughter and waste of human life—but, even more disastrous, it exterminated those who ought now to be ruling our national destinies according to the pre-War liberality of thought in which they had been reared. We started at that time to walk backwards instead of forwards, and have retreated steadily ever since. A fear of expressing opinions which then began to seep in has gradually helped to impose censorship and further intolerance.

I was neither pro-Ally nor pro-German but, using common sense, was distressed at seeing German achievements torn into shreds. Intelligence in Germany had been focused on all fronts; she had the lowest illiteracy of any country and had invested heavily in mass education from which the rest of the world was benefiting at little cost. She had offered the best training for graduate students in medicine; foreign travel had been accelerated by German linguists; commerce had been able to carry on international contacts through German interpreters; any foreign industry which had needed technical advice had usually employed a German scientist, engineer, or chemist who knew how to do his job and do it well. Germany could not continue this policy without wanting to receive some tangible return.

I was convinced the primary cause of this war lay in the terrific pressure of population in Germany. To be sure, her birth rate had recently begun to decline, but her death rate, particularly infant mortality, had, through applied medical science, likewise been brought far down. The German Government had to do something about the increase of her people. Underneath her rampant militarism, underneath her demand for colonies was this driving economic force. She could hold no more, and had to burst her bounds.

Blossom's defection was one of the heart-breaking things that can creep into any endeavor, even the most idealistic. I have seen so many young crusaders come galloping to show me the way, joining the procession and blowing horns for "The Cause," panting with enthusiasm to reform the world, willing to teach me how to put the movement on a "social" or "sound practical and economic" basis. They were going to get vast contributions so that money would roll unceasingly into our coffers. But if they lacked the necessary patience and forbearance, or were there for personal aggrandizement, they became discouraged at the first show of thorny, disagreeable obstacles, retreating or deserting rather than fighting through.

In the birth control movement supporters have come and gone. When they remained they found work, work, work, and little recognition, reward, or gratitude. Those who desired honor or recompense, or who measured their interest by this yardstick, are no longer here. It is no place for anything except the boundless love of giving. Blossom was the first illustration to me that the ones to whom authority is handed over are likely to expand and explode unless they have selflessly dedicated themselves.

Now, I believe the three chief tests to character are sudden power, sudden wealth, and sudden publicity. Few can stand the latter; nothing goes to the head with more violence. Seeing this all around me, I did not subscribe to a clipping bureau until it seemed necessary for historical purposes. I did not even read the papers when unsought advertisement was great, remembering that this could be but a nine days' wonder. Furthermore, news items were often distracting because the facts were constantly embroidered just to make a good story, to paint a situation according to the policy of the paper, or because they reflected the inhibitions of the reporters. Hours could have been entirely given over to denials and contradictions.

In the midst of any emergency such as a police raid or the stopping of a meeting my own emotions generally kept an even tenor; they did not go hopping up and down like a temperature. A nurse cannot afford to lose her head, and the control I had won in that training helped me, as did also my father's philosophy, "Since all things change, this too will pass."

Consequently, during this feverish period, neither public praise nor public blame affected me very much, although the type of criticism that came from friends was different. Just because they were friends and I wanted them to understand, I was unhappy if they did not. But, since persons one likes can have great influence and friendships take time, I refrained from making many new ones. Nevertheless, those I had then are as good today; when we meet we pick up the threads where we dropped them.

The War halted the progress of the birth control movement temporarily. The groups that had before been active now found new interests. The radicals were convulsed and their own ranks torn in two by the opposition to conscription. Influenza swept over the world and in its passage took off many of our old companions. Governor Whitman's promised commission blew up. One bright bugle sounded when

I learned that the section on venereal disease in *What Every Girl Should Know,* which had once been banned in the New York *Call* and for which Fania had been fined, was now, officially but without credit, reprinted and distributed among the soldiers going into cantonments and abroad. At home all felt there was little to do but wait until people came back to their senses; the *Review* was the only forward step I could take at the time.

Late in 1917 a new recruit was enlisted. Nobody ever knew Kitty Marion's true name. She had been born in Westphalia, Germany, and when she was fifteen her father had whipped her once too often and she had run away to England, where eventually she had headed a turn at a music hall.

The London slums had aroused Kitty's social conscience, and she had abandoned her own career to enroll with Mrs. Pankhurst in the suffrage crusade, becoming one of the most determined of her followers. When put in jail she set fire to her cell, chewed a hole in her mattress, broke the window, and upon being released threw bricks at Newcastle Post Office. Seven times she went to prison, enduring four hunger strikes and two hundred and thirty-two compulsory feedings, biting the hand that forcibly fed her. Since it was distasteful to the Government to have any suffragette die in prison, Kitty, under the so-called Cat-and-Mouse Act, was once released to a nursing home until she should have strength enough to return to confinement. Friends visited her there, exchanged clothes with her, and she escaped. On another occasion the Bishop of London personally begged her to give up her struggle. At the outbreak of war, the Pankhurst forces hustled her over to America rather than have her run the almost certain risk of deportation or internment.

Selling *The Suffragette* on the streets of London had been part of the initiation which duchesses and countesses and other noble auxiliaries to the Pankhurst cause had had to undergo. Kitty had stood side by side with them. Since we had so experienced a veteran ready for service we began to offer the *Review* on the sidewalks of New York. Our more sober supporters objected because they considered it undignified. But men and women from here, there, and everywhere passed through the commercial centers of New York, and this was a real means of reaching them.

All of us took a hand, but Kitty was the only one who stood the test of years. Strong, stoutish, tow-headed, her blue eyes bright and keen in spite of being well on in her fifties, she became a familiar sight. Morning, afternoon, and until midnight—workdays, Sundays, and holidays—through storms of winter and summer, she tried every street corner from Macy's to the Grand Central Terminal. But her favorite stand was Seventh Avenue and Forty-second Street, right at Times Square. In her own words she was enjoying "the most fascinating, the most comic, the most tragic, living, breathing movie in the world."

Many people still think I must be Kitty Marion. Everywhere they say to me, "I saw you twenty years ago outside the Metropolitan Opera House. You've changed so I wouldn't know you."

Street selling was torture for me, but I sometimes did it for self-discipline and because only in this way could I have complete knowledge of what I was asking others to do. In addition, I learned to realize what possible irritations Kitty had to encounter. Notwithstanding the insults of the ignorant, the censure of the bigots, she remained good-humored. They said to her, "You ought to be ashamed of yourself, you ought to be arrested, to be shot, to be in jail, to be hanged!" or, "It's disgraceful, disgusting, scandalous, villainous, criminal, and unladylike!" When someone asked, "Have you never heard God's word to 'be fruitful and multiply and replenish the earth'?" Kitty replied, "They've done that already," and, knowing her Apocrypha as well as her Bible, retorted in kind, "Does it not say in Ecclesiasticus: 16; 1, 'Desire not a multitude of unprofitable children'?"

During the War it was astonishing how many men, in and out of uniform, mistook Birth Control for British Control. "We don't want no British Control here!" they exclaimed. Kitty would correct them, "Birth Control," and someone would call, "Oh, that's worse!"

Who bought the *Review?* This question was invariably asked, and the answer was—radicals, the curious, girls about to be married, mothers, fathers, social workers, ministers, physicians, reformers, revolutionaries, foreigners. A psychological analysis of reactions of passers-by when they saw the words "birth control" would have been interesting. I never could credit the power those simple words had of upsetting so many people. Their own complexes as to what sex meant to them appeared to govern them. Many were disappointed at its staidness; some were highly indignant, others highly amused, regarding it as a joke; some bought with the set faces of soldiers going over the top; some looked and looked and then strolled on. Others walked by only to return with the money ready, hastily stuff the magazine in their pockets, and move away, trying to seem unconcerned. The majority bought with the utmost seriousness in the hope that it might solve their personal problems.

"Jail" was the instant reaction of every new policeman on the beat. Kitty, who knew she needed no license, would contest the point with him while a crowd gathered. But few of her arresters were familiar with the law in the name of which they hauled her off to the station. Time and again my night's slumbers were broken to go and bail her out. J.J. was always able to have the case dismissed, but only after it had been argued and proved in our favor.

Once Charles Bamberger, the *agent provocateur* of the Society for the Suppression of Vice who had brought about Bill Sanger's arrest, worked much the same ruse on Kitty. His society was supposedly designed to promote purity, which was to its members synonymous with good. But in order to do this they induced people to break the law by appealing to their deepest human sympathies, a form of trickery not to be condoned by any moral code.

Bamberger, on repeated visits to Kitty at our office, poignantly described the condition of his unfortunate wife whose health depended absolutely on her getting contraceptive information. Anna's sense, like Fania Mindell's, was unfailing in recognizing such decoys; I never went against it. But in vain did she warn Kitty, who gave him the information. He had her arrested, and she was not allowed to tell in court the means by which he had obtained his evidence; she had to serve a term. Kitty's sentence did not have adequate publicity, but so violent was the war temper, that, in view of her German birth, even well-disposed newspapers practically ignored it.

In addition to selling the *Review* we tried another experiment in street propaganda. During the warm evenings of one summer Kitty, Helen Todd, and I, often accompanied by George Swazey, a friendly Englishman, proceeded to the neighborhood of St. Nicholas Avenue above 125th Street, where many white collar families lived. We used to buy a soapbox at the nearest delicatessen and Helen, who had a lank, swarthy picturesqueness which attracted attention, mounted it; Swazey, standing behind, held aloft an American flag. Though not a soul might be in sight except our little group with its bundles of literature and Kitty with her *Reviews,* Helen began in her beautiful voice, "Ladies and Gentlemen," bowing to the trees, "we welcome you here tonight." When nobody appeared she began again. "Ladies and Gentlemen," and this time one or two strollers usually lingered. Immediately we raised our pasteboard banners with "birth control" printed in black letters. She was off in full swing, and in a few minutes we had our audience.

In the course of our various trials people had sent checks and made donations to the special Defense Fund account, and we sent anybody who gave money, no matter how much or how little, a mimeographed report of all contributors. We had also accepted almost two thousand paid-in-advance subscriptions, and had therefore incurred an obligation to continue the *Review* for twelve months.

One May morning when I put my key in the office door and swung it open, Anna Lifshiz and I stood and gazed at each other. Only the telephone perched forlornly on top of a packing box relieved the bare and empty room—files, furniture, vouchers, checks, and business records were gone. We still had to supply the subscribers with nine issues more, yet we had no equipment and not one cent in the bank account of the *Review.*

It was a challenge. We hurried over to Third Avenue and for twenty dollars refurnished the office. The loss of the contributors' cards, however, was irreparable. I could never, in spite of my best efforts, recover either them or the missing funds.

The strain to finance the *Review* was so great that after June no more issues came out until December—the printer trusted us as far as he was able from month to month. Often the bank account was down to the last hundred dollars, just enough to hold it open. Yet it might be necessary to mail letters; the call might be urgent. I was hesitant to spend that last amount, but I believed faith could bring anything to realization. Invariably when I operated on that principle and did what I was impelled to do, money poured in perhaps ten times over. Always we cleaned the slate at the end of the year.

This was one of the periods of getting roots in and waiting for the organism to grow, of quiescence before the new beginning and quickening. I kept going, conscious that with every act I was progressing in accord with a universal law of evolution—moral evolution but evolution just the same.

This belief seemed at times to force locked doors. It enabled me to dictate hundreds of letters, to interview dozens of people, to debate, or to lecture, all in twenty-four hours. Day after day I attended parlor meetings, night after night open forums, returning home too tired to eat, too excited to sleep. Frequently at seven in the morning the telephone started ringing; somebody wanted to catch me before I left the house.

For the purpose of having a more solid and substantial basis on which to operate the *Review,* the New York Women's Publishing Company was incorporated in May, 1918; shares were sold at ten dollars each. The women who gave both monetary and moral support were the wives of business men who advised them how to conduct this organization in the proper fashion. Each month Mary Knoblauch opened her charming apartment for the regular meetings any corporation was required to hold.

The movement can never be disassociated in my mind from Frances Ackermann, who, at the suggestion of Mabel Spinney of Creenwich House, came to us as Treasurer. She was exceptionally able and was soon one of our bulwarks, remaining with us eleven years. Her family was wrapped up in orthodoxy—church and Wall Street and the status quo in politics—but Frances' interests were much broader, and she was not content to lead the usual type of life ordained by her social and financial standing.

Tall, very thin, wearing her clothes with an air, Frances was one of the finest persons I have ever known. To her, fair play amounted to a religion; she was so highly sensitive that she lay awake at night after merely reading of an injustice done to anybody. To hundreds of conscientious objectors who were incarcerated during the War because of pacifist or strike activities she sent cigarette money, magazines, stationery—always anonymously—assisting their families and suggesting plans for their own futures. Her death was not only a blow to us but a blow to any endeavor that was seeking understanding. Many lifers who depended on her for brightening luxuries must now wonder what has become of her.

In 1920 Anne Kennedy came to help boost the circulation of the *Review* and gain further financial aid for it. She was a Californian with wide club experience, and had two children. Fair, in her thirties, cheerful, and a good mixer, she was most maternal-looking with her soft gray hair and sweet face; you felt you could lay your head on her bosom and tell her the story of your life.

The incorporation had heralded a new trend wherein we could have a recognized policy. When the *Review* had first been started I had had to beg authors to write. Free speech was their favorite theme, and their pieces were inferior, but they were the only things I could fall back upon. I used to ask possible contributors, "Don't you agree that these poor mothers should have no more babies?"

"Of course, but where's there any article in that?"

Then I had to suggest ideas, show them how to link these up with larger sociological aspects, until they began to cast into the arena legal, medical, eugenic compositions. The material on free speech continued to come in, but we did not need to print it any longer.

Incidentally, we now secured second-class mailing privileges. Soon afterwards I happened to be talking to a cousin who worked in the Post Office, a very young boy in his early twenties, who kept assailing me with questions about the *Review*. I could not understand his unprecedented interest, and asked, "Why are you so curious?"

"Well, I'm the official reader. It'll save my having to wade through every issue if you'll tell me ahead of time just what your policy's going to be."

"Do you make the decisions?"

"That's my job. If any seem objectionable I send them on to Washington."

I was horrified to find this adolescent in a position which permitted him to pass judgment on such serious matters, but I was able to reassure him; the course we had adopted would in no way interfere with retaining our second-class mailing privileges.

Many of the buyers of the *Review* had been disappointed because it contained no practical information. "I have your magazine. All in there is true but what I want to know is how not to have another baby next year." Thousands of letters were sent out explaining that the *Review* could not print birth control information. Nevertheless, some of the appeals, particularly from women who lived on lonely, remote farms, were so heart-rending that I simply had to furnish them copies of *Family Limitation,* though urging them to go to their physicians.

Every once in a while I had a telephone message to come down to the Post Office at an appointed hour. I did so, wondering and uncertain. Was the interview to be about the *Review, Family Limitation,* or what?

The official in the legal department whom I always saw, fatherly though not old, used to say, "Now, Mrs. Sanger, you're still violating the law by sending your pamphlet through the mails. If you keep this up they'll put you in jail again."

I objected, "The Government and I had this out years ago. The Federal case was dismissed."

"It never can be settled while we get these protests."

To prove the Post Office was not having such an easy time of it, he pulled open a drawer and inside was a little pile of pamphlets and letters from religious fanatics, self-constituted moralists of one kind or another, women as well as men, who had received their copies and then complained. He showed me envelopes addressed to the Governor of New York, to the President of the United States. I studied the handwriting to see whether I could recognize it as identical with any that had come to me. Perhaps the postmark was Wichita, Kansas; there could not be many from a town of that size, and presently I remembered the request. It was a shattering thing to see that drawer. I had been earnestly trying to aid despairing mothers, and had been betrayed.

"Here's this proof against you, Mrs. Sanger. What are you going to do about it?"

"Nothing. As long as these women ask me to help them, I'm going to do so."

I intended to continue to the limit of my resources whether or not I had help from those whom I had originally counted upon. In order to make women's clubs feel the need as I did I had often gone miles at my own expense to present a topic that had taken me years to prepare and then had had to express it to the accompaniment of the clatter of dishes or the stirring of spoons in after-dinner coffees. The members had seemed to have their minds on hot rolls or had been fidgeting to get on to the bridge tables. Sometimes a few, who had come to dabble in sentimentality, had experienced a pleasant emotional response, "Oh, the poor things," but that had been as far as it had gone.

The continued apathy of such organizations disappointed me intensely; the desire to build up a structure appeared to dominate them all. I had lost faith in their sincerity, respect for their courage, and at this time had no reason to anticipate assistance from them. To upbraid, accuse, or censure them for not doing what I had hoped was useless, but I resolved that I was never again going to talk to them, and, when it seemed necessary that they be addressed, I sent others to do it.

My nervousness ahead of lectures continued to be akin to illness. All through the years it has been like a nightmare even to think of a pending speech. I promised enthusiastically to go here or there, and then tried to forget it. The morning it was to be delivered I awakened with a panicky feeling which grew into a sort of terror if I allowed myself to dwell on it. It was fatal to eat before a meeting.

Some people can keep an audience rocking with laughter and yet get over a message. But I cannot. Seldom do my hearers have anything merry from me. Advisers often say, "Lighten up your subject." I have always resented this; I am the protagonist of women who have nothing to laugh at.

Heywood Broun once remarked that I had no sense of humor. I was surprised at him, but I could understand his statement in a way; he had been at only a few meetings as chairman and I had been serious to the point of deadliness, purposely bringing forth laborious facts and dramatic statistics. I was grasping at an opportunity to reach his audience because, whenever he was moved by anything deeply, he wrote a story in his column which by reason of its effective irony and smooth prose swayed others to the same extent.

I have had much fun, although it may have penetrated only to the intimate circle of friends. Once after giving what I thought was a very up-to-date, spirited talk at the Waldorf-Astoria, a dear old lady, at least in her middle eighties, tottered towards me with the aid of a cane and in trembling voice quavered, "I have traveled across the country to hear you speak, Miss Sangster. My mother used to read your poems to me when I was a little girl, and I feel this is a great day for me to be able to clasp your hand." She had confused me with the poetess, Margaret E. Sangster, who in the mid-Nineteenth Century had been a regular contributor to religious magazines.

Inevitably I have been constantly torn between my compulsion to do this work and a haunting feeling that I was robbing my children of time to which they were entitled. Back in 1913 I had had some vague notion of being able to spend all my summers with them at Provincetown. That visionary hope had been immediately dissipated because too many painters began to discover it and the place became littered with easels and smocks. Gene O'Neill's plays were being produced on the wharf opposite Mary Heaton Vorse's house, and these brought many more people. I wanted to get away even further, and so did Jack Reed, who had also sought sanctuary there. A real estate agent took him to near-by Truro where the feet of New Yorkers had not yet trod, and I was invited to come along. We saw a little house on a little hill, one of the most ancient in the village. Below it the Pamet River wound like a silver ribbon to the ocean. An old sea captain had squared and smoothed and fitted the timbers, brought them up from the Carolinas in a sailing vessel, and fastened them tightly together with wooden pegs. The kitchen was bright and warm, and seemed as though many cookies and pies had been baked in it.

Jack bought the cottage, but he was never able to live there. As a staff correspondent of the *Metropolitan Magazine* he was dashing from the Colorado Fuel and Iron strike to the European War and back again to New York. In 1917, knowing I, too, had looked at it with longing eyes, he asked whether I would like to buy it; he was starting for Russia the next day and had to have ready money. By a lucky chance I had just received a check for a thousand dollars in payment for some Chicago lectures. We exchanged check and deed. He left the next day for the land of promise whither Bill Haywood, his friend, had already gone and whence neither was to return.

Big Bill, who had steadily advocated resistance to conscription, had been arrested and freed on bail furnished by Jessie Ashley. She had forfeited it gladly to have him safely out of the country. I had had a long talk with him before he had made up his mind definitely to leave. The conversation brought back to me the picture of the times he and I had walked up and down the Cape Cod sands and he had given me such good counsel about not jeopardizing the happiness of the children.

Those who had opposed Bill for his "hands in the pocket" advice at the Paterson strike were the same who were opposing his jumping his bail. Since the day we had together visited the C.G.T. meetings in Paris, Bill had come to see the virtues of expediency; that, rather than languish in jail where he could accomplish no useful purpose, a revolutionary should, if he could, exile himself. "He who fights and runs away, will live to fight another day." This, according to the American idea, was cowardice—you should stay and be a martyr. But to Bill it was now merely shortsighted. He had concluded that the average worker when he went in for rioting and hand-to-hand combat was beaten before he had begun. He realized the workers had been split by the War; they had not united and stood up against conscription with any backbone. They could not as yet be depended upon as a force, but some day he hoped to return and reorganize them.

Truro provided the children with three carefree months every summer in what still seems to me one of the most beautiful spots in the world. For several years I hung on to this dream of being with them constantly, but it was only a dream. I used to go down to open the house and perhaps snatch a week or so there before being obliged to hurry back, but father and my sister Nan were good foster-parents. This house was eventually to burn as had the one in Hastings; fate seemed to decree I should not be tempted to slip back into peaceful domesticity.

Nor did I have all those hoped for years of watching the boys grow from one stage to another. I had had to analyze the situation —either to keep them at home under the supervision of servants who might perhaps be incompetent, and to have no more than the pleasure of seeing them safely to bed, or else to sacrifice my maternal feelings and put them in country schools directed by capable masters where they could lead a healthy, regular life. Having come to this latter decision I sent them off fairly young, and thereafter could only visit them over week-ends or on the rare occasions when I was speaking in the vicinity. If the desire to see them grew beyond control, I took the first train and received the shock of finding them thoroughly contented in the companionship they had made for themselves; after the initial excitement of greeting had passed away they ran off again to their games.

At times the homesickness for them seemed too much to bear; especially was this true in the Fourteenth Street studio. When I came in late at night the fire was dead in the grate, the book open on the table, the glove dropped on the floor, the pillow rumpled on the sofa—all the same—just as I had left them a day, a week, or a month before. That first chill of loneliness was always appalling. I wanted, as a child does, to be like other people; I wanted to be able to sink gratefully into the warmth and glow of a loving family welcome.

The winter of 1917-18 was particularly hard; the snow drifted high and lasted long, and it took forced cheer to keep your spirits up. Dr. Mary Halton assured me that with ceaseless financial worry, inadequate rest, incessant traveling, improper nourishment, I could not survive long. When, therefore, a publisher asked me for a book on labor problems, I snatched ten-year-old Grant out of school and set off for California, taking a small place at Coronado where I sat myself down for three months to write and to get acquainted with my son.

I loved the sunshine. It was a pleasure to be out-of-doors, to have peace and quiet and the leisure to arrange my thoughts and put them on paper. I had no inclination towards a labor book, but thoroughly enjoyed letting loose my pent-up feelings on *Woman and the New Race*. It was good to classify reasons and set them in order. My opinions did emerge, and it was a great release.

I was vividly reminded of prison one day when Grant came home from the school he was attending, both his eyes pretty dirty-looking. I asked him why he had been fighting.

"I don't want to tell you."

"I'd like to know."

"Well, this boy told all the fellows my mother'd been in jail."

"What did you do?"

"I hit him, and he hit me back. He said, 'Your mother's a jailbird,' and I said, 'She's not.' Then another fellow said, 'My mother says your mother went to jail too.'"

Grant had replied, "That wasn't my mother, that was another Margaret Sanger."

"How could you say that, Grant? You know it wasn't true."

"Mother," he replied profoundly, "you could never make those fellows understand."

Chapter Twenty-one

THUS TO REVISIT

THE event of my visit to London in 1920 was the beginning of my friendship with H. G. Wells. There was no aloofness or coldness in approaching him, no barriers to break down as with most Englishmen; his twinkling eyes were like those of a mischievous boy. I was pleased to find he had no beard and no white hair, because it seemed to me I had heard of him since I had begun to think at all.

Wells had ranged every field of knowledge, had dared to invade the sacrosanct precincts of the historian, the economist, and the scientist and, though a layman in these fields, had used his extraordinary gifts to interpret the past and present and even prophesy the future; in novel after novel he had shocked England by championing women's right to a freer life.

We in the United States were just beginning to be affected by sociological concepts; only Henry George and Edward Bellamy had previously opened up this new world of the imagination. Now here was Wells giving a fresh picture of what could be if man had an ideal system of society that was workable. At Columbia Colony he had been quoted repeatedly. On my lecture tour in 1916 his name had been on everybody's lips, and he had signed the letter to President Wilson protesting against the Federal indictment. I believed he had influenced the American intelligentsia more than any other one man.

For good reason countless faithful friends had attached themselves to Wells, and he included in his varied, intricate, and unpredictable personality a capacity for loyally loving both individuals and humanity.

People who had never met Wells always thought they knew him best, especially Londoners. I was stopping with three maiden sisters in Hampstead Gardens, and a great furor arose as soon as it was known in the household that Mrs. Wells had sent me an invitation for what was to be my first week-end at Easton Glebe in Essex. What was I to wear? Was I going to take the blue net or the flowered chiffon? They were greatly disappointed when I carried only a small bag in which there was no room for fluffy evening gowns.

Wells himself was waiting on the platform at Dunmow Station, and we drove in his little car, called the Pumpkin, to Easton Glebe, a part of the Warwick Estate on which he held a life lease. The former rectory was built of old stone, ivy-covered; lovely lawns were spread around it. Early morning tea was served in your room, shoes put out at night were properly polished, hot water was plentiful for your bath, and extra pitchers were brought with towels wrapped around carefully to keep in the steam.

During the course of the next two days I realized more than ever before how sensitive H.G. was to the slightest intonation. To be with him meant you had to be on the alert every second lest you miss something of him. He could be amusing, witty, sarcastic, brilliant, flirtatious, and yet profound at once, all in his thin, small voice, speaking high up into the roof of his mouth, as do many English, instead of back in the throat as we do.

I returned Monday evening about midnight to my room at Hampstead, having spent the day in town seeing people. But no sooner had I closed the door than steps pattered in the hallway and a soft hand tapped. In came the three ladies, hair in braids, warmly and most modestly swathed in voluminous, white cotton nighties, long-sleeved and tight around the neck. They had stayed wide-awake to hear all about my week-end. I told them as much as I could remember of the place and the stimulating fellow guests, one in particular with whom I had been having an interesting discussion. When I had finished the eldest leaned forward and hesitatingly but loudly whispered, "Did he try to kiss you?"

"What? Who?" I asked, having in mind the man I had just been praising.

"Why—why—don't you know?"

"Know what?"

She looked a little abashed at this, and another voice explained apologetically, "Sister means that Wells has a magnetic influence over women!"

"Was he fascinating?" the youngest eagerly took up the catechism.

For two solid hours I was bombarded with questions; H.G. was the Don Juan of spinsterhood in England. That there was a Mrs. Wells for whom Mr. Wells cared deeply did not matter in the least to them.

I wish I could do justice to Jane, as Catherine Wells was affectionately called. This devoted mother, perfect companion, was the complete helpmate, managing H.G.'s finances, reading the proofs of his books, seeing that all editions were up-to-date, letting no publisher be delinquent in his royalties. She did not pretend to be a Feminist; she was there to protect him, performing the duties of an English wife towards her husband and appearing with him so that they might make a united front to the world. The relationship between them was on a fine plane.

Although H.G. had told me once "the sun would set if anything ever happened to Jane" I felt that he had never put her adequately into his books as the great woman she really was; he was too close to her. After she died, his touching introduction to *The Book of Catherine Wells* proved that he realized what she had been in his life.

Jane was always mothering people and looking after their comfort. At a later time when I happened to be at Easton Glebe, she was distressed and anxious that I was taking it for granted I had to have an ice-pack on my neck every night because my tubercular glands were bothering me. She insisted and insisted something must be done, until finally my tonsils were removed, the true source of my trouble. I owed this tremendous relief to Jane's interest, which would not let me go on being sick.

The gay wit and gift for mimicry were not confined to H.G. alone. On one of my visits I was shown a new bathroom, and we viewed solemnly the tiny, almost microscopic, tub. Jane was slight and small, and I was quite sure it was meant for her and not for H.G.'s rotund frame. She maintained, however, it had been installed for his convenience, and made funny suction noises as though a large and deep well were being pumped dry. I was hilarious, but he, pretending to be irritated, yet laughing too, growled at her, "What are you trying to do? Make my bathing an international joke?"

The little things H.G. said, many of them jibes at himself, were always amusing. Even more so were the drawings with which he decorated his letters. If he did not want to go somewhere he might perhaps illustrate his reluctance by picturing himself being dragged off, or, if he desired the absence rather than the presence of a person at a meeting, he would portray him being pushed out unceremoniously. These ingenious caricatures allowed many subtleties which even he would not like to put into words over his own signature.

Jane was unsurpassed when it came to charades, and never minded having the house turned upside down in the search for properties. But the Wells family did not have to depend upon orthodox pastimes; they often made up their own. H.G. had invented a ball game which was played Sunday mornings in a barn made over into a sort of indoor court. Unlike tennis, many could take part at once and the sport was so exhausting that when they finished they were usually dripping with perspiration. I did not play; other novices seemed to be doing badly enough without me. If you did not feel up to anything so strenuous, you could take a short walk through the charming garden which Jane had so lovingly arranged, or a long one through the woods, by the lakes, or bordering the streams of the Warwick Estate, of which H.G. had free use. Every season had its different aspects of beauty.

Sunday afternoons and evenings were especially merry. The atmosphere at Easton Glebe was like nothing else, something that does not exist here, where the elders have their bridge and their conversation and the young go dancing or to the movies. There, all ages mixed together in fun, in laughter. The two sons, Frank and "Gyp," who were then at Cambridge, might bring from ten to fifteen friends home for tea, a great function over which Jane so graciously presided. The maids went out after setting the table for supper and preparing cold meats on the buffet, and the party then took care of itself, everybody serving everybody else. The boys were full of devilment and it was most uproarious.

I often wondered how the unexpected arrivals were provided for, but Jane was a remarkable hostess; I have known her to have a houseful at Easton Glebe for lunch and give a brilliant dinner in London that same evening. Every guest was planned for, no one was ever huddled with another, appropriate games were produced or friends invited who might be interesting or helpful. When they were ready to leave, all were put on the most convenient trains and returned to town with as little trouble to themselves as possible.

From 1920 on I never went to England without spending part of the time with H.G., and many of the most attractive people I met were at Easton Glebe. I always came away enriched by these contacts and the talks we had together. Conversation was a combination of current topics, science, philosophy, history. The English might not have had the same light flippancy or such a scattered fund of information as the average American, who usually qualified his statements with, "I read that—" or "I know someone who—," but they did speak out of their own experience. Furthermore, they could toss the ball of repartee back and forth objectively and not become irritated or let creep into their voices that personal note which implied they had now settled the whole thing.

Each one at Easton Glebe had his turn in the spotlight; it was never a monologue, which a man in H.G.'s position might have made it. No subject could be mentioned that he did not have its complete history and a definite opinion on it as well, including Neo-Malthusianism in all its implications.

These week-ends were inspiration and recreation. The serious duty which called me to England was lecturing. The Neo-Malthusian League had few speakers at that time to address women audiences, and wished me to test out the response to their propaganda.

English public sentiment on birth control had vastly changed since I had been there in 1915, largely because Marie Stopes' book had had such wide circulation during the after-War period; her voice had made articulate the feelings of the millions of unemployed. That people now knew what birth control meant was due in part also to Harold Cox, one of the finest orators of his generation, who had been the first to point out that its condemnation by medical men and Anglican clergy should carry little weight, because the birth rates among them were lower than those of almost any other classes. Notable exceptions who had come out favorably were Sir James Barr, ex-President of the

British Medical Association, Dr. C. Killick Millard, Health Officer of Leicester in the North, Dean Inge of St. Paul's, and the Bishop of Birmingham, who was Chairman of the English National Birth Rate Commission; England was accustomed to clarifying new and controversial subjects by such bodies, summoning experts to testify.

Dr. Alice Vickery arranged for me to give a series of talks, many before lower middle-class workers' wives who belonged to the Women's Co-operative Guild. In different districts of London they came together, paying their little bit, perhaps sixpence a month, to listen to speakers, afterwards serving tea and conversing in a friendly way among themselves. Though their economic uncertainty made them resigned to having ten or twelve children, the fact that the Guild had just brought out a book describing some of the tragic cases of its own members and the deaths from over-childbearing helped to pave the way.

Of all the slums I visited in trams, on buses, via the Underground, the one of worst repute at the time was the dockyards section of Rotherhithe. I held a small demonstration clinic there—in a sense the first of its kind in England. The eager women who came, amazingly ignorant of any possible beauty in marriage, were envious of a few in the community who, though the fathers were receiving no higher wages than their own husbands, had had only two or three children and consequently could afford to send them to the trade school. They themselves were, if not sliding backward, at least no more than holding their own, but those few families were definitely on the way up in the social scale. And it had all come to pass because Dr. Vickery and Anne Martin, a friend of hers who had labored there for two decades as a social worker, had given some contraceptive information about ten years earlier.

Although Dr. Vickery had on numerous occasions raised the question of birth control before gatherings bent on other matters, it fell to my lot to discuss it first as a public health issue. I was told I might have three minutes to address a national health Conference on Maternal and Infant Welfare to be held at Brighton. Considering the four hours required in transit this might seem a short time, but I was happy to have even as much as that. So I went.

With the prospect of reaching university students I traveled to

Cambridge. In the midst of the weathered spires, the ivied halls, and the storied dignity of Trinity and Kings, Noel Porter and his wife, Bevan, had converted an old public house, The Half Moon, into a home, yet had managed to keep its original atmosphere of convivial hospitality. The tap-room had once opened directly on Little St. Mary's Lane; now the bar had been removed, but the ancient sign still swung back and forth and the smoky ceilings and mildewed paneling were the same as when former generations had congregated there over mugs of ale.

Opposite was a tiny, old-fashioned graveyard, no longer used, and I went out there and let the sun beat against my aching back. It was amusing to have to resort to a cemetery for privacy, but the house was constantly filled with hatless students coming and going through the enormous downstairs room which served as rendezvous for all. In the afternoons these youths on the threshold of manhood came to talk over the questions which were perplexing them; in the evenings they had little meetings, at one of which I spoke.

Guy Aldred, who was in Scotland, had planned my schedule there, and I had three weeks of a Scottish summer—bluebells so thick in spots that the ground was azure, long twilights when the lavender heather faded the hills into purple.

When I had been in Glasgow before, I had encountered only officials, but on this occasion I met the people in their homes and found them quite opposite to the stingy, tight-fisted, middle-class stereotype. They were hospitable, generous, mentally alert, just as witty as the Irish and in much the same way, which rather surprised me.

Fourth of July, Sunday, we had a noon meeting on the Glasgow Green. Nearly two thousand shipyard workers in caps and baggy corduroys stood close together listening in utter, dead stillness without cough or whisper. That evening I spoke in a hall under Socialist auspices, Guy Aldred acting as chairman. One old-timer said he had been a party member for eleven years, attending Sunday night lectures regularly, but never before had he been able to induce his wife to come; tonight he could not keep her home. "Look!" he cried in amazement. "The women have crowded the men out of this hall. I never saw so many wives of comrades before."

The men were there, partly through curiosity to hear the American and partly through interest in the subject, ready to fight the ancient battle of Marx against Malthus. Efforts of the English Neo-Malthusians to introduce birth control to the masses had been hampered not only by the opposition of the upper classes, but more especially by the persistent hostility of the orthodox Socialists.

Marx, dealing with problems after they had arisen, had taught that any reform likely to dull the edge of poverty was bad for Socialism because it made labor less dissatisfied. It followed that if a man had to fight for the hungers and necessities of ten or twelve children, he made a better revolutionary. "Let 'em have as many as they can," was the cry. On the other hand, if birth control were practiced by the working classes, the wage earner who could support two children and knew how not to have more was going to be content and would not struggle against conditions of economic insecurity. Hence he was likely to forget "the Revolution."

Knowing that the Scotch took mental notes of items on which to debate, I had tried to prepare myself well, and I produced the unanswerable argument to this theory. "Why do you demand higher wages then," I asked, "when what you really want is privation? If misery is your weapon you should not insist on an eight-hour day but on a twelve- or fourteen-hour one. You should pile up your grievances, and pile them up higher. However, in spite of your best efforts I believe your hunger-revolution will, as it has always done, capitulate to whatever force or government will fill your stomachs."

Socialists, like anarchists and syndicalists, were used to contesting Malthusianism on economic grounds, but, unlike the others, they had as a part of their platform the freedom of woman. I pointed out that she could have the sort of freedom they desired for her right here and now through birth control.

When I ended, Guy Aldred asked, "Now are there any questions?" After a few somewhat irrelevant ones, silence fell; confronted by their own philosophy they could see it. One man finally rose, "We'd like to hear what the Chairman thinks of all this. Does he believe birth control will do what the lady speaker claims for it?" Apparently they were waiting for their cue. But Guy Aldred was not to be drawn. After giving him an opportunity to express himself they plunged in and said their say. Even some women who had never been on their feet before got up to tell dramatic, vivid, personal stories.

The next day I was on my way to a town not far from Dunfermline, Andrew Carnegie's birthplace. I arrived about four o'clock in a driving storm, lacking both umbrella and raincoat. No taxi had ever graced the railroad station, and we trudged through the rain to the cottage of one of the "most advanced friends of labor." I was soaking wet up to the knees. A hurry-call was sent to neighbors for dry clothing, but among that population of five thousand not a single woman had an extra skirt to lend, and only after long search was a new pair of Sunday shoes forthcoming.

Because there was not an inn within miles, I slept that night with my hostess in the one bed the house contained; the husband stretched himself out on two chairs in the kitchen. Since Sylvia Pankhurst had been similarly accommodated just a few months before, I knew I was having the best the village afforded.

The inhabitants had been dispatched from Lancashire factory towns during the War for special munitions work, and here they had stayed and made their homes. Practically all had been apprenticed to the mills at the age of eight or nine. Girls, because they were destined for marriage and therefore needed no education, had worked ten or twelve hours a day throughout their adolescence, and even after their weddings up to the time pregnancy was well advanced. As a result, the young mothers, who had never, from childhood to maturity, had a chance to become rested and get the fatigue out of their systems, had apparently transmitted their weariness to their children; the firstborn were sleepy, inert, and always tired. A doctor told me it was common for boys and girls of five, six, and seven to fall asleep at their school desks and have to be awakened.

When I had arrived in England I had gone to see Havelock in the quaint old Cornwall village where he was living alone since Edith's death. Winding pathways, well-trodden and embraced on either side by rambling shrubbery and verbena, led from his house to the sea hundreds of feet below. The waves dashed continuously against the crags and rocks, and thousands of gulls shrieked or sailed majestically almost in front of my eyes.

We had then talked about going to Ireland where I could make a foray into my own genealogy. Mother's ancestors at some stage had been the same as Edward Fitzgerald's and I thought I might find some of the places from which they had sprung. I had no exact information —just tradition from childhood days. Now, after my strenuous lecturing, I needed a brief holiday, and Havelock also wanted a vacation; so we joined forces.

My primary purpose was frustrated because after half a century nobody in any of the little villages seemed to know anything definite. At Glengariff they said, "Sure, and I thought it was Killarney your grandfather was born in." But at Killarney I was told, "Oh, it was Cork your family came from. My grandmother knew them very well."

More difficult to surmount than the vague discursiveness of these good people was the Sinn Fein Rebellion, in the thick of which we found ourselves. The night before we reached Cork there had been a raid and the leaders were in hiding. Everywhere we went we could sense a subtle, surreptitious undercurrent—in the hotels, in the restaurants, among small, whispering groups which dispersed when any stranger approached.

Ireland had great natural beauty, and I was sorry to see the beginnings of ugly, modern industrialism cropping up, especially in Cork with the Ford factory. The mustard-colored kilts of the men astonished me; I had never known the Irish wore them, but they were trying to bring back their ancestral dress along with the Gaelic language. Always their kindness and interest and the sadness in their voices moved me deeply. They were never too sad, however, to give a quick turn to a phrase. One morning the tram in which we were riding suddenly stopped. Nobody knew why; everybody was complaining. Then from a side street came a handful of Black and Tans with bayonets fixed. I asked the Irishman sitting beside me, "What does that mean?"

"You should know," he replied. "Those are Wilson's Fourteen Pints."

Havelock was a delightful companion, not loquacious, but keenly interested in everything, and forever jotting down his copious notes. We hired a two-wheeled jaunting car in which we sat back to back, and in this way bumped from Glengariff to Killarney. Occasionally the sun broke through for half an hour, but it was wet that year—potatoes and hay were rotting on the ground because the sun did not shine long enough to dry them.

We arrived at the inn, drenched and sopping. Havelock, with his typically English dread of a cold, went to bed, but I stayed up talking with a young woman and three equally young traveling priests—Sinn Feiners all. We chatted desultorily until I happened to mention I had a letter to the widow of the hero, Skeffington, who had been killed in the disturbances.

The company, assuming me to be one with their cause, immediately became most friendly. The girl began discussing higher education for her sex. I asked her how she could keep on when she married and had the inevitable succession of offspring. The priests, somewhat to my surprise, fell in with my ideas by deploring too large families; some of the older sons and daughters had to emigrate, and even those who were left could not care adequately for their parents. It would be better for the Catholic Church as well as for the world if they could help people to have only a few children and bring them up decently. I felt hopeful because they were speaking of birth control as solving some of their own problems; they were saying exactly what I most wanted them to say.

Several happy days we spent at Killarney, exploring on foot, on horseback, and in boats. The men who drove the cart or rowed us through the lakes always knew the old myths of the mountains and poured into our ears tales of leprechauns and other "little people." You heard the word "divil" more than any other. Here the divil, so they told us, had left his step, there he had run away. The shape of every mountain, the twist of every stream had their stories.

Wherever we went women, lean and elderly, wearing tiny shoulder shawls and calico print dresses, fairly started out of the hillsides, bareheaded, barefooted, complexions like roses, and eyes as blue as the sky. Yet their faces were hungry and worn. Getting on in years as they were, they could and did run faster than our ponies. When we spurred forward they came right along, flattering, cajoling, uttering prayers and "God bless you's," calling on all the saints to preserve you if you would buy a drop of "Mountain Dew," which was so good for your health. If you bought this Irish whiskey from one, another took her place, and, quite undiscouraged, began again the flow of sales talk.

One of our last days, when the wraiths of the lake dimmed the emerald hills, we walked to red-bricked Killarney House, to which, as Havelock said, nature was adding her own wild beauty to the beauty that man had made.

All of Ireland had seemed draped in mist and sadness and, lovely as it had been, I never wanted to go back.

Chapter Twenty-two

DO YE HEAR THE CHILDREN WEEPING?

AFTER the Irish interlude I was ready to go on to Germany to carry out the most important objective of my journey abroad. It had become obvious that progress depended on finding a means of contraception, cheap, harmless, easily applied. Way back in 1914 Havelock had seen in some of the last medical journals to come out of Germany an advertisement of a chemical contraceptive. He had mentioned it to me, and ever since I had been eager to track it down. In pre-War Germany every advertised product had been required to live up to the claims made for it; the public must not be misled. Thus I was convinced that if the notice had stated it was to prevent conception, the assertion was true. No news of it had come since the War, and I wished to ascertain whether it was still being manufactured. Perhaps this formula would be the solution to our problem.

I had a secondary reason also for going to Germany—to investigate the decline in the birth rate. It was said half the married women had become barren during the blockade for lack of proper food. I was always looking for evidence to support and strengthen our arguments, and, consequently, wanted to discover what had been learned of the relation between vitamins and fertility.

Berlin was cold and dark when Rose Witcop and I, about eleven at night, arrived at Neuköln, a special proletarian section of the city. The train was late, an unusual state of things in efficient Germany, but this was the period of her greatest disorganization. The telegram which had been sent to Rose's sister and brother-in-law, Milly and Rudolph

Rocker, had apparently not been delivered; nobody met us. There were no taxis, no carriages, no lamps, no lights in the windows to relieve the pitch blackness. A sleepy, disgruntled porter led us across the street to an insignificant hotel. He knocked at the door; a head popped out of a window above. "Two ladies want to stay overnight." The proprietress said she could give us nothing to eat, but that we could have a room. We accepted gladly, climbed up a ladder into the same bed, piled high with feathered mattresses above and below us, and settled ourselves to comforting sleep after the long and tiresome journey.

In the morning, refreshed, we took a tram to the Rockers' small apartment. Rudolph was a syndicalist, a friend of Portet, and had been interned in a concentration camp near London during the War. Both Milly and Rudolph had suffered great privations after their return. But, although food was very scarce, they were more than prodigal and kind in sharing with us.

Germany was still no place for casual visitors in 1920. She seemed dead, crushed, broken. Street traffic, even in a metropolis the size of Berlin, was slight. I noted particularly the grim silence everywhere; people had forgotten how to smile. They were thankful for the Revolution, but it had not brought much relief, and the winter to come was dreaded. Instead of displaying food or clothing, the windows of shop after shop on street after street were decorated only with streamers of colored paper.

Everybody was ravenous for fresh vegetables; money meant nothing, food everything. I saw old peasant women coming in from the country with bags of potatoes on their backs. Fifteen minutes after emptying them on to pushcarts they were sold out. The only fruit to be had were plums, and that is how I remember it was late summer in Berlin; it is curious how such memories crop up.

Ordinarily I could go without eating if I had plenty of water, but in Berlin I found myself haunting grocery stores like a hungry animal, examining each new article avariciously. I cannot as a rule bear tinned milk and will not give it to babies, yet here when I saw a can of American evaporated milk, I found myself viewing it with glowing eyes. I was disgusted with myself. Nothing satisfied my appetite except eggs, and these, along with milk, could be purchased only on prescription from a doctor. Meat was reduced to half a pound a week for each person, but I had no ration card. A neighbor of the Rockers obtained some bread for me and gave me her potatoes although she and her three lovely daughters had only rice as a substitute. I was in tears over her generosity.

For months many families had existed on nothing but turnips. They ate turnip soup, turnips raw, turnips mashed, turnip salad, turnip coffee, until their whole systems revolted physically against the sight of turnips. The contact with other persons in trams, halls, churches, even streets, was nauseating; in a few minutes the fumes of turnip from their bodies was so offensive that they became almost unendurable to themselves.

I went into a two-room home, clean but overflowing with ten children, five born since the War, starvation horribly stamped on their faces. The oldest was twelve—still too young to work. The father, a locksmith, had no job. All were living on a hundred marks received every week from Government Unemployment Insurance. It was now Saturday, and not one crumb or morsel remained to tide them over until the next payment on Monday. They had eaten no breakfast, no dinner, and the father had gone to the woods to search for mushrooms to keep them alive.

Even men who had employment were working only three days a week, averaging a hundred and fifty marks for a family, and marks were fifty to the American dollar. The best food had to be given to them because they were the earners. Women were the real sufferers; they had to go without or subsist on what they could scrape together. They nursed their babies beyond two years to supply milk, and all their time was occupied in a constant hunt to find nourishment for the older ones.

I heard countless stories from mothers who had been tortured by watching their children slowly starve to death—pinched faces growing paler, eyes more listless, heads drooping lower day by day until finally they did not even ask for food. You saw a tiny thing playing on the street suddenly run to a tree or fence and lean against it while he coughed and had a hemorrhage. Others like him were dying of tuberculosis from lack of eggs, butter, and milk—so many cows had been sent to France. Yet they came up to me and offered to sell their prescriptions thinking that I, as a foreigner, had money to buy them; they themselves had none for these luxuries.

The old-fashioned warrior who entered with the sword and killed his victims outright had my respect after witnessing the "peace conditions" of Germany.

The Quaker food stations admitted only children who were ill and only mothers who were more than seven months pregnant or who were nursing babies less than four months old. The spectacle of one of these women bringing two or three of her brood, not sick enough to be regularly fed, to share her own soup was too sad and overwhelming to bear. Those in charge of the distribution wanted each mother herself to eat for the benefit of her unborn child or nursing infant, and were already crowded to capacity, feeding three and four hundred at a time on cocoa and rolls made from white flour. But they could not bring themselves to exclude the little scarecrows with large, starry eyes, pipestem legs, and hands from which the flesh had fallen until they were like claws. On one of my visits the "sister" had them stand up and then asked, "Where have you been?"

"To America," they chorused.

"What have you to say?"

"We love America. We thank America."

I did not instantly comprehend, but it was explained to me that they called the station *Amerika* in token of their gratitude.

To account for the sorry state in which they found themselves the Germans were groping to fix the blame either within their country or on some foreign power. All seemed of the opinion that had the United States not entered the War, none would have been victor and none vanquished; this, they said, would have meant a lasting peace. Yet they felt little animosity towards us. What there was had been largely wiped out by the aid of the Hoover Commission. Furthermore, they still hoped we might be an influence in loosening the Treaty chains which kept them helpless and bound. When I asked them why they had accepted the humiliating terms at Versailles of which they complained so bitterly, they replied they had been told that, had they not done so, vast territories which supposedly had been mined would have been blown up and huge populations would have been annihilated.

The military party accused the Socialists of having stabbed them in the back and brought about defeat through the leadership of such pacifists as Karl Liebknecht and Rosa Luxemburg, who had paid with their lives; the Socialists and workers regretted they had not united with Russia and, combining their own scientific and technical knowledge with her raw materials, conquered the world and thus molded all civilization to their ideals.

Both classes sincerely believed that France wanted to destroy them utterly. I saw something of the reason for their feeling one day when a tram stopped to let off passengers, and a French automobile filled with French officers, instead of halting the prescribed number of feet away, plowed right through, knocking down two people and never even pausing to see what havoc it had created. The spectators gazed at the bodies lying there waiting for the ambulance. They did not dare shake their fists, but anyone could tell from the pitch of their voices, their expressions of passion and anger, how bitter was their resentment.

The women broke down all the reserves of my emotion. They had been at one time the most advanced in Europe, politically, economically, and socially, and, although they had had to work harder at the gymnasiums than the men because higher marks had been required of them, they had been really on a par. But now a frightful retrogression had occurred. Working women had been forced down to a state beside the lower animals; they had become drudges in the fields in place of draft horses. I saw one who could not have been past twenty-five carrying a huge basket of vegetables strapped to her back, the weight of which threw her forward so that I expected any minute to see her go on all fours.

An impressive and tragic poster by Käthe Kollwitz was displayed on various corners. It showed a woman with head thrown back, eyes closed, arms crossed over breast, and was captioned simply, "Waiting." The human figures you saw on the streets looked out of eyes dried by suffering and deepened by hunger. They had no faith, no hope, no philosophy; they were resigned to love or hatred, peace or war, a living death or a sudden end.

Throughout Europe, governments were clamoring for bigger populations; France was offering bonuses for large families. "Our babies are dying; give us more babies." Among European labor groups only the syndicalists of France had recognized excessive population as detrimental to the working classes.

The deficiency in Germany of two million lives sacrificed in the War had been made up by the thousands returned from Alsace-Lorraine, from the former province of Posen, and the deportees from England, France, and Italy. There were not nearly enough positions to go round. Yet the nationalists, who had tried to cover the bitter pill of imperialistic ambitions with a sugar-coating of patriotism, still estimated the world in terms of numerical greatness and women as mere machines in the cradle competition of human production. Even the German Socialists, following in the footsteps of Marx, opposed Malthusianism vigorously in and out of season.

A Neo-Malthusian congress had been held in Dresden in 1912, but the movement then organized by Maria Stritt had practically gone out of existence and its place taken by a more popular demand for the right to abortion. For a single year the statistics of Berlin indicated that out of forty-four thousand known pregnancies twenty-three thousand were terminated by this means, though it was technically illegal. Women were now campaigning for a bill before the Reichstag to permit operations to be performed lawfully in hospitals, where fatalities could be reduced by proper sanitary care. Not one of those with whom I talked believed in abortion as a practice; it was the principle for which they were standing. They were resolved to have no more babies for cannon fodder, nor until they could rear them properly.

Most of the doctors whom I interviewed said that what Germany needed was children and lots of them. I asked one if the medical profession, as a whole, were doing anything to prevent entrance into the world of those children whose backs were so weak that they could never sit up straight, whose bones were too soft to hold the weight of their bodies. He answered abruptly, "By aborting the mothers we are doing our best to cope with conditions as we find them. It is not our work to change them."

I was hounding everybody to learn the whereabouts of the contraceptive formula for which I was searching, and was finally given the name of a gynecologist who should know, if anybody did, where it could be found. I made an appointment, and he greeted me in the most cordial way. When I questioned him about the reported sterility of German women, he agreed with the argument that, the situation being what it was in the country, the population should be checked for the next five years. "Here is a friend indeed," I said to myself.

I then gently brought up the subject of abortion. "Doesn't this seem a ridiculous substitute for contraceptives?"

The doctor rose, his chest sticking out; he buttoned his coat, bowed formally, and inquired, "Where did you say you came from?"

"New York City."

"Are you sure you are not from France or Belgium?"

"Certainly not."

"Nobody who has the welfare of Germany at heart could talk to me as you have this morning. Only enemies could come here to give such information to our women."

I wished he would sit down; he made me nervous. But I went on. "Why is it such an act of enmity to advocate contraceptives rather than abortions? Abortions, as you know yourself, may be quite dangerous, whereas reliable contraceptives are harmless. Why do you oppose them?"

To my horror he replied, "We will never give over the control of our numbers to the women themselves. What, let them control the future of the human race? With abortions it is in our hands; we make the decisions, and they must come to us."

That was not the tone of this doctor alone but also that of most of his confrères.

Thinking that Dr. Magnus Hirschfeld might know about the formula, Havelock had given me a letter to him, and I presented it at the Institute of Sex Psychology, where abnormalities were being studied and treated. This most extraordinary mansion, bestowed by a prince of Bavaria who had himself been cured of inversion by Dr. Hirschfeld, was furnished sumptuously. On the walls of the stairway were pictures of homosexuals—men decked out as women in huge hats, earrings, and feminine make-up; also women in men's clothing and toppers. Further up the steps were photographs of the same individuals after they had been brought back to normality, some of them through adaptation of the Voronoff experiments in the transplantation of sex glands. It was not a place I particularly liked, although I was interested to see how a problem which had cropped up everywhere in the post-War confusion was being attacked.

Dr. Hirschfeld was kind and gave me the address of a firm in Dresden which he believed might be manufacturing the formula, so off I went to that city. It was memorable for my meeting with Maria Stritt, a darling little old lady, as quaint in her way as Dr. Vickery in hers. This tiny aristocrat, like one of the dolls for which her city was famous, had a fine vigorous mind, and spoke English with care and a better choice of words than most Americans. Again I made the rounds of the doctors and again found none concerned over birth control; I went to the address where the formula was supposed to be, only to be directed on to Munich.

Munich, to me the most lovely city in Germany, seemed the most prosperous of any I had visited. I noticed a difference immediately; the streets were cleaner, the people less hungry-looking. There was more food, more clothing in the shops, and much greater activity. It had always been synonymous in my mind with music and *Liebfraumilch,* and I was delighted to be asked to dine at a hotel which I was told was the smartest and gayest in town. "Oh, we envy you. You'll have dancing, you'll have wine, you'll have everything." But it turned out to be a night club in the most blatant New York style, one table elbowing another, the people—Germans, not tourists—dancing to last year's jazz, the whole place shrieking nouveaux riches. This, too, was part of post-War life.

Bavarian *gemütlichkeit* could not be altogether downed. On Saturdays the trams were literally jammed with men and women, young and old, who had put on their climbing clothes, donned their packs, and here hieing themselves away to near-by resorts or to the hills. With them went their guitars or accordions, and when the singing began everybody knew all the words—no tum-de-tum-de-tum. If they did not have their own instruments there was sure to be a wandering musician to play, and the floors of every hostelry or open-air *biergarten* were literally filled with whirling, waltzing figures. Everyone seemed able to enter into the folk dances, although to me they appeared complicated—many steps, much precision, and a great deal of dignity.

Hunger and poverty existed in plenty, however, in the city. Hospitals were lacking in the simplest and most ordinary articles—no soap, no cod-liver oil, no rubber sheets, insufficient clean linen. Even the babies had to lie all day in wet diapers, and consequently the poor little waifs were a sad, miserable lot. Another tragic thing which gave me nightmare for weeks was to see children's mouths covered with running sores, because the sole available meat and milk came from cattle suffering with hoof-and-mouth disease.

Here at Munich the "birth strike" was most violent. The former medical chief of the Communists told me the women of Bavaria were determined to stop having babies; he himself had given information to thousands and had intended to establish clinics all over the state had the Communist Republic remained in power.

Only the preceding spring the Communist red flag had for three weeks flown from the house tops of Munich. I met representatives from both sides of the political arena. The middle- and upper-class conservatives claimed the revolutionists had not been capable of managing affairs, being good agitators but not good organizers—able to start things but not knowing how to finish them. They had not given up their guns; money had been put aside and peasant costumes and boots were ready for escape, because the existing bitterness made it likely the struggle was not yet settled. Communist leaders, on the other hand, claimed they had allowed their enemies to flee and then had been tricked and fooled, and knew at last they could expect no quarter. Their ideals, their faith in humanity, their consideration, had cost them their lives and liberty, and they would not forget this valuable lesson.

At a meeting of the Communist Party I was introduced to Mrs. Erich Mühsam who, with her husband and their friend Landau, had gone to the front and distributed leaflets to call the boys back home. Landau, a gentle soul who so believed in the goodness of man that he had pleaded with the soldiers to be brothers and not to take life, had been kicked and clubbed to death by the White Guard, which had afterwards marched to the Mühsam apartment and, when they could not find anybody there, had wrecked it with machine guns. Fortunately for the Mühsams they were already in jail.

Though the Revolution was supposed to be over, Erich Mühsam was still imprisoned. In every country during such upheavals thousands are cast into jail and, unless some other upheaval occurs to get them out, they remain there; many pacifists in the United States were not freed until long after the Armistice.

In 1928 I saw Erich Mühsam—every inch a poet, an artistic and delicate organism, almost helpless-looking. In 1935, under Nazi rule, he was returned to a concentration camp—a hangover on the black list.

The account of his fellow prisoners ran something like this: One afternoon he had been told to "report at headquarters and bring a rope."

"Where can I find a rope?"

"I don't know. Get it!"

"They're going to kill you," he was warned as he started out, still lacking a rope.

"Oh, it's just one of their jokes—a form of torture."

"You may be right; you've scarcely lifted a voice."

But that evening his comrades discovered him dangling by the neck from a beam. They said he could never have climbed up himself and that, furthermore, he had been beaten to death before he had been hung there.

Nevertheless, officially he had committed suicide.

I met in Germany probably a hundred thorough-going conservatives and only one Mühsam, and yet he it was who stood out spectacularly.

My own interests were keeping me busy enough. I finally found that the formula I was seeking was made in Friedrichshaven, on Lake Constance. I initiated a correspondence with the chemist, asking him to come to Munich, and enclosing stamps to make sure of his reply. He could not make the journey but, instead, invited me to Friedrichshaven.

All the passengers on dismounting at the station seemed to have someone to meet them except myself. I noticed a smallish man with what appeared to be bangs under his hat, front and back, standing on the platform and holding a tight bunch of wild flowers wrapped up in a newspaper, a matching one in the buttonhole of his coat, but as far as I could see he was serving no special purpose there. I went to a hotel, and in a very short while the little man himself arrived, having identified me as the American lady he had come to greet. His quaint bouquet was my welcome to Friedrichshaven.

The chemist, with his father and brothers, ran an unpretentious factory which, in addition to other products, was making the contraceptive in the form of a jelly. It had been put out before the War, then dropped, and was now just starting up again and beginning to find a market in Germany. He feared to let me go near his establishment, suspicious that America might steal his formula. But he showed me a picture of it, and gave me a few sample tubes, saying I could obtain others from his sister, who was going to act as his agent in New York. Thus was inaugurated a new phase in the movement—the use of a chemical contraceptive.

I had letters of introduction to several people in Russia, and had hoped to be able to go there, but I had commenced handing out my extra dresses, underwear, stockings, shoes in Berlin; my friends had so little and were so generous that I could not endure it, and now, in the face of an approaching winter of hardship, without wardrobe and no prospect of securing one or even sufficient food, I had to abandon the Russian plan.

I had talked clinic, clinic, clinic while I was in England. Having myself been convinced, I wanted the Neo-Malthusians also to believe that it was a better way than advice through literature. A few of them were assembling to meet me in the Netherlands, and thither I turned my steps. As soon as the train north was over the border, cream was brought and delicious fruit; the contrast between one side and the other was too obviously brutal and awful. It almost made me ill to see so many delicacies in the Dutch shop windows when children in Germany were starving.

With the Drysdales, to Amsterdam came Dr. Norman Haire, Australian born, a gynecologist who had settled in London, sensed the public interest in birth control, informed himself thoroughly on the subject, written a great deal about it, and become prominent in the movement, advocating contraception from his Harley Street office.

As Dr. Haire and I went around visiting clinics we found that the countless stores where contraceptives were sold had fitting rooms in back with midwives in charge. They did not maintain the old Rutgers standards. I was disappointed to see the deterioration which had taken place since 1915. During the reorganization period of Europe the tendency, under Russian influence, was for young laborites to be in charge of things, and they aimed to turn out Dr. Rutgers and the Dutch Neo-Malthusians and put clinics, which were dedicated to the workers, on a strictly utilitarian basis. Here as elsewhere they could agitate and tear apart but lacked executive ability. The new board, composed mainly of laymen, did not realize that such technical knowledge and experience was required as only a physician like Dr. Rutgers possessed. He was a sad and unhappy man, profoundly discouraged over the odds against which he had to struggle.

Nonetheless, my English friends were converted to the idea of clinics, and Bessie Drysdale and Dr. Haire planned to open one soon in London.

Chapter Twenty-three

IN TIME WE ONLY CAN BEGIN

"Enough, 'tis the word of a Grand Bashaw;
You needn't to bother about the law.
He told me they wasn't to speak at all,
You don't need a warrant to clear a hall.
He told me to tell them to stir their stumps;
When 'Clubs!' is the order, then clubs is trumps.
What else would it be when I'm just a cop
And he is a Reverend Archbishop?"
　　　　　　　　　　　ARTHUR GUITERMAN

IN confirming my conviction in 1918, Judge Frederick E. Crane of the Appellate Division of the Supreme Court of New York had for the first time interpreted the section of the state law which permitted a licensed physician to give contraceptive advice for the "cure or prevention of disease"; and, further, he had taken from *Webster's Dictionary* the broad definition of disease as any alteration in the state of body which caused or threatened pain and sickness, thus extending the meaning of the word far beyond the original scope of syphilis and gonorrhea. But, never satisfied, I wanted women to have birth control for economic and social reasons.

Therefore, in January, 1921, Anne Kennedy and I went to Albany to find a sponsor for a bill which was to change the New York law. It was not only a question of amending it, but also a means of educating the public, of explaining our cause through the medium of legislation. Months of preparation were required, hours of tramping the floors of State buildings at Albany, interviewing one person after another, securing promises of help, breaking down hostility.

When people said that women who would not have children were selfish and preferred lap dogs, I replied, "All right. Then it is better for the children not to be born." That type of woman should die out biologically, just as did the different species that were caught in the mire and slime and could not reproduce themselves. It is a principle that applies to human beings also, that they must work through their environment in order to survive.

As soon as you could get out of people's minds what birth control was not, they almost invariably said, "Why, yes, certainly, that sounds reasonable." Many of the lawmakers themselves believed that the measure might be of great benefit, but the party whip cut too deeply.

Birth control was once described by Heywood Broun as dynamite from the point of view of the politician. If he supported it, he might lose votes; if he opposed it, he might lose votes. "There is nothing a politician hates more than losing votes. He would much rather the subject never came up."

One assemblyman from Brooklyn at first agreed to introduce our bill and then wrote, "I very much regret, but after consulting with some of the leaders of the Assembly, I have been strongly advised not to offer your bill. I am told it would do me an injury that I could not overcome for some time." Another refused on the ground of "levity from his associates." But a few years later we found a young, courageous legislator who introduced a bill and secured hearings. Although it was defeated, the atmosphere was clarified.

Mrs. Hepburn, who had been in the suffrage movement early and had been one of the sponsors of Mrs. Pankhurst's tour of the United States, now lived in Hartford, Connecticut. Although the mother of six, including the actress, Katherine, she retained her youthful face and figure, being almost like a sister to her children, playmate and companion for them at tennis, golf, and swimming. Young men asked her to dinner with the same pleasure that they asked her daughters.

Closely associated with her was Mrs. George H. Day, Sr., a grandmother in 1921. She always came from Hartford for every Board meeting of the League and, in turn, her house was a place of refuge for poor, worn-down friends of causes. They could go there and be ministered to by a staff of servants and come back, rested and rejuvenated.

With two such seasoned campaigners to back us, we carried our legislative activities into Connecticut, the only state where "to use a contraceptive" was a crime—as though it were possible to have a policeman in every home! A mere six years had elapsed since the movement had begun; consequently, that we were now able to get a hearing was in itself a triumph. Nevertheless, no easy task faced us; so much red tape had to be broken through. But here at Hartford we did succeed in finding an introducer who could hold his own under ridicule. Then we had to educate him, feed him with facts—medical, social, historical—so that he could defend his bill.

A young priest stood forth as our chief opponent, basing his objections on the laws of nature, which he claimed were contravened by birth control. Fortunately the committee had a sense of humor. In my ten-minute rebuttal I was able to answer the "against nature" argument as Francis Place had done a hundred years earlier. I turned the priest's own words on himself by asking why he should counteract nature's decree of impaired vision by wearing eyeglasses, and why, above all, was he celibate, thus outraging nature's primary demand on the human species—to propagate its kind. The laughter practically ended the "unnatural" thesis for some time.

In New Jersey another attempt was made. The law there allowed doctors to give information for "a just cause," but they were fearful of including minor ailments under this interpretation. The bill introduced at Trenton had a hearing, but it also failed to pass.

The whole thing was nerve-wracking but was part of the experience we gained. And, furthermore, whenever we had hearings, the local work progressed much more rapidly as a result. Nothing was lost, however expensive the plowing and sowing. Apparent defeats were victories in the long run.

It then seemed to me from glancing over current clippings and publications that people all over the world were discussing birth control. The English Baron Dawson of Penn had been Court Physician to Edward VII and had continued in this same post during the reign of George V. But he had broader interests, too. One of the great events in the history of the movement was his speech at the Church Congress at Birmingham in answer to the doctrine promulgated by the Bishops at Lambeth that sexual union should take place for the purpose of procreation only:

Imagine a young married couple in love with each other being expected to occupy the same room and to abstain for two years. The thing is preposterous. You might as well put water by the side of a man suffering from thirst and tell him not to drink it. Romance and deliberate self-restraint do not to my mind rhyme very well together. A touch of madness to begin with does no harm. Heaven knows life sobers it soon enough.

His speech caused an immense sensation throughout England. Headlines and streamers announced, "King's Physician asks Church to sanction birth control." The deduction was that His Majesty was endorsing it, and stolid Britishers were all agog at the idea that Buckingham Palace was now talking about the subject; it was hinted Queen Mary was not overpleased.

On this side of the Atlantic Major General John J. O'Ryan, who had commanded the Twenty-Seventh National Guard Division, lectured on overpopulation as a cause for war. Frank Vanderlip, once Assistant Secretary of the Treasury and later President of the National City Bank, had just returned from Japan, proclaiming that population must be controlled because some countries could no longer feed themselves. Here was an army man on the one hand, and a financier on the other, unprimed, uncoerced, even uninvited, speaking out of their independent experiences. They were voices in the wilderness, oases in the desert, and certainly encouraging historical landmarks.

Among uneasy experts the sentiment was growing that population pressure in Japan would soon create an inevitable explosion. Indeed, one of the familiar arguments in the United States brought forward against birth control was the "menace of the Yellow Peril," by which was meant specifically, Japan. What folly to reduce our birth rate when Orientals were multiplying so appallingly fast that the downfall of Western civilization might soon be looked for! India and China were teeming indiscriminately, but their peoples were feeble, inert, and diseased; whereas the Japanese were being reared under German health traditions, were ninety-seven percent literate, and were technically equipped for battle.

Naturally I was eager to learn as much about this situation as possible, and welcomed the opportunity to meet the Nipponese friends of

Gertrude Boyle, who had married a gentleman of Japan. They always appeared in pairs or groups of three, four, five at a time, talking busily in asides with each other while I exchanged opinions with one. They were helpful in furnishing me with unpublished facts; the older, conservative, nationalist, militarist party advocated greater numbers, but the young, liberal intellectuals, many of whom had attended Occidental universities, could see the clouds already lowering on the horizon and hoped the storm could be averted by controlled population growth. Atro, a reporter on a New York Japanese paper, had been supplying the last-named group, which in Tokyo called itself Kaizo, meaning reconstruction, with clippings about birth control, and several of my articles had been printed in their publication.

The women's point of view was graphically described to me by the Baroness Shidzué Ishimoto, daughter of the head of the great Hirota clan and wife of Baron Keikichi Ishimoto, a young nobleman who had put in practice his ideals of service. This charming, youthful and gracious matron, tall for her race and equally beautiful by our standards, very smart in her American street costume, had in 1919 come from her own land where suffrage for women was still mentioned in awed tones. She had studied our language at a Y.W.C.A. business school, and in three months had performed the extraordinary accomplishment of mastering it sufficiently to speak, write, and even take dictation in English.

We quickly became friends and she at once foresaw the possibilities of birth control in bringing Japanese women out of their long suppression in the family system. She said she intended to form a league immediately upon her arrival in Tokyo, and did so in 1921.

During that year also clinics were started in England. That of Marie Stopes proved popular, although instruction, given by a midwife, was limited to mothers who had already had at least one child. Shortly afterwards Dr. Haire and Bessie Drysdale, with Harold Cox as chairman of a lay group to finance the work, established Walworth Center, which had a fine gynecological thoroughness and set an example which later clinics in England followed.

It was high time clinics were started in the United States as well. After the Crane decision I had anticipated that hospitals were going to give contraceptive advice. But in 1919, under Dr. Mary Halton's direction, two women, the first with tuberculosis, the other with syphilis, had been taken from one to another institution on Manhattan Island. All had refused such information, although most had agreed that the patients, if pregnant, could be aborted. The officers in charge had said they were obliged to protect their charters, and the staff physicians their licenses and reputations.

Anything depending on the organized medicine is hard to put over; though individual doctors may break away, in the long run most medical progress proceeds by group action.

Since the hospitals were laggard in this matter, I decided to open a second clinic of my own. It was to be in effect a laboratory dealing in human beings instead of mice, with every consideration for environment, personality, and background. I was going to suggest to women that in the Twentieth Century they give themselves to science as they had in the past given their lives to religion.

In addition to the usual rooms I planned to have a day nursery where children could be kept amused and happy while the mothers were being instructed. A properly chosen staff could enable us to have weekly sessions on prenatal care and marital adjustment. Gynecologists were to refer patients to hospitals if pregnancy jeopardized life; a specialist was to advise women in overcoming sterility; a consultant was to deal with eugenics; and, finally, since anxiety and fear of pregnancy were often the psychological causes of ill health, a psychiatrist was to be added. I intended, furthermore, that it should be a nucleus for research on scientific methods of contraception; domestically manufactured supplies of tested efficacy could not, at that time, be procured.

Because organized medical support was lacking, I tried to see what could be done with individuals, writing to various doctors to inquire whether they were willing to sponsor such an undertaking. Several asked me what methods I was recommending, but Dr. Emmett Holt, then the outstanding pediatrician of New York, whose book, *The Care and Feeding of Children,* was the bible of thousands of mothers, invited me to come to his office; before making any endorsement he wanted to know more about it.

I packed up all my European supplies and showed them and explained them to Dr. Holt, who had called in also an obstetrician and a neurologist, Dr. Frederick Peterson, for the discussion. The usual attitude of the child specialist was, "Our living depends upon babies. Why should we advocate limiting the supply? The more the merrier. If you cut down, you're taking our maintenance from us." But Dr. Holt said, "A thoroughly reliable contraceptive would be a godsend to us. If the family cannot afford a nurse we must rely on the health and strength of the mother to keep her baby alive. If pregnancy can be postponed for a few years, not only the baby who has been born, but the baby who comes after is much more likely to survive."

Dr. Holt lent us his name, one of the first important physicians to do so, thus setting an example which eventually others followed. Five or six men and women doctors agreed to stand behind the clinic.

But I had to have more than verbal approval. Unless the clinic were to be conducted by a doctor with a New York practicing license, it would not be there to stay. In early autumn I brought together an interested group to discuss the possibility of a location on the East Side near Stuyvesant Square, and Dr. Lydia Allen de Vilbiss, whom I had met at the Indianapolis social workers' conference, was going to form her own medical committee behind her and build it up. On the basis of her promise, I signed a year's lease for a small suite of rooms at 317 East Tenth Street, from which a dentist had just moved out, appropriately situated on the ground floor in a densely populated section.

The legislative activities and planning for a clinic had taken much of my attention during the year, but the central theme was the determination to hold the First National Birth Control Conference, November 11–13, 1921, at the Plaza Hotel in New York. I timed it purposely to coincide with a meeting of the American Public Health Association, hoping that if we could only convince these officials of the need for birth control, they would use it in their own work.

In addition to the health aspect, we planned to treat of population and also have a doctors' meeting on methods and technique. But "flaming youth" was having its fling, and the great clamor of the moment was directed towards the moral issue. Opponents were constantly hurling the statement that immorality among young people was to be the inevitable fruit of our efforts. This I did not believe. I knew that neither morality nor immorality was an external factor in human behavior; essentially these qualities grew and emerged from within. If the youth of the post-War era were slipping away from sanctioned codes, it was not the fault of birth control knowledge any more than it was the fault of the automobile, which made transportation to the bright lights of the city quick and easy. Immorality as a result should not be placed at the door of Messrs. Ford or Chrysler.

In order to have a free and fair hearing we proposed a large open meeting to wind up the Conference, and invited ministry and clergy of all denominations, including Archbishop Patrick J. Hayes, who was the spokesman of the Catholic Church in New York.

The movement was older in England and had already established its dignity there. Consequently, the presence at the Conference of such an outstanding Englishman as Harold Cox was certain to carry weight. To persuade him to take the sea voyage I sailed for Europe. When I arrived in London I found him unwell, and his doctors at first refused him permission to travel. Under the circumstances it was very fine of him to promise to come. J. O. P. Bland also said he would look in on the Conference if only to give it his blessing. He was a dark-haired, witty, amusing North-of-Irishman who had lived much in the Orient and become an authority on Far Eastern matters, an internationalist in all his thinking. He was one of those who always helped to hold up your right hand.

My object in England having been attained, I went on to Switzerland with a definite aim; I had formed a habit in my nursing days, when I was waiting in the night to give medicine or treatment to a patient, of occupying the time putting down experiences and thoughts that came to me. The same habit continued. After lectures, while I was still sizzling with excitement, I often relieved the tenseness by writing down answers to questions I feared I had not covered adequately. Before I knew it I had material gathered for a book, and even some chapters in rough draft. They needed pulling together and polishing off and I went to bed in Montreux for a month to do this. I had regarded *Woman and the New Race* as my heart book; this, *The Pivot of Civilization,* was to be my head book. I brought it back with me to the United States and Wells, who was reporting the Washington Disarmament Conference for the New York *World,* wrote an introduction.

To make our Conference a success it had to be under the auspices of an organization. I had always had a dread of them. I knew their weaknesses and the stifling effect they could have. They seemed heavy and ponderous, rigid, lifeless, and soulless, often caught in their own mechanism to become dead wood, thus defeating the very purposes for which they had initially been established. Even the women who were able and clever at systematizing such bodies terrified me with their rule-and-rote minds, their weight-and-measure tactics; they appeared so sure, so positive that I felt as if I were in the way of a giant tractor which destroyed mercilessly as it went.

In spite of this dread I had reasoned out the necessity for an organization to tie up the loose ends. Although it might be limiting and inhibiting to the individual, it had other advantages of strength and solidity which would enable it to function when the individual was gone. Therefore I sent a questionnaire to leaders in social and professional circles, asking them whether the time had not come for such a national association; the replies almost unanimously confirmed this decision.

The evening before the Conference was to open, a few friends gathered together to launch the American Birth Control League. Its aims were to build up public opinion so that women should demand instruction from doctors, to assemble the findings of scientists, to remove hampering Federal statutes, to send out field workers into those states where laws did not prevent clinics, to co-operate with similar bodies in studying population problems, food supplies, world peace. After the dinner, given at Mrs. George F. Rublee's home, we talked over specific plans for the year and set in motion the machinery for having the League incorporated.

Juliet Barrett Rublee had been one of the pioneers, a member of the original Committee of One Hundred, and all the way through the years she has never wavered from my side. No more inspired idealist was ever initiated into a movement. The imagination of this picturesque, romantic wife of a conservative lawyer had been so fired that she dedicated to it her entire devotion, loyalty, partisanship. Others had rallied their own personal friends around the idea, but Juliet's influence brought in her husband's associates—the Cravaths, Morrows, Lamonts, Dodges, and Blisses.

Juliet's parties were always gay and interesting, with an atmosphere nobody else could create. Her small, engaging dining room was as colorful as she herself—the only woman I ever knew who dared to wear bright greens, reds, yellows, all together. For lunches, teas, and dinners in behalf of the cause she practically turned over her home in Turtle Bay Gardens.

A goodly number attended the opening of our Conference, which, appropriately, coincided with that of the great disarmament conference at Washington. The medical meeting, where contraceptive technique was discussed, was so crowded that latecomers could not squeeze in. The doctors who did find places, each apparently surprised to see his confrères there, expected us to have a hundred percent sound methods; they seemed disappointed because we had no magic up our sleeves and told them quite frankly we had not. The best we could do was show what devices were being employed, including those from the Netherlands and the preparation I had found at Friedrichshaven, with the warning that they had not been tested for efficacy.

After two full days nothing remained but the Sunday evening mass meeting on "Birth Control, Is It Moral?" For this we had selected the Town Hall on West Forty-third Street, a new club designed as a forum for adult education; the auditorium was often used for discussion of questions of civic interest. Harold Cox was to deliver the first speech and I was to follow.

Always, when I am to speak, I attempt to visualize the hall and the audience in order to feel my way into the subject. When I cannot do so, I have invariably been met by blocked doors. Throughout Sunday, try as I would to "tune in" to the approaching event, I could not do it. I kept remembering a dream I had had the night before in which I was carrying a small baby in my arms up a very steep hill and came rather abruptly to a slope which became a mountain side of rock and slippery shale; I had nothing to grasp to prevent me from sliding. The baby cried continually and I wanted to comfort it, but I dared not use my right hand because it was held up like a balancing rod which saved us both from falling. That miserable dream made me drowsy all day. My brain seemed numb. I simply could not think of what I was going to say.

Anne Kennedy had gone ahead to the Town Hall at about seven o'clock. Harold Cox and I had dined at Juliet's but I could not eat; I was interested neither in the food nor the conversation. I still had an absolute blank in front of me. Juliet was congratulating me that soon, with the Conference over, I could have a rest. Ordinarily when I am approaching the end of a particular job I begin to feel released, but this time I could not reassure her; I was nervous, anxious, and apprehensive.

Our taxi swung into West Forty-third Street and crept cautiously along through a swarming aggregation. "Heavens!" I said. "This *is* an overflow with a vengeance."

We dismounted and pushed our way to the Town Hall doors. They were closed and two policemen barred our path when Mr. Cox and I attempted to enter. "This gentleman is one of the speakers and I am another," I said. "Why can't we go in?"

"There ain't gonna be no meeting. That's all I can say."

I had not the faintest idea of what was happening. A newspaper man standing near by suggested, "Why not call up Police Commissioner Enright and see what the trouble is?"

Juliet and I rushed across the street to a booth and she telephoned police headquarters. No one could say where the Commissioner was. As far as they knew no orders to forbid the meeting had been issued.

Then I put through a call for Mayor Hylan. While I was waiting for the connection I kept my eyes on the Town Hall entrance and saw that policemen were cautiously opening the doors to let out driblets of people. If they could get out I could get in, so I abandoned the telephone and wove my way through the throng until I reached the doors, slipping in under the policemen's arms before they could stop me. Dignified health officers from all over the country, lawyers and judges with their families and guests were standing about, grumbling, vague, reluctant to depart, wondering what to do.

I fairly flew up the aisle but halted in front of the footlights; they were as high as my head and another blue uniform was obstructing the steps leading to the stage. Suddenly Lothrop Stoddard, the author, tall and strong, seized me and literally tossed me up to the platform. A messenger boy was aimlessly grasping flowers which were to be presented after my speech. Stoddard grabbed them briskly, handed them to me, and shouted, "Here's Mrs. Sanger!"

"Don't leave!" I called to the audience. "We're going to hold the meeting."

A great scramble began to get back into the seats. The hall was in a turmoil; the front doors had been stampeded and those in the street were pressing in, only to find their places gone. The boxes and galleries were soon filled, the stage was jammed, hundreds were crowded in the rear. I cried, "Get in out of the aisles!" I knew the meeting could be legally closed if they were blocked, and I did not want fire regulations to be used as a pretext.

I still had no idea of what had gone on earlier when I commenced my lecture, but had uttered no more than ten or twelve words when two policemen loomed up beside me and said, "You can't talk here." A thundering applause broke out as though it were the only relief for angry, indignant, rebellious spirits.

"Why can't I?"

I started again but my voice could not be heard. I then suggested to Harold Cox, "Perhaps they'll let you speak. Try it." This white-haired and pink-cheeked gentleman walked to the edge of the platform with a dignity of bearing about as distantly removed from immorality as could be imagined. "Ladies and gentlemen," he began, "I have come from across the Atlantic—" but that was as far as he got before he was led back to his seat by a policeman.

Then Mary Winsor, an ardent suffragette, sprang up, but they stopped her also. As soon as one was downed, another jumped to his or her feet. I did not know the names of some of the volunteers, who were not even allowed to finish their "Ladies and gentlemen."

Meanwhile, Anne Kennedy was telling me as best she could what had happened prior to my arrival. When the house had been half filled, a man had come to the platform and asked, "Who's in charge?"

"I am," Anne had answered.

"This meeting must be closed."

"Why?"

"An indecent, immoral subject is to be discussed. It cannot be held."

"On what authority? Are you from the police?"

"No, I'm Monsignor Dineen, the Secretary of Archbishop Hayes."

"What right has he to interfere?"

"He has the right." Here he turned to a policeman. "Captain, speak up."

"Who are you?" Anne had demanded.

"I'm Captain Donohue of this district. The meeting must be stopped."

Capable and cool-headed Anne had replied, "Very well, we'll write this down and I'll read it to the audience. 'I, Captain Thomas Donohue, of the Twenty-sixth Precinct, at the order of Monsignor Joseph P. Dineen, Secretary to Archbishop Patrick J. Hayes, have ordered this meeting closed.' "

The listeners had sat petrified while she had read them this strange admission. No hissing or booing then. They had just sat. It was one thing to have the hall shut by a mistaken or misguided police captain; a very different thing to have it done by a high dignitary of the Roman Catholic hierarchy.

Monsignor Dineen was now stationed in the back of the hall, and Anne pointed him out to me, of medium size, in plain attire, calmly directing the police by a casual nod of the head or a whisper to a man who acted as runner between him and the Captain on the platform.

Confusion and tumult continued for at least an hour. Newspaper men were scribbling stories; those who could not get in were creating commotion outside; the reserves had been summoned. It was bedlam. Miss Winsor tried to speak two or three times; I, at least ten. But I knew that I had to keep on until I was arrested in order that free speech might be made the issue. To allow yourself to be sent home at the order of the police was accepting the police point of view as to what was moral. Moreover you were bound for the principle of the thing to carry it into the court for a legal decision; if the pulpit and press were denied you, you must take it to the dock.

Captain Donohue kept repeating to me, "Please get off this stage before you cause disorder." Police now began to hustle the audience towards half a dozen exits, and finally Miss Winsor and I were put under arrest; Robert McC. Marsh, Mrs. Delafield's son-in-law, offered to act as our counsel.

Juliet said to an officer, "Why don't you arrest me too?"

"Well, you can come along if you like," he agreed. So we walked together up Broadway to the station at West Forty-seventh Street, policemen flanking us. The crowd, still jeering the reserves, who had been trying vainly to clear the way, fell in line and marched behind us. A patrol wagon then took us to night court where we were arraigned before Magistrate McQuade. Someone had telephoned J.J. and he came up later, but Mr. Marsh had already taken care of the necessary formalities. We were released on our own recognizances, to appear at court the following morning.

It was now some time after midnight, but we all went back to Juliet's apartment. Harold Cox was shocked, not only by the roughness of the police, but also by the supineness of the audience, which had done nothing but make a noise. "Had this been in London, they would never have been able to stop the meeting! We would have defended our rights, used every chair and door and window to barricade the place, even though we might have been beaten in the end."

Anne Kennedy had brought the reporters, and they were waiting for us. They wanted to make out a story of police stupidity and let it go at that, unable to believe her when she told them it was the Archbishop who was responsible. A *Times* reporter called up the "Power House," as St. Patrick's Cathedral was colloquially termed, reached Dineen himself, and asked for verification. "Yes," said the Monsignor, "we closed the meeting."

Then and there we decided to hold a second one as soon as possible at the same place.

It was well on towards five o'clock when at last I fell in my bed. I sank to slumber, but it was only to find myself still carrying that same baby up the steep and sliding mountain, balancing myself with upraised hand. The sky was dark, the way unmarked. Wearily I stumbled on.

Chapter Twenty-four

LAWS WERE LIKE COBWEBS

*"And heard great argument,
About it and about; but evermore
Came out by the same door wherein I went."*
EDWARD FITZGERALD

PROMPTLY at nine the morning after the wretched Town Hall affair Miss Winsor and I appeared before Magistrate Joseph E. Corrigan and the case was dismissed in five minutes. Neither Monsignor Dineen nor Captain Donohue was in court. Here was a ridiculous thing—the Catholic Church held such power in its hands that it could issue orders to the police, dissolve an important gathering of adult and intelligent men and women, and send them home as though they were naughty children—and then not feel called upon to give any accounting.

The papers expressed the greatest indignation. Even the most conservative were placed in the trying situation of defending birth control advocates or endorsing a violation of the principle of free speech, which "must always find defenders if democracy is to survive." It was to be expected that the *World* would be up in arms, but the *Times* carried a headline that Archbishop Hayes had closed the meeting, and the *Tribune* was spurred on by the indignation of Mrs. Ogden Reid, who had been present at the Town Hall.

Apparently the Church had not expected to render any explanation whatsoever. Then, faced with a battery of reporters, Monsignor Dineen made a statement:

The Archbishop had received an invitation from Mrs. Margaret Sanger to attend the meeting, and I went as his representative. The Archbishop is delighted and pleased at the action of the police, as am

I, because . . . I think any one will admit that a meeting of that character is no place for growing children. . . . The presence of these four children at least was a reason for police action.

He had not improved his position. The scoffing was redoubled when it was learned that the four "children" were students of Professor Raymond Moley's class in sociology at Columbia University; Monsignor Dineen had not seen beyond their bobbed hair.

Only a small section of the public had been aware of our modest little conference; even fewer had known of the proposed Town Hall meeting. Now the publicity was tremendous. Many Catholics themselves condemned Church tactics, and Archbishop Hayes had to defend himself:

As a citizen and a churchman, deeply concerned with the moral well-being of our city, I feel it a public duty to protest . . . in the interest of thousands of . . . distressed mothers, who are alarmed at the daring of the advocates of birth control in bringing out into an open, unrestricted, free meeting a discussion of a subject that simple prudence and decency, if not the spirit of the law, should keep within the walls of a clinic. . . . The law was enacted under the police power of the Legislature for the benefit of the morals and health of the community. . . . The law of God and man, science, public policy, human experience, are all condemnatory of birth control as preached by a few irresponsible individuals.

The seventh child has been regarded traditionally with some peoples as the most favored by nature. Benjamin Franklin was the fifteenth child, John Wesley the eighteenth, Ignatius Loyola was the eighth, Catherine of Siena, one of the greatest intellectual women who ever lived, was the twenty-fourth. It has been suggested that one of the reasons for the lack of genius in our day is that we are not getting the ends of the families.

This statement appeared synchronously with our second meeting. The Town Hall had been booked ahead for several weeks; consequently, we had engaged the big Park Theater in Columbus Circle. It was packed fifteen minutes after a single door was opened. Dr. Karl Reiland of St. George's Church was a new recruit on the platform; otherwise our program was the same as before, and a balanced and poised discussion proceeded without acrimony or excitement. Outside, however, two thousand people were clamoring to get in, even climbing up the fire escapes. Orators were haranguing from soapboxes, men were pounding each other with their fists, Paulist fathers were selling pamphlets against birth control.

In my open letter of reply to Archbishop Hayes I said:

I agree with the Archbishop that a clinic is the proper place to give information on birth control. . . . I wish, however, to point out the fact that there are two sides to the subject under consideration—the practical information as distinct from the theoretical discussion. The latter rightly may be discussed on the public platform and in the press as the Archbishop himself has taken the opportunity to do.

And then, citing Scripture:

If the Archbishop will recall his Bible history, he will find that some of the more remarkable characters were the first children, and often the only child as well. For instance, Isaac was an only child, born after long years of preparation. Isaac's only children were twins —Jacob, the father of all Israel, and Esau. Samuel, who judged Israel for forty years, was an only child. John the Baptist was an only child, and his parents were well along in years when he was born.

Archbishop Hayes delivered his final pronunciamento in his Christmas Pastoral:

Children troop down from Heaven because God wills it. He alone has the right to stay their coming, while He blesses at will some homes with many, others with but few or with none at all. . . . Even though some little angels in the flesh through moral, mental, or physical deformity of parents may appear to human eyes hideous, misshapen, a blot on civilized society, we must not lose sight of this Christian thought that under and within such visible malformation there lives an immortal soul to be saved and glorified for all eternity among the blessed in Heaven.

Heinous is the sin committed against the creative act of God, who through the marriage contract invites man and woman to co-operate with him in the propagation of the human family. To take life after its inception is a horrible crime; but to prevent human life that the Creator is about to bring into being is satanic. In the first instance, the body is killed, while the soul lives on; in the latter, not only a body, but an immortal soul is denied existence in time and in eternity. It has been reserved to our day to see advocated shamelessly the legalizing of such a diabolical thing.

A monstrous doctrine and one abhorrent to every civilized instinct, that children, misshapen, deformed, hideous to the eye, either mentally or constitutionally unequipped for life, should continue to be born in the hope that Heaven might be filled!

General opinion was that controversy gave us free publicity, and it did, column after column, but to my mind it was of the negative kind. The truths falsified and motives aspersed had to be debated, corrected, and argued away, and this took time from constructive work. The press wanted to keep up the excitement and manufacture news, but I did not. As a matter of fact the hullabaloo was usually done for me; the blundering of the opposition often saved my voice.

The correspondence through the press was dropped, but meanwhile the American Civil Liberties Union, spurred on by Albert de Silver, from whom we had previously sought advice and who had helped us raise funds, had urged me to institute action for false arrest. This I knew would be a fruitless task, but I did consent to the demand for an investigation. Commissioner Enright was said to be out of the city, but Chief Inspector Lahey, acting in his place, was to determine whether charges should be preferred against Captain Donohue for having stopped the meeting.

On December 2nd, in a small room closed to the press, Mr. Lahey sat at the head of a long table. On his right was a chair to which I was called. On his left, opposite me, was a heavy man with a big bulldog head, wearing a black alpaca coat. He fixed his eyes straight on mine as though he intended to hypnotize me and influence by sheer terror what I was to say. His features were so set, his expression so immobile, that I sensed animus. I refused to return his gaze but faced the Inspector instead.

The interrogation, prompted by this sinister individual, who bent over occasionally to murmur into Mr. Lahey's ear, held bitter malice. Nevertheless, I answered every query as completely and as honestly as I was able. I had nothing to hide, and still believed that my interlocutor could arrive at no decision unless he heard the truth in its entirety. I was all for telling it.

But never throughout any of the hearings could either the examiners or police be kept to the point. They were not genuinely trying to find out who had given the orders and why, but attempting to justify the illegal proceedings; and always they went off into vague irrelevancies extraneous to the issue, such as trying to embarrass dignified, elderly witnesses by asking, "What are you doing with birth control?"

Chiefly the investigation focused around the Brownsville clinic raid. I denied emphatically that certain contraceptives for use by men only had ever been there; they were of a type which I did not recommend, and had been brought in by the police themselves.

"Do you mean to say, Mrs. Sanger," went on Mr. Lahey, "that this statement of the police officer as written into the records was untrue?"

"I do."

Mr. Lahey lifted an official finger to an attendant. The door of the anteroom opened and Mrs. Whitehurst, who had been the leader of the raid, was dramatically framed before us.

"Do you say that if she," he waved to her, "made the statement referred to in the police records, she lied?"

"She did," I affirmed. This was the first time in all my life that I had ever called a person a liar. I felt as though I had stepped down into the lower brackets of common decency, but the police are accustomed to such words, and I had to meet the circumstances.

Mrs. Whitehurst was instantly dismissed. I, too, was dismissed, and Juliet took my place. She had learned from her husband and other lawyers how witnesses could protect themselves, and tossed off her answers readily, now and then returning, "I don't know," and, frequently, "I don't remember." The black-coated gentleman who had hoped to trip her up but was getting nowhere, became exasperated and said roughly to Mr. Lahey, "Oh, stop this! Ask her if she's read the law."

Juliet admitted she had read Section 1142, but, to further questioning, replied she did not recall when, she had not read it in my presence, she might or might not have talked it over with me.

Mr. Lahey rose and left the room. Then the Unknown shouted to a young Irishman who had been busily taking notes, "Arrest that woman!"

We could not have been more astonished if a thunderbolt had struck the place. For a few seconds, which seemed longer, everyone was paralyzed. At last Mr. Marsh asked, "On what grounds is Mrs. Rublee arrested?"

"She has violated Section 1142."

"She said she had read the law—is that a crime?"

No answer.

Mr. Marsh then inquired, "On whose authority is Mrs. Rublee arrested?"

Dead silence. No reply while the Unknown and the stenographer muttered together. Finally, when Mr. Marsh repeated the question, the latter replied, "I do. I arrest her on my own authority. Patrolman Thomas J. Murphy."

Mr. Marsh said to the Unknown, "It's customary for brothers of the law to give each other their names. Mine is Robert Marsh, practicing attorney. May I not know with whom I am speaking?"

"I'm just a bystander."

"Well, Mr. Bystander, won't you instruct the police officer to be more explicit in his statement of facts?"

"Look here, Marsh, I'm telling you the officer is arresting this witness on his own initiative."

He, too, left the room.

Juliet, Mr. Marsh, and I entered her car and young Stenographer-Patrolman Murphy, obviously ill at ease, sat beside the chauffeur. At the Elizabeth Street Court, Magistrate Peter A. Hatting smiled cheerfully at us from behind his desk, "Well, where's the prisoner?"

Murphy made a feeble gesture in Juliet's direction and said in a whisper which we could overhear, "It's a birth control case."

"Oh, I see. Well, what was she selling—where are the articles?"

Murphy could produce none.

"Well, well, where is the evidence?"

Murphy looked even more embarrassed, mumbled that he didn't have any.

"Well, the court is adjourned anyway, and we'll have to wait until this afternoon."

I was turning my back on Murphy, very cross at him, but Juliet asked him to lunch with us. "He didn't want to arrest me, did you, Mr. Murphy?" And Mr. Murphy shook his head most decidedly.

While we ate, he explained that our Unknown was Assistant Corporation Counsel Martin W. Dolphin, with offices in the Police Department, that he himself was Mr. Dolphin's private secretary, that he had been brought to the inquiry merely to take dictation, that he had been only ten months on the force, that he had never arrested anybody before, and that when Mr. Dolphin had said to arrest Mrs. Rublee he had protested, "Why, I can't arrest her. I haven't seen her do anything to be arrested for!"

"I'm awfully sorry," he went on, addressing Juliet, "but I had to obey orders. If I didn't, I'd be in an awful mess. Gee, why didn't they get some of the old fellows down there to do it?"

When we returned to court, Assistant District Attorney Wilson said to Magistrate Hatting, "Your Honor, I have no evidence in this case. The police have furnished nothing to the District Attorney's office. If I have not sufficient evidence by three-thirty I'll dismiss the whole thing."

Then we waited. Eventually the expected "minutes and statement" arrived. Murphy swore that they were true—to Juliet's wholehearted disgust. Her faith in human nature had been betrayed; she did not see why he preferred to keep his job rather than his self-respect. Magistrate Hatting seemed anxious to make everybody comfortable—Juliet, the Catholics, the police, and the public—and to convey the impression nobody was really to blame.

Since the wife of a prominent lawyer had become involved, people in high places in New York had an obligation to protect their own. Publicity had been great before; now it was multiplied tenfold. A letter was addressed to Mayor Hylan:

> The action of the Police Department . . . constitutes such a wilful violation of the right of free speech as to cause grave alarm to the citizens of New York, who have a right to know why such outrages have taken place, what motives and influences are behind them, and whether any conspiracy exists in the Police Department to deny the right of free speech and the equal protection of the law to citizens of New York. This obviously is a matter of the gravest concern.
>
> We, therefore, ask an immediate and full investigation to be followed, if the evidence warrants, by such disciplinary measures against the officials found to be guilty as will discourage similar offenses hereafter.

This demand was signed by Henry Morgenthau, Sr., Herbert L. Satterlee, Paul D. Cravath, Lewis L. Delafield, Charles C. Burlingham, Samuel H. Ordway, Pierre Jay, Paul M. Warburg, Charles Strauss, Montgomery Hare.

As a result, Mayor Hylan delegated David F. Hirshfield, Commissioner of Accounts, to supervise an investigation into the previous investigation. The first session was diverted into a discussion of the merits of birth control. The Commissioner was facetious, and, when Mr. Marsh kept after him for interrupting witnesses and getting off the subject, finally said he had been insulted and refused to continue as long as Mr. Marsh represented us.

At the three subsequent hearings Emory R. Buckner took charge of our interests. Dolphin, although summoned, did not appear at any of them. Captain Donohue testified that Desk Lieutenant Joseph Courtney had received the information over the telephone, and had passed it on to him. So far as he knew it was the telephone operator who had given the orders to close the meeting. But he would, he said, have done so anyhow.

"What law did Mrs. Sanger violate?" asked Mr. Buckner.

"She was disorderly. I requested her several times to leave the platform and she defied me and said she would not do it. She caused quite a commotion and people were all hollering and yelling, a general commotion."

"You think it was a crime for her to commence to speak after a Captain of Police had told her not to?"

"Yes."

"Was Miss Winsor also arrested because she attempted to speak after being told to keep quiet?"

"She said she knew a woman who had nine children and the audience commenced to holler and try to pull the policemen off the stage."

Even the Commissioner was becoming annoyed at Donohue's inanities. He said to Mr. Buckner, "You do not have to put any witnesses on to show the intelligence and the lack of sight or foresight of the Captain. You and I, I think, will agree on that point." And then he turned to Donohue. "Now, Captain, will you tell me the reason for acting in the Hall as you did to prevent that meeting? You see, I do not know whether you understand me or not. You policemen, you do not usually understand ordinary language. I want to know what was in your mind; why did you act as you did, that is all."

"Because I had orders to do so." But he would not admit they came from any further back than the Desk Lieutenant.

Officer Murphy was put on the stand next, and the Commissioner gave him a chance to explain what had prompted him to make the arrest. "I figured this way. If it would be a crime to run such a meeting or hold such a meeting in the City of New York according to the Penal Law, if Mrs. Rublee was an assistant with Mrs. Sanger or anybody else in running such a meeting, and there were distributed circulars regarding prevention of conception, Mrs. Rublee was just as much responsible for the distribution of these circulars as anybody else."

"The circulars stated there would be a public mass meeting at Town Hall on birth control," said Mr. Buckner promptly. "Is that a crime?"

The Commissioner interrupted. "Mr. Buckner, you do not expect this young man to be interested in that. He is too young to know about birth control. The old, bald-headed ones are the only ones that are interested in it."

And late in the afternoon he said, "I am too busy and have too much work to do, so we won't have any summing up."

At the concluding session Desk Lieutenant Courtney disclaimed all liability, saying the only order given to Captain Donohue was to take a number of policemen to the meeting and see that the law was not violated; thereafter the Captain had acted on his own responsibility.

As far as I was concerned the final scene in the farce took place before the elderly and firm Judge John W. Goff, one of the official referees of the Supreme Court who was to hear the charges before the New York Bar Association as to whether Dolphin should be disbarred. He was summoned again in vain until Judge Goff said angrily, "Unless he comes within the hour, I'll subpoena him," and at last, still in his alpaca coat, he put in an appearance. I was on the stand almost an entire afternoon during which the attorney representing Dolphin was attacking me personally instead of inquiring into Juliet's arrest.

"Do you know Carlo Tresca?"

"Yes."

"Do you know Alexander Berkman?"

"Yes."

I could now see what was coming; radicals were always made the whipping boys and, in lieu of specific charges, any acquaintance with them was made to seem incriminating.

"Do you know Emma Goldman?" Here the attorney's voice rose in outrage, and he looked at Judge Goff as though to say, "There you have it."

"Yes," I reiterated, "but I also know Mrs. Andrew Carnegie and Mr. John D. Rockefeller, Jr. My social relations are with people of varying ideas and opinions."

The next attempt was a subtle sort of third degree, aiming to confuse me and imply I was an inaccurate witness. "What was the precise time you entered the room where Mrs. Rublee was arrested? How large was it? How long, how wide, how high, how many windows were there? Who was called first? Where were you sitting? How far was Inspector Lahey from your chair? Were you second, third, or fourth on the right side or left side? How wide was the table, how long? Where was the door located relative to the table?"

Usually I could not have remembered one such immaterial and unnecessary detail. But that afternoon I was given second sight. I could visualize the room; my mind seemed to be projected into it so that every particular stood out with the utmost clarity. It was an excellent lesson to me; thereafter I observed much more carefully.

After hours of this cross-examination I was physically exhausted, as though I had been flung back and forth, beaten and pounded from the bottom of my feet to the top of my head. I almost looked at my arms to see whether they were black and blue, they ached so.

It was all useless. The police went unreprimanded, Donohue was promoted when things had quieted down, and Dolphin, though Judge Goff recommended prosecution and the Court of Appeals stated that his conduct was "arbitrary and unlawful," was not disbarred because he had not been acting in an official capacity when he had ordered the arrest. In spite of the inconvenience, the humiliation of halls closed covenants broken—exactly nothing happened.

Chapter Twenty-five

ALIEN STARS ARISE

IN the summer of 1921 I had signed a contract with the Kaizo group, which had arranged a series of lectures in Japan by four speakers: Albert Einstein was to explain relativity, Bertrand Russell the consequences of the Peace of Versailles, H. G. Wells his version of international accord, and I was to discuss population control, delivering in March and April eight to ten lectures of five hours each. The five-hour clause I innocently believed to be merely a mistake on the part of the translator, but I had faith in the common sense of human nature and expected the error to be taken care of when I arrived.

January and February were months of feverish activity. I spoke in city after city—Boston, Baltimore, Philadelphia, and elsewhere—rushing back to New York to Town Hall hearings and farewell luncheons and dinners. The prolongation of the Town Hall episode had been entirely unforeseen. If bookings had not already been made requiring my departure in February, I should have postponed the trip. But I had promised, and lecture dates were binding obligations.

Stuart was at Peddie Institute where my brother Bob had gone, captain of his football team, preparing for college, having a full and rich time. Grant was there also but he was barely thirteen; I could not bear to put the broad Pacific between us. The headmaster warned me that he was only beginning to adjust himself to the school and his studies, and would be set back at least a year if I took him with me. I agreed to reconsider, but I am afraid I had made up my mind beforehand.

With scant ceremony and scarcely enough clean shirts, I bundled him up and away, leaving the turbulence of New York behind.

Since Grant was to travel on my passport, I had to have it renewed, and had telegraphed Washington for it to be sent to the West Coast where the detail of a visa could also be attended to. At San Francisco it was waiting. With the little book and Grant in tow I presented myself to the Japanese Consul. Instead of stamping it as the usual mere formality, he examined it carefully and then, apologizing profusely, regretted very much that the Japanese Imperial Government could not give me a visa.

Here was a state of things. I asked him whether he could find out the precise reasons. Was it that I as a person could not go there, or was my subject taboo? The next day, after a cable to Tokyo and much polite bowing, he notified me it was both. In varying degrees of amusement and indignation the papers published the fact that the Japanese were turning the tables on the United States; by our Exclusion Act we had implied they were undesirable citizens, and now it was an American who was undesirable to them.

The steamship company would not sell me tickets on the *Taiyo Maru* without the visa. Two days previous to her sailing a Japanese who had been in the United States for the Washington Conference proffered a letter of introduction. He deplored the action of his Government and was desirous of being helpful. "The *Taiyo Maru* is going on to Shanghai. Why don't you get a Chinese visa?"

I always chose to go forward, and there was always a chance that a way might open. A hundred and fifty Japanese who had been at the conference—delegates, professors, doctors, members of the diplomatic corps, secretaries—were returning by this same vessel. Once on board I could meet them simply and informally, and I was sure I could convince them I was not dangerous. The Chinese Consul granted a visa without question, our tickets were delivered, we sailed on the *Taiyo Maru*.

I had never before been on a Japanese liner. The segregation between whites and Orientals horrified me. Here were the aristocrats of a people by nature intelligent, well-bred, well-clothed, inclined to be friendly, taking Grant under their wing, and teaching us both, amid much laughter, to eat with chopsticks. They had made valiant efforts to adapt themselves to Occidentalism; they had altered their dress and fashion of eating—substituting coats, collars, shoes for loose kimonos and soft felt slippers, forks and knives for chopsticks; they sat on chairs instead of kneeling comfortably on the floor. Yet my compatriots kept themselves aloof. Never did I see the two groups together in conversation; they joined only in sports.

At night members of the crew wrestled in the moonlight, and I gazed down at their deck, marveling at the grips, the holds, the stoutness of legs, the strength of backs and arms, the quickness of action, the primitive, guttural calls of the umpires. Others of the crew stamped their feet and, for good luck, threw pinches of salt towards their respective champions.

Two days out the Japanese asked me to address them. I willingly complied, and the dining room was closed off for the purpose. Admiral Baron Kato, who was later to be Prime Minister, and headed the delegation, talked to me afterwards. He had the culture, courtesy, restraint, and suavity of a true gentleman, rather than the mien of the war lord his title seemed to imply.

Equally genial was Masanao Hanihara, then Vice Minister of Foreign Affairs and destined to be Ambassador to the United States. He knew American ways and manners, or mannerisms, if you wish to name them so; he was understanding, and perhaps one of the most fluent of the Japanese I met in the ease of his English. He told me his people were not likely to accept the idea of birth control as a social philosophy, though they were bound to accept the economic aspects, and all the young would be interested as individuals.

Not until later did I learn how happily my contact with these two gentlemen had resulted. They had separately cabled their Government asking that I be allowed to lecture in Japan.

At Honolulu I had one short afternoon into which to crowd so much. With leis hung about my neck I was whisked off for lunch to a magical house at Waikiki, then to a big meeting. What surprised and pleased me most was the complete absence of race prejudice. I looked out over faces, mostly American but with a liberal sprinkling of Chinese and Japanese in their native costumes and Hawaiians in bright Mother Hubbards. Honolulu was the only place I had found where, class for class, internationalism did exist.

Two Japanese correspondents followed my zigzag trail, notebooks in hand, pencils working furiously. They even inserted questions as I was swept towards the boat where, breathless and almost in a daze, we were garlanded once more. They had a scoop and were going to cable their favorable impressions to their papers in Japan.

Their efforts had definitely produced a favorable reaction on board ship. Individuals and delegations of Japanese came into my stateroom at any time—morning, afternoon, or evening—"to be informed." Although they did not knock, this was not considered an invasion of privacy, provided they bowed profoundly on their way in; on entering and on leaving they bowed and bowed, again and again. They seemed to know more about my affairs and my children than I did myself, mentioning things I had completely forgotten, even reminding me of my unspoken thoughts of long ago.

Past experience had taught me that when a despotic and arbitrary screen was interposed between birth control and the people, the desire for knowledge was immeasurably enhanced. This was particularly true in Japan, where the recent renaissance had quickened the public mind. At the announcement I could not land, officialdom was subjected to frank criticism.

A little, round-faced boy called me each morning, murmuring something in a voice so soft and melodious it almost lulled me back to sleep. With the coffee, which tended to wake me, he announced, "Madam Sanger go in maybe. Yes, Japanese Government let her go in." In ten minutes he would return with the reversal of this news. He was aware of the contents of the radiograms which kept the aerials crackling even before they had been delivered to me. One read, "Thousands disciples welcome you." Another, "Possible land Yokohama; impossible discourse." From the ship's daily I learned first that I might lecture, but not publicly; and then, a day later, after continuous derision on the part of the press—all right, I might talk publicly if I wished, but under no condition on birth control. The last word I received was that I could land but speak only in private. From the Ishimotos came the message, "Anticipate your staying with us."

March 10th was so dripping and foggy that when we reached Tokyo Bay I could not see Japan. The arrival of the *Taiyo Maru* bearing such an array of distinguished passengers as the conference delegates was bound to call forth unusual activity. A veritable flotilla met the ship—police and health officers' launches, mail tenders and press dispatch carriers. Two officials came on board to interrogate me, and the three of us retired to my cabin, where our bags had been hopefully packed. I showed my passport, told the purpose of my visit, explained how I happened to know the Ishimotos and Mr. Yamanoto of the Kaizo group. Inspector and interpreter alike smiled amiably as they plied their questions, ending with the polite query, "Who is paying your expenses?" The implication was that I might be a secret agent sent by the United States Government to deplete the population of Japan and to prepare the way for an American invasion. This was particularly amusing, since I was one of the persons thoroughly disapproved of by my Government.

At the end of the lengthy catechism it was agreed that the ban would be removed if I, for my part, agreed not to lecture publicly on birth control, and provided the American Consul General Skidmore formally requested permission for me to land. I had sent him a wireless message from the *Taiyo Maru* saying I would like to visit the country, if not as a lecturer at least as a private citizen, and asking him to use his influence. Though I had had no reply I sent off a telegram to him immediately, and Grant and I sat down on the luggage to await developments.

The two officials had no sooner taken their departure than the little cabin was filled to bursting with the gentlemen of the press. We started and blinked with each rapid-fire, flashlight explosion. The room was literally smoking with the acrid powder, and not an inch of standing room remained. Seventy were all trying to get in at once; whatever I said had to be relayed and translated to the unsuccessful ones who brimmed over into the corridor.

Meanwhile, we had docked at Yokohama and, when the reporters were finally disposed of, my friends, who had been patiently enduring the rain, greeted me—Mr. Yamanoto, Mr. Wilson of the British Embassy, Baroness Ishimoto, and "the missionary who lived next door." After welcoming me they left, the last named carrying with him my briefcase laden with my most private papers and pamphlets, which I did not wish seized at the Customs.

Now came the tapping of clogs along the passage, and in the doorway were framed slight, doll-like figures, pale white faces, crimson lips, black glossy hair beautifully coiffured, butterfly-looking obis. The trials of the day vanished before their bobbing little bows. Here was a Japanese fairy tale come true.

In precise English the leader introduced the others; this one represented the silk manufacturers, that one the weavers; each of the twenty-five was appearing for some laboring organization. She explained they had been there all day, but it was nothing—they were so proud to be the first to welcome the herald of freedom for women. The Industrial Revolution which had put them to work was still so young that they were in virtual slavery. Yet, she said, they were so accustomed to subservience that it would be a long time until they learned to rebel against their wrongs. Suffrage was slow—Japanese women found it difficult to see its advantages. They could not be stirred by offers of economic independence; it was a higher ideal to have husbands take care of their wives than have them battle for themselves. She was certain no inspiration was to be found in that quarter.

Then, with eyes sparkling, she added, "But when the message of birth control came to us from Honolulu, like the lightning we understood its meaning, and now we are all awakened."

We were served with tea, and I continued to await a reply from Mr. Skidmore, but none ever came. Finally, at seven-thirty, due to the British Mr. Wilson's intercession, the Imperial Government at last opened its gates to me without the sponsorship of my own Government.

I still had to go through Customs. Papers and books, including forty copies of *Family Limitation,* were confiscated. Thereafter I usually left spaces in my diaries instead of writing out names, because I never knew who was going to see them.

The Customs men further minutely examined my clothes, accessories, even necklaces and ornaments, holding them up, laughing at them, calling each other to come and look, in order to inform themselves as much on the composition and design as to determine whether they were dutiable. The data they gleaned thus from incoming travelers they stored away like squirrels—and cheaply-manufactured replicas shortly appeared on Woolworth counters, stamped in purple ink, "Made in Japan."

When I emerged, tired and damp, more crowds pressed around seeking autographs. Everywhere in Japan people wanted your signature. One man, who spoke some English, said he represented the Ricksha-men's Union and apologized for the trouble to which I had been put. "Sometime Japanese Government he little autocratic." For that matter everybody apologized for the Government.

After the torrents of rain, logs blazing in fireplaces warmed us in the Ishimotos' charming house at Tokyo. Grant and I were both in a large room, almost bare of furnishings, exquisite in its simplicity. The fragile walls of painted silk gave an impression of airiness.

Next to us was the huge bathroom, the floor and lower walls of burnished, shining copper. In the center, raised on legs, stood a great wooden tub with a top that closed down, and a hole for your neck. Five or six basins were ranged around the room and, beside each, brush and soap. You were supposed to scrub and scrub and then rinse by throwing pans of water over you. Finally you entered the steaming tub to relax. It was not etiquette to leave any trace of soap in the bath or any evidence of its use, because everybody in the family soaked in that water before the night was over—guests, hosts, and servants in order.

I sank gratefully on one of the mattresses borrowed for our comfort and laid on the floor; the rest of the household slept on mats with wooden blocks in place of pillows, a custom which allowed the ladies to keep their coiffures intact for a week at a time. Through the frail partitions we could hear the servants laughing and chatting until late into the night, men and women together, carrying on their bathing as though it were a function of eating.

Our days were tremendously busy, beginning early with the ringing of the antiquated telephone on the wall. People came silently in rickshas and departed after conversing with the Baron and Baroness.

Old Japan had extended esthetics into the realm of ordinary existence, and undoubtedly had produced a thing of beauty. The gestures of ceremony might have meant little, but they made delightful the arranging of any affair whatever. The Japanese always greeted each other with a bow from the waistline, hands gliding down to the knees.

The difference between one and another was so subtle that a foreigner could hardly distinguish it, but it was there all the same. A particular mark of respect was the triple bow, graduated according to the social rank—an inclination, a slight pause, a deeper inclination, again a pause, and then down further until the back was nearly horizontal.

Grant, who was very affectionate, had been accustomed to kiss me when we met, whether it were in a restaurant, hotel, on the street, or anywhere else for that matter. But he had to forego this salute in Japan when we observed that kissing was a shock to Japanese sensibilities, and, indeed, was considered immoral. Instead, he took over Japanese manners and became marvelously courteous. Practically every time he spoke to me he made the three bows, and unconsciously I soon found myself returning them with equal formality.

Politeness in behavior, impersonal and ritualistic, was most noticeable in those relationships where we naturally expected habitual and conventional reserve to be thrown aside. When the Baroness Ishimoto's mother and sister were coming for lunch, she donned a special kimono, set out special vases and screens, greeted them with the prescribed bows, wordings, and gestures. Even I noticed the civilities accorded the two were not the same. The effect was that the mother occupied the place of honor as though she were receiving.

Men came also to the Ishimotos' to plan for the various meetings and entertainments. A member of the House of Lords telephoned to say he was a "disciple." The press sought interviews. Early in my career I had realized the importance of giving clear, concise, and true concepts of birth control to those who wished to quote me. This simple policy served my purpose particularly well in the Orient, where technical phrases in English were hopelessly confusing. Under any circumstances our language was peculiarly difficult for the Japanese, and their phraseology was sometimes convulsingly funny. One letter from a dismissed government employee to the head of his department was making the rounds of Occidentals in the East:

Kind Sir, on opening this epistle you will behold the work of a dejobbed person, and a very bewifed and much childrenized gentleman, who was violently dejobbed in a twinkling by your goodself. For Heaven's sake, sir, consider this catastrophe as falling on your own head, and remind yourself on walking home at the moon's end to savage wife and sixteen voracious children with your pocket filled with non-existent pennies and pity my horrible state. When being dejobbed and proceeding with a heart and intestines filled with misery in this den of doom, myself did greedily contemplate culpable homicide, but Him who protected Daniel (poet) safe through the Lion's den will protect his servant in this home of evil. As to reason given by yourself esquire for my dejobment the incrimination was laziness.

NO SIR. It were impossible that myself who has pitched sixteen infant children into this vale of tears can have a lazy atom in his mortal frame, and a sudden departure of eleven pounds has left me on the verge of the abyss of destitution and despair.

I hope this vision of horror will enrich your dreams this night and good Angel will meet and pulverize your heart of nether millstone so that you will awaken and with such alacrity as may be compatible with your personal safety, and will hasten to rejobulate your servant.
So mote it be, Amen,
Yours despairfully,
Akono Subusu

And on the bottom of the letter the district officer had noted:

Gentle Reader, do not sob—
Akono Subusu has been rejobbed.

I myself had a letter from a gentleman who wrote, "How I am unavoidably in need to execute your 'Ism' and hope to know your effective method."

Had it been allowed, I should have given forth practical information. Since it was not, I believed if I could make plain to the authorities that I was not going to break this rule in my lectures, they could find no fault with them.

Accordingly, the morning of our second day in Tokyo an appointment was made with the Police Governor. In spite of the early hour the hard little official, his close-cropped hair revealing all the bumps and developments, served us tea. The Japanese always handed you tea as we pass cigarettes—in embarrassment, for relaxation, or just to tie up loose moments. Disregarding the vital subject completely we discussed current topics through an interpreter. Though all the people were intensely serious, they were remarkably fond of plays on words. Merrily I was told my name had created much confusion owing to its similarity to *sangai san,* which meant "destructive to production."

Birth control was thus delicately introduced. For the first time I heard about the Dangerous Thought Law, which had been sponsored in Parliament by a group called the "Thought Controllers," who aimed to exclude from the country all ideas not conforming to ancient Japanese tradition. The Police Governor assumed he knew exactly what I had planned to talk about, and I could not move him from the conviction that I wanted to present a Dangerous Thought.

I was not, however, going to let the matter drop. I went higher up to the Home Affairs Office. A courteous gentleman informed me the Minister sent his regards and hoped to have the pleasure of seeing me some other time. There was no tea. I was politely bowed out.

My next stop was at the Kaizo office, where the entire staff was called into consultation. They were bristly and burly enough to be taken for Russians; only their kimonos identified them as Japanese. One and all decided we should go in person to the Imperial Diet. There, on presentation of our cards, couriers started running around to find the Chief. In a few moments the door of the room into which we had been ushered was opened, and in came the very same man with whom I had conversed at the Home Office that morning. Profoundly embarrassed I explained this was the way of impatient Americans, who were bent on hurrying things along. He was very kind, and said he had been on the point of giving me permission to speak publicly provided I did not mention birth control. When I sketched an outline of a possible population lecture we laughed and agreed the Empire of Japan was not, as a result, going to fall.

Almost from the time of landing I had been deeply conscious that I was in one of the most thickly populated countries of the world. The Ishimotos' automobile honked, honked, at every turn of the wheels to squeeze through rickshas, pedestrians, and children in the narrow, unpaved streets.

In any traffic danger the first concern was always for the baby. I never saw one slapped, struck, scolded, or punished. I never heard one cry; they all seemed happy and smiling, though I must admit a few of them needed to have their little noses wiped. I could not believe any country could contain so many babies. Fathers carried them in their arms; mothers carried them in a sort of shawl; children carried babies; even babies carried smaller babies. I saw a land of one-story houses but of two-story children. Boys with babies on their backs were playing baseball, running to bases, the heads of the babies wobbling so that you thought their necks were surely going to be broken.

The momentum that had come from the high birth rate was felt in every walk of life. Peers, business and professional men were all having large families. One told me he wanted twenty children. When I asked him how many he had already he replied, "Two," and he was offended when I suggested that perhaps his wife, instead of himself, had had those.

The density of population in tillable areas of Japan averaged two thousand human beings to the square mile, and it was increasing at the rate of almost a million a year. Although they built terraced rice paddies on their hillsides with tremendous labor they could not feed themselves. Furthermore, lacking ore, petroleum, and an adequate supply of coal, they could not develop their industries to a point where they could exchange their products for enough food.

The Government should itself have been disseminating contraceptive information, but the army faction was not friendly to it and claimed Japan could never be respected in the eyes of the world until she possessed a force sufficiently powerful to make might right. It was even then too late for birth control to offset the inevitability of her overflowing her borders; the population pressure was bound to cause an explosion in spite of the safety valve of Korea. How long this could be delayed was a matter of pure conjecture.

Chapter Twenty-six

THE EAST IS BLOSSOMING

AFTER I found out where I stood with the Government, the silent friends who had come and gone so frequently from the Ishimoto home produced plans for various meetings. In each one the address was to a particular class which did not mingle with others—commercial, educational, medical, parliamentary.

The Kaizo group were intensely disappointed that I could not deliver the lectures I had prepared and for which they had invited me to Japan. As a compromise we agreed that I should have to focus my War and Population talk around Germany and the Allies. It was going to be difficult, because I was not satisfied with the European facts and figures I had.

My first meeting was at the Tokyo Y.M.C.A. Shortly before one o'clock I was escorted with great ceremony into a room behind the auditorium, pungent with smoke from a charcoal stove. Then I was presented to a gathering of about five hundred—prosperous-looking men, well-dressed women, students, a number of foreigners, a Buddhist priest or two, and a liberal sprinkling of the Metropolitan Police to make certain my audience thought no dangerous thoughts as a result of my speech.

Most of the auditors apparently understood some English, because while I was speaking they leaned forward attentively, laughing in the proper places, but when I paused for the translation they relaxed, rustled papers, and whispered to each other.

I had discovered that the five-hour clause in my contract was no mistake and no joke. Standing from one until six was a frightful strain. The lecture with interpretations took three hours, although I could have delivered it in one, and questions took two more. Many of these were on subjects entirely alien to my own. "What do you think of missionaries? What do you think of Christianity? Are you yourself a Christian?" This last was naïvely posed, and, thoroughly aware of the significance of what it meant truly to be a Christian, I replied, "I'm afraid I'm not a very good one."

My questioner put out his chest and said confidently, "I am."

I seemed to recall my adolescence when I had exacted the last ounce of righteousness from every breathing hour. Many of the Japanese converts had this spirit. They were trying to change their ancestral ideas of morality and, instead, adopt wholesale the Christian code without having had time to assimilate it.

The most painful experience I had in Japan was in addressing the Tokyo medical association. The volunteer interpreter was a young doctor who had been on a three weeks' tour of America, and his command of English was correspondingly slight. From the attitude of the audience I could tell whenever he was not conveying my meaning as I had intended it, though I did not always know what specifically was wrong. The Baroness, unable to bear his mis-translation of "prevention of conception" as abortion, which she knew would distress me intensely, finally rose and attempted to correct the erroneous impression he was giving. But the meeting was over before she could make it clear.

Nothing had been said about remuneration. I expected none. But the next day an army of ten rickshas appeared. The officers of the society, laden with packages and bundles, presented themselves. One by one they offered boxes in which I found an elaborate kimono, an embroidered table cover, a purse, a fan, a cloisonné jar, and, in conclusion, the President offered me the smallest package of all, wrapped in tissue and tied with a paper tape on which were the characters wishing me health, happiness, and longevity. Opening it I found crisp new bills in payment. This delicate gesture was typically Japanese.

At other meetings we usually sat on clean, fresh mats; the room might be chilly, but a little charcoal burner was beside you and occasionally you warmed your hands over it. I liked the service and the food which the maids silently brought all at once on a tray, covered over and steaming hot. After *saké* in diminutive porcelain cups the group was ready to converse, and it was cozy and interesting. Often we did not get away until midnight because, although the discussion was carried on in English, each remark was translated for the benefit of those who did not understand. The Baroness always went with me, and it was a revelation to them to have one of their own countrywomen present.

I had heard much talk of the Elder Statesmen, but nobody at the Peers' Club, where I gave an afternoon address, seemed to be even elderly. They were curious to know why women were divorced, whether they wanted more than one husband, whether they really could ever care for more than one man, the nature of their love for children, how long it could continue. They were like Europeans in the frankness with which they regarded the relationship of the sexes. Yet they were not satisfied with the accepted Japanese tradition—on the one hand geisha girls who played and coquetted and amused them, and on the other wives whose place as yet was definitely in the home. They asked, "Is it not true that the American woman can be all things to her husband—his companion, mother of his children, mistress, business manager, and friend?"

I agreed with them that this was the ideal, but had to confess that by no means every American wife fitted into this picture.

Many of the Japanese had themselves forgotten that in the heroic and epic days women had enjoyed freedom and equality with men. Only with the rise of the powerful military lords in the Eighth Century had this most rigid, most persistent, and most immovable discrimination arisen.

The *Ona Daigaku*, the feudal moral code, counseled:

A woman shall get up early in the morning and go to bed late in the evening. She must never take a nap in the daytime. She shall be industrious at sewing, weaving, spinning, and embroidery. She shall not take much tea or wine. She shall not visit places of amusement, such as theaters or musicals. She must never get angry—she must bear everything and always be careful and timid.

The resultant upper-class Japanese lady, exquisite and decorative, was a living work of art particularly created by the imagination of numberless generations of men. My original conception of all Japanese women had been fashioned out of romantic fallacies—partly by the three little maids from school who simpered through the *Mikado*, and to no small extent by the gaudy theatricalism of *Madama Butterfly*. The unrestrained exoticism of Pierre Loti and Lafcadio Hearn had strengthened my illusions, as had also the color prints that had aroused so much enthusiasm towards the end of the century.

But I soon found the cherry blossom fairyland was being destroyed by the advent of machinery. In Yokohama and Kobe you heard factory whistles and saw tall smokestacks, new shipyards, and great steel cranes. The Industrial Revolution, accomplished in our Western countries gradually, had invaded the Island Empire with an impact and a shock the repercussions of which were still evident. It had not brought freedom to the women whose low status was admirably suited to the purpose of manufacturing with its ever-increasing demand for cheap and unskilled labor.

Practically half the female population, some thirteen millions, were engaged in gainful occupation though few were economically independent. In the mill districts mothers scolded their small daughters by threatening, "I'll sell you to the weavers." These *kaiko*, or "bought ones," served as apprentices generally from three to five years. Modern Japanese industrialism had been able to take advantage of an ancient Oriental habit of thought which placed slight value on the girl child.

I spent half a day as the guest of the Kanegafuchi plant, the largest cotton mill in the Empire and the ideal industrial institution which was to be a model for others, comparing favorably with one of our best. But Kanegafuchi was the exception. On the average, employees in other mills worked a twelve-hour shift, day and night, amid the deafening roar of relentless power engines. Dust and fine particles of fabric fell like minute snowflakes upon them. Their growth was stunted, their resistance to infection and malignant disease broken down. In a silk-spinning mill at Nagoya conditions were only slightly better. I found over seven hundred girls, some no more than ten years of age, swiftly twirling off the slender threads from the cocoons and catching them on the spindles. They were pathetic, gentle, homeless little things, imprisoned in rooms with all windows closed to keep them moist and hot. A quarter of their seven dollars a month wages had to go for board.

Only by the graciousness and charity, in a sense, of the upper classes were the household servants saved from institutions. When the Baroness, for example, had married, some of them—cooks, maids, and nurses—had stayed with her parents, some had gone to another sister, some had come to her and been set to training the new ones. With her they had a home for life. This system accounted in part, at least, for the fact there were no beggars or mendicants in Japan.

Essentially conservative, essentially the product of a strange and scarcely understood past, the Japanese woman in my opinion did not possess in her typical psychology any strong leanings towards rebellion. This was true even among the many women writers on papers and magazines. Those who interviewed me were intelligent, but I was constantly amazed at their ancient and domesticated outlook.

I did not believe the woman of Japan would discard her beautiful costume or sacrifice her esthetic sense upon the altar of Occidental progress and materialism. The kimono was her chrysalis. Outwardly it was often of some thick serviceable goods, dull brown or black, shot through with threads of purple or blue. Yet underneath were silks of the brightest and most flaming hues, formalized for each particular occasion. Only a fleeting glimpse was caught of these as she walked. They were symbolic of her present position in society.

From the lowest serving maid to the finest aristocrat, certain indelible traits immediately impressed themselves. First of all was the low, soft, fluttering voice, like art and music combined. They were too modestly shy to talk out loud; you could scarcely hear them in a small room. Perhaps one reason men did not take their opinions seriously was because they did not speak up. I heard on every side of the New Woman—but I never saw her. Only those who had turned Christian showed any signs of thinking independently. To be a Christian seemed to imply being a rebel or radical of some kind. They told me it with great secret pride.

This was the single place where I had found men rather than women responding to the potentialities of birth control. The former wanted to learn and thereby make of themselves something better. They were more and more in touch with the ideas of the Western world, and were broadening themselves through travel. I was confident a shifting environment was going to extend the masculine point of view and, if birth control could be proved of benefit to them, they would practice it. At that time I did not agree that East and West could never meet.

Japan was undoubtedly a man's country. Wherever we went, Grant was Exhibit A. He was a tall, dark, rather gawky youth, with adolescent manners but always cheerful. In private houses butlers and maids paid him much attention, and, in hotels, as soon as we entered the dining room everybody, because he was a man child, rushed to anticipate his wishes, to see that he was made comfortable. I straggled on behind. At our first appearance in one of these, the little girls who were being trained as waitresses and whose duty it was to bow the guests in and out were obviously confused. When we were seated at the table the proprietor apologized, "You must excuse them because they are so young, and they have their minds too much on this young gentleman."

The Yoshiwara, to which some missionaries escorted me, was certainly an integral part of this man's world. First we visited the unlicensed quarter, winding in our rickshas among alley-like streets lined with small houses. The dark eyes of the girls peered out through slits in the screen walls. Working men were standing in the muddy roadways, chattering, scrutinizing the prices which were posted in front like restaurant menus—so much per hour, so much per night. A door opened to admit a visitor. The light in the lower story vanished and soon another twinkled upstairs; or a light went out above and reappeared below, the door opened again and a figure emerged. Hundreds of lights behind paper windows seemed to flicker on and off constantly, low to high, high to low. The sordidness, the innumerable, shining eyes made me shiver involuntarily.

After we crossed a bridge to the licensed quarter the scene changed immediately. The wide thoroughfare, with a row of trees down the center festooned with electric globes like a midway, was clean and inviting. The amply-built houses had an air of spaciousness and luxury, their lanterns sent out a soft, alluring gleam, and carefully cultivated gardens produced a profusion of flowers in the courtyards. This part of the Yoshiwara appeared a delightful place. Its attraction for the girls was obvious; they would rather seek a livelihood in this fashion than in the dismal factories. Nor was it odd that they should find more romance here with many men than drudging for one all their days as the "incompetents" they became after marriage under the domination of their mothers-in-law.

Through portals as broad as driveways the patrons, much better dressed than those in the unlicensed quarter, strolled up to view the photographs of the inmates, posted like those in the lobby of a Broadway theater. In some frames was only the announcement, "—— just arrived, straight from ——. No time for picture." The clients did a great deal of "window shopping." Newcomers from the country might have eight or nine visitors an evening, an older one but two or three. Many of the girls came from good families, frequently to lift their fathers or brothers out of debt. They sent their earnings back and, as soon as they had accumulated a sufficiency, often went home, married, and became reputable members of society.

But in spite of the Yoshiwara's artificial glamour, the crowd of men swarming like insects, automatically reacting to the stimulus of instinct, was unutterably depressing.

We walked home at midnight through the sleeping city, mysterious and quiet, not like a city at all—no jumping signs or illumination, but more like a nice, low-ceilinged room trimmed with old, brown-stained oak, and only here and there a glow.

Nothing else in my travels could compare with that month in Tokyo. The language was strange and unfamiliar. The bells in the shafts of the rickshas, ringing for pedestrians to get out of the way, added a bizarre note. The queer, clicking sound of the wooden geta was different although somewhat reminiscent of the clop, clop, of the Lancashire wooden shoes, which also were taken off at the door and exchanged for slippers. All the smells and the sights were quite new, even the signs on the shops were unreadable. In Europe, you could usually guess from some root word what kind of merchandise was for sale within. But not so in Japan. One day I stopped, totally puzzled, to inquire the whereabouts of a store the address of which had been written down for me. I showed my slip of paper but nobody there could help me. I went on. Fully three minutes later the pattering of hurried steps behind me caused me to turn. Here was one of the clerks. He had gone to the trouble of looking up the address I had asked for and had come to act as guide to make sure I arrived.

Throughout Japan the custom of greeting you and seeing you off was touching, and gave you a charming remembrance of a world where friendships were worth time and consideration. When a Tokyo doctor heard I was leaving Yokohama eighteen miles away at eight o'clock in the morning, he presented himself at seven to bring me a box of choice silk handkerchiefs. He must have risen at five to do so.

From the window of the train for Kyoto the faces of the old men trudging along the road looked curiously like the drawings of them. Everywhere were small village houses and, since I could see through from front to rear, I wondered where the peasants and their numerous offspring ate and slept.

The former capital was fascinating. The shopkeepers appeared to esteem their visitors more highly than the goods they had to sell, though Kyoto blue and, more especially, Kyoto red were like no other colors anywhere. If ever you see the latter, buy it if you can, cherish it among your treasures, save it for your children, because it is the most beautiful of all reds.

It was now April, the festival of spring and of the geishas, the jealously guarded and chaperoned entertainers, singers, players. Everybody was anticipating the flowering of the cherry trees, and with the rest of Kyoto I went to see the enormous, spreading, willow cherry, then in dazzling white blossom. It was several hundred years old, its limbs which grew out and drooped towards the ground were propped up with care, and around it was a superbly groomed landscape garden. The proprietors of hotels near such trees erected unpretentious tea houses, temporary in character, where hundreds of people kept vigil. You could not help having respect for a people whose love of a tree brought them from miles away and who waited day and night throughout the duration of its brief blooming. They paid deference to it as they did to a great artist who they knew could live just so long.

The Japanese designed their gardens with the mood of the individual in mind. Some were filled with music, water, birds, activity, and there you could go to be cheered when gloomy and despondent. As soon as I entered the Golden Temple grounds its influence fell upon me. Everything was planned for thought and concentration. No color, no noise, no rushing of water, no singing birds distracted the attention. Only at certain hours could you even walk about, because movement was disturbing to meditation.

Japanese hospitality reached its finest flower in Kyoto, and the supreme day of entertainment was offered by a generous and considerate doctor. On inviting me to luncheon he said he would call with his car at ten in the morning. This seemed a bit early, but it appeared he wanted me first to visit the Museum of Art. Here was no wandering through miles of rooms so that the eye was wearied and no lasting impression was gathered. Instead, I was shown only the one most prized specimen of paintings, porcelains, and rare screens. Afterwards, I was ushered into the library to see a collection of precious manuscripts, then back through the city for a few especially renowned views, and finally at noon to the doctor's home. His wife and two daughters greeted me and I was introduced to the guests. Little short-legged trays were put before our floor cushions, and we all picked up our chopsticks. I envied Grant his dexterity.

After the trays had been removed, we conversed until the business men had to return to their offices. But a fresh group of guests took their places, and with them appeared a painter. An easel was set up and each of us in turn made a single brush line on the rice paper—some straight, some curved, some vertical, some horizontal, criss-crossing each other in every direction. Then the artist took his brush and, amid exclamations of wonder and appreciation, with a few expert strokes converted the mélange into a flower pattern, a lake, or a mountain.

An hour or so of this pleasure and the easel was swished away, the painter vanished with his colors, and a sculptor was substituted. We were now supplied with dabs of clay which we began to mold, the sculptor going from one to another to give assistance. If you were clever, as several of the Japanese were, works of art resulted. I created a plain jug with handle and lip, was taught how to draw a design upon it and how to paint it. Next day it was delivered to me, baked and glazed.

Later we were escorted to the garden where we congregated beneath an open tea house perched high on a rock. There the younger daughter tended a tiny fire and brewed a ceremonial tea—no simple brew, but leaves of a special sort, beaten until the beverage was bright green. When we had enjoyed this delight we strolled about, admiring the brooklets, the dwarf pines, the shrubs, the iris in bloom.

We returned to the house to find, as though in a play, that the scenery had all been changed. Different screens were up, fresh flowers in the vases, the women of the household in more elaborate costumes, and new visitors waiting. Grant and I alone seemed to remain static.

Now on the immaculate matted floor appeared little charcoal stoves. The evening meal was served by the mother and daughters as a marked honor to their guests. This time I was brought a spoon and fork; apparently I had not been very deft at lunch in handling my chopsticks. After dinner came yet more people and yet more conversation. I had been talking steadily since early morning, the topic being selected according to the type of gathering. In the evening it was population, and more serious. Sometimes I forgot myself and spun out involved English phrases, then, realizing they had missed fire, had to go back and choose key words more easily comprehended.

This continued until midnight or later. At last we had to excuse ourselves and ask to be taken home, because we were leaving for Kobe the next morning.

The doctor and his wife, accompanied by some of their friends, were at our hotel betimes, all with boxes and bon voyages. This reversal of the Occidental custom of bestowing presents on one's host or hostess was an enchanting way of conducting the amenities of life. They wanted no return for their hospitality. I had arrived in Japan with one small trunk and departed with five, laden with gifts.

Chapter Twenty-seven

ANCIENTS OF THE EARTH

NEW and different places, strange countries, peoples, and faces have always appealed to me. I did not have to be in London for the Fifth International Conference until July. When I had secured my Chinese visa it had occurred to me that it might be much better to go on around the world than retrace my steps.

On a misty day, the sun not bright enough to clear the sky completely, we sailed from Kobe through the glorious Inland Sea, threaded its innumerable islets, like the Thousand Islands of the St. Lawrence, only more delicate. The boat was small and out-of-date. A few of the English had chairs but Grant and I wandered between crates of ducks, chickens, and livestock, and hundreds of Japanese squatting stolidly on the deck. When we emerged into the Yellow Sea it became very foggy and Grant was sick to his toes. I put on a brave face and ate, though with long teeth, as the old phrase goes.

We landed at Fusan one evening. Koreans stood about in their white robes which fell to their ankles, pale figures outlined against the night in the subdued light of their mysterious paper lanterns. The next morning as I glanced out over the countryside on the way to Seoul it appeared an Oriental desert, odd but seemingly familiar. I felt at home within its gates. White-robed coolies smoking long thin pipes with minute bowls drove oxen, worked in the fields. They had North American Indian faces, uncut, ragged hair, reddish skins, and curious, wooden structures strapped to their backs to carry burdens of any kind—soil, coal, rocks.

The streets of Seoul were broad, dimly lit. The tall Korean men were unique, a combination of priest, patriarch, and grandee, so formal and elegant with their pointed beards a trifle larger than Van Dykes. They were utterly indifferent to other people, managing to preserve a proud and aloof air in spite of their idiotic, silly-looking hats, dinky-crowned and wide-brimmed, from which hung strings of amber beads, valuable family heirlooms.

I wondered again at the universal white costumes. Everywhere on the banks of rivers women were eternally pounding laundry; you could almost feel the threads parting company with the terrific beating—washing with stones and ironing with sticks.

The Korean was held in contempt by the Japanese, who declared his Government had built schools, roads, railroads, brought cleanliness. It was true that the houses of the Koreans were not so well-kept, their habits not so sanitary, but they were a separate race, and they accepted scouring and scrubbing and sweeping only under pressure. Hatred and rebellion had been the result of denying them their language and customs. They claimed they were taxed out of existence to pay for such luxuries, and nourished antagonism and stubborn resistance against anything Japanese. They maintained further that they had no personal liberty, even being required to have passports to move about in their own country.

Koreans also resented the speeding up of production in the silk factories through the exploitation of little girls. I saw them there, shoulders bent, crouched up over their work, hair braided down their backs; they were almost like babies. Their job was to put their tender, delicate fingers into boiling water to pull out the silk cocoons—the hands of older people were not sensitive enough. But the Japanese said they did not feel the pain.

Even though I had a large luncheon meeting attended by foreign missionaries and officials, Korea was but a stepping stone to China. The Celestial Kingdom had an indefinable odor of its own, peculiar and inimitable, which waxed and waned, varying with each city and with each district of a city. It might be a compound of sauces, onions, garlic, incense, opium, and charcoal, but who has ever succeeded in putting an odor into words? It marched upon you, at first faintly and indistinctly like a distant army, and then closed in relentlessly, associating itself with memories, making you gasp in protest or pleasure.

At Peking I wanted to change into fresh clothes all the time. I was haunted by dust—dust in my body, in my ears, up my nose, down my throat, between my teeth. Some of the streets were paved, but the dust was suffocating. After every sight-seeing sortie I bathed and bathed and bathed in a desperate effort to rid myself of the diabolical dust.

We were seven days viewing palaces, native quarters, night life, sing-song girls, hospitals, factories, silk mills. We heard the mechanical chanting and beating of drums by Buddhist priests, mostly young boys dressed in soiled yellow robes; gazed with amazement at the funeral processions—great floats, fantastic gods, food, flowers, possessions; visited old Chinese gardens and museums. I shopped for jade and lapis lazuli and was well cheated.

Beggars, many of them crippled and on crutches, were hobbling along in the gutters or sitting on corners, gaunt and filthy. Children were turning handsprings, doing anything to attract your attention; they edged beside you, and you had the feeling they had been born with palms upward.

You could not set foot out of doors without being besieged by ricksha boys clothed only in scant, cotton trousers and jackets, always short at ankles and wrists. The moment you stepped in they picked up the shafts of their little vehicles and began the dogtrot journey. I could not become accustomed to the eager running of these half-naked creatures, so weak, so underfed, so much less able than the rest of us. It had been bad enough in Japan, but there you felt the runners were sturdy; in China they usually were suffering from varicose veins, heart disease, and, forever, hunger. Often, as the wind blew some of the rags and tatters aside, I saw pock marks and wondered how close we were to the manifold diseases of the Orient.

I was going about a good deal and it worried me to be pulled around by a human being so emaciated. One morning our regular boy was missing. Another replaced him, cheery and smiling. Three days later the first returned. He had been sick, he said; he had had smallpox. The scabs had not yet peeled off.

I spoke to the doorman at the hotel, who managed the rickshas. "This boy is not well enough to work."

"Oh, yes, he's used to it. He feels a little bad, but he's all right."

Nevertheless, I sent him home to rest up. Nothing save famine and pestilence and plague seemed to give the Chinese any breathing spell. It was said the average ricksha coolie lasted but four or five years—the remainder of his life he merely subsisted. I was submerged in a strange despondency and questioned "the oldest civilization in the world" which still, after so many thousand years, permitted this barbarism.

Grant rode a donkey when we went to the Ming tombs, and the guide did also. I was carried in a chair for miles and miles through an arid, dusty plain. Two coolies held the lengthy bamboo poles on their shoulders and a third jogged alongside waiting to take his turn. I felt so sorry for them I wanted to get out and walk. I wished I could carry myself. All the way these poor, starved creatures made animal noises, "Aah-huh, aah-huh," nasal, interminable, varying the tone but slightly; even their words sounded like grunts to me.

China was not yet past the story-telling age, as you saw in the theater, where someone recited the news from the stage; for a copper anybody could hear what was going on in the world. The ancient classical forms of the Chinese language were intelligible to scholars alone, and Dr. Hu-Shih had been instrumental in devising a literary vernacular which the people could use. This philosopher who at three years old had been familiar with eight hundred characters, now in 1922, while only in his late twenties, was already reputed to be the initiator of the Chinese Renaissance. He asked whether I would speak to the students of the Peking National University and, though he was to act as chairman, volunteered also to interpret, which I esteemed an almost unheard-of honor. His outlook, coinciding with mine, recognized what birth control might mean for civilization.

Dr. Tsai Yuen-Pei, the Chancellor of the University and a leader of the anti-Christian movement, had gathered into his fold the most brilliant students of Young China, all of them bubbling over with interest at Western ideas, which were sweeping the globe. A great turmoil was going on in their lives and a revolt against rigid Chinese tradition.

Due to the translation difficulties I had encountered in Japan, I had decided I could not afford to speak in China unless I went over the subject first with my interpreter and knew he understood the spirit as well as the words. Therefore I showed Dr. Hu-Shih my lecture material in advance. He suggested, "These students will want to know everything about contraception as it is practiced."

"But I've never given that except at medical meetings."

"China is different from the West. Here you may discuss contraception as an educational fact as well as a social measure. You will be listened to respectfully, laughed at if you do not, and will surely be asked for definite information. I think you should prepare yourself for this."

It was not simple to digress from principles and theories and go into methods that needed diagrams and technical knowledge to secure understanding, and I felt diffident about following his advice. But these young people, responsive and alert, received my first practical lecture with earnest attention. Dr. Hu-Shih translated accurately and quickly, interjecting amusing stories and improving, I imagine, upon my own words.

Afterwards he and I were escorted across the campus to the home of Dr. Tsai. I have always been interested in foreign foods. I like to try them out, and have brought home dozens of Hawaiian, Chinese, Indian, Japanese recipes which can be made at home. This dinner was an Arabian Nights experience. It began at seven and lasted until one in the morning—bird's-nest and quail egg soup, fried garoupa, ducks' tongues and snow fungus, roast pheasant, rice and congee, lotus nuts and pastry, sharks' fins, and various kinds of wine.

There must have been well over thirty guests invited for the evening, among them an American woman, Mrs. Grover Clark, whose husband was on the faculty of the University. Some of the students had been to her between the lecture and dinner time and given her the transcribed notes which they had taken down in shorthand. Would she correct them? They wanted to get the information published. When they came to the Chancellor's home to call for them so that they could deliver them to the press, I could see at a glance that this was not at all what I desired to leave behind me; my spoken words never sound adequate or complete in print. Therefore, I sent a boy to the hotel for a copy of the old stand-by, *Family Limitation*. The students set to work at once to translate it. Mrs. Clark offered to pay the expenses, and the next afternoon five thousand copies were ready for circulation.

This little incident was significant of Young China; an idea to them was useless if only in the head. Their motto was to put it into concrete reality.

Symptomatic also of new China was the abandonment of bound feet, although women of advanced years still were to be seen leaning on each other for support as they tottered by. Amahs were carrying nurselings about when they themselves seemed scarcely able to stand up. However, I was glad to see only a few of the small children had these lily feet. Fathers realized their daughters could not earn a living if thus deformed. At the Peking Union Medical College, combining the modern equipment of the Occident with the artistry and traditions of the Orient, no girl was accepted for training unless her feet were normal.

One day Dr. Hu-Shih asked me to lunch in an old Manchu restaurant where his friends were accustomed to gather and ponder. Many were business or professional men, but all, with their little beards and intellectual faces, had the appearance of professors. It was an unusual combination of Wall Street and university. In our private dining room were seven English-speaking Chinese with families of from four to nine children. Each said the later ones had not been wanted; nevertheless they had come.

The conversation took a scientific turn. Since man had through breeding brought about such changes in the animal and vegetable kingdoms, why could he not produce a class of human beings unable to procreate? Was there any reason why the particular biological factors that made the mule sterile could not be applied further? They discussed the interesting possibility of creating a neuter gender such as the workers in a beehive or ant hill.

The implications of this colloquy formed a fascinating climax to our sojourn in Peking. Our train was the last one south for several days. Soldiers cluttered the landscape—not alert or even military-looking, but men or boys put into uniform and told how to act. The Tuchuns were all trying to "unite" China, each in his own way. We read in the papers about the war clouds hanging over the country, but nobody seemed to be excited. We were not worried; being foreigners, we were assured, meant protection.

The valley of the Yangtze Kiang was green and luxuriant; every inch of ground was being utilized. Even space which should have been employed for roads was given over to food production, and thousands of people were born, lived, and died in boats on the river. Some water buffalo waded in the mud of the rice fields, some horses worked the water treadmills, but human labor predominated. Overpopulation and destitution went hand in hand. In this land which Marco Polo once described as "a pleasant haven of silks, spices, and fine manners," all the hypothetical Malthusian bogeys had come true.

Foreigners at the International and French Settlements of Shanghai enjoyed much the same life as at home. Their hotels were the same, they met the same sort of people, dressed in the same clothes, ate the same meals; in fact, it was difficult to get Chinese food unless you knew exactly where to go. They came in droves, herded together, most of them bored to death. You could see they had appropriated the best of everything—the houses with gardens and walls, the clean rickshas, the well-fed boys, the prosperity. The Chinese, in their own country, lived on what was left, which was practically nothing. They huddled wistfully on the fringes—horrible, abject, dirty.

It amazed me to see that Americans, French, and English could be so near and yet close their eyes to the wretched, degrading conditions of devastating squalor in the native quarters. Once while a missionary was guiding me through the Chinese City, we noted a crowd, children included, gathered in curiosity around a leper woman. She was on the ground, sighing and breathing heavily. Nobody offered to help her. "Maybe she's dying," said my companion. Just then the woman gave a fearful groan and took a baby from under her rags. She knew what to do, manipulated her thighs and abdomen, got the afterbirth, bit the cord with her teeth, put the baby aside, turned over, and rested. No trace of emotion showed on the faces of the watchers.

In their respective countries Europeans would have made an effort to improve such conditions. But here they seemed to have lost many of their former standards and qualities of character and conscience. It was said that China, psychologically speaking, swallowed up the morals of all those who came to reside there.

One young American secretary related to me the joys of living in this section of the Orient. She said her salary was far smaller than any she would have received in the United States, but her comfort, on the other hand, far exceeded what she could have had in Boston at double her present wages. Among them she mentioned her ricksha boy, who cost her only five dollars a month, out of which he had to support himself and his enormous family. During the three years he had been working for her she had never raised his pay, nor did she ever expect to. He dared make no request, because in China it was almost impossible to get a job by one's self. When a servant was dismissed he faced practical starvation. I really formed a bad impression of people who wanted to live in China because of the cheapness of its luxuries.

The Grand Hotel was elegantly appointed, but the boys who served in the rooms did not seem friendly in their hearts towards any foreigners. Hostility was percolating throughout the country. Deep in the Chinese mind lay the memory of many invasions, of the Boxer Rebellion, and the intrusion of business men and, particularly, missionaries.

In Shanghai the American missionaries dominated Chinese education, such as it was. I was surprised to find families of eight or ten children the rule rather than the exception among them. Their salaries were raised with each new infant, and that may have been the reason. Nevertheless, there were many who wanted birth control information. When they learned of my presence they called on the telephone, sent cards, came to see me. But, apparently apprehensive of criticism, they took me if possible into a secluded room or, if we had to meet in a public place, backed me into a corner and stood in front to conceal the fact they were talking with me; they acted as though they were turning up their coat collars so that they should not be recognized.

The only method of family limitation known to the poor Chinese was infanticide of girl babies by suffocation or drowning. The missionaries were co-operating with the Government, which had enacted a law forbidding the practice. They went from home to home to see whether any woman were pregnant. If one were obviously so, her name was jotted down in a notebook for a call soon after birth was due. At the same time both father and mother were informed of the severe penalty they would incur unless the baby itself or a doctor's certificate of death from natural causes were produced. After two years' work ninety-five percent of pregnant mothers showed either their babies or good reasons for not doing so.

But the Chinese had so low a margin of subsistence that, if the law forbade them to dispose of one child, another was starved out. Sometimes two little girls had to be sold to keep one boy alive; in dire necessity even he might have to be parted with to some sonless man who wanted to ensure ancestor worship. Because the elder girls could begin to help in the fields or become servants in some rich landowner's household, usually it was the three- and four-year-olds who were turned over to brothels. There they stayed until mature enough to be set to working out their indenture. If they ever tried unsuccessfully to find freedom, the proprietors might beat them unmercifully, sometimes even breaking their legs so that they could not walk, much less ever run away again.

When infanticide was stopped, the corresponding increase in sing-song girls making their living by prostitution was almost immediately evident. It was estimated Shanghai had a hundred thousand. Many were Eurasians, the results of unions with white men who were in Shanghai on small salaries as representatives of foreign business firms. I glimpsed some of the Chinese women who had been bought as housekeepers and mistresses as well saying good-by at the train to their American or English masters summoned home.

Desiring to see the worst of the city I went to the prostitute quarter in company with Mr. Blackstone, a missionary from the Door of Hope, a house of refuge for escaping girls. In Shanghai, as in Tokyo, we found in the Japanese section soft, low lights and an undercurrent of music in the air. The inmates were fully grown, gay and hearty, the interiors were immaculate and restrained in their decoration, the streets were swarming with sailors who apparently preferred this district to the depressingly dark and gloomy Chinese one near by.

Here and there the Chinese prostitutes could be seen through the open doorways, heavily rouged, gowned in vivid colors, limned like posters against the meanness of the background, their frail, slight bodies at the service of anyone who came. Each took her turn upon a stool outside, using her few words of English to attract the sailor trade. I thought I would never recover from the shock of seeing American men spending their evenings at such places with what were obviously children.

In one house we found half a dozen girls looking much younger than their theoretical fifteen seated on hard benches around a room not more than six feet by nine. A little one holding high a lamp so that we should not trip and fall, escorted us to her cubicle, which had only a bed for furniture. A chair was brought in for me.

Mr. Blackstone began to talk to her in her own dialect. Why had she come?

"Too much baby home—no chow." She said she was sixteen and had been there since she was twelve.

"Why she can't be a day over ten," I expostulated.

The child was visibly frightened, aghast at her own loquacity. We might be from the Government. When we had at last gained her confidence, however, she responded eagerly to this unusual sympathetic contact, talking freely about herself—the long time it took to pay herself out, the precariousness and physical fatigue of her calling; some days she had no visitors, but when a ship was in maybe as many as ten or twelve a night. She seemed as old as the ages in her knowledgeableness; "No want baby," she told us. Yet her poor little frame had the immaturity of fruit picked green and left to shrivel.

We gave her money and left in spite of her urgent and kind invitation to stay.

All sing-song girls were not necessarily prostitutes; most hotels hired them to entertain guests. Only their lips were made up, their faces remaining pale. They wore flowers in their hair and although not so soft-voiced as the geisha had greater independence. Certainly their weird, shrill songs accompanied by the tinkle of a lute were not attractive to Western ears.

Echoes of my visit to Japan had permeated throughout the colony of Japanese, who aimed to give me an extra-cordial welcome, trying their best to make up for what they thought had been an unpleasant experience in their country. I had not realized the power of ancient feudalism over the Japanese woman until I met her away from home, where she blossomed into an intelligent, outspoken human being. I noticed she expressed herself much more frankly in the presence of men, but underneath the conversation I often sensed a propaganda which had resulted in deep prejudice; from the horrible stories you heard of the savagery of the Chinese you received the impression all were cannibals.

Since my plans to include China in my itinerary had been made so late, I had few letters of introduction there. Consequently, to my regret I did not see many Chinese women. I had not expected to do much speaking and had had very little press in Peking. Dr. Hu-Shih, however, had arranged for me to meet about fifteen newspaper men and women in Shanghai. We sipped our tea, nibbled our cakes, and then they began to ask questions, taking down the answers with the utmost care. They wanted to set forth the pros and cons of birth control in their own vernacular, but unfortunately could not reach the illiterate masses. They asked me to speak at the Family Reformation Association, an organization which was under missionary auspices. The rules were no smoking, no drinking, no gambling. Its membership, therefore, remained small.

The young woman who interpreted paragraph by paragraph had just returned from America, but did not prove the expert her traveling had indicated. The chairman said I was to give both theory and practice, but when I came to the latter my translator's courage took flight entirely. She whispered, "I'll get a doctor to say that." I gave up and switched to something simpler. My audience, however, knew without her assistance what I had been trying to convey, and was much diverted by her predicament.

Of all lands China needed knowledge of how to control her numbers; the incessant fertility of her millions spread like a plague. Well-wishing foreigners who had gone there with their own moral codes to save her babies from infanticide, her people from pestilence, had actually increased her problem. To contribute to famine funds and the support of missions was like trying to sweep back the sea with a broom.

China represented the final act in an international tragedy of overpopulation, seeming to prove that the eminence of a country could not be measured by numbers any more than by industrial expansion, large standing armies, or invincible navies. If its sons and daughters left for the generations to come a record of immortal poetry, art, and philosophy, then it was a great nation and had attained the only immortality worth striving for. But China, once the fountainhead of wisdom, had been brought to the dust by superabundant breeding.

This was my conclusion when at last we were back again in the modern age on the American ship *Silver State* bound for Hong Kong; we had comfort, hot water, baths, heard the softness of the little chimes as the steward went through the corridors announcing meals. It was almost with a sense of awe that I asked for any service. After being some time in the Orient you were a bit embarrassed by having an American wait on you. Soon, however, the plumbers, the carpenters, the painters who kept the vessel trim, the sailors who swabbed down the decks at night, gave me a feeling that in the Western countries we had gone far towards dignifying manual labor.

Chapter Twenty-eight

THE WORLD IS MUCH THE SAME EVERYWHERE

⋙ ⋙ ⋙ ⋙ ⋙ ⋙ ⋙ ⋙ ⋙ ⋙ ⋙ ⋙ ⋘ ⋘ ⋘ ⋘ ⋘ ⋘ ⋘ ⋘ ⋘ ⋘ ⋘ ⋘

A FAVORITE sales promotion method of astrologers is to send partial readings to people whose names appear in the papers, in the hope of piquing their curiosity to the point of demanding fuller details regarding their future lives and conduct. From time to time I used to receive these and paid no attention. But just before I had sailed from California a friend of birth control had sent me one based upon arrests and prison. This forecast told me I would have a great deal of difficulty in starting, and that on a certain day in May the same signs would prevail over my House as at the Town Hall Meeting —that I should, therefore, be prepared for police interference.

While packing in Shanghai I was looking through my briefcase and happened to note that the date was one on which the *Silver State* would still be at sea; she was not due at Hong Kong until the next day. I laughed to myself and said, "Here's where I prove it wrong." As it turned out, however, the ship was ahead of her schedule and arrived in Hong Kong twelve hours early.

We were steaming up the long reach towards the Kowloon piers when, to my utter surprise, the immigration officer who had come on board handed me a notice instructing me to visit the Chief of Police.

"Is this a special invitation for me, or is everybody included?"

"Only for you, Madam," was the smiling response.

The harbor was crowded with junks and fishing boats. Children in sampans were holding out nets for whatever might come overside, fishing up each bit of refuse from the water. Adjoining ships were being coaled by women coolies, hundreds of them, their faces strained and bodies stringy as though made up entirely of tendons. They carried their two baskets on bamboo poles across their shoulders, and clambered like ants in their bare feet over the barges—not singing as the men coolies of the North, but making much *wallah-wallah*—jabbering and shouting.

After settling Grant in a hotel I took a chair from around the corner, because police headquarters was part way up the Peak, and rickshas could not negotiate the steep ascent. The Chief was not there. I inquired whether anything were wrong with my passport. Since my British visa was perfectly correct, they said there must be some mistake; they had no information about any summons. I left my card.

The next day the Chief called at my hotel but we missed each other because I was out with Grant ordering his first pair of long trousers. When I returned I found a calling card and another request to come to headquarters that afternoon. Again I obeyed, and again I found no Chief and no message for me. I left another card and the officials whom I had seen before laughingly reiterated they still knew of no complaints.

"Well, I'm going tomorrow morning. If the Chief wants anything he'll have to come to the hotel." He never did.

Once more we were off, this time on a British liner. The sea was smooth, the air cool. It was the ideal ocean voyage I had always longed for. I was relaxed and enervated but it was good to be so. I had nothing to do all day but sit in the glorious breezes on deck and watch the romping children, about fifty of whom were on board. Many had been born in the Orient and were accompanying "pater" who was going home on leave. One little boy might come tearing by pursued by another, both followed by anxious Chinese amahs, thin, dark, slick-haired, wearing glossy, black trousers and coats buttoned down the side. They seemed in constant distress over the antics of their energetic charges.

When we dropped anchor at Singapore, agitation and excitement were again manifest among the inspectors at the sight of my passport. I was politely asked to stand by while they consulted, and then was ushered off the ship to an upstairs office where I was questioned by a pleasant young Englishman as to my intentions in going to India.

"But I'm not planning to stop in India."

"Lectures by you are announced in Bombay and Calcutta."

"This is the first I've heard of it," I assured him. "But if I were to go, would there be any objection?"

"That would depend on the subject of your lectures."

"I'm interested in only one subject."

He pressed a button. Miraculously, almost like a scene from a mystery play, and as though everything had been rehearsed in advance, an attendant entered and placed on the desk a large, closely typewritten paper.

"Am I on the blacklist?"

"Not exactly, but you said you were interested in only one subject. Then what about this?" He actually read me from that document details of a small reception I had given five years before in my own apartment in New York for Agnes Smedley after her release on bail.

For a moment I was speechless with amazement. Then I ejaculated, "Why shouldn't I be interested when she was arrested for a cause that is my own? Besides, you must remember the charge was later dismissed."

"Then what about serving on the Committee for the Debs Defence and for the Political Prisoners Defence?" He mentioned other gatherings I had attended during that parlor meeting era, such as when Mary Knoblauch had had Jim Larkin talk on Irish Home Rule or Lajpat Rai, the Indian sociologist, express anti-British tendencies. Wherever my name had appeared on the stationery of any committee he had it on his record. My public life was there spread out, showing how careful was British espionage.

I brought forth from my arsenal some of my most trusty arguments, and the official ultimately agreed that if the vast millions of India wanted birth control he was all for my going there and would visa my passport. However, since I did not propose to include it in my trip the discussion was purely academic.

Although Singapore when we reached it seemed to combine so many nationalities that it was like Europe, America, and the Orient all mixed together, Malays, whose land it once had been, appeared to be in the minority and their dialect little used. I could not escape that fatal horoscope, because when their language was described to me as easy and simple, the example given was *mata*. By itself it meant eye. But, *mata mata*, in addition to being the plural, also meant policemen, who were the eyes of the government, and *mata mata glap* meant secret eyes, hence detectives.

How Europeans made themselves understood in Singapore was a wonder to me. The Chinese ricksha boys apparently comprehended no tongue, nor knew where any place was. You stepped into a ricksha and pointed to where you thought your hotel was, praying your finger was extended in the right direction. If you did not point he ran in any direction of the compass. Even so, at the first corner he was inclined to turn into a more shady street. After a while, since he seemed to be arriving nowhere, you spoke to him sharply and he pulled up to a traffic officer, who told him where to go. Still pointing and saying "hotel" loudly, you eventually were delivered in front of the door by a much pleased coolie, grinning from ear to ear at his own cleverness. The poor fellows were so cheerful and willing that you could not help smiling, too.

The weather continued balmy to Penang, to Ceylon, to Aden. I had been dreading the heat of the Red Sea, but the passage was surprisingly cool; the facing wind was really enjoyable.

At Cairo, where we made a longer pause, Grant came down with dysentery and his temperature shot to a hundred and four degrees. A Czechoslovakian doctor spent three nights with him but could not reduce the fever. Each morning when I rose early to act as nurse, I stumbled over about six natives, our own guide Ali among them, kneeling on prayer rugs in front of his door. All the fortune tellers had said a death was pending in Shepheard's Hotel and were assuming he would be the victim. The fourth day, after the doctor had gone to his office, I ordered a dish pan full of ice and sponged Grant off with the frosty water. Two hours later his temperature was normal and he began to show signs of recovering. I never divulged that cold bath to the doctor.

Ali was a handsome, dark-faced Arab with large luminous eyes and fine-cut features which made American ones seem crude and weak in comparison. Wearing his long black robe to the ground and topped by a red fez, he used to come to his duties bearing great armfuls of flowers from his mother. We held lengthy conversations. "Have you been married?" I asked.

"Yes, five times."

"Weren't any of them happy?"

He began enumerating. The first one had been young and inexperienced; she had not been properly brought up and did not know her position as his wife. Although she had cost him a hundred dollars, he had dispatched her to her parents because she was too independent. Number two had not been clean and had been too old for his mother to train; he had made amicable arrangements with her father for her return, and had lost no money on this transaction. Number three had been sickly, and a great expense; she also had gone back. Number four had not loved him; it had been shortly evident her heart was with another man and the agreement had been broken by mutual consent. Number five, the latest, he had sent home because she would not wait on his mother.

"Why should she?"

"Madam, my mother carried me in her belly for nine months. Should I have a wife who would not work for her after that?"

He was now casting about for his sixth.

Ali haunted our footsteps and, in order to collect his five percent commission on all our purchases, noted every place we went. Merchants made a social affair of their customers' calls. You went to a perfume shop in the Bazaar. The proprietor said, "Yes," sat down, and handed you a gold-tipped, aromatic cigarette. He lighted it for you, took out a pile of letters from a bag, and opened them for your inspection. They were testimonials that a certain gentleman had sent similar cigarettes to Hartford, Connecticut, or Pelham, New York. Of course, you bought some. Then a cup of Persian tea was brought you, and you wanted some of that. At last you recalled that you had come for attar of roses. By this time he had sensed your "aura" and knew what you could pay. He was willing humbly to mention the price.

Our tour had been a wonderful experience for Grant. He had studied the Baedekers, planned our trips when we were coming to a new city or country, looked into their histories and, although he was only thirteen, shown a highly awake and intelligent attitude towards everything we had seen.

He had had all sorts of wares hurled at him—ostrich feathers, fans, baskets, sapphires, scarabs. He was satiated with strange sights and lore—Buddha's Temple of the Tooth at Kandy, caravans of bullocks, the English club at tiny Port Swettenham in Malaya, the enormous porters of Egypt who picked up trunks as though they were handbags, women veiled and women unveiled, mosques, the Coptic church where Joseph and Mary were supposed to have hidden Jesus from Herod, the date trees along the road to Memphis, the underground Temple of the Bull, the remains of an old proud world at Alexandria where Cleopatra had once held court, the primitive ferry-raft on which we had crossed the Nile to see the place where Moses had been found in the bullrushes, the wonderful ride, weird and lovely, across the Sahara to view the Pyramids and Sphinx. On his way to Switzerland he had traveled by gondola along the canals of Venice, had been trailed through the art galleries of Milan.

After a few weeks at Montreux Grant was fully recovered, but he was now homesick for the first time since we had left New York eight months before. All he wanted was to see Tilden play in the tennis matches at Wimbledon, and then go home. Because I did not think he should miss the reception which H.G. was giving, I had him fly across the Channel to London, and afterwards, appreciating his longing to be among his own age and kind, I shipped him off on the maiden voyage of the *Majestic* to a camp in the Poconos. By the time he was back at Peddie he was up with his class, his mind vastly enriched, and able to approach his studies in a more mature manner. I have never regretted taking him with me.

I myself remained in London for the Fifth International Neo-Malthusian and Birth Control Conference to be held July 11–14. The inclusion of the words birth control was a definite concession on the part of the Neo-Malthusians to the new trend of thought. It was a delight to be amid conditions where tolerance reigned and the atmosphere was unblighted by legal restrictions. The scientific candor of the discussion was reported in the newspapers with sincerity and sobriety.

John Maynard Keynes, who had become famous almost overnight as the result of his book, *The Consequences of the Peace,* presided at one of the afternoon meetings. Later, I had lunch with him. He was tall and well-built, with clear, cold, blue eyes, a fine shapely head, brow, and face, a brilliant bearing and brilliant intellect. I was impressed by the fact he did not smile. Because he gave each question of yours so much consideration, he seemed constantly perplexed, but when he once started to talk you knew he had already put aside the thing as having been solved, and gone on in advance. You were probably more puzzled at his next question than he at yours.

In the two years that elapsed before I saw Keynes again he had married Lydia Lopokouva of the Russian Ballet. He had become an entirely different person—his serious mien and countenance had been changed to a buoyant, joyous happiness. His knowledge of the problems of money, population, and economics were of a nature far above the grasp of an ordinary intelligence, yet in his conversation with his wife he always implied she knew the subject as thoroughly as he, and answered her queries as though their minds were together. He was the only Englishman, perhaps the only man, I ever knew to do this.

Unlike Lydia Lopokouva, most women had a strenuous battle trying to prove themselves equal to men; this marriage conflict was inseparable from modern life. I could sense it frequently when coming in contact with a married couple—on her part the years of rebellion, and on his of trying to put her down as a weakling.

Sentiment has extolled the young love which promises to last through eternity. But love is a growth mingled with a succession of experiences; it is as foolish to promise to love forever as to promise to live forever.

To every woman there comes the apprehension that marriage may not fulfill her highest expectations and dreams. If in the heart of a girl entering this covenant for the first time there are doubts, even in the slightest degree, they are doubled and trebled in their intensity when she meditates a second marriage.

J. Noah H. Slee, whom I had known for some time, was what the papers called "a staid pillar of finance." He was South African born but had made his fortune in the United States. In customs and exteriors we were as far apart as the poles; he was a conservative in politics and a churchman, whereas I voted for Norman Thomas and, instead of attending orthodox services, preferred to go to the opera.

An old-fashioned type of man, J.N. yearned to protect any type of woman who would cling. Complications, therefore, confronted us. I had been free for nearly ten years, and, for as long, had been waging a campaign to free other women. I was startled by the thought of joining my life to that of one who objected to his wife's coming home alone in a taxi at night, or assumed she could not buy her own railroad tickets or check her baggage. Nevertheless, despite his foibles, he was generous in wanting me to continue my unfinished work, and was undeterred by my warning that he would always have to be kissing me good-by in depots or waving farewell as the gangplank went up.

I had to consider also that I had two boys to be educated, and that children were much more to a woman than to a man. Yet I knew he would be kind and understanding with them. Furthermore, he had faith both in individuals and in humanity; his naïve appearance of hardness was actually not borne out in fact. He kept his promises and hated debts; we attached the same importance to the spirit of integrity.

Hundreds of people who scarcely knew me were delighted when the news of our marriage eventually became public. Within one week letters began to arrive from all over the United States and Canada. One man wrote he had helped me get up a meeting at San Francisco and now needed a printing press—would I mail him the trifling sum of three thousand dollars? Another brought to mind I had had dinner at his home when lecturing in his city, and now that he had painted enough pictures to hold an exhibit, would I finance it? Dozens of ministers, old men, old ladies, writers, sculptors wanted me to set them up in business, musical concert work, bookshops, recalling the time they had taken me in cars to meetings, or that I had slept in their beds. Parents requested me to send their children to schools, to Europe, to sanatoriums—heaven knows what. I never knew people could need so much. I longed with all the desire in me to make out a check for every lack and wave a magic wand and say, "So be it."

But all I could do was write back that I had no more wealth than before—my husband's was his own. And I still required as many contributions to birth control as ever.

I had not wanted the worry or trouble of handling money, nor do I want it today. The things I valued then I value now, not for what they cost, but for what they are. To me dollars and cents are only messengers to do my bidding, and nothing more. To use them properly and get results is my responsibility.

When I asked J.N., "Why do you lock things up?" he replied, "I always do, don't you?"

"Never. I haven't anything worth locking up."

That is the way I still feel.

It seemed so final when again I started a home, but there had been a gathering loneliness in my life—not seeing the children except on holidays, never having time to spend with old friends or to make new ones, and with such rich opportunities constantly offering themselves. I knew very well, however, what sort of a house I wanted—a simple one, something like Shelley's in Sussex.

In 1923, with stones gathered from the fields we built a house near Fishkill, New York, cradled in the Dutchess County hills, beside a little lake. On it we tried out swans, but they did not work; although they looked picturesque, they were too messy. So we changed to ducks and stocked the water with bass. I planned a blue garden which grew up and down and threw itself about the house and altered with the seasons. Pepper, a cocker spaniel puppy of two months, came the first year and bounced and leaped around us as we walked through the woods or rode horseback over the hills.

Willow Lake was only sixty miles from New York. I could make out the menus for a week ahead, leave directions for the gardening, be in my office fairly early and back again for dinner at night. Later, for working purposes, we built a studio among the treetops on the edge of a cliff from which I could look far off across the majestic valley of the Hudson.

Domesticity, which I had once so scorned, had its charms after all.

Chapter Twenty-nine

WHILE THE DOCTORS CONSULT

AFTER coming back from around the world I found nothing had been done about the Tenth Street clinic, which I had expected to be in operation. No members of the Academy of Medicine had come forth to back Dr. de Vilbiss, and I had paid the rent for the last twelve months while vainly waiting.

Now I gave it up and decided to start afresh. The more I had studied, the more clearly I had recognized that it was not possible to advise a standard contraceptive for all women any more than it was possible to prescribe one set of eyeglasses for all conditions of sight. Only upon examination and careful check-up could you determine the most suitable method. No detailed statistics had ever been kept except at Brownsville, and those case histories had never been returned to me by the police. I wanted to collect at least a thousand such records for a scientific survey before any opposition could interfere with the plan.

Many women were still coming to me personally for information at 104 Fifth Avenue. The best thing to do was have a woman doctor right there to take care of them—a quiet way to begin. It was hard to locate one foot-loose and free; I could have no shying or running off at the first indication of trouble. In making inquiries I heard of Dr. Dorothy Bocker, who held a New York City license though she was at present in the Public Health Service of Georgia. This single, cordial, and enthusiastic young woman knew practically nothing about birth control technique, but was willing to learn. The difficulty was that she wanted five thousand dollars a year.

At first this appeared an almost unsurmountable obstacle. Here was just the person I had been looking for, but it seemed beyond my power to raise so large a sum. I was loaded with the financial weight of the *Review* and the League. That organization had been admitted as a membership corporation and hence could not secure a license to conduct a clinic, which in New York was synonymous with a dispensary. No clinic, therefore, could be included in its budget; it would remain a department of the League by courtesy only, being actually my private undertaking. Where could I find someone to donate such an enormous amount?

Then I remembered Clinton Chance, a young manufacturer of Birmingham, who had prospered exceedingly both before and during the War. He and his wife, Janet, had become good friends of mine during my 1920 visit to England. Having felt the need of a more sound and fundamental outlet for his riches than that provided by charity, he had come to see that birth control information was far better for his employees than a dole at the birth of every new baby. He was not in any sense a professional philanthropist, but only wanted to help them be self-sufficient.

Clinton had once offered me money to set the birth control movement going in England, but I had refused then because England had enough co-workers, who were handling the situation well, and, furthermore, my place was in the United States. He had then said to me, "I won't give you a contribution for regular current expenses, but if ever you see the necessity for some new project which will advance the general good, call on me."

Now I cabled Clinton at length, explaining my need. He promptly answered, "Yes, go ahead," and soon arrived an anonymous thousand pounds to cover Dr. Bocker's salary for the first year. I made out a contract for two. She was to come in January, 1923, and we were to shoulder the risks and responsibilities together.

Even to choose a name for the venture was not easy. I had been steadily advertising the term "clinic" to America for so long that it had become familiar and, moreover, to poor people it meant that little or no payment was required. But the use of the word itself was legally impossible, and I was not certain that the same might not be true of "center" or "bureau." I wanted it at least to imply the things that clinic meant as I had publicized it, and also to include the idea of research.

Finally, one of the doors of the two rooms adjoining the League offices, readily accessible to me and to the women who came for advice, was lettered, Clinical Research.

It was still a clinic in my mind, though frankly an experiment because I was not even sure women would accept the methods we had to offer them. We started immediately keeping the records. Dr. Bocker wrote down the history of the case on a large card, numbering it to correspond with a smaller one containing the patient's name and address. Each applicant she suspected of a bad heart, tuberculosis, kidney trouble, or any ailment which made pregnancy dangerous, she informed regarding contraception and advised medical care at once.

In our first annual report, which attracted much attention, all our cases were analyzed. We said, "Here is the proof—nine hundred women with definite statistics concerning their ages, physical and mental conditions, and economic status."

As time went on I became less and less pleased with Dr. Bocker's system. She had no follow-up on patients, and I wished the clinic to be like a business in the thoroughness of its routine. I refused to approve methods as a hundred percent reliable until there had been not merely one but three checks on each woman who had been to the clinic. To begin with, she was to return two or three days after her initial visit; she usually did that. But if she did not come back inside three months, then a social worker in our own employ should be sent to call on her. Finally, she was to be examined once a year. Dr. Bocker did not see eye to eye with me that this was the only way to put the work on a sound scientific basis of facts, and we agreed to part company in December of the second year.

Dr. Hannah M. Stone, a fine young woman from the Lying-In Hospital, volunteered to take Dr. Bocker's place without salary. Her gaze was clear and straight, her hair was black, her mouth gentle and sweet. She had a sympathetic response to mothers in distress, and a broad attitude towards life's many problems. When the Lying-In Hospital later found she had connected herself with our clinic, it gave her a choice between remaining with us and resigning from the staff. She resigned. Her courageous stand indicated staunch friendship and the disinterested selflessness essential for the successful operation of the clinic. These qualities have kept her with us all this time, one of the most beloved and loyal workers that one could ever hope for.

The clinic could serve New York, but its practical value outside was restricted, and I was always seeking some way of remedying this. We took the preliminary step in Illinois, where no laws existed against clinics. I had arranged a conference in Chicago at the Drake Hotel, October, 1923, the first of a regional series. Mrs. Benjamin Carpenter and Dr. Rachelle Yarros, who had been with Jane Addams at Hull House, had to obtain a court decision before Dr. Herman Bundesen, Commissioner of Health, would issue a license for the second clinic in the United States.

Meanwhile, between 1921 and 1926, I received over a million letters from mothers requesting information. From 1923 on a staff of three to seven was constantly busy just opening and answering them. Despite the limitations of the writers and their lack of education, they revealed themselves strangely conscious of the responsibilities of the maternal function.

Childbearing is hazardous, even when carried out with the advantages of modern hygiene and parental care. The upper middle classes are likely to assume all confinements are surrounded by the same attention given the births of their own babies. They do not comprehend it is still possible in these United States for a woman to milk six cows at five o'clock in the morning and bring a baby into the world at nine. The terrific hardships of the farm mother are not in the least degree lessened by maternity. If she and her infant survive, it is only to face these hardships anew, and with additional complications.

In the midst of an era of science and fabulous wealth reaching out for enlightenment to advance our civilization, with millionaires tossing their fortunes into libraries and hospitals and laboratories to discover the secrets and causes of life, here at the doorstep of everyone was this tragic, scarcely recognized condition.

It was an easy and even a pleasant task to reduce human problems to numerical figures in black and white on charts and graphs, but infinitely more difficult to suggest concrete solutions. The reasoning of learned theologians and indefatigable statisticians seemed academic and anemically intellectual if brought face to face with the actuality of suffering. When they confronted me with arguments, this dim, far-off chorus of pain began to resound anew in my ears.

Sensitive women of our clerical staff were constantly breaking down in health under the nervous depression caused by the fact we had so little knowledge to give. One who went to Chicago to help rehabilitate soldiers wrote me, "I'm feeling much better. These men who have lost a leg or arm come in, apparently disqualified forever, but something is being done about them, and it is happy work, not forlorn like yours."

To prove that the story could be told by the mothers themselves, ten thousand letters, with the assistance of Mary Boyd, were selected and these again cut to five hundred. Eventually this historical record appeared in book form as *Motherhood in Bondage*.

Whenever I am discouraged I go to those letters as to a wellspring which sends me on reheartened. They make me realize with increasing intensity that whoever kindles a spark of hope in the breast of another cannot shirk the duty of keeping it alive.

Woman and the New Race, which sold at first for two dollars, had a distribution of two hundred and fifty thousand copies, and it made my heart ache to know that poor women who could ill afford it were buying the book and not finding there what they sought. To the best of my ability I tried to supply general information, but the only way of extending genuine aid was to persuade doctors to give it professionally.

By a happy chance I met Dr. James F. Cooper, tall, blond, distinguished, a fine combination of missionary and physician, who left no stone unturned when a patient came to him, but devoted his whole attention to her—everything in her life was important to him. He was recently back from Fuchow, China, and was establishing himself in Boston as a gynecologist. Since he was thoroughly convinced of the vital necessity for birth control and could talk technically to his profession and interpret to the layman as well, my husband pledged his salary and expenses for two years, and I induced him to associate himself with us as medical director to go forth and try to convince the doctors throughout the country that contraceptive advice would save a large proportion of their women patients.

In January, 1925, Dr. Cooper started on a tour which covered nearly all the states in the Union. In the course of the two years he delivered more than seven hundred lectures. Occasionally he was suspected of ulterior motives, of attempting to advertise the products he recommended, but this did not sway him from his persistence. Where he found laxity on the part of medical organizations he spoke to lay associations, which applied pressure on their own physicians, demanding information. As a result of this trip, doctors really began to awake to the problem of contraception, and when it was ended we had the names of some twenty thousand from Maine to California who had consented to instruct patients referred to them.

At this point began the huge and difficult process of decentralization, so that the New York office need no longer be a clearing house. Each request which lay outside the pale of the Cooper influence required voluminous correspondence. One letter, enclosing a stamped, return-addressed envelope, was mailed to the woman, asking her to furnish us the name of her doctor. We then wrote him to inquire whether he would give her information, and offered to send supplies if she could not afford them. If he said yes, we notified her to that effect; if he said no, we gave some other doctor in her vicinity an opportunity to co-operate.

We were immediately confronted with the situation that even willing doctors had little to recommend. Literally thousands of women reported that such ineffective methods had been tendered them they had refused to pay. We ourselves did not have a great deal, and this put us in a weak position; the acceptance of the theory was ahead of the means of practicing it.

The jelly I had found in Friedrichshaven had turned out to be too expensive, because it was made with a chinosol and Irish moss base, and the price of the former was prohibitive in preparing it for poor women. Dr. Stone and Dr. Cooper, therefore, devised a formula for a jelly with a lactic acid and glycerine base, which was within our means. Most of their cases, however, were sufficiently grave for them not to feel justified in using it alone experimentally. Consequently, they took the precaution of having a double safeguard by combining the chemical contraceptive with the mechanical—jelly with pessary—which proved ninety-eight percent efficacious.

At this time we could not import diaphragms directly. Although I had given various friends going to Germany and England the mission of bringing them in, this could not be done in sufficient quantity.

Furthermore, since bootlegging supplies could not continue indefinitely I had to find out how they could legally be made here.

Two young men came to help in whatever way was most necessary. Herbert Simonds, who had been in advertising, began to investigate the possibility that some recognized rubber company should make our supplies. When one and all were fearful, he and Guy Moyston, who did some publicity for us, concluded they would form the Holland-Rantos Company, selling only to physicians or on prescription. They spent their own time and thousands of dollars personally on research, in the end perfecting a quality of rubber that could stand the variations of climate in the United States—hot houses and cold winters, Florida dampness and Western dryness.

Meanwhile, Julius Schmid, an old established manufacturer, had been importing from his own concern in Germany a few diaphragms, but only on a modest scale because he did not want to run afoul of the Comstock law. As soon as he saw a potential market in the medical profession he fetched from the Fatherland several families who had been making molds there, gave them places to live in, and set up a little center, expanding gradually until eventually he sold more contraceptive supplies than any firm in the world.

But this was all in the future.

Soon after we had developed an organization in which economists, biologists, and other scientists could be articulate, they came into the movement. Dr. S. Adolphus Knopf, a tuberculosis specialist, who had been one of the first to greet me when I came out of jail, never missed an opportunity to contribute articles to medical journals and to write letters. Professor Edward Alsworth Ross's books continued to popularize the sociological and economic aspects. Professor E. M. East of the Bussy Institute of Harvard University published a study of population titled *Mankind at the Crossroads,* which obtained wide circulation. His one-time pupil, Dr. Raymond Pearl of Johns Hopkins, was carrying on the same work showing exactly how much food a certain number of acres could produce at what cost. Universities generally began to show an interest; students wrote asking for scientific and historical data upon which to base their theses.

Young people in colleges, partly because their ideas were not yet biased, offered a fallow field for my personal campaign of education through lecturing. I particularly enjoyed their quickness and alertness and their interludes of comic relief. Nowhere has this combination been more apparent than in a recent visit to Colgate University. Four boys met me at the station and somehow or other we all squeezed into an automobile which shortly deposited me at the home of one of the professors for tea and to meet the faculty. "This is house-party night," he told me. "The girls are here, and most of the boys won't get to bed until daylight. We'll have to rout them out to hear you at chapel tomorrow." He added that during his twelve years in the University no woman had spoken on that platform.

"Have they prejudices against women speakers?"

"Oh, no, no. There's just no subject a woman can deal with better than a man."

Well! I thought, if the boys will all have been out to parties and I'm the first woman speaker, here is a challenge! No sociology or dull population figures for them from me.

The next morning, determined to make them take notice, I ransacked my bag for my smartest dress, adjusted my lipstick, and carefully set my hat at an angle. Nevertheless, I was a bit ill at ease. My anxiety was not allayed when Norman Himes, professor of sociology, said, "Now, Mrs. Sanger, we probably shan't be able to hear you in this hall. The acoustics are very bad. They can hardly hear me and I have a big voice."

This was even less encouraging. I felt I was likely to be the last as well as the first woman at Colgate. However, I replied bravely, "I can speak up and we can have some wave if they can't hear me. Anyhow, there probably won't be many; why can't they be moved up front?"

"Yes, that's what we'd better do."

We went in to find the chapel jammed. Some of the students were standing in the door, others against the walls.

Professor Himes introduced me at the top of his lungs. "Louder! Louder!" The boys waved their hands. The more he tried to make himself heard, the more restless they became. When I stood, however, they had to listen if they were to hear me. There was no waving, no calling.

They roared with laughter and clapped at everything I said. This seemed fine, but I suspected that I could not have really made so profound an impression as to deserve so much applause.

Someone afterwards commented to Professor Himes, "We've never seen the boys so appreciative."

"Oh," he remarked, "they thought if they could keep Mrs. Sanger talking long enough they wouldn't have to go to their examinations."

From the time I started lecturing in 1916 I have appeared in many places—halls, churches, women's clubs, homes, theaters. I have had many types of audiences—cotton workers, churchmen, liberals, Socialists, scientists, clubmen, and fashionable, philanthropically minded women.

Once in Detroit Mrs. William McGraw, Sr. had organized a public meeting and luncheon at the Statler Hotel. When I arrived I encountered a situation which might well have embarrassed a less doughty hostess. She had invited a dozen of the most prominent women in the city to sit at the speaker's table. Mrs. A. had asked, "Will Mrs. B. sit there also?" Mrs. B. had inquired, "Will Mrs. C. be next to me?" Each wanted social support. Mrs. McGraw had blandly refused to tell them; consequently not one had accepted. Although five hundred came, only two places were set at the great banquet table on the platform. Mrs. McGraw and I ate in solitary splendor with nothing but the floral decorations for company.

All the world over, in Penang and Skagway, in El Paso and Helsingfors, I have found women's psychology in the matter of childbearing essentially the same, no matter what the class, religion, or economic status. Always to me any aroused group was a good group, and therefore I accepted an invitation to talk to the women's branch of the Ku Klux Klan at Silver Lake, New Jersey, one of the weirdest experiences I had in lecturing.

My letter of instruction told me what train to take, to walk from the station two blocks straight ahead, then two to the left. I would see a sedan parked in front of a restaurant. If I wished I could have ten minutes for a cup of coffee or bite to eat, because no supper would be served later.

I obeyed orders implicitly, walked the blocks, saw the car, found the restaurant, went in and ordered some cocoa, stayed my allotted ten minutes, then approached the car hesitatingly and spoke to the driver. I received no reply. She might have been totally deaf as far as I was concerned. Mustering up my courage, I climbed in and settled back. Without a turn of the head, a smile, or a word to let me know I was right, she stepped on the self-starter. For fifteen minutes we wound around the streets. It must have been towards six in the afternoon. We took this lonely lane and that through the woods, and an hour later pulled up in a vacant space near a body of water beside a large, unpainted, barnish building.

My driver got out, talked with several other women, then said to me severely, "Wait here. We will come for you." She disappeared. More cars buzzed up the dusty road into the parking place. Occasionally men dropped wives who walked hurriedly and silently within. This went on mystically until night closed down and I was alone in the dark. A few gleams came through chinks in the window curtains. Even though it was May, I grew chillier and chillier.

After three hours I was summoned at last and entered a bright corridor filled with wraps. As someone came out of the hall I saw through the door dim figures parading with banners and illuminated crosses. I waited another twenty minutes. It was warmer and I did not mind so much. Eventually the lights were switched on, the audience seated itself, and I was escorted to the platform, was introduced, and began to speak.

Never before had I looked into a sea of faces like these. I was sure that if I uttered one word, such as abortion, outside the usual vocabulary of these women they would go off into hysteria. And so my address that night had to be in the most elementary terms, as though I were trying to make children understand.

In the end, through simple illustrations I believed I had accomplished my purpose. A dozen invitations to speak to similar groups were proffered. The conversation went on and on, and when we were finally through it was too late to return to New York. Under a curfew law everything in Silver Lake shut at nine o'clock. I could not even send a telegram to let my family know whether I had been thrown in the river or was being held incommunicado. It was nearly one before I reached Trenton, and I spent the night in a hotel.

In Brattleboro, Vermont, my audience was made up of another slice of America—honest, strong, capable housewives who made their pies and doughnuts and preserves before they came. When I had finished there was not a murmur of commendation from the three hundred. The minister of the church where the meeting was held had asked me to stand beside him to say how-do-you-do when they came out. They just went by, eyes straight ahead.

On the telephone afterwards, however, each was asking what the other thought. The cases I had cited were typical of their own community. "Was she referring to this one or that one?" they queried.

I returned two days later to lunch with a doctor and four or five social workers, and was surprised to hear, "The women want to start a clinic."

"But there wasn't any enthusiasm when I suggested it the other morning."

"The people around here don't express much openly. They were moved to quietness. But just the same they're starting a clinic in Brattleboro."

Chapter Thirty

NOW IS THE TIME FOR CONVERSE

SIDE by side with the clinic and education another project had been stirring for some time in my mind. Internationalism was in the air, and I wanted that outlook brought into the movement in the United States. To this end I made plans for the Sixth International Malthusian and Birth Control Conference, to be held in New York in March, 1925.

In the summer of 1924 I called a Conference Committee meeting of the League. That is, in addition to the regular Board members, other supporters were invited to attend. As soon as the matter was brought up they expostulated, "You still have to ask for money to run the *Review*. How can you pay the fares of the delegates and furnish them with hospitality? Do you know how much it will cost?"

Since I wished to have the Conference important enough to make its mark I replied promptly, "Not less than twenty-five thousand dollars."

"Have you thought of how you are going to finance it?"

"Certainly I have." I was certain that the interest of many of our contributors extended beyond the magazine, and that they would see we now had a broader field of activity. They had given before and would give again. I knew money would come in.

Any five of the outside women present could have underwritten the Conference, but they objected that funds were needed for other work. One by one they left in a hurry; the inevitable appointments were waiting for them. Their advice to the Board was, no Conference —and the wealthy members of the Board concurred.

Nevertheless, I went ahead with the details of securing backers. Even the letterhead on our stationery was significant. You could tell such a lot about an organization—quality, standards, tone—from the names, often more informative than the body of the letter. My intention was to make people stand in public for what they believed in private, and at least our list of sponsors was impressive enough—a brilliant and distinguished array.

The success of any conference was determined in great measure by the caliber of the men who took part in it. Results depended first upon the concept animating it, and second, as had been proved before, on the presence of an eminent figure to ornament the assemblage. I decided to see whether I could induce Lord Dawson to be our main speaker, and, hoping that personal persuasion might be more efficacious than written, sailed for England in September.

Havelock came up from Margate to greet me, as usual far removed from the hurly-burly of the world, aloof from the conflict of ideas which meant so much to me. Yet to talk with him again was to return to the mêlée with renewed inspiration. I managed to crowd in a motor trip to Oxford, lunch at the Mitre, a walk through Brazenose and King's, and a drive back through Buckinghamshire, where the beeches were changing to bronze and russet. I felt a regretful pang that so little of my life could be lived in England.

Unfortunately for my purposes Lord Dawson was away shooting in the North. With some temerity I dwelt upon the possibility of Lord Buckmaster, the former Stanley Owen, Chancellor of the Exchequer in the Asquith Coalition of 1915, who had become one of the most finished orators in the House of Lords. He had just returned from Scotland and telephoned me to suggest we exchange views. He was about to present a resolution that, under the auspices of the Ministry of Health, restrictions on birth control instruction be removed for married women who attended welfare centers. He was gathering practical information from people who had had practical experience, and wanted to know how methods in the United States differed from those in England and, particularly, verification of their harmlessness.

When he came to my hotel one afternoon, I did not take time to mention the Conference, because H.G., knowing the value of proper introductions, had arranged one of his most brilliant dinners for that very evening, or rather he had proposed it and Jane had arranged it. For H.G. to entertain in behalf of a cause set the seal of approval on it. Jane had invited literary luminaries and their wives: George Bernard Shaw, Arnold Bennett, Sir Arbuthnot Lane, Professor E. W. MacBride of the Eugenics Education Society, Walter Salter of the League of Nations, and Lord Buckmaster.

It had been my experience that personages gave little of themselves on formal occasions. So many people expected these lions to roar bravely, forgetting that they preferred to save their sparkling sallies for the pages of their books. Moreover, when the English came together for an evening they liked to have it light and amusing. I had received much from the books of Shaw, who had advanced civilization by breaking down barriers of all sorts, now almost nothing from him personally, although he was very diverting, with funny quips upon life and America and birth control.

I had by design been seated next to Lord Buckmaster, and after the meal had been in progress for perhaps half an hour, H.G. leaned over and whispered to me, "Have you got him?"

"I haven't started yet."

"You're no true American. You ought to work faster. You're missing out." Whereupon he focused his own attention on Lord Buckmaster, who, in answer to his direct query, regretted that the date conflicted with the opening of Parliament.

Before I could realize it the time came when I was due to sail from Southampton. Lord Dawson had just returned and could see me at three that afternoon. Promptly on the hour his secretary ushered me into his library at Wimpole Street. A fire was burning cheerfully in the grate, a gentleman, traditionally tall and handsome, was sitting leisurely on the sofa as though my boat train did not leave Waterloo Station at four-thirty, and endless days remained in which to talk about the interesting subject of birth control. He was a grand seigneur such as you rarely encountered in your travels, having a mind that could understand and meet any discussion with knowledge, facts, and comprehension. The approach, the surroundings, his courtesy, charm of manner, and poise, proved him a great English aristocrat. He asked me about the attitude of the medical profession in the United States, desirous of knowing who had identified themselves with it. I recited my past efforts to enlist the support of the leading physicians. The minutes sped relentlessly away; I had to leave, and barely caught my train. Having admired him so long from afar, I was glad to have had this brief contact, even though he was unable to attend the Conference.

I was back in New York by the end of October, and soon came a letter from Shaw cheering me with his point of view:

Birth control should be advocated for its own sake, on the general ground that the difference between voluntary, irrational, uncontrolled activity is the difference between an amoeba and a man; and if we really believe that the more highly evolved creature is the better we may as well act accordingly. As the amoeba does not understand birth control, it cannot abuse it, and therefore its state may be the more gracious; but it is also true that as the amoeba cannot write, it cannot commit forgery: yet we teach everybody to write unhesitatingly, knowing that if we refuse to teach anything that could be abused we should never teach anything at all.

Interminable correspondence began immediately with adherents and, in many distant lands, possible delegates. I sent out telegrams to the former and as fast as money arrived dispatched it to the latter for their passage over, though I did not yet have enough to get them home again. Languages and interpreters then had to be arranged for; in Europe that was difficult enough, but here it was more than perplexing. Worst of all was the eternal barrier of our laws. Topics that could be freely discussed in London were forbidden in the United States, and we could not afford to have the dignity of the occasion marred by another Town Hall episode. I had to tell delegates what their papers were to be about, and, when it was necessary to cut out a reference to contraceptives, had to apologize and explain why.

I quickly found that visitors from seventeen countries could produce more problems than statistics and theories proved. The committee sent to meet Dr. G. O. Lapouge, a French eugenist, after vainly searching through the cabins on the boat, went back to the pier whence all had fled save one inconspicuous, desolate man sitting on top of his luggage, reading, waiting patiently for someone to come for him—so unimportant-looking that no one would have suspected him of being a renowned scientist. The next morning the Hotel McAlpin, where the convention was to be held, called me up to report that Dr. Lapouge had been severely burned, and an interpreter was needed. Dr. Drysdale hurried off to find the poor little man of seventy in excruciating pain but carrying on a dissertation, highly amusing, about the hazards of America's much-advertised plumbing. Without understanding how to regulate the shower he had stood under it and turned on the hot water. The skin fairly peeled off his chest. Nevertheless, bandaged and oiled, he undauntedly attended all the sessions.

The opening night we had a "pioneers' dinner" over which Heywood Broun presided. The Danish Fru Thit Jensen, blond, vivacious, was to relate the troubles she had had in arousing interest in her own country. She made her address in English courageously enough, but it was evident at once that someone slightly familiar with American slang had helped her out. She was describing a doctors' meeting in Denmark and the first words we heard were, "When I gave my greetings to those boneheads as I am to you—" We all burst into laughter because they seemed to apply to the guests present. Her face remained sphinx-like in its determined immobility; she halted for us to subside, then continued. Almost immediately the dignified gathering went off again into a fresh peal. You no sooner recovered from one shrieking convulsion than she made another remark equally ludicrous. After each outbreak she paused resignedly before going on with her carefully prepared speech. The hilarity finally got out of hand, so whether the end was funny or not nobody knew or cared.

At every meeting Dr. Ferdinand Goldstein of Berlin, who was hard of hearing, sat in the front row. The mention of any phase of population, on which he was an expert, brought him promptly to his feet. Standing directly in front of the speaker, he cupped his ear in order not to miss a single word. The one discordant note occurred on the last day when the committee declined to embody in its program any endorsement of abortion. He not only left the Conference but went back to Germany without saying good-by to anyone.

The Austrian delegates were Johann Ferch and his wife, Betty. This Viennese printer had become interested in birth control through setting up material on his linotype. He had informed himself of methods and in a short time had several clinics started in Vienna. One morning when I found them at breakfast in the dining room, great tears were rolling down Mrs. Ferch's face. I asked her what the trouble was and she said she was weeping because the pot of coffee on the table, a simple bit of food, cost thirty-five cents, and she realized what this amount of money would buy at home; for the price of one meal in New York their starving relatives could live for a whole day in luxury. Neither of them felt entitled to indulge in such extravagance.

Dr. Aletta Jacobs walked along with me after one of the sessions. She said the fact she had refused to see me in 1915 had been on her mind ever since, and she desired to clear up the matter now; she had always been against lay people taking part in the movement, and for that reason had opposed the Rutgers method of training practical nurses and allowing them to go out in the field after only two months' instruction. She had put me in the same category as those in her own country who had wanted to establish clinics as a commercial venture. That afternoon she visited our clinic and went over methods with Dr. Cooper and Dr. Stone. Here, she said, with kindling eyes, was the system she had envisioned in the Netherlands but had never been able to make come true.

The eugenists were given their opportunity to speak at the Conference. Eugenics, which had started long before my time, had once been defined as including free love and prevention of conception. Moses Harman of Chicago, one of its chief early adherents, had run a magazine and gone to jail for it under the Comstock regime. Recently it had cropped up again in the form of selective breeding, and biologists and geneticists such as Clarence C. Little, President of the University of Maine, and C. B. Davenport, Director of the Cold Spring Harbor Station for Experimental Evolution, had popularized their findings under this heading. Protoplasm was the substance then supposed to carry on hereditary traits—genes and chromosomes were a later discovery. Professor Davenport used to lift his eyes reverently and, with his hands upraised as though in supplication, quiver emotionally as he breathed, "Protoplasm. We want more protoplasm."

I accepted one branch of this philosophy, but eugenics without birth control seemed to me a house built upon sands. It could not stand against the furious winds of economic pressure which had buffeted into partial or total helplessness a tremendous proportion of the human race. The eugenists wanted to shift the birth control emphasis from less children for the poor to more children for the rich. We went back of that and sought first to stop the multiplication of the unfit. This appeared the most important and greatest step towards race betterment.

A special round table for the eugenists was held at which we took the opportunity to challenge their theories. I said, "Dr. Little, let's begin with you. How many children have you?"

"Three."

"How many more are you going to have?"

"None. I can't afford them."

"Professor East, how many have you, and how many more are you going to have?"

And so the question circled. Not one planned to have another child, though Dr. Little has had two since by a second wife. "There you are," I said, "a super-intelligent group, the very type for whom you advocate more children, yet you yourselves won't practice what you preach. If I were to put this same question to a group of poor women who already have families, every one of them would also answer, 'No, I don't want any more.' No arguments can make people want children if they think they have enough."

When the Conference was over, a final meeting was held at my apartment to form a permanent international association of which Dr. Little was made president.

Handling everything had been something of an undertaking, but after all the delegates had been sent off we still had money in the bank. My faith had been justified that, if you started something worth while, means for its realization would be forthcoming.

Chapter Thirty-one

GREAT HEIGHTS ARE HAZARDOUS

> *"Professor East, though you may try,*
> *You fail to rouse my fears,*
> *For I don't dream that even I*
> *Will live a hundred years;*
> *But do not think I view with mirth*
> *Five billion folk (assorted)*
> *Five billion tightly packed on earth*
> *Who cannot be supported."*
> (South African Review)

AT the conclusion of the New York Conference I thought that I was never going to have anything to do with organizing another. But hardly more than a few months had gone by before my mind was dwelling on one to be centered around overpopulation as a cause of war. From the statements of Keynes and the specialists of the League of Nations, and from the status of the countries of Europe, it was inferred that international peace could in no way be made secure until measures had been put into effect to deal with explosive populations.

Between 1800 and 1900 the inhabitants of the world doubled in spite of bloody wars, thus proving they were only temporary checks. For every hundred thousand babies who died between dawn and dawn, Professor East estimated that one hundred and fifty thousand were born. These fifty thousand survivors contributed to the globe in twenty years a horde almost equal to India's three hundred and seventy-five million.

In the United States, numerically speaking, overpopulation was not of apparent importance; we still had unoccupied lands. But evidence that we were beginning to consider the quality of our citizens as well as the quantity was shown in our immigration laws. In 1907 we had barred aliens with mental, physical, communicable, or loathsome diseases, and also illiterate paupers, prostitutes, criminals, and the feeble-minded. Had these precautions been taken earlier our institutions would not now be crowded with moronic mothers, daughters, and grand-daughters—three generations at a time, all of whom have to be supported by tax-payers who shut their eyes to this condition, admittedly detrimental to the blood stream of the race.

Then our sudden closing of the doors in 1924 by placing the world on a quota, threw Europe's surplus population back on herself. Italy had to face this problem as Germany had had to do in 1914. At the Institute of Politics in Williamstown, Massachusetts, in the summer of 1925, Count Antonio Cippico, Fascist Senator, virtually demanded that, to make room for her "explosive expansion," Italy be allowed to export her half-million annual increase to foreign lands. Professor East answered him, asking Italy first to put her house in order, and setting forth with clarity the inexorable results of "spawning children on the world with haphazard recklessness." But she had no intention of doing so. Shortly afterwards Mussolini outlined his plan: "If Italy is to amount to anything it must enter into the second half of this century with at least sixty million."

Japan and Germany as well as Italy were already called danger spots in 1925. Japan's goal was a hundred million. Göring was soon to say, "The territory in which the Germans live is too small for our sixty-six million inhabitants and will be too small for the ninety million which we want to become." The three military countries were pleading with their women to bear more children, offering as inducements medals, money, lands. They claimed the right of expansion because they were too crowded at home, and were at the same time increasing their peoples in order to promote successful wars.

Populations can fall into a semi-starved state of inertia, such as that of India or China, unless they are aggressive. They have a choice of three courses: to lower the standards of living to the bare subsistence level, to control the birth rate, or to reach out for colonies as Great Britain has done.

While we had been holding our conference in London in 1922 I had met at one of Major Putnam's luncheons the Very Reverend "gloomy" Dean Inge, except that he was not gloomy at all; he was full of mischief. In his late fifties, tall, thin as an exclamation point, quite deaf, he reminded me of a Dickens character. He had commented in his usual pungent style on the real meaning of the right to expand:

It is a pleasant prospect if every nation with a high birth rate has a "right" to exterminate its neighbors. The supposed duty of multiplication, and the alleged right to expand, are among the chief causes of modern war; and I repeat that if they justify war, it must be a war of extermination, since mere conquest does nothing to solve the problem.

I was still of the opinion in 1925 that the League of Nations should include birth control in its program and proclaim that increase in numbers was not to be regarded as a justifiable reason for national expansion, but that each nation should limit its inhabitants to its resources as a fundamental principle of international peace.

On the other hand, it was all very well to say, "Cut down your numbers," but how could this be done if scientific and medical development lagged so far behind that few knew how to do it? Building up huge populations by following the way of nature was fairly simple, but it was by no means simple to reduce them again voluntarily. No long-range program was possible until economists, sociologists, and biologists alike should garner and contribute facts to the solution. Therefore the occasion was now ripe for the attention of the scientific world to be focused on the population question. I planned to bring them together at Geneva, the logical meeting place.

Dr. Little, who had accepted the presidency for the next international birth control conference, had gone to the University of Michigan as its President. He had no time for organizing, raising money, getting speakers; if this lengthy job of organizing the World Population Conference were to be done I should have to do it.

So great was the competition between the League of Nations and other groups desiring to hold conventions at Geneva during its sessions that you had to book an auditorium and rooms for delegates practically twelve months ahead. Consequently, towards the end of 1926 I went to Geneva to make arrangements for an expected three hundred guests. I had previously become acquainted with several Genevese. William Rappard, then a professor at the university there, consented to go on our committee and advise me on social details with which only a native would be familiar.

More vital to me was the Labor Office of the League, where it was not a matter of politics but of industrial problems thrashed out by people chosen for their special knowledge. Here I met Albert Thomas, a strange-looking person, short, stocky, with black beard sprouting over his face, very talkative, amazing in his energy, traveling over Europe by night, arriving in Geneva in the morning, conducting his business affairs, making speeches. But with all this activity he managed to spare hours enough to help me immeasurably when I consulted him on subjects, persons, locations, and dates.

The Salle Centrale was engaged for three days, August 30th to September 2nd of the next year, 1927. Back I went to London to enlist an English committee. Clinton Chance became my husband's assistant in supervising finances, and also provided London headquarters in his offices, supplying stenographers and secretaries. Edith How-Martyn joined us and I secured the invaluable aid of Julian Huxley, brother of Aldous, a brilliant, young, enthusiastic scientist, alive and having a mind that not only took things in, but gave them out. The Conference owed much to his fair and just opinions and the fine supporters he rounded up. Together we went over names and names and names, trying to choose a chairman of sufficient distinction around whom European scientists would rally. Professor A. M. Carr-Saunders at first accepted, but a month and a half later informed me his other obligations were so heavy he would have to limit his participation to membership on the Council.

After weeks of uncertainty, interviews, and rejections, we selected Sir Bernard Mallet, K.C.B., once of the Foreign Office, Treasury, Board of Inland Revenue, later Registrar General of Births, Deaths, and Marriages, and President of the Royal Statistical Society. Although very English, he was not too conservative. He knew well Sir Eric Drummond, then head of the League of Nations, and also had many friends on the Continent, particularly in Italy. He was typical of an individual who had climbed far, who knew where he was going and the road by which he should travel. Bored at being now in retirement, he accepted our offer willingly because, although no salary was attached, it would give him a position and an interest, and keep him socially in touch with noteworthy figures. Lady Mallet's previous experience as lady-in-waiting to Queen Victoria made her an expert hostess, and this too we needed.

Once I had to make an expedition all the way to Edinburgh to seek out Dr. F. A. E. Crew, a shining light among the younger biologists, who was making hens crow and roosters lay eggs. He readily agreed to come to the Conference and during the two days I visited him helped me build up my program.

I also wanted a paper read by André Siegfried, author of *America Comes of Age,* written after journeying some six weeks through the United States. When he invited me to tea at his home in Paris, I found him in appearance more like a mixture of American and English than French. But you could feel from his attitude and deduce from his conversation that he really envied, despised, hated Americans; by invading France with our "wealth and vulgarity," we had utterly spoiled it for his compatriots. Appreciating good food, which we never had at home, we squandered enormously, four or five times what they did. The same was true of wine; we were drinking their best, paying high for it without being able to tell the difference when we were given cheap vintages. Consequently, the Parisians were being shut out of Paris because they could not afford the prices.

"I don't see how you can blame the Americans for coming over and paying what you French ask," I replied. "You might have a complaint perhaps if we tried to undersell you or refused to buy. But it seems to me you are profiting considerably by this 'outrageous intrusion of the American dollar.'"

Although we did not get on very well and although he would not read a paper, he consented to attend.

Some of the preliminaries having been set, my husband took a villa at Cap d'Ail between Nice and Monte Carlo and near enough to Geneva, Paris, and London for trips whenever necessary. From my room the sunrise was incredibly vivid—reds and yellows mixed with the glorious blue of the Mediterranean. But it was not warm. H.G., who had a villa at Grasse, said the Riviera reputation for summer heat in wintertide was a fraud. We used to drive up to see him; the flowers for the perfume manufactories grew thick on the hillsides, so thick that the air for miles around was fragrant. Occasionally we picnicked in the tiny village on top of the mountain of Ez, a favorite haunt of artists. Once the old castle had belonged to robber barons, who could see for miles the approach of a ship; now the elder Mrs. O. P. Belmont had a palatial residence there.

The Riviera was always a Mecca for English people wanting to escape their own cold and fog and damp, and our eight guest rooms were full most of the time. It was quite novel for me to manage a household in French. We had the traditional bad luck of Americans; the maids stole from the guests and the hot water boiler only held ten gallons—not a person could have a good bath until a modern one was installed. My first cook was an expert in her field, but I soon found she was running over in her bills, even allowing for the customary perquisite of a sou for each franc she spent with the butcher and the greengrocer. Eggs and butter were on the list every day, but never how many eggs nor how much butter. I laid the responsibility on my own bad French, before I discovered it was her understanding of Americans. Then and there I told her she had to leave the following day immediately after breakfast. She received this ultimatum with tears and wailing. Somewhat uneasy I rose early at seven only to find she had gone late the preceding night, taking with her every scrap of food in the pantry and storeroom except the salt.

On one of my frequent flittings to London I went to a hairdressers' shop, unfamiliar to me but carrying the insignia of reliability, "By Appointment to Her Majesty." I was to return to Cap d'Ail in a few days and wished to appear with a wave in my hair, which I wore Mid-Victorian, very sweet and simple. After washing it, the coiffeur put an iron on a little gas arrangement in the window near by and left the room while it was drying, floating out in the wind.

Meanwhile I meditated on the subject of hair. The story of Samson seemed to have been more than an allegorical tale. I could tell from the way mine acted on being brushed in the morning how I myself was going to be. If it were strong and electric, then I was full of vitality. When slumped over my forehead so that it had to be tied down, then I dragged about spiritlessly.

It was also interesting to analyze why a woman should wear her hair in a certain style. I knew some who, at the age of sixty, curled theirs in baby ringlets; doubtless something within them wanted never to grow up. Women who had gone into the underground movement in Russia took the shears to theirs so that nothing should divert the attention to feminine appeal. I was not enough of a Feminist to sacrifice mine, but I had once come to the conclusion that the triumph of life would be to push it straight back from my forehead and tie it in a knot behind, because that was how people thought I looked. But I could not do it. No matter what was said about your feet or your figure, you could at least show your hair—in front of hats, down your back, everywhere, and so I had clung tenaciously to my long locks.

At this point in my musings I smelled something burning and turned around to find half my hair singed off to my ear. I gave one shriek, and the whole staff rushed in. But it was too late; it all had to be cut short and I actually wept.

As soon as I reached Paris I had what was left done up like a switch so that I could put it on if I felt too badly. I kept it in a box, all ready in case my husband did not want me without my hair. Eventually I had to face his disapproval. I appeared for dinner. Nothing was said. Although internally amused the guests maintained grave faces, waiting for him to notice it; not until next morning did he do so. My own attitude had changed overnight; never did I want to return to long hair.

During early spring, just when it was beginning to be most beautiful, I could spend little time at Cap d'Ail. Permanent headquarters were established in April at Geneva—four airy, spacious rooms up two flights. I had expected Edith How-Martyn to be with me, but she came down with scarlet fever in London. It was a complication to do without her until Mrs. Marjorie Martin, who had organized a pool of stenographers, secretaries, and typists at the Labor Bureau, furnished us with a most competent and experienced office staff of seventeen.

At four-thirty our large reception room was transformed into a living room where all the employees and volunteers gathered. Each in turn provided cakes, brewed the tea, and washed up afterwards. One evening at a quarter to seven some good American stopped in and, seeing everybody smiling and cheerful though still at work, asked, "Will you tell me what magic you women use to create this atmosphere? You've been at it since seven this morning."

The answer was—tea at four-thirty.

I liked being in Geneva, neat and clean and filled with watch shops. I did not even mind the great numbers of people in solemn, black clothes. If anyone died in this Calvinist city, the family wore full mourning for one year, and half for the following—in large families the process became almost perpetual.

I was not stimulated by the League sittings. There was much reading of papers and a lot of noise, but no breathless excitement during the debates. Instead, the members talked in small groups, looking very bored. The big things, just as in Washington, were done behind the scenes, at dinner tables, and in private conferences. The general meetings were merely sounding boards for public opinion. One of the most interesting features was the way a delegate could make a speech in his own language and others at their desks could plug in earphones and hear it simultaneously in theirs, coming from booths off stage.

Delegates to our Conference were all asking whether their papers were to be given in their respective tongues. I came to one swift decision—to adopt the bilingual League precedent of French and English. It was simple enough to secure interpreters who were familiar with political terminology, because they swarmed at Geneva, but to find those who understood scientific terms in German, Italian, Hungarian, Scandinavian, Portuguese, Greek, Spanish, Japanese, and Chinese was quite another affair. We tried to catch as many as we could passing through Geneva and hold them over during the time we needed their services.

In order to facilitate matters my husband generously financed the morning journal to be delivered on the breakfast tray of every person registered at the Conference, and also to members of the League of Nations. It was printed in English and French in parallel columns, containing the papers, the discussions, and any news items that might concern the delegates.

Entertainment was an important feature. A series of luncheons was to be held at the Restaurant Besson, with a host at each table, and daily the seating was to be rearranged so that each guest might be placed between those who spoke his own language or languages. M. Rappard was to give a reception. M. Fatio invited us on board the *Montreux* to visit Mme. de Staël's former home at Coppet. The chief social event was the reception and dinner at Mrs. Stanley McCormick's Fifteenth

Century Château de Prangins at Nyon. She herself could not be there, but sent a representative from America to open it, equip it with servants, and make everything ready.

Adequate handling of publicity was essential, and Albin Johnson, correspondent of the New York *World,* did this for me. He knew who was who, whom to avoid, and what persons would put the proper emphasis on what. He volunteered his services, but some of his assistants had to be paid.

We offered expenses to all speakers and certain visitors who might later be influential in their own communities. The outpouring of money was constant and I was not getting enough by soliciting from wealthy individuals. Consequently, giving up the villa in May, I came back to the United States to secure some from a foundation.

By now I knew I should be gone for at least another year, and someone had to take charge during my absence. The woman on our Board of Directors who seemed to be the most selflessly devoted, giving time and effort without stint, able to speak and to direct, was Mrs. F. Robertson-Jones. She went to meetings in blizzard or rainstorm, by subway or on foot if necessary. No dressmaker, no friend dropping in to lunch kept her from her job. But she differed from me in one respect. She could not run things unless she felt secure; she wanted a definite signing on the dotted line for so much annually instead of voluntary contributions of what people felt they could afford when they could afford it. This was quite against the spirit on which the movement had always proceeded, but I was willing to compromise. I did not then realize how serious it was going to prove in the future to have ceded this fundamental precept. She accepted the temporary presidency and I sailed back, reaching Geneva in July.

I was surprised at the rising tide of international solidarity which, in this non-industrial city, evidenced itself in astonishing fashion the night Sacco and Vanzetti were to be electrocuted. I had been working late at the office and when I came out towards midnight the crowds in the streets were so dense I could hardly move. As soon as word came in the early morning that the execution had not been stayed, they shouted reproaches before the houses of Americans, smashed the windows of the United States Consulate, and some in the League building.

Even in front of the Hôtel des Bergues, where we were stopping, they clamored their protests.

The great Dr. William Welch of Johns Hopkins was in Geneva at this time, a cheerful person, roly-poly, abounding in fun and sly, acute remarks. To listen to his unimpressive conversation you would never suspect that here was one whose name was known around the world. We had lunch together one noon. He knew how much I was depending on the Conference, how much I was hoping that the population aspect of birth control should be started in the right direction and under the right auspices. He walked a little way with me and then, putting his arm across my shoulders, said, "Perhaps you think your battles are over, but they aren't."

I felt he was trying to prepare me for something having gone wrong, though I could not imagine what it was. From then on I was aware of an unpleasant subterranean mystery insidiously disturbing the previous harmony. But nobody talked openly.

During my absence in the United States, Sir Bernard had been collecting his European friends. Not only was Italy intent on increasing her population, but the reactionary element of France also had formed a society to combat birth control. We had invited the Italians, Guglielmo Ferrero and Gaetano Salvemini, but Sir Bernard had been induced to accept as a substitute Corrado Gini, who, dark, swarthy, highly egotistical, speaking English painfully, was the perfect mirror of Mussolini's sentiments, and turned out to be a most tiresome speaker and a general nuisance.

The delegates, Gini among the first, began to gather late in August. The storm broke the Friday before our scheduled opening Tuesday, August 31st. Proofs of the official program had just come to me for my approval. Sir Bernard came into my office and looked at them. "Well, we'll just cross these off," he said, drawing his pencil through my name and those of my assistants.

"Why are you doing that?"

"The names of the workers should not be included on scientific programs."

"These people are different," I objected. "In their particular lines they are as much experts as the scientists."

"It doesn't matter. They can't go on. Out of the question. It's not done."

A long cry of dismay went up from the staff. They considered the action reprehensible and petty. The young woman who was to deliver the program to the printers would not do so. Saturday morning, secretaries and typists—twenty-one altogether—struck in a body, and without them the Conference could not proceed successfully.

While Dr. Little was trying his powers of persuasion on them, I reported the situation to Sir Bernard, saying that in justice to the women who had given so generously of their time and effort, who had raised the money, issued the invitations, paid the delegates' expenses, they should be given proper credit. All the latter had had to do was walk in at the last moment, present their papers, and take part in the social life planned for them.

Having registered my sentiments, I spent most of Sunday convincing the members of the staff that the Conference was bigger than their own hurt feelings and making them promise to return; Edith How-Martyn, however, who had joined me some time before, refused to continue because the hard labor of the workers was not to be acknowledged.

Though suspecting that the elimination of my name was the crux of the matter, I was still at a loss to know the exact reason back of this tempest until one of the delegates told me the story. Sir Eric Drummond had warned Sir Bernard that these distinguished scientists would be the laughing stock of all Europe if it were known that a woman had brought them together. Hence, in order to influence Italian and French delegates to attend, Sir Bernard had secretly pledged that I was not to be a party to the Conference and no discussion of birth control or Malthusianism would be allowed. He had hoped that the whole thing might be muddled through, and, when the delegates had come drifting in, had gone from one to another to urge, "I ask you to stand by me; do not let me down."

Only our young English friends had held out for the recognition of the women. I was not surprised at the Europeans; but it was difficult to comprehend the American attitude on this point. Perhaps Professor Pearl and Dr. Little, in agreeing to support Sir Bernard, had not realized the unfairness of the action. Clarence Little was as honest a human being as you could find, but sometimes I thought his personal allegiances obstructed his vision; he used his intelligence to make up arguments on the side of loyalty rather than on the side of principles.

At the hour designated the first meeting opened in the Salle Centrale. Each delegate had a number of extra tickets, and with the German, Belgian, and French contingents came several gentlemen with large silver crosses hanging down outside their coats. In the lobby a Genevese book concern had been permitted to set up a table for the sale of volumes by delegates. These guests immediately demanded of Sir Bernard that a certain one, of which they disapproved, be banished. Sir Bernard trotted to me and said he wished no trouble; there seemed to be some controversy. Would I have the offending books taken away?

I approached the strangers and asked who they were. They vociferated in various languages, shaking the book under my nose, getting red in the face, looking as though apoplexy might smite them. I sent for an interpreter and instructed him to say, "The hall will be for rent next Monday. Meantime, I have paid for it and will suffer no dictation from anybody as to what shall be done here."

The disturbers did not depart, and the excitement around the bookstand was so considerable that the volumes were sold out and more had to be ordered.

During the course of the Conference the Americans, British, and Scandinavians admitted the need for limiting population; the Germans and Czechs concurred, although with less assurance; the Italian and Slav voices were definitely opposed; the French, who practiced it at home, preached against it publicly. The papers of Professors East and Fairchild came perilously near mentioning the forbidden word Malthusianism, but as for birth control, it was edged about like a bomb which might explode any moment.

At the close of the three days a permanent population union was formed which is still meeting—the only international group dealing with the problem.

All the brilliant committee now took trains and steamed off for home, leaving me with the bills, the clearing up, and, most important of all, the editing of the proceedings. After a rest at a sanitorium at Glion in Switzerland I set to work, and by the end of November they had gone to press. I wanted to visit India but had to think of this trip in terms of physical fitness and, consequently, was obliged to forego it. Instead, I accepted an invitation sent me by Agnes Smedley on behalf of the Association of German Medical Women to lecture in Germany in December.

The Berlin of 1927 was far different from that of 1920. Food was plentiful, if expensive, the Adlon and other restaurants were crowded, a stirring of life and nationalism was everywhere to be sensed. At the appearance of a Zeppelin in the skies, men in the streets took off their hats as though it had been a god.

When I spoke in the Town Hall of Charlottenburg-Berlin I was reminded of the birth strike German women had been carrying on when I had last been there. German men seemed to have remembered little of this, still thinking they could keep their wives to childbearing, "their race function," as it was called. But the women had now definitely directed their thoughts from race preservation to self-preservation. As I said to my audience, "Birth control has always been practiced, beginning with infanticide, which is abhorred, and then by abortion, nearly as bad. Contraception, on the other hand, is harmless."

Almost before I had finished Dr. Alfred Grotjahn, Professor of Social Hygiene at the University of Berlin, who was seeking to present the picture of Germany's future greatness in terms of numbers, shouted out that every woman ought to have three children before she should be allowed contraceptive information. No sooner had he resumed his seat than several women were demanding recognition. I was told one of them was Dr. Marthe Ruben-Wolf. "She's a Communist. What she's saying is all on your side, but it won't do any good, because nobody has ever been able to cope with Grotjahn." Nevertheless, she answered him figure for figure, fact for fact, each based on her experience, adding that his patriotism was only skin deep. He might as well bury himself now; he would soon be buried by the rising generation and forgotten.

Then a huge shape arose, garbed in uniform and bonnet. I thought she must be a deaconess, but she turned out to be President of the Midwives Association. She bellowed in tones even louder than those of Grotjahn, putting herself on record against birth control. She could not be stopped; she would not sit down even when the bell was rung. Others answered her—the debate developed into a regular bear garden before the contestants were separated and removed.

As a result of the meeting some twenty women physicians gathered at my hotel two evenings later. Clinics were to be established at Neuköln under Dr. Kurt Bendix, the health administrator of the section; for the first time in history a government agency was actually sanctioning birth control. I promised fifty dollars a month for three years towards supplies; the doctors agreed to furnish rooms and medical services. They had a more Feminist point of view than ours in the United States; Ellen Key's liberal influence had seeped through from Scandinavia. Nevertheless, I was astonished that in the very country where we were purchasing our contraceptives, these outstanding members of their profession knew practically nothing about them. The original clinic was opened the following May and for five years contraceptive information was given in a dozen places under medical supervision. Then the Nazis came into power, they were closed, and Dr. Bendix committed suicide.

Towards the middle of the month I went to Frankfurt-am-Main where Dr. Herthe Riese was managing one of the largest of the marriage advice bureaus, of which there were about fifteen hundred in Germany. Anyone could apply to these for legal information and, for example, receive enlightenment as to who should have custody of a child if illegitimate, the amount of alimony to be paid by the husband in case of divorce, the nationality of a child if the father were a foreigner, the effect of sterilization, the results of the marriage of cousins, or any problem, including homosexuality and inversion, feeblemindedness and abortion.

In this period of great unemployment, bearing particularly heavily upon families with many children, Dr. Riese had gone to the officers of one of the big health insurance companies and persuaded them that it would be economical for them to underwrite sterilization of women carrying health insurance if this were advised by a doctor. I saw her order seventy-five of these major operations one evening between six o'clock and eight-thirty in her own clinic. Professor Grotjahn had created almost a slogan by his demand that in order to bolster up the falling birth rate every wife have three children. But the women had a counter slogan; they came in saying, "I've had my three. I want an operation." I saw also some who had returned from the hospital to report. They appeared happy and proud and pleased with themselves. Their ten days or two weeks in bed had meant food and much-needed rest.

After Germany I went vacationing to St. Moritz, to play, to skate, to ski, in that glorious high altitude. It was transcendently beautiful. I used to get up in the morning and listen to the sleighs coming up the hill with their tinkling bells, and look out at the scintillating snow; every twig of every tree was encased in ice on which the sun glistened without melting it. The scene was a white etching.

St. Moritz was much frequented by nobility and royalty on holiday. Whenever one of them arrived, like a flock of birds the hangers-on winged their way thither, settled down in all the hotels so that ordinary folk could scarcely find room.

Almost the first person I met was Lady Astor, more British than the British themselves, the Southern accent entirely gone. Her blond hair was turned sand-colored, her blue eyes were always gay, her tanned and rugged features sharp, mouth and jaw firm set, neck clean cut. She was quick-tempered and frank, and ready to take fire easily. Lord Astor, who was devoted to his wife, was much more politically astute, and usually went campaigning with her. He sat directly behind her, and, when the heckling began or a question was posed which might involve her in difficulties, he called out in a stage whisper, "Don't be drawn, Nancy, don't be drawn!"

During one House of Commons debate, Lady Astor had attempted to drive home a point by stating she was the mother of five children and therefore ought to know.

Her opponent, taking issue with her, had jumped up, saying his word should carry more weight on the subject because he was the father of seven.

Lady Astor then retorted, "But I haven't finished yet."

The British professed to be horrified at this—so vulgar and American!

Once after Lady Astor had been off skiing all day, I joined her in her room shortly before dinner. She was sitting up in bed, the windows wide open, cold cream smeared over her sunburned face, her glasses on her nose, reading *Science and Health* with the Bible near by. She had not quite ended her day's lesson.

Almost wherever I am, the subject of birth control comes up sooner or later, and it did on this occasion. Lady Astor seemed to think her religion forbade her believing in it. "If they want babies, let them have babies. If they don't want them, let them practice continence."

"Even accepting that continence is the ultimate ideal," I replied, "wouldn't you agree that contraception as an immediate necessity to help millions of women is of equal importance with wearing glasses to read the Bible? As a good Christian Scientist you should not use them. Until you get enough faith to go without, don't you think it better to read Mary Baker Eddy through some such means as glasses than not at all?"

In one second she beamed. "You're perfectly right. That's only reasonable."

If you present common-sense people with the premise that birth control is common sense, they will always react in a common-sense way. Lady Astor was a practical person, and from that time on she has been a friend of the movement.

Chapter Thirty-two

CHANGE IS HOPEFULLY BEGUN

As a cause becomes more and more successful, the ideas of the people engaged in it are bound to change. While still at St. Moritz I had been getting messages and letters about the disturbing situation in the American Birth Control League. I cabled Frances Ackermann to take it in hand, but she replied she was unable to bring about a friendly solution.

I found on my return after eighteen months that the tone of the movement had altered. The machinery I had built up to be ready for any emergency was marking time. An incident which occurred almost immediately was highly indicative. During my absence the League had been invited to participate in the Parents' Exhibition in the Grand Central Palace, and had signed a contract for a certain space. The day before the opening came a letter from Robert E. Simon, who was in charge, stating that William O'Shea, Superintendent of Public Schools, threatened to remove the Board of Education exhibit if ours were there, and he therefore requested our withdrawal.

With time so short I asked an attorney to secure a court injunction to prevent our exclusion. But one member of the Board said no step should be taken without the approval of all; a meeting should be called to discuss what course was to be adopted. I tried to reach various Directors by telephone, but before I could gather a quorum it was too late; the check which paid for our space had been sent back and the Exhibition had opened. We were left out.

Obviously, the old aggressive spirit had been superseded by a doctrinaire program of social activity; the League had settled down. I had always believed that offerings should be voluntarily measured by the individual's desire. In this way you could appeal whenever a special occasion warranted and receive anywhere from one dollar to two or three hundred. Contributors were giving to something that concerned them vitally, and they did it, not because they had signed a pledge for a limited sum, but because they wanted to help forward the movement. I could not share the League's enthusiasm over the fact that our bank account had grown to sizeable proportions—thousands of dollars drawing interest, though I admit it must have been a great relief to a Board whose previous experience had been to hear wails from the President and Treasurer as to our needs for some new project.

I knew the apathy which came from a fat bank balance. I knew also the tacit disapproval which would meet every suggestion to touch that precious fund. But my policy had been to spend, not to save, when work ought to be done. I discovered that subscribers to the *Review* had not been informed it was time for them to renew their subscriptions, and that, consequently, they had diminished from thirteen thousand to twenty-five hundred. Accordingly I told the bookkeeper to give fifteen or twenty dollars to the clerk to pay for circularizing. She said she could not do it; a bylaw had been made that nobody could direct the outlay of more than five dollars without a resolution passed by the Board.

There is doubtless a place for organizations that restrict their scope to the status quo. Most charities are like that—they live on securities, install as officers those who keep pace with but are never in advance of general opinion. Two members of the Board, with League-of-Women-Voters training, saw the movement in the light of routine, annual membership dues and a budget, going through the same ritual year after year and remaining that way, performing a quiet service in the community. I looked upon it as something temporary, something to sweep through, to be done with and finished; it was merely an instrument for accomplishment. I wanted us to avail ourselves of every psychological event, to push ahead until hospitals and public health agencies took over birth control as part of their regular program, which would end our function.

Regretfully I found the League was to side-step the greatest and most far-reaching opportunity yet offered it. It was logically equipped to enter the legislative field. But it wanted to progress state by state. I was convinced action in the Federal sphere would be quicker and much broader educationally, and that, furthermore, success there would provide a precedent for the states.

When you build an organization, you try to combine harmonious elements, but you cannot tell what they will turn out to be until a certain interval has elapsed. Some of these women were in the movement for reasons they themselves did not always understand. A few liked the sensation of being important and having personal attention; they were at their best in following an individual, yet I never felt they were doing it for me. The liberals who had started with me had never demanded a reward. What they gave was for the cause; they refused to work *for* people; they worked *with* them or not at all.

Most movements go through the phase of being brought into the drawing room. Those who disagreed with me believed the emphasis should be on social register membership, and argued that my associations had been radical. The answer was "Yes," because the radicals alone had had the vision and the courage to support me in the early days. The women who were raising objections now had only joined up after it had been safe to do so. Moreover, they were, for the most part, New Yorkers, not all of whom had even gone into neighboring states. Their attitude tended to be, "Never you mind the West; let the Empire State make the decisions."

The conflict of views which reigned in various matters was based on lives and environments which had been vastly separated. The time of some of the members of the Board had to depend on what was left from other duties—husbands, children, servants, charities, church entertainments, shopping. To me the cause was not a hobby, not a mere filler in a whirl of many engagements, not something that could wait on this or that mood, but a living inspiration. It came first in my waking consciousness and was my last thought as I fell asleep at night.

I was always willing to present my facts to experts and abide by their superior knowledge, and I gave every consideration to the suggestions of the Board. But I was no paper president. Experience had given me a judgment which entitled me to a certain amount of freedom of action, and I could not well observe the dictates of people who did not know my subject as well as I did.

June 12, 1928, I resigned the presidency of the League. Because the majority of the Directors were against this, and because I wanted to make it easier for Mrs. Robertson-Jones to take over, I stayed on the Board and continued to edit the *Review*.

But the divergence of opinions rapidly crystallized in the next few months. This had to be pondered upon and wisely dealt with. The situation was going to mean constant friction, and the League might easily disintegrate into a dying, static thing. In any event, internal discord was abhorrent. I began to ask myself whether I could pass over the *Review,* which for eleven years had been a vital part of my own being.

Then came a meeting at which the question of the editorship arose. For the first time friend opposed friend. Three voted against me; the other nine were for me. But my mind was now made up. I could fight outside enemies but not those who had been my fellow-workers; I would give complete freedom to others in order to obtain a new freedom for myself. Therefore, I surrendered the *Review* to the League as its private property. I have been sorry that this step was necessary, because the magazine changed from being a national and international medium for the expression of ideas and became merely a house organ. However, I trust that some day it will be possible to broaden its scope of usefulness once more.

The clinic, which had recently been treated rather like an orphan, still remained intact. No one in the League had ever paid any attention to it, and the doctors on the committee had been too busy with their own practices. I felt it was my responsibility, and belonged to me personally. It was an interesting angle on my own psychology. I did not regret the theoretical part of the movement going into other hands, but I would have been traitor to all that had been entrusted to me had I yielded the clinic to women who had shown themselves incapable of the understanding and sympathy required in its operation.

One of the most distressing aspects of the impasse was that members of the organization had to forswear one to choose another, and this I hated. Juliet Rublee, Frances Ackermann, and Mrs. Walter Timme came with me unhesitatingly. So, too, did Kate Hepburn, Mrs.

Day, and Dr. William H. Garth, the only minister on the Board, a forthright man who always spoke his mind.

Dr. Cooper was ready either to go with the clinic or keep on with the League in the field if I thought he could be of most use there. It seemed to me few in the country could fill his place in speaking to the profession and, consequently, I advised him to continue with the latter.

Anne Kennedy had been loyal, done her job well, served a valuable purpose. She asked whether I would approve her affiliating herself with the Holland-Rantos Company. Someone was badly needed in the manufacturing realm who was at one with our policies, who could help to instill pride in quality into the contraceptive business. Although I knew she did not like the commercial atmosphere and it would be a definite sacrifice for her, it was an excellent choice, and I was sure that any firm she was with would hold fast to ethical standards.

Mrs. Delafield called me up and I went to see her. "They've telephoned me three or four times this very day. I've refused to answer until I talked with you. What do you want me to do?"

I asked her a counter-question. "What do you want? You must go as your heart tells you."

"Well," she replied, "I realize you will now require only professionals—doctors, nurses, social workers, people who know politics—perhaps I could be of more use in the work with which I am familiar."

Thus the matter was settled.

There are many ways by which the same goal may be reached, and as a rule diverse ones must be tried out in order to find the best. I still believed we were all aiming towards this, although not seeing eye to eye on procedure.

I felt very decidedly that the future of the movement was like that of a growing child. You might guide its first faltering steps, but unless you let it run and fall it never could develop its own strength. The younger generation might need a little pushing and prodding now and then, but I was confident that eventually they were going to build toward a sound civilization.

As things recede in time they become of less and less importance. One of my absolute theories is that any movement which has been based on freedom, as this had been, is like a live cell; there is a biology of ideas as there is a biology of cells, and each goes through a process of evolution. The parent cell splits and the new entities in their turn divide and divide again. Instead of indicating breakdown, it is a sign of health; endless energy is spent trying to keep together forces which should be distinct. Each cell is fulfilling its mission in this separation, which in point of fact is no separation at all. Cohesion is maintained until in the end the whole is a vast mosaic cleaving together in union and strength.

Chapter Thirty-three

OLD FATHER ANTIC, THE LAW

⋙-⋙-⋙-⋙-⋙-⋙-⋙-⋙-⋙-⋙-⋙-⋙-⋘-⋘-⋘-⋘-⋘-⋘-⋘-⋘-⋘-⋘-⋘-⋘

BETWEEN Fifth and Sixth Avenues, practically in the shadow of the gray mass of St. Francis Xavier's College, was a shabby, brownstone building, Number 46 West Fifteenth Street. After the two years of gathering statistical histories at 104 Fifth Avenue we decided in 1925 the time had come to expand, and moved to this second home of the Clinical Research Bureau. It was next to an express agency, three steps down from the street, which was generally lined with trucks since the section was thick with lofts, factories, and warehouses—not particularly attractive, but inexpensive, and we had a happy Irish landlord who helped convert the English basement into offices and reception rooms.

The clinic was a neighborly place where mothers could congregate. We tried to keep it home-like, so that they would not feel an atmosphere of sickness or disease. The patients were accorded just as much consideration as a business house gave its clients, and not, as in many doctors' anterooms, made to wait indefinitely; they were usually nervous enough anyhow without having to endure added suspense. Moreover, they had husbands and children to feed and care for, and every hour was precious to them. As they increased, staff increased; two physicians were always on hand. We shortly included the first floor, and finally occupied the three.

About a year before we had changed our location Lord Buckmaster had introduced in the august House of Lords the memorable resolution which we had discussed when I had been last in England. Rarely had such an eloquent voice been lifted for our cause:

I would appeal on behalf . . . of the women upon whose bare backs falls the untempered lash of the primeval curse declaring that "in sorrow thou shalt bring forth children," the women with the pride and glory of their life broken and discrowned, and the flower of motherhood turned into nothing but decaying weeds; and on behalf of the children who are thrust into this world unwanted, unwelcomed, uncherished, unsustained, the children who do not bring trailing behind them clouds of glory but the taint of inherited disease, and over whose heads there may hover for ever the haunting horror of inherited madness; on behalf of them all I would appeal and as men who believe in the great future of our race, I beg of you, I earnestly entreat you, to support the motion that I seek to move.

It is said that these women whom we seek to benefit are so indolent, so ignorant, so foolish that they will not come for the information. It is not merely that they do come, but the people who make that statement do that which men so often do—they overlook the women's side of the question. What to a man may be a mere triviality, an act between a sleep and a sleep and forgotten in a moment, may bring to the woman the terror of consequences that we cannot measure, of months of sickness, misery, and ill health, ending with hours of agony that are not veiled under the cloak of chloroform's most merciful sleep. These are the people that we want to help.

We, too, were dedicated to help such women, and each day brought more to the doors of our clinic than we could provide instruction for, from all over the country and of all classes. Some weeks so many Italian women crowded in that we had to employ an interpreter. Then droves of Spanish or of Jewish arrived.

Merely judging by the letters that had come to me I was prepared to find many psychological problems presented. I often thought of the high cost of small families for women who had more or less restricted their procreative powers through other means than contraception. Although the size was limited, it was frequently accompanied by marital unhappiness and hidden psychic disturbances. But the kindness of Dr. Stone aided immeasurably in our informal "court of domestic relations."

One hot July day when I was coming out of the clinic I saw a woman, obviously pregnant, carrying a year-and-a-half-old baby, dragging another one, only a trifle bigger, crying behind her. The little girl's shoes were too short and were pinching her toes. I squirmed myself, remembering my own squeezed feet as a child. I caught up with her. "Can't I carry one of the babies? This one seems tired. Which way are you going?"

"Can you tell me where the jail is?"

"The nearest one is on Spring Street, I think."

"No, there's a jail somewheres around here."

"Didn't you get the address?"

"Yes, but I left it on the table."

"What do you want a jail for?"

"My man's there."

"What for?"

"Leaving me. He always does when I get like this."

"How many children have you?"

"Nine."

"How often has he left you?"

"This is the fourth time now."

"Do you want any more children?"

"No!" emphatically.

"Did you ever know there was a way to stop having so many?"

She almost dropped the infant, took hold of me, and said, "They won't give it to me. I'm asking everybody. They'll only give it to the rich. He wants it. He'll even have an operation. But nobody'll tell us."

I wrote down our street and number and said, "You go back to that place where I met you, and the doctor there will tell you about it."

The next day I was called up unofficially by a social worker, one of those who used to send us cases on their own initiative. She wished to explain to me: the husband would be let off if he promised to live with his family and support them; otherwise he had to serve a sentence. His wife had seen him and shown him my note; he had said he would rather go to the Island for three years than come out, unless we could not only guarantee his getting the information, but, furthermore, that it would work. He was fed up with having a new baby every year.

We suggested he talk it over with us and bring his wife. She was silent, glum, did not appear to know what it was all about. He was discouraged and doubtful. We gave him the information and he departed. "I'm the one to do this. She won't," glaring at his wife, who tagged on behind him.

We hoped for the best.

About half a year later both returned for the check-up, she with her hand on his arm. This vague, dumb, immobile woman was now in spruce jacket and skirt, head up, stepping lightly. You would never have known her for the same person. The two were off to the movies together.

Few social workers were understanding enough to smooth the lives of people in such difficulties. One agency was told by a doctor that a certain family on its rolls must not increase; the mother had already borne four babies and had a bad heart. A visiting nurse relayed this to the husband one Sunday morning when he was home from work. "If your wife becomes pregnant again, you'll be a murderer."

He was frightened. "I don't want to kill her. What shall I do?"

"Sleep alone."

The husband's disposition began to change; he became gloomy, would not talk to his wife, was ugly in sudden tempers, slapped, shouted at, and even kicked the children, rushed into the house to eat his meals and then out again, not retreating to his own bed until after she was in hers, which had been made up in the kitchen where it was warm. She was so unhappy over the metamorphosis that she made tentative approaches, whereupon he beat her and ran into the street. The next day she marched to the nurses' settlement to tell them what she thought of them. "If all you can do is keep my husband from me, stay away. I'd rather be dead than live like this!"

The case was taken to a physician, who sensibly warned, "You can't separate people by such barriers. That's not the answer."

Then she was sent to us. After she had been instructed the tension lessened and the domestic situation was remedied.

In another family of six children, the husband, part Italian and part some other nationality, was affectionate and irresponsible.

Every time he walked in the door, wreathed in smiles, his wife greeted him with frowns and scowls. She threw dishes and pots at him. He thought she was crazy and asked to have her committed. A psychiatrist talked to her and found she was in deadly fear of being pregnant again. When we saw her she really appeared to be demented.

One forenoon, six months later, as I passed through the waiting room, the nurse at the desk tendered her usual, "Good morning, Mrs. Sanger." Immediately a neat, trim woman came over to me.

"Look at me," she beamed. "You don't know me. I was the one who sat there and they said I was crazy. I don't look crazy now, do I? I wasn't crazy then—just worried to death."

For four years we went along in the clinic, working steadily, straightening mental tangles and relieving physical distress when we could. Then, early in the morning of April 15, 1929, the telephone in my apartment rang, startling me. I was pretty nervous, having been up all night with Stuart, who had mastoiditis. His temperature was running high, and he was suffering with terrible, indescribable pain.

I took off the receiver. "Hello. This is Anna. The police are here at the clinic." Briefly she related how they had descended without warning, stamped into the basement, and were at that moment tearing things to pieces.

With this meager information pounding through my brain I hastened to the street, hailed a taxi, and urged the driver to go as fast as he could to West Fifteenth Street.

The shade to the glass door was pulled down; the door itself was locked. I knocked and a plain-clothes man of the Vice Squad opened it. "Well, who are you?"

"I'm Mrs. Sanger and I want to come in."

My request was passed on to a superior and I heard someone answer, "Let her in."

Inside, in a room more than ordinarily small because partitions had sliced it up to make minute consultation booths, the patients were sitting quietly, some of them weeping. Detectives were hurrying aimlessly here and there like chickens fluttering about a raided roost, calling to each other and, amid the confusion, demanding names and addresses. The three nurses were standing around; Dr. Elizabeth Pissoort was practically in hysterics.

Dr. Stone was aloof, utterly unmoved by the tumult and the noise. I have always admired her attitude. This was the first time in her life she had been arrested, yet she treated it so lightly. "Isn't this fantastic?" she remarked. "Only a few moments ago a visiting physician from the Middle West asked one of the nurses whether we ever had any police interference. 'Oh, no,' the nurse cheerfully replied. 'Those days are over.'"

Stocky Mrs. Mary Sullivan, head of the City Policewomen's Bureau, was superintending the raid in person. Her round, thick-set face might have been genial when smiling, but was very terrifying when flushed with anger. She was giving orders to her minions in such rapid succession that it seemed impossible to keep pace with them. I tried to talk to her, asking why she had come and what it was all about.

"You'll see," said Mrs. Sullivan, and went on directing the patrolmen who were removing books from shelves, pictures and diagrams from walls, and sweeping out the contents of medical cabinets. In their zeal I noticed they were seizing articles from the sterilizers, such as gloves and medicine droppers, having no sinister significance whatsoever. They were also gathering up the various strange, weird devices patients had brought us to inquire as to their efficacy, and which we exhibited as curios.

Patrolwoman Anna McNamara, far less assured than her chief, was consulting a list in her hand and turning over the case histories in the files as swiftly as her fingers could move. Many of these contained the personal confessions of women, some of whom had entrusted us with the knowledge that their husbands had venereal disease or insanity. It ran through my mind that dire misfortune could follow in the way of being blackmailed by anyone obtaining the records.

I requested Mrs. Sullivan to show me her search warrant, and saw it had been signed by Chief Magistrate McAdoo. Nevertheless, I cautioned her, "You have no right to touch those files. Not even the nurses ever see them. They are the private property of the doctors, and if you take them you will get into trouble."

"Trouble," she snapped back. "I get into trouble? What about the trouble you're in?"

"I wouldn't change mine for yours."

"Well, this is *my* party. You keep out."

One of the policemen scooped up all the name cards and stuffed them into a waste basket to be carried off as "evidence." This was a prime violation of medical ethics; nothing was more sacred to a doctor than the confidences of his patients. Immediately Anna telephoned Dr. Robert L. Dickinson at the Academy of Medicine that the police were confiscating the case histories of patients and asked him to recommend a lawyer. He suggested Morris L. Ernst, whom Anna then called.

Doctors, nurses, and evidence were being hustled into the street. The patrol wagon had arrived, but I summoned taxicabs in which we rode to the West Twentieth Street station. On the way I heard part of the story, which accounted for my non-arrest. About three weeks earlier a woman who had registered under the name of Mrs. Tierney had come for contraceptive advice and, on examination, was found by both doctors to have rectocele, cystocele, prolapsus of the uterus, erosions, and retroversion. Although not informed of her exact condition, she was instructed, because another pregnancy would be dangerous, and told to return for a check-up. She had now done so under her rightful name of McNamara, including in her entourage Mrs. Sullivan and a police squad.

Dr. Stone, Dr. Pissoort, and the three nurses were booked for violation of Section 1142, though I attempted to explain the clinic had been active for six years quite legally under the exception, Section 1145. At Jefferson Market Court, to which we next traveled, Magistrate Rosenbluth looked over the warrant and ordered a three-hundred-dollar bond for each.

The succeeding morning I sent Stuart to a hospital for treatment; I had to attend a meeting in Boston, and the day after that go to Chicago for a series of lectures. Again I was obliged to leave him, and this time with even more misgivings. At Buffalo came a telegram saying a mastoid operation had been performed. At Chicago I telephoned the doctor and was reassured. The moment my duties were over I hurried back to be with him, and, incidentally, to attend the hearings.

I still had no idea of the fate of the case histories and had been very worried. Now I learned that the evening after the raid Magistrate McAdoo had been dining with Dr. Karl Reiland, my husband's pastor. Dr. Reiland, much upset, had remarked upon its outrageousness. Justice McAdoo, aghast and horrified to find that, without reading it, he had signed this warrant, just one of many laid on his desk, had called up the police station without delay, saying that all the twenty-four histories must be put in his safe and kept there until he arrived in the morning. He had perceived instantly that those doctors' records were going to be a serious embarrassment.

One hundred and fifty cards, our sole memoranda of names and addresses, were never restored. Catholic patients, whose records had thus been purloined, received mysterious and anonymous telephone calls warning them if they continued to go to the clinic their private lives would be exposed. They came to us asking fearfully, "Will I get in the papers?"

Immediately after the raid various doctors volunteered to go on the stand and testify as to the medical principles involved. The New York County Medical Society was aroused and passed a resolution protesting against the seizure. Through Dr. Dickinson's foresightedness and energetic interest the Academy of Medicine held a special meeting which resolved:

> We view with grave concern any action on the part of the authorities which contravenes the inviolability of the confidential relations which always have and should obtain between physicians and their patients.

Police Commissioner Grover A. Whalen, then embroiled in a mortifying, futile investigation of the murder of Arnold Rothstein, the gambler, had termed the raid a "routine matter," but when Dr. Linsley Williams, Director of the Academy, wrote a letter of protest, he decided it might not have been so routine as it had appeared, and apologized.

What had caused the raid in the first place? I employed the Burns Detective Agency to sift the affair. Approximately fifty percent of our cases were being sent by social workers on the lower East and West Sides, a conglomerate of all peoples and classes, including Irish, Italians, and other Catholics. So many had benefited and told their neighbors that others also were asking of their agencies how to get to our clinic. Catholic social workers, at a monthly meeting with officials of the Church, had sought guidance in replying to parishioners, and the ecclesiastics had been shocked to find that a clinic existed. Catholic policewomen had been summoned, Mary Sullivan had been chosen to wipe out the Clinical Research Bureau, and Mrs. McNamara selected for the decoy.

Morris Ernst, who had accepted our case, had already won a reputation for his espousal of liberal causes. It was most encouraging to discover a lawyer who was as convinced as we that the principle of the law was the important issue. Although he seemed very young, the moment I talked with him I recognized here was the person for us. He was a good psychologist as well as a good lawyer. He tried to bring everything out, but wanted the evidence correct and the minds of the witnesses straight as to what had happened.

On April 21st, when Magistrate Rosenbluth called the case, the attitude in the courtroom was far different from anything exhibited at previous birth control hearings. Only one witness was heard that day, Mrs. McNamara. In spite of the hostility of Assistant District Attorney Hogan, which was to be expected, and in spite of the Magistrate's prompting that she was a policewoman and not required to tell all, Mrs. McNamara was made to confess she had set out deliberately to deceive the clinic doctors. As she testified under Mr. Ernst's cross-examination what she had done, her stolid face turned from pink to purple. On her first visit she had learned the routine and on her second, being left alone, had copied down the number of every name card lying on Dr. Stone's desk.

Murmurs rose among the spectators, a melodious sound to ears still echoing with the harsh and suspicious accents of a mere twelve years before.

After forty minutes Magistrate Rosenbluth adjourned the hearing over our protests; if the object had been to secure a quieter and less sympathetic audience the ensuing day it failed. Now physicians took the stand: Dr. Dickinson, Dr. Frederick C. Holden, Dr. Foster Kennedy, the neurologist. The climax came when Mr. Hogan asked Dr. Louis T. Harris, former Commissioner of Health of New York City, whether he had ever given any information to a patient regardless of a marriage certificate. Dr. Harris answered, "The birth control clinic is a public health work. Every woman desiring treatment is asked whether she is married."

"Don't they have to bring their marriage certificates with them?"

"No."

The Magistrate leaned forward ponderously and heavily. "Does not the clinic send out social workers to discover the truth of patients' statements?"

Mr. Ernst interpolated, "Did you ever know of a situation where a doctor dispatched a detective to find out whether his patient were married?"

Loud laughter came from the listeners. Judge Rosenbluth pounded his gavel. "Unless there is absolute silence I shall clear the court room." Then, seeming to grow more angry, he added, "On second thought I shall clear it anyhow. Out you go."

The joke was on him. It was the doctors who had laughed the loudest and their presence as witnesses could not be dispensed with. Following a fifteen-minute recess the audience was once again in the room, more partisan than ever.

Young Mr. Hogan tried to be dramatic, but he failed before our attorney's cold uncompromising logic. He took up one of the pessaries that had been appropriated in the raid and addressed Dr. Harris. "You know that the laws of New York State are that contraception may be given only for the cure or prevention of disease. Do you dare to claim this article will cure tuberculosis? Will it cure cancer, high blood pressure, heart disease, kidney disease?"

Again came mirth. No one assumed a pessary or any other form of contraceptive could effect a cure. "But," replied Dr. Harris, "in preventing conception it may be said to cure because pregnancy can often be the cause of furthering the progress of a disease."

A month later the defendants were discharged, Magistrate Rosenbluth writing an admirably lucid, fair, and definite decision:

Good faith in these circumstances is the belief of the physician that the prevention of conception is necessary for a patient's health and physical welfare.

Mrs. Sullivan was temporarily demoted. She continued, however, to be paid the same salary as before, and was eventually restored to rank.

It was an ill wind that did not blow somebody good. After this our calendars were filled three weeks in advance, and we had to add two evenings a week to the daily routine. To our amazement among the many patients there appeared one afternoon Mrs. McNamara, who had first heard in court of her five ailments, every one of which legally entitled her to contraceptive information. She had come back to ask Dr. Stone whether she really had so many things the matter with her, and was assured the diagnosis was correct.

The raid had been one of the worst errors committed by the opposition, because it had touched the doctors in a most sensitive spot, the sanctity of records, and they were obliged to stand by us, whether they wanted to or not. Even so we were not yet certain that the question had been settled for all time. At any moment our Irish landlord might receive orders from his bishop to eject us. To avoid any such contingency and to take care of the increasing numbers, in 1930 we bought a house of our own at Seventeen West Sixteenth Street.

Our new building gave us not only more room for patients but better opportunities for research. It was a sad commentary that though medicine had evolved into the preventive state where it was causing a revolution in sanitation and health education, contraceptive technique had been little advanced since the days of Mensinga.

However, research was going on in various lands under the most diverse conditions. A modern clinic had started up again in the Netherlands, a memorial to Aletta Jacobs and bearing her name. It was based on the old Rutgers standards which had lapsed for so long. America and England, as the consequence of guiding the movement along professional lines and putting emphasis on the keeping of records, had made the greatest strides. But all accomplishments needed to be correlated, co-ordinated, unified in a scientific conference. Zurich was a central location for many countries, and, in addition, offered beautiful scenery in abundance; it was a pleasant place to be.

September 1, 1930, some one hundred and thirty physicians and directors of clinics from different parts of the world began comparing notes and reporting progress. Only the present generation was behind the times. A representative from the Netherlands one day stood up, a rather youthful person, and said, "I am glad to announce that at last we in the Netherlands have also a birth control clinic." This was extraordinary in view of the fact that the Netherlands had been the pioneer country and had inspired us all.

Even more recently I encountered a young matron, a member of the American Birth Control League and head of the state organization in New Jersey, who had again utterly disassociated herself from history. She urged, "Mrs. Sanger, can't we convert you to the establishment of clinics? You know, they're going, they're being established all over the country."

"When were you born?" was all I could gasp.

These two women epitomized a day which had not studied what had gone before; if new to their minds, then it was new.

In contrast to Geneva and its problems in tact, Zurich was a dovecote. One slight incident alone disturbed the calm. I had gone to Berlin to secure delegates and there in a public theater had seen a film which had traversed the length and breadth of Germany as propaganda for abortion under safe conditions. The scene opened with feet endlessly passing on the streets; you saw a kerchief drop, a masculine hand reach down to pick it up, the boy and girl at lunch, she looking up at him wide-eyed. Soon she was obliged to go to a *femme savante* in a filthy narrow old alley; you watched her ascend the rickety stairs, an ancient crone peeling potatoes, shoving wood in the stove with dirty hands, the agony in the girl's face. It was a succession of pictures such as this, straight out of life itself.

I had borrowed the film and rented a theater in Geneva. To my great surprise and no little amusement when the Caesarian section appeared on the screen several men and women in the audience began to faint, among them our own workers, even Edith How-Martyn. One, a young scientist, had to be led out and given a drink to brace him up. Cars and taxis were commandeered to cart the squeamish back to their hotels.

This Conference must remain a milestone because there all propaganda, all moral and ethical aspects of the subject were forgotten. The whole problem was lifted out of the troubled atmosphere of theory, where previously it had been battered by the winds of doctrine and the brutal gusts of prejudice, into the current of serene, impersonal, scientific abstraction. It was too early to tell what practical results might ensue, but at least we soon received the assurance that certain doctors would welcome efficient contraceptives.

Individual physicians in New York had since 1923 taken serious thought of the need for contraception. Mrs. Amos Pinchot had organized certain outstanding members of the Academy of Medicine into the Committee on Maternal Health. They had been fortunate enough to secure the well-known retired gynecologist, Dr. Dickinson, as secretary. He had trained many of the younger men and was able to bring into the movement doctors who would have paid slight attention to anyone less admired and honored. With the aid of various foundations, the Committee on Maternal Health had been doing a fine piece of work in publishing the findings of scientists in brochures and pamphlets.

The Academy, after the Zurich Conference, formally declared that "the public is entitled to expect counsel and information by the medical profession on the important and intimate matter of contraceptive advice."

We had been attaining small victories, and little by little and bit by bit the Protestant churches had begun to regard us favorably. In September, 1925, the House of Bishops of the Protestant Episcopal Church, meeting at Portland, Oregon, had gone on record against birth control. Later some of the wives of these same bishops had come to me in New York and asked my help in educating their husbands. A group of three had taken it upon themselves to see that every bishop was thoroughly enlightened. The consequence of the campaign was that at a subsequent meeting in 1934 they reversed their original stand.

Even the Jews had on occasion been in opposition. Rabbi Mischkind of Tremont Temple had been rebuked by his Board of Trustees for having invited me to speak one Sunday morning. Rather than surrender he had resigned and found another synagogue in which I could appear.

Now the Central Conference of American Rabbis urged the recognition of birth control. The hundred and seventieth conference of the Methodist Church sanctioned it and the American Unitarian Association did the same. A special commission appointed by the Presbyterian General Assembly to study the problems of divorce and remarriage admitted the desirability of restricting births under medical advice. And in March, 1931, the Committee on Marriage and the Home of the Federal Council of the Churches of Christ in America approved it.

Due in large measure to Lord Dawson's eloquence, the Bishops at Lambeth gave us one of our greatest triumphs by voting 193 to 67 in favor of birth control. Bernard Shaw believed the Church of England was making a "belated attempt to see whether it could catch up with the Twentieth Century."

Ever since the outburst of religious intolerance at Town Hall, it had been apparent that in the United States the Catholic hierarchy and officialdom were going to be the principal enemies of birth control. From city to city you could feel this. At Albany we could not have a hall because the police commissioner was a Catholic. In Cincinnati the Knights of Columbus almost succeeded in barring us from the hotel. At Syracuse the mayor had to veto the ordinance of the Catholic Council before we could hold a conference there. When I was to give a lecture in Milwaukee the Catholic Women's League came to protest the meeting to Socialist Mayor Hoane. He had told them, however, "If I prevent Mrs. Sanger from speaking because you protest, I shall also have to prevent you from speaking when others object to Catholic doctrine. Free speech must prevail in Milwaukee."

Tactics aiming to bring about a reconciliation between the Anglicans and Rome had been rendered futile by the endorsement of the Bishops. I suspected the demand for a clear statement from the Vatican on the question originated in the United States where Catholic women were showing a gradual yet persistent spirit of independence. In spite of Church canons they were using contraceptives, and the Church, in its wisdom, was obliged to change the law to keep its parishioners from breaking it. In December came the answer in the form of a Papal Encyclical. The world moved but the Pope sat still.

He declared that he was "looking with paternal eye—as from a watch-tower." But what was he looking at?

The Pope said over and over again that sexual intercourse, unless definitely designed to produce children, was against nature and a sin; he roundly condemned any contraceptive and he affirmed that in the matter of limiting families continence alone was permissible. Yet in the selfsame document he nullified his previous insistance that procreation was the sole justification of marital relations by countenancing them at times when pregnancy could not result. These times he made indefinite; they might refer to sterility, post-menopause, or the so-called "safe period" during the menstrual cycle; in fine, he was saying first, that you might not have intercourse unless you expected to have a child, and, in the same breath, that you might have intercourse when you could not possibly have a child. This Jesuitical inconsistency allowed a loophole for the issuance of the Latz Foundation booklet entitled *The Rhythm of Sterility and Fertility in Women*, published with "ecclesiastical approval" and recommended by Catholic societies.

It had become part of my routine to answer every challenge to the cause, just as I tried to answer every question at a meeting. Here again was the hoary "nature" argument which should have been in its grave long since. The contention that it was sin to interrupt nature in her processes was simple nonsense. The Pope frustrated her by shaving or having his hair cut. Whenever we caught a fish or shot a wolf or slaughtered a lamb, whenever we pulled a weed or pruned a fruit tree, we too frustrated nature. Disease germs were perfectly natural little fellows which had to be frustrated before we could get well. As for the alleged "safe period" which *Rhythm* now set forth, what could be more unnatural than to restrict intercourse to the very time when nature had least intended it?

But, taking one consideration with another, it seemed to me then that the birth control idea was rolling merrily along. I could sympathize with an indignant old radical who left a birth control congress sniffing, "This thing has got too darned safe for me."

Chapter Thirty-four

SENATORS, BE NOT AFFRIGHTED

"SHOULD the Federal Laws Be Changed?" was the subject of my debate with Chief Justice Richard B. Russell of Georgia, who had had eighteen children by two wives. I always welcomed a debate, although after the first few years it had been almost impossible to find anyone to defend the other side, and therefore I was pleased to be called to Atlanta, in May, 1931, for this one.

The old judge, white-haired and with white eyebrows and mustache, his figure still erect, fixed me with a glance, sometimes satiric and sometimes flaming with the rage of an Old Testament prophet. He talked of the sacredness of motherhood, the home, and the State of Georgia. "We don't need birth control in Georgia. We've had to give up two Congressmen now because we don't have enough people. If New York wants to wipe out her population, she can. We need ours. . . . I can take care of all the children God sent me. I believe God sent them to me because they have souls. Poodle dogs and jackasses don't have souls. I have obeyed the command of God to 'increase and multiply.' "

His children and their wives and their relatives occupying several rows of seats down front applauded vigorously.

On the train coming back I bought a paper and noted with surprise that I had been awarded the American Women's Association medal for accomplishments on behalf of women, and was supposed to be receiving it that night in New York. I sent a telegram of thanks to Anne Morgan saying that I had just learned about it and there was no way of my attending.

It was nice to be handed a medal instead of a warrant; at the postponed dinner, organized by John A. Kingsbury, a director of the Milbank Fund, I sat there listening to the beautiful tributes and asked myself, "Is it really true? Am I awake? Or is it a dream?" I never thought of the medal as being given to me as a person, but to the cause, the women I represented, and, representing them, went through the act of accepting it.

As I was trying to express this, a little woman who used to appear frequently on all sorts of occasions came up through the well-groomed audience, climbed to the platform, offered me a bouquet of flowers from the Brownsville mothers. "You are our Abraham Lincoln," she said, unconscious of the smiles, amused yet sympathetic, of the audience. She left a kiss upon my brow and hurriedly went back to her place. To me she embodied the spirit of Mrs. Sachs, who had died so long ago—all I was still working for, though through channels which had broadened immeasurably since then.

In the beginning of the birth control movement the main purpose had been the mitigation of women's suffering, Comstock law or no Comstock law. Its very genesis had been the conscious, deliberate, and public violation of this statute. Later, to change it became imperative, so that the millions who depended upon dispensaries and hospitals could be instructed by capable hands.

In 1918 Mary Ware Dennett had dissolved the old National Birth Control League into the Voluntary Parenthood League, which had for its aim the repeal of the Federal law. This seemed fine on the surface but repeal would permit anyone to give and send contraceptive devices as well as information to anyone through the mails regardless of standards or quality. Mrs. Dennett still looked upon the movement as a free-speech and free-press issue, just as I had done before going to the Netherlands. Now I considered no one had sufficient knowledge of the possible consequences of some contraceptives to permit them to be manufactured or distributed without guidance or direction. They might kill the birth control movement as well as some of the women who used them. No sponsor could be found until in 1923 Senator Cummins had introduced her repeal, or so-called open bill, in which the lack of safeguards was severely criticized. Therefore she had had it reintroduced in 1924 with a clause added that all literature containing contraceptive information must be certified by five physicians as "not injurious to life or health." This bill, practically impossible of application, died in committee.

Since we believed information should be disseminated only by doctors we had kept very quiet and out of it during those years. But we had our own ideas of what sort of legislation we preferred. When Mrs. Dennett retired and her organization ceased its work Mrs. Day, Anne Kennedy, and I, in January, 1926, went down to Washington on a scouting expedition to take a survey of the mental attitude of Congressmen and discover whether their reaction was more favorable towards a repeal bill or our proposal of an "amended doctors' bill." We set up headquarters and began interviewing senators until we had satisfied ourselves that personal sentiment was more in favor of our policy.

We thought it advisable also to sound out the Catholic stand. Getting together was the trend of the times. Eugenists, the Voluntary Parenthood League, the American Birth Control League, all were trying to meet each other. People of tolerant opinions had always felt the Catholic Church was too clever to oppose a movement that inevitably it would some day have to sanction, and the tumult and interference was simply the result of local ignorance and bigotry; if we could reach the scholarly heads themselves, if we could all "sit at a table and talk things over," we would find their ideals of humanitarianism were much like our own.

Consequently, Anne had an interview with members of the Catholic Welfare Conference, including Monsignor John Ryan, John M. Cooper, Ph.D., Father Burke, and other prelates. We thought we would agree on the doctors' bill—that they surely wanted the public safeguarded from the misuse of contraceptives. But they unequivocally set forth their objections; not even a physician's indisputable right to save lives swayed them. They declared it was their office to see that no "social or moral" legislation passed Congress that did not conform to the tenets of Catholic doctrine; they would attempt to prevent any such bill from becoming a law. Anne wrote out a report of the interview, including this shocking statement, and showed it to them so they might have an opportunity to correct it if they so desired. They left it essentially as written.

Considering this a fundamental issue of liberty and life not affecting birth control alone, I took the presumptuous document to H. L. Mencken, supposedly the outstanding libertarian in America. He had the power to evoke a response from thinking minds, even though they were rock-bound in patriotic dogmas; he had knocked down a great many gods, chiefly along political and religious lines.

Trusting that Mencken would make an effective protest in the *American Mercury,* I talked to him, explained the situation, predicting that if we let this go unnoticed we should all have to endure the future consequences. He admitted the Catholic action was brazen, but mentioned the fact that he had too many friends of that faith in Baltimore for him to attack their church. I gained the impression he was out to slash and hit where the cause was obviously popular, but had no intention of leading a forlorn hope or playing the role of a pioneer for freedom. He never fulfilled the expectations I once had of him; he was not a tree bearing fruit but a spoon stirring around, very much of a "Yes, but-er." He said, "Oh, yes, that is grand, but, on the other hand, there is this to be said for the other side."

In our campaign of educating the public in the necessity for changing the Federal statute I began having regional conferences in the East, South, Middle West, West, and linking them all into an organization to support the bill. One of these was at Los Angeles. At first most of the Westerners wanted an open bill such as Mrs. Dennett's, and I stood rather alone on the doctors' amendment, which was only approved on the last night of the Conference by a very narrow margin.

As the people filed out I saw at the end of the room a thin, almost emaciated woman with gray hair, somewhat shabby, but not unusually so. She held out a bony hand to clasp mine, saying practically nothing, just a word or two, and her name, Kaufman, came to me. I remembered it because Viola Kaufman had been one of the small subscribers to birth control in the past, and I was familiar with most of these names. I thought nothing further of it at the time.

Wanting all the endorsement I could get for the doctors' bill, and particularly that of the American Medical Association, I made a special trip to Chicago to see Dr. Morris Fishbein, who was a power in that organization. I asked for advice or help, and offered to draw up a bill in any way which would suit them. Dr. Fishbein appeared sympathetic and turned me over to Dr. William C. Woodward, the legislative director; we had a pleasant conversation and that was all. Though he made no comment as to its merits or demerits, I put the bill on record in their office.

Tried and true friends, whose abilities and loyalties had been tested and proved, rallied around the National Committee on Federal Legislation for Birth Control, which established its headquarters in Washington in 1931. Frances Ackermann assisted my husband as Treasurer. For Vice President we had Mrs. Walter Timme who had left the League of Women Voters, a fine speaker, a clear-thinking crusader, a devoted ally of long standing. Tall, large-framed, broad-shouldered, she could harangue audiences in the strong, convincing, and forceful fashion of the early, suffrage, soapbox days—nothing delicate or fragile. When she had an idea, it was an idea, and she stated it as an idea. More than once our bank account would have faded to a mere wraith had it not been for Ida Timme's money-raising talents.

Mrs. Alexander C. Dick was Secretary. She had the old-fashioned head of a daguerreotype, but was thoroughly modern in her verve and gay personality and her quick agility of mind. Since 1916, when I had first known her, she had been really interested in the research end of birth control, and definitely had agreed with the then new war cry that it should be under medical supervision. It was mainly due to her and her late husband, Charles Brush of Cleveland, that Ohio had had from the beginning one of the best organized and conducted state leagues.

Kate Hepburn was Chairman. In her long public career she had learned great efficiency and was so careful of minutiae that she never let our witnesses run over their time. Just as we were swinging along briskly she invariably tugged at a coat and passed over a little slip— "time up in one minute."

Best of all our lobbyists was Mrs. Hazel Moore, our Legislative Secretary, who had left the Red Cross in the South to support us. Nothing could withstand her indefatigable enthusiasm, and it took a stout Senator to harden his heart against her feminine ruses and winning manners.

We now began to be initiated into the A B C of Federal legislative procedure. After your bill had been drawn up, you had to find a Congressman to introduce it. Sometimes he believed in it a hundred percent; sometimes he believed in the individual a hundred percent; sometimes he sponsored it only to be accommodating and agreeable, in which case it was called "by request," a very weak way since you knew he was not going to fight for it. When introduced, the bill was read in the House or Senate and at once referred to a committee, those having to do with changing a law to the Judiciary. Ours was difficult to manage at first, because we were trying to alter several statutes simultaneously, not merely Section 211 and everything pertaining to mails and common carriers, but also laws relating to imports. We had a general principle back of us, but we had to keep whacking off clauses so that it would not be thrown into the wrong committee.

If you were fortunate enough to secure a Senate hearing for your bill the chairman of your committee appointed a sub-committee of about three; in the House, the entire committee might attend the hearing. A day was set and you began preparing your ammunition; the opposition was allowed an equal amount of time to the second. After the hearing a vote was taken. If they were against it, they killed it then and there; if they recommended it, it came up before the full committee and, if then approved, went to the Senate or House for debate on the floor.

To the frantic, worried, harassed, driven Congressmen of 1931 the announcement of a birth control bill was like a message from Mars, only less interesting and more remote. The mind of each Senator resembled a telephone switchboard with his wary secretary as the operator. All the wires were tied up with foreign debts, unemployment relief, reparations, moratoriums, sales taxes, prohibition, budgets and bonuses, war in Manchuria, peace conferences, disarmament, and the tariff—issues of vital concern to themselves for which they needed every vote; and their principal endeavor was not to cause conflict or get themselves disliked. What chance had we to plug in?

When the vigilant secretary found we were not direct constituents, we were told the Senator was busy—in conference, in committee, meeting an arriving delegation. Would we come back later, tomorrow, next week? Always we came back promptly and on the dot. For months it was almost impossible to see any of them. Often as many as forty calls were made, and if we succeeded in getting two interviews, we considered that a good day's work. When finally we did reach them, few of the younger, still fewer of the older, Senators knew what we were talking about. When we were able to make this clear, young and old alike, just as in the state legislatures, were full of fears—fear of prejudices, fear of cloakroom joshings, mainly fear of Catholic opposition.

Though Senator Norris had approved the repeal bill, he believed that ours had a better chance of passing because antagonism to the former was even greater than in 1926. He himself had Muscle Shoals and the Lame Duck Amendment on his hands and several more pet projects to boot, and suggested we get somebody to introduce the bill who would not be up for re-election. Our choice fell on Senator Frederick Huntington Gillett of Massachusetts, for years Speaker of the House, and now about to retire. He was a gentleman born, gray-haired, typically New England, without children or any particular philosophy regarding birth control. Our Southern helpers, notably Mrs. J. B. Vandeveer, were persistent and determined. They would not be put off with polite, routine dismissals, but asked point-blank, "Will you introduce this bill for us?" Senator Gillett, recognizing their earnestness, agreed. But we heard no more of it.

When I returned at the next session of the same Congress someone remarked, "Aren't you lucky to have had your bill introduced?"

"What?" I stared with wide-open eyes.

"Yes, Senator Gillett remembered it a few days before the session closed."

I called on him at once. "Where's our bill gone?"

It had gone nowhere. "We'll just send it around to the Judiciary Committee," said the Senator. "Norris is Chairman and he's friendly. He'll pick out a good sub-committee for you."

We gathered our witnesses together the night before the hearing, which was to be February 13th, and asked, "What do you want to say? How long do you want in which to say it?" We had eight people to testify in the space of two hours; moments had to be carefully parceled out to each. We were permitted to deduct ten from our allotment the first day to be used the following one for a rebuttal.

William E. Borah of Idaho and Sam G. Bratton of New Mexico had been assigned to us with Senator Gillett, but Borah did not appear. The audience, mostly women, crowded the committee room, imposing with marble pillars, glossy mahogany, gleaming windows.

Dr. John Whitridge Williams, obstetrician in chief of Johns Hopkins, summed up the medical evidence for birth control. "A doctor who has this information (prevention of conception) and does not give it cannot help feeling he is taking a responsibility for the lives and welfare of large numbers of people." The Reverend Charles Francis Potter, founder of the Humanist Society of New York, discussed the moral phase. "The bird of war is not the eagle but the stork." Professor Roswell H. Johnson, then at the University of Pittsburgh, stressed eugenics. "Most intelligent, well-informed people . . . are so determined in this (spacing children) that no laws yet devised succeed in forcing a natural family, which is about eighteen children, upon them." Rabbi Sidney Goldstein dealt with religious aspects. "The population is not made up of those who are born but is made up of those who survive." Professor of Sociology Henry Pratt Fairchild spoke from the economic point of view. "We human individuals cannot break laws of nature. We can, however, choose which of her laws we see fit to obey." Mrs. Douglas Moffatt announced that the twenty-seven hundred members of the New York City Junior League were overwhelmingly in favor of the bill.

The next morning the opposition began by trying to prove that we who advocated birth control, a Russian innovation, were seeking to pull down motherhood and the family as had been done in Russia. The Honorable Mary T. Norton, Representative from New Jersey, made the astounding assertion that the happiest family was the big one, and that a large percentage of the great men and women of this country were born poor; this was a blessing since it fired them with ambition. And she mentioned Abraham Lincoln, whose birthday had been but two days before. I was particularly outraged by hearing statements from other witnesses that the American Federation of Labor was against us, that the American Medical Association was antagonistic, and that the Methodist and other churches were going to help defeat our bill. Speaker after speaker representing Catholic organizations repeatedly hurled such dramatic tirades as, "I ask you, gentlemen, in the name of the twenty million Catholic citizens of the country, to whose deep religious convictions these vices are abhorrent, and of all those to whom the virtue of a mother or a daughter is sacred, to report unfavorably on this diabolical and damnable bill!"

It was difficult to gauge the impression that was being made; you could only sense that the response was one of feeling. These dogmatists, harking back to the Dark Ages, summoned to their aid the same arguments that had been used to hinder every advance in our civilization—that it was against nature, against God, against the Bible, against the country's best interests, and against morality. Even though you proved your case by statistics and reason and every known device of the human mind, the opponents parroted the line of attack over and over again; in the end you realized that the appeal to intelligence was futile.

On occasions like this the inward fury that possessed me warmed from coldness to white heat; it did not produce oratory, but it enabled me to move others. The way to meet the opposition was to keep emotions in hand and, at the same time, without stumbling or fumbling, to let them go. Every word I said was calculated and thought through, not in advance, but as it came along. I did not react this way often, but I did that day.

When my ten minutes for rebuttal came, I knew that emotional speed was required. Nevertheless, I first knocked down their false assertions: that the birth control movement had originated in this country during 1914, long before anyone had ever heard of Bolshevism; that the objections of the American Federation of Labor had referred to the repeal bill of 1925, quite different from the doctors' bill now under discussion; that the American Medical Association had taken no stand, but two of its most important branches, the Neurological and Woman's Medical, had gone on record in our favor; that Dr. C. I. Wilson of the Methodist Board had denied his church was opposed, and, in fact, its ministers had worked unofficially for us. "When someone says that the happiest families are the largest ones, and that the world's great leaders have been of large families, I would like to call to your attention that the great leader of Christianity, Jesus Christ himself, was said to be an only child." Here the Catholics crossed themselves and muttered, 'Blasphemy!'

"These opponents have had the laws with them, the wealth, the press, and yet they have come today to say they are afraid of the morals of their people if they have knowledge, if they do not continue to be kept in fear and ignorance. Then I say their moral teachings are not very deep. Mr. Chairman, we say that we want children conceived in love, born of parents' conscious desire, and born into the world with sound bodies and sound minds."

The two Senators sat there in silence. The bill was killed, due to the adverse vote of Senator Borah—who had not attended the hearings.

The next year, 1932, Senator Gillett was gone and a substitute had to be found. Believing the first woman Senator would be on the side of her sex, we asked Mrs. Hattie Caraway to introduce the bill. She said she herself was interested in the subject, but her secretary would not let her touch it.

Ordinarily Congressmen paid little attention to abstract arguments, logic, or the humanitarian needs of outsiders. But they could be reached through their constituents. One way of doing this was to get women "back home" to help themselves directly by writing letters. This required money. We sought it from a foundation which donated ten thousand dollars earmarked for this special purpose. To the still continuing stream of letters from mothers, requesting as always contraceptive advice, my reply went, "I would gladly give you the information you ask for if the law permitted. Your Congressman now has the opportunity to vote on this bill. Send him a letter telling how many children you have living, how many babies dead, how many abortions, what wages your husband receives, everything you have told me," and I enclosed an envelope, stamped and addressed to their respective Congressmen.

While walking one day through the tunnel which connected the House with the Senate, I stopped to ask a man my direction. He said, "I'm going your way. Come along and I'll show you."

We fell into conversation. He informed me he was a Senator, and asked what I was doing.

"I'm working on the birth control bill."

"That's funny. I've just had a letter from a woman five miles from where I've lived most of my life. Listen to this."

And he took it out of his pocket and read the history of the woman's abortions and operations. "I've never heard anything quite so awful, and at the bottom she says, 'You can help me by getting this law changed, and Mrs. Sanger, who has the information, will send it to me if you get the law changed.'"

These letters brought fine results. Through them Senator Henry D. Hatfield of West Virginia was persuaded to introduce the bill. At the hearing he described how as physician and surgeon and governor of his state he had seen the free mating of the unfit, and had forced through a sterilization law. We produced our usual array of experts, and the opposition produced Dr. Howard Atwood Kelly, a famous gynecologist in his day at Johns Hopkins, but now Professor Emeritus and very old, who rambled discursively on morals; his was a state of mind if not of reason. Dr. John A. Ryan, a member of the National Catholic Welfare Conference, chose economics for his discussion. Neither spoke on his own subject, but selected something on which he was not an authority.

The bill was killed in committee, and the one introduced by Representative Frank Hancock of North Carolina in the House got into the wrong committee so nothing happened.

Before you had seen it, the Congress of the United States loomed impressively in your consciousness; you had a feeling, "This is the greatest country in the world, this is its Government, I helped to send these men here." Then you watched Congress at work, listened to it, and were disillusioned. A few years of sitting in the gallery and looking down gave you less respect for the quality of our representatives, less faith in legislative action, and you wondered whether those who had already abandoned hope of obtaining relief in this way and resorted to direct action had not, perhaps, the right idea.

The same arguments went on from year to year. A certain amount of publicity was secured, a certain number were educated. Some of our followers, in face of the evidence to the contrary, still were confident that if the Catholics understood our bill they would not obstruct it. They said Representative Arthur D. Healey of Massachusetts, a member of the Judiciary Committee, although a Catholic was so liberal that if he could once be made to see the reasons back of it he would cease being openly hostile, and it might even get out of committee. Accordingly, I went to his office; we talked at length, and again got nowhere. As I was leaving this father of four said, in order to explain himself, "You see, Mrs. Sanger, I'm just one of those unusual men who are very fond of children." I was inwardly convulsed at the thought that he considered himself unusual and that we were all a lot of Herods trying to do away with babies.

At first it seemed that I was to have greater success as the result of my interview with Dr. Joseph J. Mundell, Professor of Obstetrics at Georgetown University, who advised the Catholic Welfare Conference on all their medical legislation. In a private session I conceded some things in the bill; Dr. Mundell gave up certain others. The compromise apparently suited everybody.

In 1934 identical bills were introduced in Senate and House, the latter by Representative Walter M. Pierce, Democrat, who as Governor of Oregon had burned his political bridges by vetoing a bill which permitted parochial schools. Since he had nothing to lose, he did not have to play politics.

Hatton W. Summers of Texas was chairman of the hearing. Our side led off, again specialists in each line covering the vital points. Rabbi Edward L. Israel of Baltimore made an impassioned plea. "And I say, gentlemen, if this thing we are now advocating is not morally right, let us stop being hypocrites and, in its place, put a law on our statute books that will drive contraceptive devices out of your homes and mine."

Here John C. Lehr of Michigan, sitting back in his chair with thumbs hitched in his suspenders, declared pompously, "As a member of this Committee I want to go on record there have never been any contraceptives used in my home. I have six children, too."

Malcolm C. Tarver of Georgia interrupted, "You don't mean any member of Congress has used anything of that kind, do you?" His surprise was obviously genuine.

The proponents of our bill, even elderly women, had stood while delivering their testimony. But when Father Charles E. Coughlin entered, cheeks very pink over his black collar, a chair was placed for him, because as a representative of the Church he would not stand before a representative body of the State. He began talking at random, "I have not heard one word of the testimony these ladies and gentlemen have produced, and my remarks are not addressed to them now, because I can easily handle them over the radio Sunday after Sunday. . . . You, gentlemen, you are married men, all of you, and you know more about it than I will ever know." Here he arched his eyebrows into a leer. "The Chairman, I understand, is a bachelor like myself. . . . We know how these contraceptives are bootlegged in the corner drug stores surrounding our high schools. Why are they around the high schools? To teach them how to fornicate and not get caught. All this bill means is 'How to commit adultery and not get caught.'"

Some of our sympathizers walked out of the room. Two Congressmen left the table. But we were a polite, well-behaved group that shrank from scenes, and, though furious and indignant, we allowed him to conclude his half-hour of grossness.

I could hardly believe my ears when Dr. Mundell, who shortly before had helped us formulate a bill which he said was satisfactory to him, rose and deliberately betrayed us by stating there was no need for legislation whatsoever, because a recent scientific work—by which he meant *Rhythm*—had shown that fertility in women could be reckoned with almost mathematical precision.

In the rebuttal Dr. Prentiss Willson testified that the theory of the cycle of sterility had no medical standing. Then came my turn. I had in my pocket a copy of *Rhythm,* and quoted from it. Under the heading of procreation it asked whether married people were obliged to bring into the world all the children they could, and then made answer:

Far from being an obligation, such a course may be utterly indefensible. Broadly speaking, married couples have not the right to bring into the world children whom they are unable to support, for they would thereby inflict a grievous damage upon society.

I told the committee that apparently the only distinction in the pros and cons of the birth control question was that the method we advocated was a scientific one under the supervision of doctors; that of the Catholics had *not* been proved scientifically and was open to any boy or girl who could read the English language.

Nevertheless, the bill again died in committee.

The Senate hearings on the bill, introduced by our old friend Daniel O. Hastings of Delaware, did not come until March. We presented our advocates, among them a miner's wife from West Virginia, the native state of two members of the committee, Hatfield and Nealy. She was a perfect illustration of the type which most needed birth control. When she had finished a Catholic woman asked her, "Which of your nine children would you rather see dead?"

"Oh, I don't want to see any of them dead. I love them all; but I don't love those I haven't had."

Her reply was just right; it could not have been better.

Vito Silecchia, my former coal and ice vendor from Fourteenth Street, also made his way to Washington and told his simple story. His wife had come to me when pregnant with her fourth child, and I had said I could do nothing for her until she had had her baby. Now, many years afterwards, she had no more than the four. Vito reasoned his case as a man, "I am a Catholic myself. The Catholics say we should have much children. I say different. I say it is not good to have too many children. You can't take care of them." He ended by describing the mother of six who lived next door to him. "I told her, 'I will take you to a place. It is a wonderful place.' She does not know the English language. Therefore, she has never come up to see Mrs. Sanger, but she will—but she will!"

For the first time the Senate sub-committee reported out the bill and it was put on the unanimous consent calendar. The last day of the session came, June 13th. Over two hundred were ahead of it, but there was always hope. One after another they were hurried through and then, miracle of miracles, ours passed with no voice raised against it. The next one came up, was also converted into law, another up for discussion, tabled. Twenty minutes went by. Suddenly Senator Pat McCarran from Reno, Nevada, famous divorce lawyer though an outstanding Catholic, came rushing in from the cloak room and asked for unanimous consent to recall our bill. As a matter of senatorial courtesy Senator Hastings granted his request; had he not done so Senator McCarran would have objected to every bill he introduced thereafter. It was summarily referred back to the committee and there died.

In 1935 we took the fatal step of having it voted on early in the session and it was promptly killed. The whole year's labor was lost. The following winter, when I was in India, Percy Gassaway of Oklahoma introduced a bill in the House, Royal S. Copeland of New York, in the Senate, by request; neither one reached a hearing.

Another line of attack on the Comstock law was to try for a liberal interpretation through the courts. Among the products shown at the Zurich Conference in 1930 had been a Japanese pessary. Pursuing the clinic policy of testing every new contraceptive that appeared, I ordered some of these from a Tokyo physician. When notified by the Customs that they had been barred entrance and destroyed, we sent for another shipment addressed to Dr. Stone in the hope that it would then be delivered to a physician. But this also was refused, and accordingly we brought suit in her name.

After pending two years the case finally came up for trial before Judge Grover Moscowitz of the Federal District Court of Southern New York. Morris Ernst conducted our claim brilliantly, and January 6, 1936, Judge Moscowitz decided in our favor—the wording of the statute seemed to forbid the importation of any article for preventing conception, but he believed that the statute should be construed more reasonably. The Government at once appealed and the case was argued in the Circuit Court of Appeals before Judges Augustus N. Hand, Learned Hand, and Thomas Swan, whose unanimous decisions were rarely reversed in the Supreme Court.

In the fall of 1936, while I was in Washington getting the Federal bill started again in advance of Congress' meeting, news came that the three judges had upheld the Moscowitz decision and had added that a doctor was entitled not only to bring articles into this country but, more important, to send them through the mails, and, finally, to use them for the patient's general well-being—which, for twenty years, had been the object of my earnest endeavor.

The Government still had the right to appeal inside of ninety days. Therefore, I was not unduly jubilant. We had had so many seeming victories that melted away afterwards.

But long before the period of grace had expired, Attorney General Cummings announced to the press that the Government would accept the decision as law, and, with commendable consistency, the Secretary of the Treasury sent word to the Customs at once that our shipments should be admitted. It is really a relief to be able to say something good about the Government.

In the face of the court decision there was little point at this time in continuing the Federal campaign. The money for closing it up came through a most unexpected and affecting channel. About a year after I had seen Viola Kaufman at the California Conference in 1931, I received a letter from her asking me please to write out the form in which I would like any money left so that she could designate it in her will. I took her clear, concise note to my attorney who suggested that, since organizations were many and might go out of existence at any moment, it would be wiser to have the bequest in my name to be dispensed for any purpose within the movement I saw fit. I answered her to this effect and she replied, "I am now passing over to you in my will whatever I possess."

I considered that the only courteous thing to do was to have Anna Lifshiz, who was living in Los Angeles, go to see Miss Kaufman. The address was in the Mexican district, in the poorest, most dilapidated, run-down section. In patched clothes she came to the door of her house, in which there was hardly any furniture. She was formal and rather cold.

Anna merely explained the reason for her call was that she knew Miss Kaufman as one of our subscribers. She wrote me, "That poor creature hasn't money enough to keep body and soul together."

Two years went by. I was in Washington, preparing to start for Boston for a meeting when a messenger boy delivered a telegram from the director of the General Hospital at Memphis, Tennessee, requesting me to come at once; Viola Kaufman was dangerously ill with pneumonia and asking for me. I looked up trains; it would take forty-eight hours, and so I put in a long-distance call to the director, who told me she had died during the night.

"What was she doing in Memphis?"

"We don't know. The Salvation Army brought her in to us. She has only a little cash tied up in a handkerchief. We can't do anything without you because you're the beneficiary."

The undertaker also wanted an order from me, and, since her executor, an officer of a bank in Los Angeles, had gone on a fishing trip, I arranged the details for her cremation. She had ordered that her remains be sent to me and when they arrived the clinic staff came up to Willow Lake and we held a little memorial service of gratitude and respect, spreading the ashes over the rock garden.

To everybody's astonishment Viola Kaufman had about thirty thousand dollars in Los Angeles realty. But it took a year and a half to settle the estate and by this time everything was at the lowest ebb of the depression. We received approximately twelve thousand dollars. I have never looked at the obituaries for the last twenty years without hoping to read that someone has willed a million dollars for birth control, but the only legacy ever bequeathed us was that saved from the meager earnings of this schoolteacher, Viola Kaufman, who herself lived in poverty.

With this money we wrote finis to the Federal legislation. Of the old organization all that was left in Washington was a secretary to read the *Congressional Record* daily—a watchdog to report any bills proposed which would make it necessary for us to jump into action to combat them.

Six years of this work had cost one hundred and fifty thousand dollars. It had also meant strain and worry beyond anything I had ever attempted—never being able to detach myself from it whether Congress was in session or not, always on the alert to discover any new person elected who might be favorably disposed. Now and again it had been discouraging; you could exert yourself to the utmost with pleasure if it were a matter of convincing a person and watching his mind being pried open, but here, over and over again, you saw this same conviction, yet he reverted to the same fears and refrained from doing anything.

However, the process of enlightening legislators had also unclosed the eyes of an enormous number of organizations. First to approve publicly had been the National Council of Jewish Women. Eventually more than a thousand clubs—civic, political, religious, and social, including the General Federation of Women's Clubs, the Y.W.C.A., local Junior Leagues—in all representing between twelve and thirteen million members—had given their endorsement. And, more important than anything else, the public had been educated persistently, consistently away from casual and precarious contraceptive advice into the qualified hands of the medical profession.

Dr. Dickinson had been appearing regularly at American Medical Association meetings, keeping the question constantly alive. But not until Dr. Prentiss Willson had formed a national body of doctors in 1935 to carry on legislative work had there been any action. One had stirred up; the other organized.

I was at Willow Lake one June morning of 1937 when I saw spread across the newspaper in double column the glad tidings: the Committee on Contraception of the American Medical Association had informed the convention that physicians had the legal right to give contraceptives, and it recommended that standards be investigated and technique be taught in medical schools.

In my excitement I actually fell downstairs. To me this was really a greater victory than the Moscowitz decision. Here was the culmination of unremitting labor ever since my return from Europe in 1915, the gratification of seeing a dream come true.

These specific achievements are significant because they open the way to a broader field of attainment and to research which can immeasurably improve methods now known, making possible the spread of birth control into the forlorn, overpopulated places of the earth, and permitting science eventually to determine the potentialities of a posterity conceived and born of conscious love.

Chapter Thirty-five

A PAST WHICH IS GONE FOREVER

PARENTHOOD remains unquestionably the most serious of all human relationships, the most far-reaching in its power for good or for evil, and withal the most delicately complex. I always tried to secure my sons' confidence by being honest with them, treating them as though they had intelligence, and expecting them to use it. For the sake of companionship it was essential to be honest, no matter what the cost. Fortunately, the younger generation is not crumpled up when sharply confronted with the truth. They have cut through the regard to their feelings until they can say extraordinarily blunt things to each other and yet not be hurt. And with this they have invented a new language; they can "take it."

Many times I could have forced my opinion on the boys and saved them perhaps some bitter disappointments—"Let me do it. I'll manage all this. Let me know when you need anything." But, instead, I merely stated my attitude and said, "Here are the two alternatives. You want this; I think the other is better. Neither of us can tell which is right. If you choose your own way I'll help you as long as you do it well, providing you stop as soon as you know it is wrong and go back and pick up the other. If experience teaches you a greater wisdom, you can call it square."

At Peddie Institute, Stuart was paying more attention to sports than studies. It was easy for him to be an athlete. But he also had a logical mind and a quick ability for co-ordinating hand and brain.

When he was ready for college he entered Sheffield Scientific School of Yale University. His imagination was soon captured by archaeology and medicine, but his course was already set.

Meanwhile Grant, who had been inclined to hero-worship his older brother, had also gone to Peddie. His athletics left little opportunity for bringing out his artistic talents, and he agreed to take his last two years at Westminster School in Simsbury, Connecticut, where he was encouraged to develop along his own lines. In his sophomore year at Princeton, he still had no idea of what he wanted to do with his life. Although he had a leaning towards diplomacy, which would include training in law, I explained to him that, since the family had no political influence, it might lead to being a small politician.

And so I made out a list of as many occupations known to man as I could think of, and sent them to him, telling him to mark off with a blue pencil those which he was perfectly sure did not appeal to him, and check with red those for which he felt some predilection. Out immediately went piano-mover, waiter, floorwalker, bank manager, bookkeeper, and some fifty others.

Six months later, I returned him the red-checked list for further perusal. Now his preferences were much more definite. Research, journalism, editorial work, diplomacy were again red, but almost everything else marked headed him for a scientific career.

The decision made, Grant began his pre-medical course.

After Stuart graduated from Yale he moved downtown to Wall Street and continued in a broker's office all during the depression. But, in this money making atmosphere, his attitude was changing. He had concluded that serving humanity was a higher fulfillment than profiting at humanity's expense, and medicine seemed the career which he also liked best. Having found out, he had the courage to start back at the beginning to accomplish it. We made a compact for him to go as far as he could and test whether his interest kept up. First he had to acquire sufficient chemistry and biology, going to Columbia University in the daytime for the former, to New York University in the evening for the latter, preparing his lessons until three in the morning.

The next year he passed his entrance examinations.

Following the legislative near-victory in the winter of 1934, I resolved to go to Russia to see for myself what was happening in the greatest social experiment of our age. With keen anticipation I looked forward to discovering whether the Marxian philosophy, dramatized and realized and based on an economic ideology, did not have to accept some of the philosophy of Malthus.

Grant, then about to enter his final year at Cornell Medical School, was eager to investigate the progress of medicine in the Soviet Union, and made up his mind to come along. I was taking also my secretary, Florence Rose, efficient, competent in any capacity, whether field organizing or in the office. Though but recently enlisted in the movement, she had come more with the attitude of the early days, not for what she could get out of it, but for what she could give to its furtherance. Her talents and enthusiasm, when added to her cheerfulness, made her a rare combination; always gleeful and bubbling with fun, she carried out nearly everything in that spirit.

Mrs. Ethel Clyde, an officer of the Federal legislative organization, was to be the fourth of our little group within a large group. When zeal for the "new civilization" in Russia had been at its height she had relinquished her expensive Park Avenue apartment for a smaller one on a side street, and contributed the difference in rent to sundry leftist causes and birth control.

At the last moment it seemed we might not be able to go. For some years Stuart had had a bad sinus condition, and hardly had he matriculated at Cornell in the fall of 1933 when he had been struck by a squash racket, fracturing the bone over his eye. That winter he had been operated on nine times. A week before I was due to sail his doctor advised that he have an exploratory operation. I rushed up from Washington, where the legislative work for that session was just being wound up, and would have abandoned the Russian expedition had not the operation apparently been entirely successful. Stuart insisted that I go. Since he was in no danger I continued with my plans.

It was not feasible to travel in Russia except in a party under official guidance. Three people I knew who had gone by themselves described how train after train had passed them, boat after boat had steamed down the Volga with no accommodations available. Therefore, we chose the non-partisan Second Russian Seminar.

Shortly prior to leaving I spent an evening with Maurice Hindus, Will Durant, John Kingsbury, and Drs. Hannah and Abraham Stone, all of whom had been to Russia the previous year. Maurice Hindus had returned impersonal and still unprejudiced, Will Durant utterly antagonistic, John Kingsbury full of fervor, and both Stones warmly disposed. They had all been in Moscow, practically at the same time, for approximately the same number of days, and all had received utterly dissimilar impressions. Even pictures that Will Durant had taken were not the same as those of John Kingsbury or Dr. Stone, snapped from almost identical places, thus showing me how wide might be the variety of responses, depending on the individual bias.

I expected to keep my eyes open, to think independently, to ask questions, and compare. I was going to use as much sanity and fairness as I possessed, and not be swept emotionally into any current of opinion.

Billy Barber was the manager of the Seminar, and I did not envy him his job. There were many complaints and stupid remarks and much faultfinding. Most of the party were going merely to be able to say those things were true which they had previously said were true. I asked one woman who went on every sight-seeing expedition but never got out of the bus, "Why did you come?"

"Oh, just to wipe Russia off my list."

Edward Alsworth Ross was among the leaders. He was the only person who had been there under the former regime some twenty years earlier, and had an authoritative basis of contrast between the old and the new; we all rather sat at his feet. He was a typical professor, wore enormously high, stiff collars, played checkers with anybody who would indulge him, and was upset when he failed to win. His personality was impressive, literally so because wherever you looked you spied him. One of the funniest sights was to see this Nordic giant, six feet four, walking with short dark Florence Rose, five feet two, each jollying the other.

We scooted through England across to Copenhagen, about which I recall very little. I was always trying to learn what advance the women's movement had made, but somebody was always trying to tell me how marvelous the city was. Remembering Ellen Key, I reached Scandinavia with great hopes for Feminism. But the women who were considered the most intelligent were complacently resting on their laurels. The older ones still reigned supreme and believed that, because they had won their battles of twenty-five years ago, there was nothing left to fight for. The younger group found it hard to rise above the inertia of this overwhelming prestige. Since population was not a problem in Scandinavia, they were interested chiefly in eugenics, and had almost forgotten the aspect of individual suffering.

At Oslo a number of us went on pilgrimage to the grave of Ibsen. As I stood there in silent tribute I had the feeling he had understood women and the ties they had been loosening. To my mind Nora never went back to the "doll's house"; her evolution was too complete. Or, if she did return, she entered by another door.

Mr. Barber had arranged to feed his hundred and six charges at the last Finnish railroad station. There was a particular exhilaration about the prospect of that meal, because it was to be our final one before crossing into "famine-stricken" Russia. We arrived at ten in the morning, all of us hungry. As we filed into the station our eyes met the most gorgeous panorama—long tables beautifully laid out with delicious meats, fish, breads, compotes.

While we paused, debating which of these delicacies to taste first, there came a stampede of fifty other Americans, a tourist group led by Sherwood Eddy. Never had I seen such an exhibition. The men, unshaven, hatless, coatless, pushed and shoved around, in front of, and almost on top of the tables. The best we could do was find comfortable seats from which we could have a good view of the riot. The meal prepared by the railroad with such courtesy for our party was demolished by another.

Barber and Eddy eventually discovered it was all a mistake. The train carrying the Eddy-ites had failed to stop at the town where their repast had been awaiting them, and naturally they supposed this breakfast was theirs.

At Leningrad we were met by buses and driven through streets that swarmed with imperturbable, peasant-like people. The upper parts of their Mongolian-shaped heads all looked exactly the same. I noticed how immaculate they were. Faces, necks, hands, were white as white and displayed a cleanliness simply marvelous when you took into consideration the difficulty of securing soap and water. Very few were old; many were children apparently between the ages of two to twelve. But in the expressions of all I glimpsed a sadness.

The former capital was depressing and down at heels, shabby and in need of painting. Yet it was beyond comparison in its spacious dignity; the architectural design of the houses could not be hidden. My high-ceilinged room at the Astoria was luxurious with alcove bed, bath room, and large marble tub, which, although cracked and spotted with rust, nevertheless evidenced the days of splendor when the hotel had been frequented by the aristocracy of the Old Regime.

From my window I could see the cobbled square. It was eight o'clock and the city was awakening. I watched the passing show: heavy wagons were drawn by a single and often most decrepit horse with what seemed a dark brown rainbow, arched and graceful, over his neck; queues formed in front of little stands that served rations of beer or bottled soda water; some women, the varying colors in their shawls making bright splotches, swept the car tracks with birch switches or pushed empty carts on their way to market, others carried hods of cement up the ladders to the masons on the new buildings being erected everywhere. Usually the men were doing the skilled work, and women, hardy and robust, with strong legs, bare feet, sunburned faces, were kept at the laborious, monotonous, physical labor until such time as they could qualify as expert artisans.

The Communists' apartments were much better, lighter, airier, cleaner, more modern than those for non-party members. When we asked why, in an equalitarian state, one section should be thus privileged, we were answered, "It was they who made all this possible. Why should they not have the best? What you bourgeois give to your capitalists, we give to our Communists."

We asked Tanya, our guide, if she were a Communist, and she replied, "Oh, no. That's too hard." Ordinary citizens might be excused for a mistake or even a crime, but party members could have no human frailties. They were exiled or perhaps shot for cheating, stealing, deceiving, exploiting, taking money under false pretenses, or many things which average people could do and be punished with fines alone.

Although the cost of the trip itself was relatively low, whatever we bought in Russia was excessively high owing to the peculiar situation of the ruble. In the first place, there was no ruble; it existed only in theory. Second, every foreigner was supposed to deal exclusively with the Torgsin stores through which the Government had cleverly contrived to come by a hoard of foreign currency by charging seventy-eight cents in our money for each ruble instead of its actual value of five cents. For example, the price of a stamp on a letter to the United States, which was two and a half rubles, amounted to two dollars.

Mrs. Clyde, who leaned sympathetically towards Communism, said to one of our young men, "Let me get you a little present."

"Not here," he said. "It'll be too expensive."

"Oh, yes," she insisted. "What would you like?"

"Well—a bar of almond chocolate, then."

She had to pay ten American dollars for that ten-cent bar of chocolate. Her Communism melted slightly.

Ultimately, we solved the ruble problem. One morning a boy who had been loitering around the Astoria asked Grant, "Would you like me to take you through the city?"

Grant prudently inquired, "How much?" It appeared that the boy merely desired an opportunity to perfect his English; he had plenty of rubles, which he was glad to dispose of at the rate of fifty for a dollar. Russians could obtain none but the cheapest commodities on their tickets; if they wanted luxuries such as good shirts, leather or rubber boots, and other articles sold only at Torgsin, they were obliged to surrender some treasured gold piece or use foreign money.

With an ample supply of rubles I sent long, elaborate cables to Stuart to cheer him up. He must have thought an excessive maternal solicitude was getting the better of my economic judgment. But, as a matter of fact, one of twenty words was costing me less than twenty-five cents.

Dr. Nadina Kavanoky, who had been interested in birth control in the United States, had given me a letter to her father, Dr. Reinstein, once a dentist in Rochester, New York, now in Stalin's close confidence. He came to see me about eleven-thirty one night, the Russian calling hour, and we talked until three in the morning. When he wanted to know my "impressions of Russia," I said promptly, "It seems to me your policy of overcharging us is a mistake; for the sake of a few dollars you are creating ill will, just as the French have done. In our own Seminar we have twenty librarians and perhaps double that number of schoolteachers and students, many of whom have gone without other vacations to come here. They have a unique opportunity to influence people; everybody will ask them when they get back, 'Did you like Russia?' You are trying to build up a favorable public opinion abroad, and these people are the best mediums for that purpose. If they are pleased they will fight for you and break down prejudice."

But he was not convinced, and, evoking the specter of the Tsarist debt to America, he replied, "We'll bleed you, we'll milk you, we'll get every dollar out of you we can. America demands her pound of flesh and this is how we'll pay you."

The occasions for receiving "pleasant impressions" were offered by vigorous tours to points of interest. We were given a choice of hard buses or harder ones, all, in my experience, springless and clattering noisily over the cobble-paved streets. After a few bumps we usually hit the roof and came down with headaches. Our poor little guides had to screech with full lung power to be heard over the incessant rattling.

One morning when driving back from sight-seeing, the motor gasped and collapsed on a slight hill. Passengers volunteered helpful suggestions—"Put it in low. Put it in neutral. Push this. Pull that."

The driver moved gears forward and backward and then looked around at us in perplexity, "I did, but it won't work." We waited and waited and waited and waited. Somebody ran a mile to telephone that we were stranded and needed another bus. Meanwhile, everything we wanted to see was closing, and we had already learned that whatever you missed in Russia was always the most worth while. In fact, it seemed they had visiting hours timed to end five minutes before you got there. Several other buses came along and stopped. Their drivers got out, poked their heads under the hood, began taking things apart, strewing bolts this way and nuts that. Then they, too, became discouraged, and, leaving increased confusion, climbed on their chariots again and went on.

Finally some bright young man discovered we were out of gas.

As we crossed the huge square in front of the hotel, I saw directly ahead of us an enormous pile of bricks with wide spaces on both sides. Closer and closer we came. "When will the driver turn?" I asked myself. But he never did; we went right over the top and the bricks slipped out from under. That was the Russian system. You could not go round an obstacle; you must go over it.

Enlarged portraits of Lenin and Stalin were in all public buildings. Their statues were everywhere, in every square, on every corner. A major industry of Russia seemed to be to find new poses for Stalin—standing up, lying down, writing, reading. Often just his head, definitely recognizable in spite of the predominance of red, was designed in flower beds. One of the most delicate attentions was to give him a different colored necktie on different days; the plants were kept in pots to make this charming gesture possible.

After the Revolution when peace had come, connoisseurs from various countries had been invited to examine the recovered statues, rugs, tapestries, and *objets d'art* stolen from the palaces and churches. One by one the priceless paintings were displayed, specialists rendered their opinions, commercial dealers furnished appraisals, stenographers took down every word. The same was done with the lapis lazuli tables, the snuff boxes, the court jewels.

The interesting part of the new arrangement was that the interpretation was entirely Marxian. Pictures, instead of being hung according to the orthodox history of art, were fitted into the Industrial Revolution. A certain Madonna was not admired for its qualities of color or form, or as a thing of beauty in itself; the guide explained to you that it was created at such and such a time when the Church was trying to get a hold over the people, when artists were starving and had to look for their means of livelihood to the patronage of the Church.

Later, in the Kremlin at Moscow we saw fantastic and incredible riches, jeweled saddles, a whole set of harness studded with turquoise, a huge casket cloth embroidered with thousands of pearls. In order to place the period of the latter I asked Tanya where it had come from. She replied in her precise English, "You see, it is for to cover the dead. You see, in Russia there was such a custom. When they died they put them in the ground. It was such a custom, you see, to cover them with cloths."

She spoke of the Tsarist Regime as though it had been centuries ago.

One of the pictures was a Christ removed from the cross and lying on the ground. Tanya said, "People used to come here, and they even kissed it!" This she uttered in the tone of scorn of a very youthful generation shocked and horrified at the ancient traditions.

"Our hope is in the young people," she said frequently.

"But how old are you?"

"Oh, I'm thirty-two," as though she were doddering.

Grant and I were once walking by a group of children when a small boy pointed at us and remarked, "Ah, there go some of the dying race." To them all *Amerikanski* were capitalists.

The Marxian ideology had been applied to every phase of life. H.G., accompanied by Gyp, his biologist son, had flown over from London. Since he wanted an opportunity to go around alone, he rather resented being so closely guarded and courteously guided. After talking with Stalin he had come to the conclusion that the Dictator had no understanding of economics. He was somewhat annoyed at the constant interpretation of everything in terms of politics, and of having Marx stuffed down his throat at every turn.

At the schools you might ask what kind of mathematics they taught.

"Marx."

"And what system of engineering?"

"Marx."

No matter what the question, the answer was Marx.

The Anti-Religious Museum, once a cathedral, was directly across from the Astoria. Each half-hour little girls, who seemed hardly more than ten or twelve, their sleeves hanging down over their finger tips, with great dignity conducted excursions of peasants through. Their lecture started with the fundamental principle that the earth was round. A bas-relief of the world was underneath the huge pendulum which hung from the dome. If you stood there long enough you saw it swing from one point to a further one. They were trying to show that it was within man's power to make his own heaven.

Here were kept the relics of the churches, the icons laden with silver and gold wrung from the poor peasants in the past. Actual concrete things were reduced to their simplest terms on large poster-type murals which depicted stories, a necessary practice since the muzhiks were so generally illiterate. In one a kulak was coming to the priest with a sick child in his arms, asking for prayers to cure its illness. The priest, fat and clad in rich robes, shook his head, saying, "You must bring money for the saint. The saint will not cure your child unless her arms are covered with silver." But the kulak had only his farm. "Mortgage it and get the money," the priest ordered. Soon the kulak returned with silver, and the mural showed how now the saint's arm was almost hidden. But still the child remained sick. "The saint's halo is bare," said the priest. At last the whole figure was silvered, but the baby died just the same.

Opposite this mural was pictured the Soviet way. The father carried the baby to the hospital, where nurses with gauze across their mouths took it preciously, bathed it carefully, laid it in bed. The entire sterilizing process was illustrated—the doctor in white gown and cap, scrubbing and washing each hand five minutes as marked by a clock. Finally you saw the child, healthy and well, jumping into its mother's arms.

The people stood there looking, their imaginations fired. They said, "This is what is happening to us."

Most particularly I wanted to investigate what had been done for women and children in Russia, to learn whether they had been given the rights and liberties due them in any humanitarian civilization. Grant, Rose, as she was known to me, and I went one day to the Institute for the Protection of Motherhood and Childhood, a vast establishment stretching over several miles, with model clinics, nurseries, milk centers, and educational laboratories. I was overwhelmed in contemplating the undertaking. There was no doubt that the Government was exerting itself strenuously to teach the rudiments of hygiene to an enormous population that had previously known nothing of it. Russia was also aiming to free women from the two bonds that enslaved them most—the nursery and the kitchen. All over the country were crèches connected with the places they worked.

Children were the priceless possessions of Russia. Their time was planned for them from birth to the age of sixteen, when they were paid to go to college, if they so desired. No longer were they a drain or burden to their families. Not only were teachers or parents forbidden to inflict corporal punishment, but children might even report their parents for being vindictive, ill-humored, disorderly, and in many cases they did so.

In one divorce dispute as to custody of the offspring, the father argued that the mother was bad. The Judge asked, "Of what does her badness consist?"

"She is nervous and loses her temper."

The Judge agreed she was not fit for motherhood.

Furthermore, Russia was investing in future generations by building a healthy race. If there were any scarcity of milk the children were supplied first, the hospitals second, members of the Communist party third, industrial groups fourth, professional classes fifth, and old people over fifty had to scrape along on what they could get, unless they were parents of Communists or closely associated with them.

I was eager also to find out what had been done about the study carried on by Professor Tushnov, of the Institute for Experimental Medicine, on so-called spermatoxin, a substance which, it had been rumored, produced temporary sterility in women. I made an appointment with him, but a shock awaited me. He had tried out his spermatoxin on thirty women, twenty-two of whom had been made immune for from four to five months, but now all laboratory workers had been taken from pure research and set at utilitarian tasks such as the practical effects of various vocations on women's health. Nothing concerning immunization to conception could be published in Soviet Russia, no information could be given out under penalty of arrest, and, moreover, nothing could appear in a foreign paper which had not already been printed in Russia.

Intourist, the Government tourist bureau, and Voks, the All-Union Society for Cultural Relations with Foreign Countries, had asked me when I had first arrived whom I wished to see and where

I wished to go, and had offered to call up people on my list and arrange for visits, a service which had saved me much trouble and expense. In spite of this co-operative attitude, I was suspicious that much was being hidden from us. Before I had left America I had heard I could see only what Russia presented for window-dressing, and with this in mind I was on the alert.

Both Grant and I wondered how the hospitals built under the Tsars compared with recent ones. When I asked to be taken to a certain one, I was assured it was too far away, and anyhow it was being renovated; there was nobody there. I said to myself, "Aha! here is one of the forbidden sights. Whoever heard of a hospital equipped to handle thousands of patients being utterly empty? They are not going to let us see this because it might speak in favor of the old in contrast to the new."

Politely but firmly I insisted. Again I was told there were so many other interesting things it would be a pity to waste my time going to see it. I found it difficult to say anything further without giving offense. Then Grant encountered a young American nurse from the Presbyterian Hospital in New York who spoke Russian; she also wanted to visit hospitals. We engaged a car of our own and drove a good fifteen miles out of the city over horrible roads, winding and dusty and badly paved, and even pushing on as rapidly as we could we did not get there until late in the afternoon. To our dismay we discovered not a patient, doctor, or nurse in the place, only plasterers, painters, carpenters, and cleaners, pulling down and refurbishing. We had lost half a day and were a little ashamed of our lack of faith.

The night came to take the train for Moscow. Nobody called "All aboard!" in Russia. Trains went right off underneath you when you had one foot on the platform and one on the step. They just moved and moved fast. But we clambered on and soon the leather seats were made into our beds; they were so slippery that we kept falling out.

Once at Moscow, we who were coming second-class, according to Marxian procedure, received the worst rooms at the hotel; those who traveled third had the best. I could not applaud the one selected for me. It was directly over the laundry, and the smells of cooking and suds floated through the window. I refused to stay and was accommodated on the top floor where the servants had once lived.

Moscow was as different from Leningrad as New York City from a sleepy Pennsylvania town. The people walked more quickly and seemed to be going somewhere, not simply wandering listlessly. Bedlam existed at the hotels, but by now we were beginning to learn that the Russians were so concerned with their own efficiency that they had no time to do anything. To be in a hurry merely complicated matters. I could wait, but for energetic Rose it was torture. To all specific requests they replied, "It cannot be. It cannot be." She had her own methods of coping with this, saying she did not wish to hear the word, "impossible"; she had no intention of asking the impossible. Then when they procrastinated with, "a little later," she countered, "In America we say, 'now!'"

Her triumph over dilatoriness came on Health Day. Since health was almost a god in Russia, all activities ceased on that occasion and the populace of Moscow came together on Red Square. The spectacle was to start at two in the afternoon, but before it was light you could hear the songs of men, women, and children moving towards their appointed stations.

Out of our party only thirty were privileged to receive tickets, and their names were posted. Mrs. Clyde and I were on the list, but not Grant or Rose. The previous day the numbers were cut to twenty; that morning there were but sixteen, and feeling ran high. "Why haven't I a ticket?"

Fortunately for me I had been invited to lunch by Ambassador William C. Bullitt, who entertained lavishly and was helpful to traveling Americans. When I had met him back in New England, I had never thought of him as an ambassador, nor as a man skilled in dealing with the great problems that required strategy, diplomacy, political sagacity, and a prime knowledge of economics and history. I considered him rather as amusing, an excellent dinner host, and one to whom you could go when in difficulty, sure that he would get you out. Perhaps this was what Russia wanted at that time more than anything else. No doubt he was then somewhat disappointed at the turn relations between Russia and the United States had taken. Russians on the whole admired him; they had not forgotten that, although he was not counted a proletarian or in the category of Jack Reed, he had lifted the cudgels for them in the early days when friends were needed.

The Ambassador's little daughter Ann, aged ten, officiated at the head of the table, apparently enjoying herself. The house in which they were living while the new Embassy was being built had an architecture quite befitting what I imagined the style of Russia should be—a bit of the Kremlin, a bit of a mosque, and a bit of an Indian palace.

On the way to the Square after luncheon a wave of people surged between the rest of the diplomatic party and myself, but I kept saying "diplomatique," and was bowed through to the grandstand.

Meanwhile Rose had been devoting her whole attention to tickets —and there were no tickets. The lucky holders lined up and filed off under a leader. Rose, the ever resourceful, donned a red bandanna and said to the "forgotten men" in the party, "We'll make our own battalion." She handed out slips of paper about the size of the tickets and then started, Grant and the Harvard professors following her through the blare of music and the tramping troops and the pageantry of blue trunks and white shirts, orange trunks and cerise shirts.

Whenever anyone stopped Rose she pointed ahead and repeated my open sesame, "diplomatique," and they let her by until she reached the last barrier. There the guard was suspicious of her password and challenged her. Then she spied another group coming up, dashed over to the leader, and exclaimed, "Quick, please explain that our interpreter has gone on with our tickets!"

The woman looked unbelieving, but still others arrived at that moment, and the Russian system collapsed under pressure. In they all piled, and Rose turned to her unknown benefactress, "You don't know how grateful I am to you for getting us in."

The reply was, "You don't know how grateful I am to you for getting *us* in! I'm a tourist too, and we have no tickets either."

Nobody seeing Moscow that day could have thought it a somber place. It was alive with song, happy faces, bright attire. The parade of a hundred thousand or more was one of the most marvelous spectacles for color, form, cadence, geometrical precision that I had ever seen human beings accomplish. Men and women were representing all sorts of games and sports—swimming, shooting, tennis, flying. There was nothing tawdry. Each company held aloft beautifully designed placards as it passed Stalin, who stood on top of Lenin's tomb. The Dictator looked much like his pictures, with his heavy black mustache resembling the wings of a bird of prey.

All day long and everywhere you heard the *Internationale,* over and over and over again. Each band struck up as it approached the Tomb and kept playing as it swung on. Always the stirring song from those coming up, those far away—overtones, undertones, thrilling, insistent, now loud in your ears, now dimly echoing in the distance, a rhythmic motif symbolizing the onward march of Young Russia.

Chapter Thirty-six

FAITH IS A FINE INVENTION

"There is a great difference between traveling to see countries and to see people."
JEAN-JACQUES ROUSSEAU

"TOVARISH —— wishes to see you," came a call from the hotel desk. For a moment I could not place the name, and the face had changed so completely that I could but faintly trace a resemblance to the boy I had seen before. He reminded me I had known him in Seattle as one who had assisted in getting up birth control meetings. When the Wobblies were being arrested in the United States he had hired out as a stoker on a boat, and gradually made his way to Russia, where he thought he could help to usher in the new society.

Here was one person who had not had the best of the bargain. He was shabbily dressed and looked dilapidated, evidently having seen hard times, and had a beaten expression in his eyes. Yet, disillusioned as he was, he had not come to complain. Since it was four in the afternoon, the lunch hour in Russia, I asked him to join me in the dining room, conducted like a large commons. The waiters seemed disgruntled, unhappy, inept and knew very little about service; they glanced scornfully at the man who sat down beside me. The one lively note was the orchestra, which threw itself into marches and wild and spirited Caucasian or Slavic folk dances while we ate.

My guest said this was the best meal he had had since leaving America. "Why don't you come back?" I asked.

"I couldn't get in."

"Would you if you could?"

"Just give me a chance!"

I suppose it was inevitable that in such a social upheaval many suffered. I called upon Dr. Peter Tutyshkin, who had tried to attend our 1925 Conference in New York, but had arrived too late. As was the case with most professional men of his years, he had been of the old aristocracy. He and his wife and two daughters, both physicians, had owned a beautiful home. Now the thousands of volumes of what had formerly comprised his fine medical and scientific library had been taken away, and he and his wife slept and ate in the room which had contained them. He was margined and rationed to the last degree, and I could feel his humiliation at having so little food that he could not offer us a cup of tea.

While we were in Moscow, the Eddy party and the select six whom Louis Fischer was piloting, crossed our path. Fischer, a Russian living in Moscow and writing for the *Nation,* published in the United States, invited Grant and me to go along with them to meet the Secretary of the Commissariat of Public Health, Dr. Kaminsky. We went up a wide open stairway like that of a courthouse and into a spacious room with high windows running from floor to ceiling in French fashion and a huge banquet table laden with the invariable afternoon tea.

Dr. Kaminsky addressed us. "Our worst heritage from the Old Regime was in the field of medicine. The main task before us is to unite science and practice. Our medicine is a form of social insurance, our medical policy based on prevention. We are not interested in profit, only service."

The Russians had been kind and had grasped very quickly any improvement suggested to them, even accepting criticism with great tolerance. Aware of this, when Dr. Kaminsky paused for questions, Grant inquired about doctors entering private practice.

"As Russia builds up public health work," was the answer, "more doctors will be able to find room for private practice if they so desire."

Sherwood Eddy slipped me a note. "Here's your opportunity to bring up birth control."

I took my cue. "Has Russia a population policy? Has she formulated any program for the rate of increase of her people?"

The audience stirred as though I had hurled a grenade. The interpreter leaped to his feet and shrieked, "Malthusianism! We will not have Malthusianism here! We do not need it. Do you think or imply that Soviet Russia has to advance Malthusian ideas? We can have all the children we want and Russia can do with twice the population she now has." He went on and on.

After waiting a few moments for the air to clear, I continued, "I have asked Dr. Kaminsky a simple question which I will repeat. I said nothing about Malthusianism. But I should like to know whether Russia has a population policy. She has had five- and even ten-year plans for agriculture and manufacture and everything she is making. But what has she done about the most important issue today—population, its growth and distribution?"

Fischer was whispering to Dr. Kaminsky, evidently telling him what I wanted to know. The doctor replied, "If I understood correctly, you are asking if there is any policy from the biological or economic point of view."

"I am asking whether Russia, in planning her industries, has any plan also as to the eventual control of families. I know you have much freedom for women and a fine technique for abortions. To us that is extremely significant, because after a woman has been aborted she returns to the same conditions and becomes pregnant again. Four hundred thousand abortions a year indicate women do not want to have so many children; in my opinion it is a cruel method of dealing with the problem because abortion, no matter how well done, is a terrific nervous strain and an exhausting physical hardship."

Dr. Kaminsky's answer was not encouraging. "There is no question as to the increase of population. There is no policy as to the question of biological restrictions; on the contrary there is a policy of increasing the population. For six years we have had a great shortage, not only of skilled workers, but of labor in general."

Obviously, I was not a particularly welcome visitor.

By chance I was fortunate enough to encounter again Dr. Marthe Ruben-Wolf, who with her husband and children had escaped from Nazi Germany and was then at the head of a Moscow abortorium. Because of her wide experience in Germany, where clinics had been under municipal guidance, she was one of the few Communists who was sane on the subject of population. She very kindly helped me with some of my interviews.

Any woman in Russia who requested it was entitled to abortion on application to a doctor. She was told of the dangers, warned it might result in sterility, charged about two dollars and a half. We talked to about fifty patients who had already been there three days. None had temperatures. They were very jolly and going home that afternoon to rest for another week or two. Then they would go back to work with no deduction in wages. Though some of these women had had five abortions in two years and one had had eight, they could not sing too highly the praises of their country for allowing the operations. When I asked whether they would not prefer to have some information as to how to avoid further ones by protecting themselves from pregnancy, each and all replied, "We have no such thing. We hear of it, but we have nothing. Russia is too poor. We hope she will soon get it."

In only one place did I see a clinic in the sense that we use the word here, and that was in Moscow where Dr. Kabanova had sixty women the afternoon we viewed it. Great credit is also due Madame Lebedova who organized the original establishment of the Institutes for the Protection of Motherhood and Childhood, laid down the principles to be followed, and persisted until they had been embodied in a definite program.

Dr. Abram B. Genss, assistant director, was in charge of contraceptive supplies and the administration of birth control, such as it was. He was antagonistic, disagreeable, unpleasant, shouting "Malthusianism" into my ears more times in one hour than I had heard it before in twenty years. The methods in the Moscow clinic were antiquated, and I suggested sending a physician to instruct them, but my proposal was not acceptable.

I considered Russia's situation very serious. Her population was a matter of mathematics; it had increased some fifty million since the downfall of the Empire. Unless she looked ahead and educated her people in the problems which arose out of population, within two generations she would find herself with the same differential birth rate then existing in England and the United States. It would, however, have much more tragic consequences since it would lower the augmentation of the capable, skilled, shock troops of industry, the idealists and active, selfless workers, and would multiply from the bottom unskilled, ignorant, dull-witted workers, the superstitious element which even the greatest efforts of a Soviet dictatorship running at top speed could not pull up and out of their evolutional environment.

I really began to see Russia under another guise after we stepped on the train from Moscow to Gorky, the former Nizhni Novgorod. Around the big, city hotels vendors had been trying to dispose of soft, warm sables and gold-embroidered altar pieces evidently reft from churches, asking good prices for them. But now the peasant women offered tea cozies, wooden boxes, carved and painted, dolls, leather, brass, knickknacks for the tourist, quite unlike anything obtainable elsewhere in Europe, and always, of course, Russian blouses.

The side-wheel steamer *Kommunistka,* small but comfortable, was waiting to carry us down the Volga to Stalingrad. Our party occupied practically all available cabins, but hundreds of Russians were jammed on the decks. At some points the river was a mile wide as it slid between flat landscapes, limitless as far as the eye could reach. Often we overtook rafts of logs, some at least a quarter of a mile long, each bearing a diminutive house where the captain and his family lived. You could see the children scampering back and forth and the crew pushing it leisurely into the current.

We were four days in transit, passing many villages and a few towns—Kazan, Samara, and Saratov. I do not remember the cities clearly. Some places are indelible in your mind; others amount to very little. If you are searching for something and do not find it, the scene vanishes.

At every stop men and women accompanied by children and baskets of belongings were collected in hundreds. They had come a week or more early to make sure of catching the boat, spending the nights on the ground, subsisting on a loaf of bread, a tomato, or a cucumber. Their children were taken care of in the station crèche, bathed, dressed in fresh clothing, taught, directed in play, delivered to the parents just before the *Kommunistka* landed.

Then came the mad scramble. It was like the old days on Ellis Island when the peasants from Europe arrived, thousands of them, carrying huge bundles on their heads, shoving and rushing and jabbering in strange tongues, attempting to squeeze in. You wondered how so many people could ever get on board. They had no comforts, no room to sleep such as we. They appeared stark and hungry, while we had marvelous food, in fact too much of it. Any American planning to lose weight in Russia was badly disappointed.

Stalingrad, near the mouth of the Volga, was Russia's greatest industrial city. Here I saw a hotel which was going up in front and falling down behind with about equal rapidity; the building material was lying in the streets. In the one in which we lodged we had to dodge spigots. Plumbing had been laid on all over the country, but the stream from any tap never by any chance landed where it was intended to. You approached cautiously, not knowing whether it would get you in the eye, in the nose, or shoot over your shoulder and hit your suitcase. The bathroom had no lock, and the attendant insisted it was his job to help patrons take a bath. I pushed on one side of the door; he on the other. I won.

At Stalingrad, as everywhere I had been before, I was looking for Russian contraceptive methods, but having been discouraged both by Dr. Kaminsky and Dr. Genss, I went at it rather carefully. When I visited the impressive new hospital I asked the superintendent, who was a gynecologist and spoke good English, whether he gave contraceptive advice.

"I do not, but we have a department of consultation."

"May I see it?" I had already surveyed about fifteen such, where I had found nothing save exhibits on the wall.

"It's just across the road."

"Will you go with me?" I asked. "Elsewhere it's been hard to get information."

He agreed readily. As we entered, an attendant was displaying lengthy diagrams to some tourists being shepherded through, and telling them birth control was taught in hospitals throughout Russia. Someone I knew came up to me. "This is wonderful, Mrs. Sanger, the people are being taught birth control by the Government."

The posters were there to prove this, but the consultation room itself was locked. "Who is in charge here?" demanded the superintendent. "I've been sending patients over. Who takes care of them?"

"I do sometimes," a woman assistant volunteered. She let us into the room. There were the same cases I had seen everywhere, probably untouched since 1925, the articles within moldy and cracked.

"What do you use?" I asked.

"We have nothing. We've asked and asked Moscow, but we get nothing."

The superintendent was much embarrassed; he inquired how long it had been since supplies had come.

"Two years."

"Why?"

"We don't know."

"Well, what about the patients I send over here?"

"We just tell them to go home and wait. We have nothing for them."

From Stalingrad we took the train to Ordzonikidze, the beginning of the Georgian Military Highway through the Caucasus to Tiflis. After the usual breakfast of Russian tea, black bread, and fresh caviar, which I found delicious, we climbed into four open-topped char-à-bancs, filling them to capacity. Enormous trucks came behind with our luggage. For about two hours we rolled along by the side of the river Terek, which was running dark and going so fast that the only thing I could think of was the streams from Swiss glaciers, but instead of being ice-green, this was muddy, splashing up on the road. The guides told us there had been a two-day, torrential rain, the worst the Caucasus had ever known.

About ten we stopped to stretch our legs at a village. Groups of lusty mountaineers stared at us, grinning good-humoredly as though we were as odd as any freaks in a circus. They gave us cheese and bread; some of us bought wine and tea, not knowing when we might leave. After three hours we were still at the village when finally men with great high hats and military-looking, astrakhan capes rode up on horseback and spoke to our guides who, not being Georgian, had difficulty divining they were trying to say our cars could not pass.

We thought it was just like the Russians to fuss about a few little obstacles, and said there must be some way to get through. Off we went, and our drivers were magnificent. With the stubbornness of tractors we plunged across streams and over rocks; when trees blocked the road, they lifted the trunks, branches and all. We drove on and on, slowly, and at last, towards five o'clock, came to a spot where there was nothing before us—nothing but the mountain side sheer to the swirling water.

Out clambered the eighty tourists, youthful and aged, tall and short, thin and fat. We could see the road begin about a quarter of a mile beyond, a sultry sun smiling on the peaks of the mountains. The river was still rising. One of our guides waded in to test whether we could ford it, and was soon practically up to his middle in the turbid flood. Grant began ferrying old ladies over the deep places and a couple of boys carried the two-hundred-and-ten-pound Professor Ross. The current was terrific, and people kept falling.

After nearly three hours everybody was across. Our leader found a horse, galloped off to secure new buses, which arrived and took us to the town where we were supposed to have lunch. But it was now dark and lunch became supper. More conversations, more consultations, more delay, more mystery. Why did we not start? The answer was that three strange men were sitting in one of our cars—Russians who wanted to get to Tiflis. They were going to have their rights. When pleading, arguing, reasoning could not move them, the G.P.U. had to be invoked; still no results. Not until they had been promised that a bus would leave immediately did they descend and make room for the three of our group whose seats they had usurped.

We rattled off again, only to be turned back. Another long halt and more conversation. Ultimately, since buses had been dispatched from Tiflis to meet us and were waiting about six miles away, it was decided to push on.

Then began the real drive through Godaur Pass, up and over rocks and embankments, roots of trees, sand and water, precarious detours in a night as jet as any I have ever seen. The militia had been ordered by Moscow to keep the route open—green skyrockets for us to come ahead, red ones to stop, and swinging lanterns in front of the worst danger spots—great drops down into ravines. At last we reached the end and mounted a new set of buses, but only three of them.

Grant was among those who stayed behind. We arrived at Tiflis at two in the morning. Dinner was ready as well as clean beds, and we slept until the humid sun stirred us out for breakfast, just as the rest came straggling in.

It was Sunday morning. Lining the steps of the old Georgian cathedral were beggar women—lame, blind, filthy—never had I seen any others in Russia. Children were curiously looking on at the Mass, but we were told parents were forbidden to make them go to church. The few elderly women attending were carrying flowers and had twined them also around the frames of the saints' pictures. We tourists presented an incongruous contrast to the priests with their long beards and splendid robes.

Tiflis had slipped the yoke of Moscow. Here among the mosques and the camels and the bazaars, which gave it a definitely Oriental tinge, we finally saw signs of private enterprise. Back in the mountains were tribes the Soviet was trying to civilize—warlike, uncultured, barbaric. Stalin, sentimental for the country of his origin perhaps, was choosing as many Georgians as he could for high places and sending in teachers and moving pictures to educate the others, but the task was herculean.

It was hot, torrid noon when we arrived at Batum on the Black Sea. The sun was pouring down; we wanted to go swimming to cool off, and were directed to a stony beach. The water was darkened by the heavy, rich deposit which coated the bottom, and the sand, of the same color, was strewn with masses of people just like Coney Island, thousands of them on the seaweed-covered rocks. It did not look pleasant and we walked further. A partition of slats through which there was perfect visibility was supposed to divide the women from the men, but despite having heard so much about the nude bathing there, we discovered everyone had on suits—astounding, old-fashioned garments.

Mrs. Clyde declined to go in, but sat watching in her hat and glasses. Tanya kept on pink panties and a brassiere. The rest of us determined to throw off our inhibitions. Once you did this you were freed from them for the time being; it was the doing that was so hard. Most surprising were the New England schoolteachers, who had certainly never before removed their clothes in public. They dashed their long, lean bodies boldly into the water as though to say, "Russia, here we come!"

The steamer on which we left Batum was dirty, loaded with passengers who had to be stepped over as they slept on deck. If you left your stateroom even a few moments somebody grabbed it and took your bed.

But the scenery of the Russian Riviera was very lovely. The spurs of the Caucasus along the coast glittered with marble palaces. I shall always remember the mighty, sable cypress trees, slender columns silhouetted against the creamy white walls; they were not funereal to me, but more like sentinels.

Only the chosen of the chosen, the executives and the intelligentsia, could stay at Yalta for holidays. Many individuals, Agnes Smedley, for one, had reason to be grateful to the Soviet for their rest periods. Although not a Communist she had written sympathetic articles, and the Russian Health Department, hearing she was ill in China, had sent her an invitation to come and recuperate, and here she had stayed a year without cost, recovering from a strained heart.

I spent a day in the majestic Byzantine summer palace of Nicholas II at near-by Livadia. It was perfectly landscaped with statues, fountains, terraces. As we drove up multitudinous shaved heads popped out open windows. In the marvelous ballroom were a hundred and fifty enamel cots, side by side, the sleeping quarters of the men on vacation. We saw the room belonging to the former Tsarina, with fragile, brocaded walls and delicate panels. In the center of the parquet floor, bare of any covering, stood a deal table with checked gingham cloth.

Now and then you caught a glimpse of people in the palace, but mostly they were reclining in the gardens. As we wandered round and round we came upon a cluster of twenty-five asleep, pale, and not too well-fed. They did not twitch an eyelid as we approached. I asked Tanya, "Who are these?"

Touching one of them on the shoulder, she said, "Tovarish, these tovarishes want to know who you are."

At that not only he but all of them jumped to their feet, as though at military drill. One after the other gave his name, each with a "vich" or a "ski" on the end of it, stating also his occupation. As he finished he turned his head to the next, who took up the recital. The little woman with bobbed black hair and a curious bodice of blue proudly said she wore the Cross of Lenin on her dress because with him she had fought for Russia. This was the highest honor any woman in Russia could be paid; only a hundred had it.

Then the first man bowed politely to Tanya and with dignity said something to her. She interpreted to us, "They want to know who *you* are."

"Tell them we're Americans."

"North Americans?" with great enthusiasm.

"Yes."

Then question after question spattered like a machine gun. "Are you from Seattle? Portland? How did you get here? What way did you come? How long did it take you? How much did it cost? What has happened to Dillinger? What's the latest news of the seamen's strike on the Pacific Coast? How soon comes the Revolution?"

We were rather dazed at the degree of current information they had gleaned—chiefly from posters in the parks. Their bombardment continued. "Do women in America have as much freedom as men?" We all disagreed on that. "Can married women work for the Government? Can they teach school?" Some of us answered "No," others, "Yes." On every inquiry of theirs we were divided, but on whatever we asked them they were united.

"Who is your favorite American author?"

I answered, "I like Sinclair Lewis."

The woman looked at me accusingly, "Not Theodore Dreiser?"

"Oh, yes," I agreed, "he's good."

A man suggested, "Not Upton Sinclair?"

They were apparently sadly disappointed in us.

At last one of them, making a sweeping gesture, said to me, "Your American Government has never built anything like this for its workers, has it?"

"No," I replied, "we never had a Tsar," which was very tactless of me.

He answered something to the effect, "You people have opinions but no convictions. We have been to prison for ours."

Tanya volunteered, pointing to me, "This lady has been to prison eight times for hers."

Astonishment was registered, and one man spoke hurriedly to Tanya who translated, "He wants to know who you are. Shall I tell him?" She then explained I was advocating birth control.

"Well, we have that. Haven't you visited any of our hospitals? Thousands of women have it."

"No, that's abortion. We don't want that. Birth control is different."

The conversation had shifted to something concrete and real; we had struck up an *entente* that was very *cordiale*. The group gathered closer. "Come on. Come on. This is important." They had never heard of contraception. How could anyone have put me in jail for that? What a crazy government! Worse than they had thought!

The woman said, "We need you over here. Come and work with us. Don't waste your life in America."

From the impatient bus came horns, whistles, bells, summoning us away. The whole twenty-five followed us to the char-à-banc, waving farewell.

Tanya was a most discerning little person, ordinarily impassive but springing up animatedly the moment music started. One of our party invited her, "Come on to America. You'll have pretty clothes, and for anyone who can dance like you, fame is waiting."

"Pretty clothes? I have two dresses, which answer their purpose. And as for fame—this is my people. I enjoy dancing, and they enjoy me. Why should I go to America?"

Before I left I wanted to do something for her, give her some sort of gift in return for her many services. She was going to be married and, because her mother was old-fashioned, have a registered ceremony, call in all her friends, and even don special raiment. I had some new stockings with me and presented them to her. She looked at them, handled them as though treasuring some lovely thing she longed for but could not possess.

"I wouldn't dare wear them. I would be ashamed because my friends could not have the same."

Tanya was willing to go without until silk stockings were to be had by all. It was necessary to grasp this attitude to understand Sovietism. It gave you slight personal freedom, and you had to ask yourself honestly whether exploitation by government or by individual was basically different. But what you did have was security for your old age and the hope that when the rewards came you would have your share.

The Russians were a mass of contradictions. One moment I was irritated enough to tear them limb from limb, the next prostrate before their sincerity and zeal. The more than one hundred and fifty races and forty-five languages made for problems that challenged man's intelligence. Perhaps no other nation had had a lower order of serfdom to arouse from lethargy and put to work on a new civilization. Nothing but admiration could be accorded their attempts and achievements.

But most of the time they were entranced by their own drug of idealism. They had swallowed so much of it that they were self-hypnotized, and bumped into reality without understanding it. Like the Spanish, it was enough for them to say, "It will be," without taking sufficient thought as to how to bring it about.

At Odessa we boarded what then seemed to us by contrast the most beautiful ship in the world, the Italian liner *Campidoglio*, entering into another domain. A neat, white cloth was spread for you, yourself; no longer did you have a soiled napkin folded for indefinite use; spotless coats adorned the waiters; our chairs were pulled out; everybody had a proper bed and cabin. It was only a simple ship, but it signified Western refinement, and I must say I welcomed it. No matter how much proletarian sympathy you might have, you appreciated clean tables, dishes, sheets, towels, and a bathroom that worked.

In order to hurry back to school Grant separated from me in Rumania and my husband joined me in Naples to go to Marienbad. I had barely reached there when Grant cabled that Stuart was ill again; I left for home the same day. On arrival I found the doctors contemplating a radical operation, but I refused to let him have another. As an alternative Tucson, Arizona, was suggested for its dry, warm climate. His wound was still unhealed when we started.

Being stowed away in Stuart's small Ford coupé for days on end gave us the best possible opportunity to catch up in our talks and experiences and place trivial and unimportant events in the pockets of memory where they belonged. The joy of thus familiarizing myself with my grown-up son made me envy mothers who had leisure to grow along with their children or, at least, to watch them develop. But it is possible we are all the better friends in adult life; at least we adhere to the rights of individuality for ourselves and for each other.

It was nearing the close of October when one bright morning we left El Paso and came across miles and miles of brown and yellow desert, up to the hills and mountains. Through the heat waves we saw mirages; we were positive they were lakes. Arizona was so unlike any place I had been before; you either had to be enthralled by it or hate and dread it. Not being quick to come to conclusions I was not at first sure. But I knew there was a delight in the cool nights and the translucent, sunny days with a lovely tang in the air. In the beginning it was the people who won me, particularly Mrs. Robert P. Bass, daughter of Mrs. Charles Sumner Bird, one of our early pioneers. We stayed with her for a short time, and then took a pink adobe house out where the desert met the foothills. Stuart grew better. In the spring we packed our bags once more in the little car and drove away, looking back regretfully at the indescribable Catalinas, on which light and clouds played in never-ending change of pattern.

Chapter Thirty-seven

WHO CAN TAKE A DREAM FOR TRUTH?

"Divinity sleeps in stones, breathes in plants, dreams in animals, and awakes in human beings."
INDIAN PROVERB

SEVERAL times I had approached the idea of going to India, and always something had prevented me. In 1922 when I was near by, it was the hot season and everybody had gone to the hill stations. In 1928, when I had also made tentative plans, I was not well. I think I had, in addition, been reluctant because Katherine Mayo's book had left me with such an aching pain I felt powerless to help lift the inertia she described.

Finally, in 1936, I had word from Margaret Cousins, pioneer in the Indian women's movement, wife of a poet and university professor, who asked whether I would accept an invitation to attend the coming All-India Women's Conference. The previous conference had passed a resolution favoring birth control in theory, but now they wanted me to assist them to "put teeth in it," to draw up one which would outline a practical plan applicable to all castes, to present it, and to argue for it.

Since such a resolution would mean that the movement had now gone beyond the point where we had to break in to be heard, and would start things in the right direction, I arranged to spend three months in India, from November to January, under the auspices of the International Information Center, which had been set up in London after the Geneva Conference so that various peoples and countries interested in the subject might have some means of contact.

Mrs. John Phillips, who had fought many battles in Pittsburgh for birth control, suggested that her daughter, a graduate of Vassar and a newspaper woman, might come along as my secretary. All the way a fine young crowd rallied around the lively Anna Jane, who had as great a capacity for laughter as any human being I ever knew. Nothing was too hard for her, nothing too big or too small for her to do; altogether she was a perfect companion, beginning with our voyage to England, and ending in Honolulu.

Temporarily in London was Gandhi's appointed successor, Pundit Jawaharlal Nehru, of a family noted for scholarship. He was the youthful leader of the more radical elements in India, much more inclined towards Communism than Gandhi. After having been in jail for four years he had now been released to see his wife who was ill and dying in Germany. I was unable to be present at a reception for him, so Anna Jane telephoned to say I was sorry. "Why should Mrs. Sanger be sorry?" he said, with the simplicity of the truly great. "She can come any time." I did so the next afternoon.

Nehru was quiet and poised, with a thoughtful manner which impressed you immediately as one of controlled intelligence. His intention was to establish in the mind of Young India that Gandhi's spiritual doctrines would only be effective if knit with economic and sociological principles.

More recondite than the Indian was the Englishman, Paul Brunton, small and dark, with a solemn, intense, almost mystic expression in his eyes. He was attempting to find what virtue lay in fakirs and holy men, combing India for them, and had embodied the result in his book, *The Search in Secret India*. He told me, "Not many holy men remain; most of them have gone back into the mountains, inaccessible to Westerners. The one for whom I have the greatest regard is the sage of Arunachala, the Maharshi of Tiruvannamalai. My wife and I have a little hut southwest of Madras, and if you will visit us when you reach that section of India, I will see that you come into his presence."

Naturally I accepted his offer eagerly and put it on my "must" list.

Shortly before my departure from London, a farewell banquet was given at the Barber-Surgeons' Hall, a relic of old London known to few, and to which you could be admitted only by invitation. It was on Monkwell Street in the City near the London Wall and Aldersgate. Well aware of the difficulties of threading that maze, even by daylight, I inquired of the carriage attendant at the Savoy whether the taxi-driver were familiar with it.

"Certainly, Madam."

Off I went with Mrs. Kerr-Lawson, the painter's wife, somewhat pressed for time. As usual in November, it was raining. After we had serpentined in and out for twenty minutes we began to surmise that the driver was lost, and I called to him, "Don't you know the way?"

"Well, I thought it was down 'ere, but it don't seem to be."

"Why don't you ask somebody?"

"W'ere's Barbers' 'All?" He addressed a mail carrier, who paused to think, and then said, "Well, it's along there," pointing back from where we had come.

We turned about but had no better luck. The driver stopped at least ten people, each in uniform or livery of some kind or other, "W'ere's Barbers' 'All?" and all we heard was the echo, "Barbers' 'All?" He drew up beside a bobby; even he did not know.

Finally, we saw smart-looking cars going in a certain direction. We said that must be it, and, sure enough, there on the corner was the sign. For our own peace of mind we were not last. H.G. was close behind us, frothing with fury because he too had been driving around Robin Hood's barn.

Much of the building was locked up, but what we saw was beautifully preserved. Evidently the Guild of the Barbers had prospered in the days when their members did bleeding and leeching, and attended to other annoyances of humanity, such as pulling teeth.

The dining room, once the operating theater, was now the fairest setting for a dinner that one could have—the service presented by Queen Anne, crystal goblets, a silver rose-carved finger bowl, the vast Royal Grace Cup given by Henry VIII, like a chalice with a six-inch stem, everything used only on rare occasions. The table was like an E with the middle left out, and in the center sat Harry Guy in his high-backed chair above the rest of us. I was on his right and next me was a man whose name had performed almost a miracle for birth control in England—Baron Thomas Horder, then physician to the Prince of Wales.

Sidney Walton, the member without whom this banquet could not have taken place, opened the affair as ancient custom prescribed by declaiming, "Pray, silence for the King!" After the toast to His Majesty, one was drunk to the President of the United States, and then my health was proposed; the loving cup, containing about a quart of red wine, began to make the rounds. During the toast, three people had to be standing—the one holding the cup, the one who just had it on the left, and the one on the right who was to receive it. The waiter came to wipe the lip hygienically when each had swallowed his sip; this was the sole modern touch.

London offered me many courtesies. The Italian invasion of Ethiopia was now in full swing. Rumors were abroad that British ships were avoiding the Suez Canal; therefore, I booked on a Dutch line. When I mentioned this to Sir John Megaw, former director of the Indian Medical Service, he practically stopped breathing and bristled in every hair of his head. "What! a P. and O. boat not go through the Canal for fear of Italy?"

"So I've heard."

"My dear Mrs. Sanger, you can go through the Suez Canal on a British boat if the British Navy has to escort you through!"

Sir John's report calling upon the British Government to make some plan for population growth, increase, and distribution for India was one of the most intelligent issued by any health officer in this age. Although entirely in sympathy with my project, yet he doubted whether it would be possible for me to do anything. That I was an American, however, he thought might obviate the antagonism which would inevitably follow the mention of birth control by anybody from the British Isles.

Almost as soon as the *Viceroy of India* sailed, we seemed much nearer the East. Indian deck hands moved about, distinguishable by their slim bodies, brown faces, and turbans, but the English were in command of all departments. It must have been a source of resentment to the Indian passengers to be ignored or treated as inferiors by the English Civil Service going to rule them in their own land.

The ship was second-rate, rocky in a heavy sea, and raucous. The blast of bugles for rising and meals had long since been outmoded on most passenger liners but was retained here. I was awakened at eight or earlier every morning by the most awful thud, thud, thud overhead. After I had had a headache for two days I went up to the sports deck and found the English were getting exercise by throwing quoits around directly above my stateroom.

The Suez Canal was bright with yellow sand and blue sky. We slowly steamed past two Italian transports with bandaged soldiers on the decks, invalided home from Ethiopia. As far as conversation on our own vessel went, no one would have suspected there was a war. Not an Englishman brought up the subject, and, if drawn into a discussion, he eluded it by saying his country could jolly well look after itself.

Once we were in the Red Sea, passengers and officers emerged in white; the decks were roofed with canvas so that the games might go on. Most of these British had traveled so much they had a seafaring routine. They indulged in sports in the morning, dressed appropriately. From two to four in the afternoon a pall of silence descended. All the chairs on the deck were occupied by dozing, browsing loungers. But as soon as the tea things appeared, life began to be interesting. Music burst forth from the orchestra, babies were brought up from the nursery, everybody hurried to and fro from chair to table, picking and choosing cakes or buns, sandwiches or plain bread and jam. After dinner again the full, blazing lights gave ample illumination for the interminable deck tennis and quoits.

Bombay from the distance was a city of tall buildings. Not until very close could you see the sizzling heat on the water; the hot sun and heavy air made it unpleasant to stand on deck. The wharf was filled, the British easily recognizable by their sola topees, the ugliest headgear in the world. All were waving with great excitement, and many carried flower garlands for visitors or those coming home. Amid scrambling and confusion coolies swarmed aboard for luggage. A delegation of about fifty welcomed us, including Edith How-Martyn, who had been sounding out popular and religious sentiment, and Dr. A. P. Pillay, editor of the magazine, *Marriage Hygiene,* the man most active in eugenics and birth control in India.

I had written to Gandhi and a reply from him greeted me at the boat, "Do by all means come whenever you can, and you shall stay with me, if you would not mind what must appear to you to be our extreme simplicity; we have no masters and no servants here."

The evening was hot and oppressive indoors but mild and balmy outside, and I sauntered under a lovely, deep sky. The women, small of body, ankles, and wrists, with well-formed features, and softly spoken as the Japanese, whether poor or not, wore bracelets, anklets, rings in the ears, and some a button jewel in the side of the nose. Seldom were any in Western costume; almost always they wore saris, graceful folds draped over their heads. Men and boys were stretched out on the walks, their only belongings the mats on which they lay. It was revolting to see something stir in the dust, and watch rags change into a human being sleeping there.

The next afternoon I had my first meeting in Cowasji Jehangir Hall, the largest in Bombay, and clamorously noisy. It was open to the street, and trams went wobbling by, pedestrians talked loudly, and dozens and dozens of electric fans purred round and round and round. You had to speak at the very top of your throat in order to be heard; Indians were accustomed to the British enunciation and the British pitch and found American English difficult to understand. Looking down on the audience was like gazing at a choppy sea; it was a broken mass of Gandhi white caps, shaped rather like those worn by our soldiers overseas. They were not removed in the house, in shops, or even at table. Everywhere in India you saw them, showing how large was his following.

I had been told that unmarried women did not exist in India and none of the cultured class worked for wages. However, the very day I landed I met three girls who were still single, gave their time to help the outcasts, and had small apartments of their own. Two of them were trying to be independent; another received an allowance from her father who, though disapproving, supplied her livelihood.

It had been predicted also that only Eurasians and the lower classes would listen to me on birth control, but the question turned out to be not, "Shall it be given?" but "What to give?" and it came from all strata. The Mayor of Bombay invited me to address a gathering of city officials. Mrs. Sarojini Naidu, the famous poetess, outstanding for her loyalty to India and next to Gandhi the most beloved person in the country, talked with me about holding a meeting in Hyderabad, where her husband was head of the medical profession. Lady Braybourne during luncheon at Government House told me that she and the Governor were anxious to prevent the fifteen hundred people on their own compound from doubling their numbers within a few years. What would I suggest?

The answer was complicated by many factors. First and foremost was the unspeakable poverty which prevailed. A contraceptive so cheap that it could be available to everyone had been invented in the form of a foam powder which could be made from rice starch; enough for a year should not cost more than ten cents. But as yet we had not tested it sufficiently to guarantee its harmlessness and efficacy.

The poorer women of Bombay, sober-faced and dull-looking, who particularly needed this method, lived in the grubby and deadly *chawls*—huts of corrugated iron—no windows, no lights, no lamps, just three walls and sometimes old pieces of rag or paper hung up in front in a pitiful attempt at privacy.

I soon learned that when traveling through the country we had to have a servant, or bearer, to secure railroad compartments, make up the beds, see we had food at various stations, and keep the vendors off. Mattresses, blankets, sheets, pillows, towels, and soap had to accompany us on trains. From Cook's we acquired Joseph, an extraordinary character, dressed always in a black alpaca coat and colorful turban. We paid him about a dollar a day, considered a very good salary. However, since he spoke not only Hindustani, but also Bengali, Tamil, and English, we thought him an excellent find. He waited on us, brought us tea in the morning, went with us on calls.

Joseph's respect for us was enormously increased when he heard we were going to visit Gandhi. He became our devoted adviser, sleeping outside the door at night. Because of his position it was beneath his dignity to carry anything. Consequently we were obliged to hire a coolie for his luggage as well as several for our own. India was undoubtedly the place for the white man to lose his inferiority complex, should he have one; the serving class was obsequious, and the educated, aloof and superior.

We were met at the station at Wardha by a covered, two-wheeled cart, a tonga, very clean with little steps leading up and drawn by a cream-colored bullock. Since there were no seats, we sat flat on the bottom and were pulled leisurely and slowly along dusty roads to the *ashram*.

Gandhi was cross-legged on the floor of a room in a large squarish structure, a white cloth like a sheet around him. He rose to greet me as I entered with an armful of books and flowers and magazines and gloves that I had not realized were there until we tried to take each other by both hands. He beamed and I laughed.

Perhaps even more exaggerated than his pictures was Gandhi's appearance: his ears stuck out more prominently; his shaved head was more shaved; his toothless mouth grinned more broadly, leaving a great void between his lips. But around him and a part of him was a luminous aura. And once you had seen this, the ugliness faded and you glimpsed the something in the essence of his being which people have followed and which has made them call him the Mahatma.

This was Monday, Gandhi's day of silence, of meditation and prayer. He was so besieged by problems and difficulties on which he had to decide that this one twenty-four hours he reserved for himself without interruption. Therefore, he merely smiled and nodded his head and then Anna Jane and I were escorted along a gravel path to the guest house, perhaps a hundred yards away, a building of four rooms, rough-hewn, white-plastered walls, the upper section open for ventilation. On the uneven stone floor stood two mattressless cots on which our bedding was spread. A roof pole in the center had a circular shelf which served as table or chairs according to need.

Bowls of porridge and milk were brought, sweetened with either honey or burned sugar—I could not tell which, but it was very pleasant. I asked no questions about its being boiled, or whether it was goats' or cows' milk; although I happened not to be hungry, down it went just the same.

From tiffin on we inspected the cotton-growing, the paper-making, the oil press, and the irrigation by means of old-fashioned turn wheels. I was not enthusiastic. It seemed so pitiable an effort, like going backward instead of forward, and trying to keep millions laboring on petty hand processes merely in order to give them work to do by which they might exist.

In the evening Gandhi wrote on his slate that next morning I could join him in his walk. This was his regular exercise, occupying about an hour. He took quite good care of himself physically, observing rules of health and diet rigidly and strictly. He had to in order to perform the tremendous quantity of labor always facing him.

After we had ascended to the roof for evening prayers, our cots were moved out on the terrace under the moon and stars and the glorious, limitless sky overhead. Lights shimmered along the path to the main house but, for the rest, all was darkness. I never was more conscious of nature's stillness or of more constant stirrings from human beings—the echoing chant from the village near by, singing, calling, laughing, dogs barking, the sounds wafted clearly through the cool and crisp air while not a leaf on the trees trembled. At four the bells rang out for morning prayers and at six Joseph came to tell me the hour and I arose and dressed.

Gandhi and I walked with his other two women guests; they deemed sacred every moment they spent with him. Men, women, and children waited for him as he passed, several prostrating themselves as to a holy person. Stepping over the debris we traversed narrow byways through the open fields where families huddled in their tiny huts together with dogs and goats. People were bathing and washing and cleaning their teeth. Little spirals of smoke were drifting from the fires for the morning meal.

At eleven we all went to our breakfast across the court, leaving our shoes outside. Everybody was ready, and great shining trays of silver-looking metal were placed before us on the floor. Gandhi was trying to persuade the Indians to utilize native-grown vegetables in different ways and thus increase their vitamin consumption. Mrs. Gandhi supervised the culinary department, and herself served the meal, of which there was a goodly and varied supply—no meat, but plenty of fruits and vegetables in curious combinations, such as tomatoes and oranges in a salad. All picked up their food with their fingers, mixing it and scooping it in very cleverly without dropping a morsel.

So numerous were Gandhi's adherents, so deep his influence, that I was sure his endorsement of birth control would be of tremendous value if I could convince him how necessary it was for Indian women. After breakfast I set myself to the task.

He spoke fluent English in a low voice with accurate intonations, never lacking for a word, and could apparently discuss any subject near or far. Nevertheless, I felt his registering of impressions was blunted; while you were answering a question of his, he held to an idea or a train of thought of his own, and, as soon as you stopped, continued it as though he had not heard you. Time and again I believed he was going along with me, and then came the stone wall of religion or emotion or experience, and I could not dynamite him over this obstacle. In fact, despite his claim to open-mindedness, he was proud of not altering his opinions.

Gandhi maintained that he knew women and was in sympathetic accord with them. Personally, after listening to him for a while, I did not believe he had the faintest glimmering of the inner workings of a woman's heart or mind. He accused himself of being a brute by having desired his wife when he was younger, and classed all sex relations as debasing acts, although sometimes necessary for procreation. He agreed that no more than three or four children should be born to a family, but insisted that intercourse, therefore, should be restricted for the entire married life of the couple to three or four occasions.

I suggested that such a regimen was bound to cause psychological disturbances in both husband and wife. Furthermore, when respect and consideration and reverence were a part of the relationship I called it love, not lust, even if it found expression in sex union, with or without children.

Gandhi referred me to nature, the great director, who would solve our problems if we depended on her, but said what we were doing was to inject man's ideas into nature.

To this I replied, "How can you differentiate? Here is cotton growing on your land and lemons also. That's nature. Would you object to dipping cotton into lemon juice and using that as a contraceptive?"

He said positively that he would. For every argument I presented he countered with "I would devise other methods," but proposed none that was not based on continence. He reiterated that women in order to control the size of their families must "resist" their husbands, in extreme cases leave them.

Those who listened to the interview declared that the Mahatma made concessions he had never made before. He himself said to me, "This has not been wasted effort. We have certainly come nearer together." Nevertheless, I knew it was futile to count on Gandhi to help the movement in India; his state of mind would not change. After reading his autobiography, I thought I saw the cause of his inhibitions. He himself had had the feeling which he termed lust, and he now hated it. It formed an emotional pivot in his brain around which centered everything having to do with sex. But there remained his kindness, his hospitality, his arrangements for your comfort, which he duplicated again and again for visitors who gave nothing, but instead received inspiration from him. And, furthermore, since humanity as a rule does little for itself and the inert mass has to be upheaved to a point where it can gain initiative, anyone who can arouse a nation of all classes and ages out of the incredible lethargy into which it has long been sunk and can stir up a people to hope is a great, even noble, person.

Nevertheless, in contrast to Gandhi's attitude towards birth control, Rabindranath Tagore's was a comfort. With Anna Jane and Joseph I set out on the long trip to Calcutta—two-thirds of the breadth of India. Now you really saw the country—the palms and banana trees, the natives getting on trains, living in their tiny huts. These were of bamboo plastered with mud and whitewashed; the floors were soaked with cow dung to harden the dirt, and the roofs were thatched with straw. As we passed through village after village, I observed cows, goats, dogs, bullocks, all with their young, rambling in the streets, freely mixing with the people and scrambling out of the way when a whistle or bell sounded. Peddlers, balancing on their heads trays heaped with oranges, walked up and down the station platforms, calling their wares in a fascinating, singsong meter.

We arrived at Bolpur beyond Calcutta at seven-thirty of an early December evening. Tagore's son had been on the train and we went with him to Santineketan, House of Peace, where Tagore lived and taught. The grouping of buildings in the thousand-acre estate resembled that of an ancient monastery, not so cozy or individual as

Gandhi's, but rather cold and bare. Before sunrise again I heard the chanting prayers of the students. Boys and girls together then went at six o'clock to study in the mango grove or under the banyan trees, all in the open air.

His former luxurious home Tagore had turned over to his son, and himself occupied a small clay house designed like a temple in modern style. The room into which I was shown in the afternoon was full of books and papers, like the office of a busy executive. Tagore, in a long, rough, handmade robe of homespun, was seated behind his desk. I had been told I would find him greatly aged, but, although he was slightly thinner than when I had seen him in New York in 1931, he did not seem much older. True his beard and hair were scantier, but his face, almost unlined, had the same repose, and his finely modulated voice expressed the same understanding when he spoke of the importance of birth control to his country, and sincerely hoped I would be able to reach the villagers, which he said must be done were it to bring any benefit to India.

Tagore knew I had been to see Gandhi, but did not mention it. He had tact combined with his grace and intellect; he drew, painted, directed dancing, even sculptured and acted. Appealing to more moneyed classes than Gandhi, he guided his school towards furthering culture and the arts as well as improving agricultural necessities.

The medical building in Calcutta had been selected for my first lecture there, but Mr. O'Connor, who was in charge, refused permission. Since the edifice belonged to the British Government, birth control became at once popular with the Indians, and the meeting was transferred to Albert Hall. I was warned we needed as chairman a good strong man with a domineering personality, because it was a rowdy place and trouble-makers always haunted it. However, the association which had asked me to speak had already chosen a woman, Mrs. Soudamini Mehta, who was managing the clinic in Calcutta. I talked against the noise for forty minutes and then Mrs. Mehta, whose voice scarcely carried over the footlights, opened the forum for questions.

Two bearded patriarchs looking like Messiahs were sitting in the front row. One of them hopped up and, without asking a question, began haranguing in unctuous tones. Mrs. Mehta tried to stop him, but could not. The audience tried to yell him down; a few were with him but most were not. Then a fist fight broke out and the second sexagenarian rose and demanded recognition. Someone caught his hands from behind, and another row began.

Finally I said to Mrs. Mehta, "Perhaps they can hear me. Let's ask them whether they want to listen to these men."

At once a mighty roar of "No!" went up. Then both the old men erupted again, shrieking. Mrs. Mehta, anger lending strength to her vocal chords, at last called out indignantly, "You're naughty, and the meeting is now dismissed!" And so, amid shouts of merriment, we broke up.

I had no more lectures scheduled for a time, and accepted with pleasure the invitation of Mrs. Norman Odling to visit her at Kalimpong, in the shadow of Mt. Everest, three hundred and fifty miles north of Calcutta.

In preparing for this excursion I had to decide whether to take Joseph. He was a silent man. Whenever I had requested him to perform any service, from getting the laundry together to looking after the luggage, he had never answered yes or no but had only shaken his head—not a regular shake, but a nodding from side to side as though he were saying, "Well, well, well!" I had usually sighed, "Never mind." I had grown rather exasperated with what seemed his deplorable lack of enthusiasm, although Anna Jane appeared to like him; being busy in other directions, especially with beaux, she had left many things for him to attend to. Finally I informed Cook's that we were departing for the North and would like somebody else. When their representative came around to investigate, he said to Joseph, "Do you wish to go with Mrs. Sanger?" Joseph shook his head.

"There you are!" I exclaimed. "He doesn't want to go."

At that Joseph put up pleading hands and spoke in Hindustani.

"Yes, he does," said the Cook's man. "When he shakes his head 'no' he means 'yes.'"

Before we started Joseph mentioned to me how wintry it was in the Himalayas; he must have an overcoat. I asked whether he had ever been there.

"Yes."

"Did you have a coat then?"
"Yes."
"Did someone buy it for you?"
"Yes, always buy it for bearers."
"Well, where's that coat?"
"Worn out."

I questioned Cook's about that also and was told, "He's trying to do you. Probably he already has two or three, and if you give him another he'll just sell it."

We hardened our hearts, and Joseph had to get along without his coat.

As we progressed north the nights grew cold, the mornings cold, four in the afternoon was cold. Joseph had changed to a hideous black hat which he said was warmer than his turban, but he had no overcoat and began to cough.

We arrived at Siliguri at six of a brisk morning, just in time to watch the rose-colored dawn break over the snow-covered mountains. After a cup of hot but vile coffee we wrapped ourselves in rugs and off we went on the full hour's drive to Kalimpong, up and around hairpin curves, mostly following the river, often through bits of jungle whence you knew a tiger might spring out on the road any minute. The scenery was the most superb I had ever seen, grander than the Rockies or Pyrenees or Alps, a blend of green tangle and white peaks touching the clear sky, with wreaths of clouds far below.

As we neared Kalimpong there was a distinct difference in the type of native; Thibetans and Nepalese were frequent. The swarms of women looked like squaws, although, instead of papooses, they carried on their backs huge baskets of charcoal or from six to eight massive blocks of stone, all for six cents a day. No horses, no mules, no wagons, only women as beasts of burden hauling these rocks from the quarry to the site, jingling with rings on their ankles and rings on their toes. What struck me as most peculiar was that many of them wore ugly shawls, assuredly products of Scottish mills; the entire hillside was dotted with plaids.

As soon as I reached Mrs. Odling's home and heard the accent of her medical missionary father, I knew the answer. "We never think of going home to Scotland without bringing some back," she said. "They much prefer plaids to their own designs."

Mrs. Odling was a darling, born there in the hills, and was intensely interested in cultivating the industries of the Thibetans, whom she encouraged to come across the border with their handsome silver boxes and brass bowls studded with turquoise. They were not a pleasant-appearing people. It was almost ludicrous to see this delicate woman slapping some of the worst-looking characters heartily on the shoulder and talking to them in their primitive language; it was evident they adored her and would do anything for her.

Kalimpong itself was lovely and sunny, perched on an outer spur of the eastern Himalayas; in the background soared up the mighty, snowy barrier of Kinchenjunga, which screened it from Thibet, and past it ran the high, chill, rocky road to Lhasa.

To reach Darjeeling, which was on the far side of a mountain range, it was necessary to retrace our steps to Siliguri and then go along a magnificent but treacherous road up another valley. Darjeeling itself disappointed me, a hodgepodge of everybody and everything—tourists, riffraff, exorbitant prices on worthless articles, scarcely a few good ones in gift shops. But I had the opportunity of buying for Grant the skin of a tiger shot in a recent hunt, and this beauty was packed in moth balls and sent directly to the ship. Also a case of Darjeeling tea from one of the choicest gardens was delivered to me in Calcutta, whither I now returned.

There a certain Dr. Ankelsaria, an Indian lecturer who had spoken in America on psychology and psychic phenomena, established himself as my interpreter and guide and dragged me willy-nilly to see such sights as the Jain Temple and Crystal Palace. He overheard me telephoning for an appointment with Sir Jagardis Chandra Bose, famous for his ingenious theory that plants breathed. He promptly said, "I know Sir Jagardis very well; I'll take you there."

I intimated that Anna Jane and I were the only ones invited, but he said, "Oh, that's nothing. We all go there to tea quite often." But when he did not arrive at the designated hour we set off in a taxi, somewhat relieved.

Sir Jagardis was a person of great dignity—elderly, polished, the scientist pure and simple. He seemed to me like a person trying to keep his life clear, without having externals crowd in upon him too closely.

We had hardly finished our tea when to my surprise Dr. Ankelsaria appeared in the doorway and Sir Jagardis inquired, "Do you wish to have this gentleman?" We explained he had offered to bring us in his car.

Soon we walked out to see the garden, where plants of every description were carefully tended, each treated like an only child—this one put to bed early, that one awakened by the sun, this shrank from noise, that loved running water, this craved a moist atmosphere, that needed a desert in which to thrive; he understood the characteristics of each. He himself was disturbed because his flowers did not like the presence of Dr. Ankelsaria and would be affected by it.

From there we stepped into the laboratory, where Sir Jagardis demonstrated the working of his machine. When he placed either nitrogen or carbon on the plant the instrument, which had been almost quiescent, made tiny marks, much as a person's heartbeat was shown on a cardiograph.

Dr. Ankelsaria pushed in and got out a pencil and notebook. Sir Jagardis at once froze, ceased talking, and asked, "Are you a newspaper reporter?"

"No, I'm a doctor."

"What are you taking down? I'll not have it!" Then, turning to me as though I had been guilty of treachery, "My conversation with you was personal and confidential."

I was profoundly embarrassed and, as severely as I knew how, requested Dr. Ankelsaria to stop his writing immediately.

The night I was leaving Calcutta for Benares, the worthy doctor insisted I have dinner at his sister's home, a real Indian feast. Among the guests was an amazing individual who greeted me as though we were old friends, and I wondered where in heaven's name I had ever known him. Then suddenly I remembered—Carnegie Hall four years earlier, jammed to the doors, some woman relinquishing her seat because she thought the subject of the lecture was more important for me than for her, then the appearance of the thick-set Swami from California, black hair hanging to his shoulders, and my amazement that in good old America in the days of the great depression five thousand people could be induced to chorus after him in unison, "I am love, I am love," swaying, hypnotized by their own rhythm, until the lofty hall vibrated and thundered. At the end of five minutes I had thanked the lady who had given me her place and tiptoed silently out.

Now here in Calcutta I met again the Swami, clad in his ochre-colored robe, back in India for the first time in many years. He inquired after my health, assured me he had been aware of what I had been doing in America, was so sorry I had not seen his home in Los Angeles. I said I would visit him when next I went to California.

Instead of being taken to the train in Ankelsaria's unpretentious car, I was transported in the Swami's elegant Rolls-Royce with the top lowered. As we went swishing through the streets, passers-by jumped on the running boards, dozens of others followed us, all wanting to touch the hem of the Swami's robe. By the time we had reached the station there were a hundred in our wake. I caught sight of Joseph at the gate, and on the platform, with one eye out for me, was Anna Jane surrounded by her formal English friends in evening dress; the train was to depart in a few minutes. When she saw me approaching with the Swami and his retinue she dashed into the compartment to compose her features. Then we stood at the doorway as we pulled out to watch the Englishmen turning away a little stiffly, and the Swami, one of the incongruous but well-wishing acquaintances whom birth control attracts, waving a vigorous good-by.

Chapter Thirty-eight

DEPTH BUT NOT TUMULT

⋙-⋙-⋙-⋙-⋙-⋙-⋙-⋙-⋙-⋙-⋙-⋙-⋘-⋘-⋘-⋘-⋘-⋘-⋘-⋘-⋘-⋘-⋘-⋘

OF all the cities of India Benares left the worst impression on me; so many things exaggeratedly extolled do not live up to expectations. I never encountered more confusion of religious symbols—the Temple of Gold, the Monkey Temple, the Snake Temple —quite out of place in a holy city. I did not like temples. They made me feel queer in the middle, so smelly and such relics of ages gone by. Worshipers bowed low, resting their foreheads on the wet and slimy floors where thousands of people were walking in and out. Around the doors were beggars—blind, maimed, diseased. In the grounds were animals of every kind—monkeys, oxen, buffaloes, goats for the sacrifice; vultures and crows were flying overhead.

Most foreigners disliked the Ganges, floating with horrors, but I found it at dawn comparatively clean, and by far the most attractive thing there. We had risen early to see the Brahmins, the first-comers, men and women, old and young, bathing in the holy water. Mourners were sitting on a hillock some twenty feet away from a burning ghat, still aflame, waiting until the fire died down and the ashes could be swept into the river. This seemed to me a more wholesome manner of dealing with the dead than the Western custom of burial.

Later Joseph, whose cough was increasing, led us through the narrow streets to the bazaars. Screaming mobs of vendors lured you towards lace shops or to buy brasses or silks. They came up to offer you cards. If you took one, competitors shouted and yelled, "He's a liar, a thief, a robber, don't go with him! His goods are fake!" Although some of the wares were exquisite, this ferocity again did not coincide with my conception of a holy city.

Allahabad was more like a college town, and there I visited Mrs. Ranjit Sitaram Pandit, the sister of Jawaharlal Nehru, whom I had met in London. Her home was old and spacious, a nucleus of intellectual thought and activity.

She sponsored a meeting to which about six hundred students came. It was inspiring to see fine young people attempting to weave together your philosophy and theirs. They were extremely sensitive —more than most audiences, I think. But, as was the case with youth elsewhere, they made light of anything that could be made light of. After the meeting free literature was announced, and in two minutes it was a regular football rush. We had to throw the pamphlets over their heads to keep them from stampeding the platform in their headlong scramble.

At the Purdah Club the audience, of course, was entirely women; many, in their early twenties, already had large families. They were little accustomed to frank examination of such subjects, but, on the other hand, did not want mere theories. By the time questions were in order they had recovered from their giggling and were ready to talk seriously. As usual, some came up afterwards to query me personally on matters that could better and more profitably have been discussed with all.

On reaching Agra we reserved the Taj Mahal for sunset. Fortunately, only a few people were there, so that the quiet was intensified. Words are inadequate to describe its dignity and chastity; it seemed to breathe the essence of beauty. It was not overwhelming, as were some of the world's wonders, but it had a perfect simplicity. I stayed until the sun sank, and in the afterglow the marble shone in a mystic effulgence, like something in another dimension reflected in the still, translucent pool. There was not a cloud in the sky, just radiance everywhere. Before daybreak I climbed again to the top of the gate tower and watched the rising sun cast its shadow on the dome. With reluctance I turned away to catch the train for Baroda.

After a long journey we arrived at the capital at three in the morning. I had been invited as a state guest, and, in spite of the hour, we were met by the secretary under a handsome hat of red and gold and black. Immediately you felt a touch of Paris in the way clothes were worn in Baroda.

Arrangements had been made for my audience with the Gaekwar, who had been put on the throne by the British Government. He was a most progressive ruler for his two and a half million subjects, aiming at compulsory education and the abolition of caste restrictions. In the immense anteroom of the Palace were ten or fifteen tall Indians with gorgeous turbans, who must have been more than just ordinary officials. The Gaekwar, short, vigorous, alert, shook hands and recalled that he had been President of the World Fellowship of Faith at Chicago, which he said had been the greatest honor of his life, and that he remembered my talk there.

"Her Highness wishes to meet you this afternoon. She is beginning to spend much time on health work and you must get her interested in what you are doing. She will be a good friend to you."

At the appointed hour I went to see the Maharani, quite different from her husband, very grave, only recently out of purdah and still keeping a separate palace. She knew hardly anything about birth control, but maintained a welfare center for mothers and infants.

I had heard from many sources that this class, that class, and the other class would welcome or oppose birth control, none of which statements had hitherto proved to be accurate. The State Medical Officer, who was very close to the Maharani, had a further thesis which he stated as he was taking me to the Maharani's settlement, a little place where forty or fifty women, each one with a child, were sitting. "These women have been brought up to the duty of having children and are so shy and modest that they would not listen to anything on birth control."

He sounded as though he were antagonistic, but he was merely indicating the difficulties as he saw them. I replied that I had never yet encountered women who, when the subject was put to them in a way they could understand, were not eager to hear more. I suggested, "There's a Mohammedan who has a sickly baby. How old is she?"

"Twenty."

"How many children has she?"

"Three."
"Did she have more?"
"Two died."
"How old is this one?"
"Five or six months."
"Wouldn't she prefer to wait until this baby is strong and well before she has any more?"

The woman had no opportunity to answer. The whole flock moved up. "I do! We do! Has this lady something like that? That's what we want!"

The medical officer was genuinely astonished. "I must tell this to her Highness." When I myself saw the Maharani for the second time she spoke far more favorably of birth control.

Eventually I was on my way to Trivandrum, capital of Travancore, to lend whatever support I could towards the resolution for birth control at the All-India Women's Conference. The larger part of the population of this semi-independent southern state was of Dravidian origin, among whom child marriage scarcely existed. Here widows were allowed to remarry, divorce was permissible for either party, and women occupied a unique position because property descended to the children of a man's sister rather than to his own.

Some of the other state guests had already arrived. One charming girl especially attracted me. She was warm-hearted, kindly, longing to serve humanity, and prepared to dedicate her life to Gandhi's teachings. When I asked her to what she intended to devote herself, she answered, "Show the depressed classes that women of my type can clean their latrines. If I can do it, then they will see that it is not such an unworthy occupation after all."

Believing this futile, I said, "Don't you think perhaps you're wasting your efforts? Why not do something constructive, teach the mothers to wash and feed their children properly?"

She was determined, however, to sacrifice herself. "Gandhi wants the latrines cleaned."

The Maharani of Travancore, Sethu Parvathi Bai, was titular head of the Conference, but the guiding spirit was a Parsee from Hyderabad, Mrs. Rustomji Feridoonji, a woman in her fifties, hair almost white, a scholar with command of English, German, and

French, with the polish of India and the West as well, alert and aware of everything going on in the world. She and several like her were an inspiration to others of the East and could put to shame many Westerners in their courage and vision. They had seen immediately the necessity of having the movement under the control of public health. In what was virtually a form of socialized medicine municipalities were already sending out midwives, nurses, and doctors to the poor classes. Wherever vaccination went, the birth control advocates planned to follow with contraceptive information. With Mrs. Feridoonji and the rest of the committee I helped to draw up a resolution to this effect.

The second afternoon the Maharani entertained at a garden party. Fountains were splashing, lakes and pools were lustrous in the sunlight. The dancing was executed by children and older girls, the couples moving round and round, precise little steps this way and that and up to each other without apparently lifting their feet from the ground.

The Maharani and I took a short stroll together and she asked me particularly to come to her palace the next morning at seven o'clock. I had really no idea why she wanted to see me, and was uneasy, because the debate over our resolution was to begin at nine. Nevertheless, I obeyed her behest. We started our conversation with a pleasant chat about bringing up children, especially when they were alone in the family without playmates. I realized she was hesitating over coming to the point. All the time the minutes were slipping by.

Eventually she took the plunge; her situation as President of the Congress was very delicate. She had been warned that the Catholics would withdraw from the Conference if the resolution were passed, and hoped, therefore, I would not find it necessary to speak for it.

"But," I protested, "I've been invited especially to present this question."

"You could substitute another subject which might be of greater importance to India."

"But what?" I asked.

"Well," she suggested, "why not brothels? It's a disgrace to have brothels in India—mind you, there are none in Travancore. Indian women won't mention them, but you're an American—you can. What we need most is to do away with brothels."

I could readily see the Maharani's position. Her social secretary was a Catholic, and large numbers of her Eurasian subjects were of the same faith. But I said the needs of millions of women in India were more urgent than the demands of a few Catholic missionaries. She took it beautifully and agreed. "I shall stay here because I feel the discussion ought to be full and free," she said. "I only want you to tell Mrs. Feridoonji to give your opponents two speakers for every one on your side."

There was considerable heat. No Indian women were against it, only converted Eurasians; all mothers were for it and all those against it were unmarried. Never had I heard so much talk of the lusts and passions of men as from the latter. They put forth the same old arguments, absolutely as though a phonograph record had been sent around the world. Nothing could have been more monotonous, repeated as they were from press, platform, and books. You might challenge them, break them down, correct them, but to no avail. The greater the vehemence, the more brilliant the opposition thought it had been. You had to ask yourself, "How did I phrase that answer twenty years ago?" We were utterly tired out when the vote was at last counted; we had won by eighty-four to twenty-five. The Catholics kept their word. None came back that afternoon. But, since it was the end of the Conference, this also did not matter.

The following day I was off to lecture in Madras, Anna Jane to visit in Ceylon. The solicitous Joseph intimated he was needed more to pick up after her than after me. "All right," I agreed. "But you don't have to take the luggage with you. Put it in my compartment." Joseph, however, made a mistake and established me on the wrong train; it went no further than Madura. The next morning about eleven everybody was told to get out, and there I was with seventeen pieces of luggage of my own and as many more of Anna Jane's.

It so happened that a young doctor of Calicut, Manjeri Sundaram, had at Trivandrum invited me to speak in his city. When I had replied that I could not at this juncture, he had pleaded, "I'll go wherever you go. I must talk to you lots and lots and lots. Whenever you're not sleeping if you'll allow me please to come with you and talk to you." I had discouraged him in a most thorough manner, but now he came up to help with my luggage and secured coolies to sit on it while we saw some thirty acres of temple.

At Madras, in the Tamil country, the turbanless natives were much darker, the costumes white and uninteresting. Sir Vepa Ramasan took me in charge. He was a retired judge of the High Court, a very imposing man of means who had devoted much of his wealth to a little Malthusian magazine and stirred things up ever since 1930. As was customary, the meeting he had arranged was from five to six, a period which by Occidentals is spent ordinarily over tea, cocktails, or apéritifs, but put by the Indians to good use. The men had left their offices by that time; it was cooler and still they could get home for dinner.

Sir Vepa, handsome, dominant, erect in bearing, not at all appearing his age, was chairman. Once my forty-minute talk was over, he called for questions in his rich, clear voice. A man produced one I thought was simple, but Sir Vepa eyed him severely, "That is not allowed!"

"I'll ask it in a different way." And he did so.

"I still say it is not allowed!"

"May I ask another?"

"Let me hear it."

Sir Vepa heard it, and dismissed it. "That's in the same category—argument!"

The man jumped up and protested loudly. "Sit down!" roared Sir Vepa, and the man sat as though he had been hit on the head.

Someone else, five or six seats off, brought up a new question, which also seemed easy enough to answer. But again Sir Vepa ruled, "That does not belong to the subject!"

The man wilted.

Now the first questioner was passing a paper over his shoulder to a third Indian who shook his head violently; he declined to be mixed up in it.

Query after query was disallowed. Finally a weak voice on the side asked about the French birth rate. Sir Vepa turned on him and said, "You look like an intelligent person, but if you have sat for forty minutes listening to this address, and you have not understood it, then you are not intelligent enough to warrant a lady's coming ten thousand miles and wasting her breath!"

The audience was laughing at Sir Vepa's judicial sternness. I, on the other hand, was rather depressed. As we were leaving I said to him, "I wish you had let me reply to them."

His expression held surprise. "I've been answering them and battling with these same people for twenty-five years. They only come to confuse. They are enemies of the cause and I give them no quarter!"

That settled the situation in Madras.

Since I was no more than an hour by motor from Adyar, the former home of Annie Besant, who had been such an influence in the movement, I made a pilgrimage there. As I walked down winding pathways under huge banyans, cocoanuts, and bananas, ever and again glimpsing the lovely water of the Bay in the distance, I imagined I caught an echo of her words reaching across the decade since I had heard her explain the philosophy of reincarnation: the more you have evolved here on earth, the less certain it is that you will have to return to undo your mistakes—best clear them up as you go along.

Annie Besant, as soon as she had become a Theosophist, had withdrawn her books on population. I was interested to find out the attitude of present Theosophists towards birth control, and discovered that those at Adyar were persuaded of its importance. Among their beliefs was that great souls did not reincarnate unless the bodies of parents, their vehicles for birth, were perfect. If they were to perform their missions, they must wait for purity in their physical vestures.

I had determined to take advantage of Paul Brunton's offer and visit Sri Ramana Maharshi, the sage of Arunachala, the quondam Hermit of the Hill of the Holy Beacon, and one of the last of Hindustan's race of noble rishis. Consequently, one evening a little after six, the train came around the bend and I beheld the sacred mountain, according to ancient lore the heart center of the god Siva and, therefore, of the world. I knew it must be *the* mountain even without being told so. The sun had just set, and the afterglow gave a lovely, serene effect.

The Maharshi's secretary, Shastri, met me, and we walked through the gathering dusk to the guest house about a half-mile away, a simple room with veranda in front. Paul Brunton had not been able to come because it was the Maharshi's birthday and thousands of devotees had to be fed. Shastri was very loquacious, and wanted me to realize that the apparent success I was having was only with the educated classes; the masses knew nothing of it. This, I said, would come in time.

After breakfast I looked out at the great tamarind trees on the lawn, up and down which monkeys ran. Often twenty, from babies up to grandparents, were in sight all at once. The windows had to be barricaded at night to shut them out of your room; they especially loved bananas but did not disdain cakes of soap.

While I was watching them scamper about, Paul Brunton pedaled up on a bicycle accompanied by a tonga for me. The driver cried out continually, "Haiee! Haiee!" which seemed to mean both for people to get out of the road and for the white bullock to move faster; he shouted himself hoarse at other drivers, who went higglety-pigglety this way and that through the streets. We stopped at the market for a few bananas as a gift for the Maharshi; he preferred food to flowers, because this he could give away. Then we trotted along through the thickly settled village, always hearing far and near the rumbling of the carts and the screeching of the drivers, "Haiee! Haiee!"

At last we reached the *ashram* at the bottom of the Hill. Shastri gathered up the bananas in his hands, but no sooner had he turned to help me out of the tonga than a temple monkey leaped from a neighboring tree, snatched two of them, and as quick as a flash had the skins off and had gobbled them down with no concern whatsoever as to the ethics of his conduct. Instead, he peered around for another grab.

Shoes and sandals were left outside the *ashram,* and Shastri went ahead to announce my arrival. I bowed in the entrance and took my place on the floor just within, crossed my legs under my skirt, and looked about me to feel and sense the atmosphere. The Maharshi, naked save for a loin cloth, was sitting cross-legged on a silk-covered couch, pillows behind him and a leopard skin thrown over the foot. A small charcoal fire and incense, which attendants kept burning all day, sweetened and made heavy the air. The Maharshi's luminous eyes were fixed in a trance, although sometimes his fan lifted a bit and his stare widened.

At first it was nicely quiet; then some women began to sing in a high-pitched tone, much through the nose and head, doubtless good for the pineal gland, once supposed to be the seat of the soul. The men chanted aloud and someone played a stringed instrument.

Towards eleven the Maharshi shared his gifts among those who sat in reflection, and shortly afterwards a man from Kashmir, six feet tall and massively built, entered, prostrated himself as hundreds had done already, falling full length, hands outspread above him on the floor, touching his brow three times. As he rose again his whole body shook, tears streamed down his cheeks. To see women cry from excess of emotion did not bother me, but when a man of such a type as this, in no sense a weakling, went into paroxysms of ecstasy, it was beyond my comprehension. With no critical intent, but curious to know why he had been so moved, we asked what had happened to him.

"When I came into the Maharshi's presence it was as though electricity had passed through my body. I felt when I bowed I would be calmed, yet when I looked into those eyes, he was like a flame."

This pilgrim had come with financial problems, illness in his family, and other troubles, but two or three hours of contemplation had wiped them out; he knew they were insignificant and trivial in contrast to his regeneration. In faith, the people in the *ashram* were comparable to those who cast away their crutches at some miracle-working shrine, except that they had come for inner illumination rather than healing for bodily ailments. They visited the Maharshi to receive the radiance of his soul, just as we sought the sun to be warmed.

Only when children or babies were made to prostrate themselves did the Maharshi smile, somewhat skeptically it seemed to me. He appeared amused when a boy of three or four began a prayer in Tamil but forgot the rest. Otherwise he remained apart from it all. He was gradually withdrawing himself and letting go material things. He wanted spiritually to fade away, leaving the shell behind.

The second day the Maharshi slept; nothing save an occasional singer broke into the hush, or a monkey had the temerity to dash in and seize an orange.

For the third day I attended the *ashram*. Now the meditation was like a linking up of mind and emotion, where even breathing was stilled. I could understand why the yogis went into the silence. Even the noises next door, the clatter of dishes, sounded remote and very far away. It was a state of consciousness rather like that which precedes sleep.

I regretted that I did not feel the Maharshi's power. His utter indifference—sitting all day in a semi-trance, engaging in no activity—seemed to me a waste. Nevertheless, I was most grateful to Paul Brunton for the experience, and understood the Indians better thereafter. They saw within and beyond the external appearance; this was at the very basis of their character, akin to the sensitivity of the grapevine telegraph. All people in the Orient spoke of it. Something happened to you or to me and before you could get to another place by the fastest conveyance it was known. Perhaps it was a primitive function of mind, this form of thought transference, but it existed there.

Dr. Sundaram, who popped up again when I returned to Madras, was still insistent that I go to Calicut, and I finally gave in. I was glad I had done so, because this city of forty thousand, ringed around a bay on the Malabar Coast and caressed by gentle breezes, was a beautiful spot with forests of palms. The almost-black women wore saris of vari-colored blues and greens, violets and yellows, with garlands of jasmine about their necks, plump, formal bouquets of roses in their hands, and in the center of every forehead was a circular red caste mark.

The meeting was held in the courtyard of a Buddhist temple. The sun was setting and part of the shell-pink sky was melting into deep carmine, like a flower. Directly in front sat three priests, each with shaved head, orange robe, and thick stave. Hundreds of rooks were chattering and other birds twittering in the trees, children were shouting at their games, the shrill chant of pilgrims walking through the streets saturated the dust-filled dusk. Mainly you heard the tinkling of the bullocks going up and down the road. The audience sat in utter silence surrounded by all these sounds.

Two days later we motored through the heavy woods to Mysore. Joseph, still coughing until it racked his frame, had rejoined me. I took my little drug shop and administered Vitamin A and D tablets, curing him and achieving thereby a reputation. Other Indians began hunting up colds and asthma and pains, and coming to me to give them some American medicine, in which they had much faith.

Soon I was on the train to Bangalore, again as state guest. The Dewan of Mysore, Sir Mirza Ismail, knew everybody in Europe, was well informed on Western methods of health, and was full of ideas about public buildings, roads, streets, industries, and the great dam which was to furnish electricity for the state. He was the first person in India who inquired after Katherine Mayo. I had been expecting to meet antagonism because of *Mother India*, which I myself now considered misleading. Certainly the conditions when I was there seemed vastly different from those she had depicted only a few years earlier.

The British believed every word true, but most of the Indians I saw looked upon Miss Mayo as having gone into their homes and then betrayed their confidences. They claimed she was definitely prejudiced, and, like the clever craftsman she was, had fixed her statistics. For example, when she discussed the age of marriage, she made sweeping statements and quoted on page so and so of such and such a report; you turned there and they were correct, and that was the reason for the astounding acceptance of her book. Nevertheless, she had violated the spirit, because two pages further in the same report followed an explanation of, or exception to, her conclusions.

Mirza Ismail, a Mohammedan, thought she had benefited Indians by shaking them awake, and that the facts she had brought out, even if not true of all the country, should be corrected; that India had to defend herself was good for her.

After visiting Hyderabad, which was pleasant and social, and after seeing this startling landscape in which the mountains seemed to have been smashed by a giant maul into enormous pieces, I started towards home. India was a land of dramatic contrasts—the highest mountains, the hottest plains, the densest jungles, the most violent rains. The loveliest architecture in the world was set against a background of nauseating squalor. Wealth beyond calculation existed alongside poverty that was living death, dazzling mental attainments beside an ignorance utterly abysmal. I could not tell precisely what the results of the trip had been; these rarely came immediately. And, if you had to hammer away and hammer away for years in the United States, you had to do it ten times over in India.

A terrific change in temperature froze me at Hong Kong; the poor huddled around little fires in the streets. Dr. Arthur Woo, a Rockefeller Foundation protégé, enthusiastic, full of energy, like magic procured quarters for me in one of the crowded hotels on the top floor, quiet and restful but, oh, how cold!

According to my schedule I was to remain twenty-four hours, into which were to be crammed a lunch, a tea, a lecture, a Chinese supper, and a public meeting. Then I decided to stay over a day for a medical gathering. Ho Kum Tong, a wealthy Chinese, provided another luncheon in his beautiful home.

In Hong Kong I heard rumors of a practical scholar in eugenics, in which the Chinese were very much interested. He was said to have, in addition to a wife, thirty concubines, by each of whom he had had three children. One of the Negro offspring—tall, kinky-haired, and oblique-eyed—was a most extraordinary-looking youth; he did not appear to belong anywhere. The daughters were much larger of stature than the average Chinese; all were educated and doing excellent work. Not only the features of the cultured types on the Island, but even those of the coolies, the longshoremen, struck me as growing less Oriental and more Anglo-Saxon, the foreheads fuller, the eyes less slanting.

When I reached Japan I found that Westernization had leaped ahead. Tokyo was not the same city I had seen in 1922—automobiles and wide-paved streets, many bicycles, many men and small children in European dress. Everywhere also was an atmosphere of tenseness on account of the assassination of the cabinet members about ten days before. Telephone communication in English was forbidden; people in Yokohama were unable to get to Tokyo because all transportation was cut off. War seemed inevitable. Baroness Ishimoto told me the activities of her organization had been curtailed, but articles and discussion and the spreading of knowledge had continued. The dissemination now was as it had been in France—from house to house, family to family, by word of mouth instead of under proper auspices.

At the end of a dismal voyage to Honolulu, I had hardly registered at the hotel when I heard a feminine voice in my ear, "Are you Mrs. Sanger?"

"Yes."

Dr. Muriel Cass, as this welcoming committee turned out to be, knew that I was recently out of a hospital, and disappeared for a few moments to telephone for a doctor. When he arrived she said, "All we want of you is to give Mrs. Sanger something to keep her going. She's got eight lectures to deliver."

I felt like a poor old war horse being fed the last measure of oats. I had a horrible memory of two weeks of fog and rain and cold at Memorial Hospital in Hong Kong, and now here I was to die in Honolulu.

But Dr. Cass, an efficient, self-sacrificing manager, did the most amazing things for me. She ordered the telephone operator to switch every call to her. There I was, quite alone. Nobody could see me or even talk to me; I must conserve my strength for the meetings. Repeatedly she rushed me to and from halls, put me in cars, and trundled me off to bed. Really I was better after each lecture than I had been before. When I left Honolulu she herself was so worn out she had to take a vacation, but I was nearly well.

The hospitality and luxuriance of this Pacific paradise were almost indescribable. Hula-hulas at the hotels, bathing on the beaches, outriggers swooping in, the native women in great flowered Mother Hubbards twining leis, the songs they sang, the air of leisure and fun and play, these made Honolulu a city apart. It was the sounding board of the Orient, people going, people coming back, but all there to enjoy themselves.

In Honolulu I repacked and, to save space, stuffed Grant's tiger skin in the trunk around my box of Darjeeling tea. When, four weeks later, I ripped off the cover at Willow Lake, it was reeking with camphor. I tried to aerate the leaves, dry them out, fumigate them with sunshine, but it remained moth ball tea. One package I had given away before I discovered the tragedy. Its receipt was ignored. No thank-you letter, no mention of it. The other friends to whom I had planned to present this choice gift had to go without.

I spent the summer at Willow Lake and in the winter, remembering Arizona from the time I had been there with Stuart, went out again in response to the summons of the desert. My husband and I found a house near Tucson of adobe, trimmed in blue. The mountains, not distant or aloof or towering over all, reached into the sky, but they were also somehow intimate, cupping the town gently on all four sides.

You settled there in the Catalina foothills and felt such a part of the whole. The first thing when you opened your eyes, before actual dawn, you beheld the gold and purple and then the entire sky break into color. In the evening the sunsets were reflected on the mountains in pink-lavender shades; sometimes the glow sprayed from the bottom upward, like the footlights of a theater, until the tips were aflame. Sunset vanished as quickly as sunrise, never lingering long.

When the marvel of spring came to the desert, you saw the cactus and the flowering, saw the brown floor change to delicate pale yellow, stood in awe of nature daring to live without water. You were reminded of the futility of wearing out your life merely providing food and raiment. Like the challenge of death, which so many of the people there were gallantly facing, the desert itself was a challenge.

Chapter Thirty-nine

SLOW GROWS THE SPLENDID PATTERN

"There is no force in the world so great as that of an idea when its hour has struck."
VICTOR HUGO

⋙⋙⋙⋙⋙⋙⋙⋙⋙⋙⋙⋙⋙⋘⋘⋘⋘⋘⋘⋘⋘⋘⋘⋘⋘⋘

LOOKING back at the past is like peering from some promontory upon a varied landscape. The years run through it like a road winding through a valley. With the passage of time you get a far-sweeping view, and the small details become blurred and difficult to recall. I wonder whether there should not be a school course to emphasize the importance of keeping diaries, so that you would know the really momentous happenings to put down. Mostly you scribble notes intended to call up a picture rather than an actual account of what has happened—memoranda of dates, engagements and events, leaving the results to recollection. Some inequality in this chronicle as to what is significant and what is not—some gaps in my remembrance of events—may have been the result.

It is strange what tricks the mind can play. My father, the person who had done most in shaping my growth, died in 1926 at the age of eighty. The day he was buried in Corning I was passing the bank on the corner of the town square with my brothers Dick and Bob, and we chanced to glance simultaneously at the clock tower. Faintly startled, we gazed at each other and Dick exclaimed, "Look at that little tiny thing! I've always thought it was as big as the Eiffel Tower!"

In all of our travels each of us had been convinced that nothing ever was so tall as that tower. That can happen to so many youthful memories. Months and miles that seemed so long then are so short later.

The same year that took my father summoned also my sister Mary, whose cruel immolation at the shrine of family duty had obliged her to forego marriage; even though I had seen her but seldom, she, too, had had an important influence over me and remained a dear presence whose loss I felt deeply. Out of eleven children seven are still living. Families have a separate and distinct role in your existence. They are closer yet more apart than friends, but often you discover that you have nothing save the ties of childhood to keep you together.

What I have been able to contribute to the birth control movement has been the result of forces which set a clear design almost from infancy, each succeeding circumstance tracing the lines more sharply: my being born into a family so large as to be in part responsible for my mother's premature death; my preparation as a nurse, which awoke me to the sorrows of women; the inspiration of having come into contact with great minds and having claimed many as friends. It may have been destiny as some have said—I do not know.

To have helped carry the cause thus far has been at times strenuous, but I have never considered it a sacrifice. Every conscious hour, night and day, in any city, in any country, has brought its compensations. My life has been joyous and exulting and full because it has touched profoundly millions of other lives. It is ever a privilege to be a part of something unquestionably proved of value, something so fundamentally right.

From time to time wonder is expressed that so much has been accomplished in so short a period. The fact remains that in an era when huge fortunes have been spent in alleviating human misery progress has been painfully slow. Countless women still die before their time because the bit of knowledge essential to very life is still not theirs. Birth control must seep down until it reaches the strata where the need is greatest; until it has been democratized there can be no rest.

It is true that great advances have been made in the realm of theory. You can almost tell people's age now by their attitude towards birth control. To the young it is merely one of the accepted facts; if questioned, they assume the whole matter must have been settled long ago.

Over and over again in the past a new epoch has adopted a concept censured by the preceding one, and has wondered derisively how its forefathers could have been so blind to anything so obvious. The use of anesthetics for mothers in childbirth was once condemned as an unholy attempt to escape the Biblical curse pronounced against all women, and, similarly, evolution as striking at the roots of Christianity. Battles over impiety, heresy, blasphemy, obscenity have been fought, temporarily lost, and finally won. Science whittles away such obstructions little by little. "The Moving Finger writes; and having writ moves on." In January, 1937, in that same Town Hall where fifteen years before I had been forbidden to speak, and whence I had been haled into court, I was honored with a medal. Pearl Buck said on one occasion, "The cause conquers because youth is for you. I have lived in China so long, and know what it is to wait until the old ones die and the young can do what is necessary to be done." I am glad both my sons are doctors with a background of human interest to which has been added a scientific quality of mind that can aid in pushing the horizon of service further into the future.

I am often asked, "Aren't you happy now that the struggle is over?" But I cannot agree that it is. Though many disputed barricades have been leaped, you can never sit back, smugly content, believing that victory is forever yours; there is always the threat of its being snatched from you. All freedom must be safeguarded and held. Jubilation is unwarranted while the world is in warring turmoil, each political unit trying to hold on to what it has—some threatening to take it away and others looking covetously towards outlets in countries not yet completely filled. The application of the movement to nations which should, in the interests of peace, control their populations, must endure.

Before 1914 the world trend was towards unity and peace. But a typhoon then caught us and turned us upside down. We began to whirl violently in one direction—that of individual and national emancipation, until at last the great wind blew crowns from the heads of Tsars and Kaisers, sweeping power into the hands of the populace.

When that War had first burst upon a shocked world people everywhere stood aghast and wept for the slaughter of men they did not know. But after four years, in self-defense, they armored themselves against the emotion which should be aroused by any cruelty, and became calloused and hardened until the deaths of thousands left nations unmoved.

Then came the vortex, the center, of the storm, and we awaited breathless the approach of the opposite edge. Everything had been lashed down in readiness, the life lines had been strengthened. Finally, all we had considered constant in rational thought, morals, ethics, started to go with equal violence in the other direction towards dictatorship and nationalism and race prejudice—a giving over of individual freedom. The immediacy of the deaths of women in childbirth seemed so small in comparison, of so little consequence; no longer were felt the pains of problems which used to be of such deep concern.

Over and over again I hear, "How do you fit birth control into a world in which dictators are clamoring for more and yet more people?" I can only answer that momentum must now derive its power from some other source than arousing sympathy. The present insensitivity is due to a horror of hovering peril. Many will be swept away and destroyed but when the battered hulls of the various ships of state emerge into calmer seas, a lesson may have been learned, perhaps, whereby these vessels may be made more seaworthy.

The Greeks, with their innate genius for dramatizing basic truths in images of telling beauty, established of old the relay torch race, or Lampadephoria, in honor of the Titan Prometheus, who had bestowed the divine gift of fire upon humanity. The contest was held at night, the great flambeaux being appropriately kindled at the altar of Eros. Participation was not a distinction indiscriminately conferred; those elect were fitted by discipline to hand on the vital flame, just as parents need training before becoming eligible for their grave responsibilities. The figures speeding around the course symbolize the passing on of the spark of life from generation to generation. Each runner must deliver his torch undimmed to his successor.

"Build thou beyond thyself," said Nietzsche, and this the birth control movement is doing. All peoples will in the future have greater regard for the quality of the bodies and brains which must be equipped for the task of building the future civilization; birth control will be the cornerstone of that great structure.

INDEX

Abbott, Leonard, 74
Abortion, 89ff., 217, 285, 449, 450
Academy of Medicine, 181, 358, 404, 405, 410
Ackermann, Frances Brooks, 188, 260, 261, 392, 395, 417
Adams, Maude, 37, 38
Agra, 479
Albany, N.Y., 208, 292, 411
Aldred, Guy, 136, 274
Allahabad, 479
Allison, Van Kleek, 207, 211
American Birth Control League, 300, 359, 369, 392ff., 409, 415
American Civil Liberties Union, 309
American Federation of Labor, 78, 80, 421
American Medical Association, 416, 421, 430
American Public Health Association, 298
American Women's Association, 413
Ankelsaria, Dr., 476ff.
Anti-Religious Museum, Leningrad, 440
Arizona, 459, 460, 491
Armory Exhibition, N.Y., 68
Ashley, Jessie, 71, 96, 100, 101, 207, 232, 234, 252, 264
Astor, Lady Nancy, 390, 391
Atlanta Ga., 413

Bamberger, Charles J., 176, 258
Barber, Billy, 434
Barber-Surgeons' Hall, 462, 463
Barcelona, 154ff.
Baroda, 479ff.; Maharani of, 480, 481
Barr, Sir James, 272
Bass, Mrs. Robert P., 459
Batum, 455
Bavaria, 287ff.
Bedborough Trial, 135
Bell, George H., Commissioner of Licenses, 252
Bellamy, Edward, 268

Bellows, George, 74
Belmont, Mrs. O. P., 381
Benares, 476, 478ff.
Bendix, Dr. Kurt, 389
Bennett, Arnold, 186, 371
Berger, Victor, 83
Berkman, Alexander, 71, 314
Berlin, 1920, 280ff.; 1927, 388
Besant, Annie, 127, 142, 172, 485
Bijur, Justice Nathan, 252
Bird, Mrs. Charles Sumner, 460
Birth Control, history of, 125–129; morality of, 298, 301; origin of name, 107, 108
Birth Control Review, 252ff., 393, 395
Bland, J. O. P., 299
Block, Anita, 76, 96, 180
Blossom, Frederick A., 198, 210, 251, 253ff.
Bocker, Dr. Dorothy, 358ff.
Bombay, 466ff.
Borah, Senator William E., 420, 422
Bose, Sir Jagardis Chandra, 475
Boston, Mass., 207
Boyce, Neith, 96
Boyd, Mary, 362
Boyle, Gertrude, 208, 296
Bradlaugh, Charles, 127, 142
Brattleboro, Vt., 368
Bratton, Senator Sam. G., 420
Brevoort Hotel dinner, 187ff.
British Museum, 124f., 130, 142
Brooklyn Eagle, 221
Brooklyn, Raymond Street Jail, 221ff.
Broun, Heywood, 263, 293, 373
Browne, F. W. Stella, 129
Brownsville, clinic, 213ff.; mothers, 231, 244, 414
Brunton, Paul, 462, 486
Brush, Charles, 417
Bryan, William Jennings, 39
Buck, Pearl, 495
Buckmaster, Lord, 370f., 398

INDEX

Buckner, Emory R., 313ff.
Bullitt, Ambassador William C., 443ff.
Bundesen, Dr. Herman, 361
Bureau of Social Hygiene, 78
Burns Detective Agency, 406
Byrne, Mrs. Ethel, 95, 186f., 208, 216, 224–234
Byrne, Jack, 42

Cairo, Egypt, 352ff.
Calcutta, 471ff.
Calicut, 488f.
Call, New York, 74, 76ff., 109
Cap d'Ail, 380
Caraway, Senator Hattie, 422
Carlile, Richard, 114
Carpenter, Alice, 187
Carpenter, Mrs. Benjamin, 361
Carpenter, Edward, 121, 130f., 139, 186
Carr-Saunders, Sir A. M., 379
Cass, Dr. Muriel, 491
Catalans, 162ff.
Catholics, 19ff., 218, 294, 303ff., 411ff.
Catholic Welfare Conference, 415
Caucasus, 454ff.
Chance, Clinton, 359, 379
Chautauqua, 34, 39
Chicago Conference, 361
Chicago, speaking experience in, 196
Clapp, Elsie, 118
Claverack College and Hudson River Institute, 35ff.
Clayton, Judge, 186, 189
Clinic, anecdotes, 399ff.; Brownsville, 213ff., 310; Dutch, 143ff., 290; English, 296; Massachusetts, 211; New York, 211, 298, 358, 398–407; origin of term, 143; plans to establish, 190f.; Rutgers system, 146
Clinical Research Bureau, 360, 398
Clyde, Mrs. Ethel, 433, 437, 444, 455
Coghlan, Father, of Corning, 20, 21
Colgate University, 365f.
Columbia Colony, 61, 268
Committee of One Hundred, 229, 231, 300
Communism, Bavaria, 288ff.; Russia, 436ff.
Comstock, Anthony, 77, 176
Comstock Law, 77, 111, 130, 182, 414, 427
Confédération Générale de Travail, 101
Conference, Chicago, 361; First National Birth Control, 298ff.; Fifth International, 337, 354; Los Angeles, 416; Regional, 416; Sixth International Malthusian and Birth Control, 369ff.; World Population Conference, Geneva, 376–388; Zurich, 408ff.
Connecticut, birth control legislation, 293f.
Content, Assistant District Attorney Harold A., 115, 120, 180ff., 189
Contraception, 104, 143, 290, 363f., 407ff.
Cooper, John M., Ph.D., 415
Copeland, Senator Royal S., 427
Cornell Medical School, 433
Corning, N.Y., 11, 19, 24, 27f., 43, 493
Corrigan, Magistrate Joseph E., 306
Coughlin, Father Charles E., 425
Courtney, Lieutenant Joseph, 313
Cousins, Margaret, 461
Cox, Harold, 172, 272, 296, 299, 303f.
Crane, Judge Frederick E., 292, 296
Crew, Dr. A. F., 380
Cummings, Attorney General, 428

Darjeeling, India, 475
Darrow, Clarence, 185
Dave, Victor, 100f.
Davenport, C. B., 374
Dawson, Baron, of Penn, 294f., 370f., 411
Day, Mrs. George H., Sr., 293, 396, 415
Debs, Eugene V., 69f., 351
Delafield, Mrs. Lewis L., 230, 304, 396
Dennett, Mary Ware, 180f., 189, 414, 416
Denver, Colo., 201
de Silver, Albert, 309
Detroit, 366
de Vilbiss, Dr. Lydia Allen, 298, 358
Dick, Mrs. Alexander C., 417
Dickinson, Dr. Robert L., 404f., 407, 430
Di Gregorio, John, 81
Dineen, Monsignor Joseph P., 304ff.
Dodge, Mabel, 72ff.
Dolphin, Martin W., 312ff.
Donohue, Captain Thomas, 304ff.
Drummond, Sir Eric, 379, 386
Drysdale, Bessie, 128, 290, 296
Drysdale, Dr. Charles R., 128, 143
Drysdale, Dr. C. V., 128ff., 178, 290, 296, 373
Drysdale, Dr. George, 128
Dunlop, Dr. Binnie, 129, 170
Durant, Ida Kaufman, 75
Durant, Will, 75, 434
Dutch Neo-Malthusian League, 143ff.

INDEX

East, Professor E. M., 364, 387
Eastman, Crystal, 108
Eastman, Max, 182, 185
Eddy, Sherwood, 435, 448
Egypt, 352ff.
Ellis, Edith, 137ff., 176
Ellis, Havelock, 75, 94, 133-141, 166, 276ff., 286, 370
England, 1914, 122ff.; 1915, 169ff., 268ff.; 1922, 354f.; 1924, 370ff.; 1927, 379, 381; 1936, 462ff.
Enright, Police Commissioner, 302
Equi, Dr. Marie, 205f.
Erie Railroad, 25
Ernst, Morris, 404, 406ff., 427
Esther, 36, 45
Ettor, Joe, 80, 83
Eugenics, 374f., 415

Fabian Hall address, 170
Fabian Society, Liverpool, 122
Fairchild, Professor Henry Pratt, 387, 420
Family Limitation, 112, 117, 119f., 121, 176, 182, 184f., 206, 232, 253, 262, 321, 342
Federal Council of Churches of Christ in America, 411
Federal Legislation, 414-428
Feminists, 187
Ferch, Johann and Betty, 373f.
Feridoonji, Mrs. Rustomji, 481ff.
Ferrer, Francisco, 74, 123, 162f.
Ferrer School, 74
Fischer, Louis, 448
Fishbein, Dr. Morris, 417
Fishkill, 357
Fitzgerald, Adelaide, 54
Fitzpatrick, George, 68
Flack, Principal of Claverack, 39
Flynn, Elizabeth Gurley, 72, 79
Flynn, Tom, 79
France, 99ff., 153
Freschi, Judge John J., 229
Frick, Henry Clay, 72
Friedrichshaven, 289f.
Frohman, Charles, 36f.
Fruits of Philosophy, 126f.
Fuller, Orson, phrenologist, 19

Gaekwar of Baroda, 480ff.
Galdós, Pérez, 164
Gandhi, 462, 465, 467ff., 481

Garth, Dr. William H., 396
Gartz, Kate Crane, 214
Gassoway, Percy, 427
General Federation of Women's Clubs, 430
Geneva, Switzerland, 378ff.
Genss, Dr. Abram B., 450
George, Henry, 17f., 204, 268
Germany, 253f., 377, 388
Gillett, Senator Frederick Huntington, 419, 422
Gilman, Charlotte Perkins, 108
Gini, Corrado, 385
Giovanitti, Arturo, 80, 83
Giovanitti, Carrie, 81
Glasgow, Scotland, 96ff., 274ff.
Globe, New York, 74, 90
Goff, Judge John W., 314f.
Goldman, Emma, 72, 203, 207, 314
Goldstein, Dr. Ferdinand, 373
Goldstein, J. J., 224-238, 258, 305
Goldstein, Rabbi Sidney, 420
Gompers, Samuel, 78, 83
Grotjahn, Dr. Alfred, 388
Guy, Harry, 463

Hague, Netherlands, 145
Haire, Dr. Norman, 290
Hall, Bolton, 207, 234
Halton, Dr. Mary, 188, 212f., 266, 296f.
Hancock, Representative Frank, 423
Hand, Judge Augustus, 427
Hand, Judge Learned, 427
Hanihara, Masanao, 318
Hapgood, Hutchins, 74, 96
Harman, Moses, 374
Harris, Dr. Louis T., 407
Harum, David, 44
Hastings, Senator Daniel O., 426f.
Hastings-on-Hudson, 61ff., 96
Hatfield, Senator Henry D., 423, 426
Hatting, Magistrate Peter A., 311
Hawthorne, Charles, 96
Hayes, Archbishop Patrick J., 299, 306ff.
Haynes, E. P. C., 172
Haywood, William (Big Bill), 70, 75, 80, 84, 96, 100f., 104, 264
Hazel, Judge, 115, 118, 120, 180
Healey, Representative Arthur D., 424
Health Day, Moscow, 444
Henri, Robert, 74
Hepburn, Mrs. Thomas, 188, 293, 395, 417

Herrmann, Justice Moses, 229
Higgins, Anne Purcell, 11, 16, 27, 41
Higgins, Bob, 493
Higgins, Dick, 493
Higgins, Ethel, 22, 26, 42ff.; *see* Byrne
Higgins, Henry George McGlynn, 29ff.
Higgins, Joe, 27
Higgins, Mary, 14f., 34, 63, 494
Higgins, Michael Hennessey, 12ff., 27ff., 41ff., 114, 208, 265, 493
Higgins, Nan, 34f., 59, 63, 265
Himes, Professor Norman, 365f.
Hindus, Maurice, 434
Hirschfeld, Dr. Magnus, 286f.
Hirshfield, David F., 313
Hogan, Assistant District Attorney, 406
Holden, Dr. Frederick C., 407
Holland, *see* Netherlands
Holland-Rantos Co., 364, 396
Holmes, John Haynes, 253
Holt, Dr. Emmett, 297f.
Hong Kong, 348ff., 490
Honolulu, 318f., 491
Horder, Baron Thomas, 463
Houghton family of Corning, 28; *see* Hepburn
How-Martyn, Edith, 170, 379, 382, 386, 409, 465
Howe, Marie, 108
Hu-Shih, Dr., 340, 342, 347
Hull House, 196
Huxley, Julian, 379
Hyderabad, 489
Hylan, Mayor, 312f.

Ibsen, 435
India, 351, 461-490
Indianapolis, 199
Industrial Workers of the World, 69, 80, 102, 204f., 265, 447
Inge, Dean, 273, 377f.
Ingersoll, Colonel Robert G., 20f.
Institute for Experimental Medicine, Russia, 441
Institute for Protection of Motherhood and Children, Russia, 441, 450
Institute of Politics, Williamstown, 377
International Information Center, 461
Ireland, 277ff.
Ishimoto, Baron Keikichi, 296, 319
Ishimoto, Baroness Shidzue, 296, 319f., 322f., 491
Ismail Mirza, 489

Israel, Rabbi Edward L., 424
Italy, overpopulation, 377

Jacobs, Dr. Aletta, 142, 148, 374, 408
Jacoby, Dr. Abraham, 181, 188
Japan, 295f., 317-336, 346, 377, 490
Jaurès, Jean, 101, 143
Jensen, Fru Thit, 373
Johnson, Alvin, 384
Johnson, Professor Roswell H., 420
Junior League, 420

Kahn, Dr. Morris H., 226
Kaizo, 296, 316, 320, 325, 327
Kalimpong, 474
Kaminsky, Dr., 448ff.
Kato, Baron Admiral, 318
Kaufman, Viola, 416, 428f.
Kavanoky, Dr. Nadina, 437
Kennedy, Anne, 261, 292, 301, 303, 305, 396, 415
Kennedy, Dr. Foster, 407
Key, Ellen, 111, 389, 435
Keynes, John Maynard, 354f., 376
Killarney, 277
Kingsbury, John A., 414, 434
Knights of Labor, 20
Knoblauch, Mary, 252, 260, 351
Knopf, Dr. S. Adolphus, 364
Knowlton, Dr. Charles, 126
Knox, Assistant District Attorney, 189
Kollwitz, Käthe, 284
Komroff, Manuel, 74
Korea, 327f.
Krishnavarma, Shyamaji, 102
Ku Klux Klan, 366f.
Kyoto, 334ff.

Lahey, Chief Inspector, 309
Lapouge, Dr. G. O., 372
Larkin, Jim, 351
Latz Foundation, 412
Lawrence textile workers' strike, 80ff.
League of Nations, 378f., 383
Lebedova, Dr., 450
Lectures, Albany, 208; Boston, 207; Brattleboro, Vt., 367f.; Calcutta, 472; Calicut, 488; Chicago, 197; Colgate University, 365f.; Denver, 201; Detroit, 366; Glasgow, 274ff.; Indianapolis, 199; Ku Klux Klan, 366f.; Los Angeles, 203; Madras, 484; Minneapolis, 198; Pittsburgh, 196; Portland,

INDEX

Ore., 204; St. Louis, 198; San Francisco, 203; subject matter, 193ff.; Tokyo, 327; Women's Co-operative Guild, London, 274
Lehr, Representative John C., 424
Lewis, Burdette G., 228
Liebknecht, Karl, 284
Lifshiz, Anna, 210f., 258, 259, 428
Lippmann, Walter, 74, 188, 199
Little, Clarence C., 374, 378, 386
Livadia, 456
Liverpool, 1914, 122ff.
London, 124, 268; see England
Lopokouva, Lydia, 355
Los Angeles, 203
Lusitania, 176
Luxemburg, Rosa, 112, 284

McAdoo, Chief Magistrate, 403, 405
McCann, Warden Joseph, 240, 245
McCarran, Senator Pat, 426f.
McCormack, Mrs. Stanley, 383
MacFadden, Bernarr, 145
McGraw, Mrs. William, Sr., 366
McInerney, Justice, 177, 226
McNamara, Patrolwoman Anna, 403, 406
Madras, 484ff.
Maharani, see Baroda and Travancore
Maharshi, Sri Ramana, 462, 485ff.
Mallet, Sir Bernard, 379, 385f.
Malthus, Thomas Robert, 94, 125, 433
Malthusian League, 127; see Neo-Malthusian
Malthusianism, 387, 449
Manhattan Eye and Ear Hospital, 55
Marion, Kitty, 256ff.
Married Love, 171f.; see Marie Stopes
Marsh, Robert McC., 304, 312
Martin, Anne, 273
Martin, Mrs. Marjorie, 382
Marx, Karl, 68, 275, 439f.
Maternal Health Committee, 410
Mayo, Katherine, 461, 489
Megaw, Sir John, 464
Mehta, Mrs. Soudamini, 472
Mencken, H. L., 416
Mensinga, 143, 408
Methodists, 35f., 38, 421
Mill, John Stuart, 125
Millard, Dr. C. Killick, 273
Milwaukee, 411
Mindell, Fania, 197, 214ff., 230, 258
Minor, Robert, 200

Mischkind, Rabbi, 410
Missionaries in China, 344
Moffatt, Mrs. Douglas, 420
Moley, Professor Raymond, 307
Montserrat, 162
Moore, Mrs. Hazel, 417f.
Morgan, Anne, 414
Morrow, Dr. Prince, 78
Moscow, 439, 443ff.
Moscowitz, Judge Grover, 427
Motherhood in Bondage, 362
Mother India, 489
Moyston, Guy, 364
Mühsam, Erich, 288
Mundell, Dr. Joseph J., 424f.
Murphy, Patrolman Thomas J., 311ff.
Mussolini, 377
Mysore, 489

Naidu, Mrs. Sarojini, 466
National Birth Control League, 108, 180, 189, 196, 414
National Catholic Welfare Conference, 423
National Committee on Federal Legislation for Birth Control, 417
National Council of Jewish Women, 429
Nehru, Jawaharlal, 462, 479
Neo-Malthusian League, 124, 128, 169, 272, 290
Neo-Malthusian movement, 103, 107, 146ff., 169, 285, 290
Netherlands, 142-149
New Jersey, legislation, 294
New York County Medical Society, 405
New York Society for Suppression of Vice, 77, 176, 258
New York State Birth Control League, 211
New York State law, 211, 224, 292
New York Women's Publishing Company, 260
Norris, Senator, 419
Norton, Hon. Mary T., 420
Nursing training and experience, 46-57, 86-92

O'Brien, Joseph, 96
Odling, Mrs. Norman, 473ff.
O'Keefe, Judge George J., 229
O'Ryan, Major General John J., 295
Osborne, Thomas Mott, 198, 242

INDEX

O'Shea, William, 392
Owen, Robert, 126
Owen, Stanley, *see* Lord Buckmaster

Pandit, Ranji Sitaram, 479
Pankhurst, Emmeline, 112, 256, 293
Pankhurst, Sylvia, 276
Parents' Exhibition, 392
Paris, 99, 153
Park Avenue subway explosion, 57
Parker, Robert Allerton, 252
Parsons, Elsie Clews, 189
Paterson silk strike, 84
Pearl, Dr. Raymond, 364, 386
Peddie Institute, 431f.
Peking, 339ff.
Peking National University, 340
Peking Union Medical College, 342
Pepper, 359
Pessary, 143, 427
Peterson, Dr. Frederick, 297
Philips, Anna Jane, 462ff.
Philips, Mrs. John, 461
Physical Culture, 145, 152
Pictorial Review, 180
Pierce, Representative Walter M., 424
Pillay, Dr. A. P., 465
Pinchot, Amos, 192, 233
Pinchot, Mrs. Amos (Minturn), 229, 232f., 410
Pissoort, Dr. Elizabeth, 403
Pittsburgh, Pa., first state league, 196
Pivot of Civilization, 299
Place, Francis, 126, 294
Pollock, Simon H., 118
Pope, 411ff.
Population, Chinese, 347f.; conference at Geneva, 376-387; historical résumé, 125ff.; Japanese, 298, 326; Russian, 450; United States, 376; world, 376ff.
Porter, Noel, 274
Portet, Lorenzo, 123, 153ff.
Portland, Ore., 204
Post Office, New York, 110, 261
Potter, Rev. Charles Francis, 420
Prison experiences, 221ff., 240-250
Prostitution, Chinese, 345f.
Protestant Episcopal Church, 410
Provincetown, Mass., 95ff., 264
Putnam, Major General G. P., 172, 377

Queens County Penitentiary, 240-250

Rabbis, Central Conference of, 411
Rai, Lajpat, 351
Raid, Brownsville, 310; Fifteenth Street Clinic, 402ff.
Ramasan, Sir Vepa, 484f.
Rappard, Williams, 378
Raugh, Mrs. Enoch, 196
Rauh, Ida, 207, 234
Raymond Street Jail, 221ff.
Reed, John, 70, 84, 182, 264
Reedy, William Marion, 199f.
Reid, Mrs. Ogden, 306
Reiland, Dr. Karl, 307, 405
Reitman, Ben, 207
Reynal, Eugene Sugney, 54
Rhythm of Sterility and Fertility in Women, 412, 425
Ridge, Lola, 74
Riese, Dr. Herthe, 389
Riviera, 380ff.
Roberts, Walter A., 252
Robertson-Jones, Mrs. F., 384, 395
Robinson, Dr. William J., 171, 181, 207
Rockefeller, John D., Jr., 78, 315
Rocker, Rudolph and Milly, 280ff.
Rodman, Henrietta, 108, 187f.
Roman Catholic, *see* Catholic
Roosevelt, Theodore, 201
Rose, Florence, 433, 444f.
Rosenbluth, Magistrate, 404ff.
Ross, Edward Alsworth, 94, 364, 434
Ruben-Wolf, Dr. Marthe, 388, 449
Rublee, Juliet Barrett, 300ff., 310ff., 395
Russell, Chief Justice Richard B., 413
Russell, Lillian, 37
Russia, 290, 433-459
Rutgers, Dr. Hoitsema, 143ff., 290, 408
Ryan, Monsignor John A., 415, 423

Sacco-Vanzetti, 384
Sachs case, 89ff.
St. Moritz, 390
San Francisco, 203
Sanger, Grant, 65f., 76, 95, 97, 99, 116, 266f., 316ff., 332, 340, 350, 352ff., 431ff., 437, 443f., 459, 475, 491
Sanger, Margaret, Arizona, 459f., 491; Brownsville clinic, 213-223; Cape Cod, 94ff.; childhood, 24ff.; China, 337-348; Columbia Colony, 61; dramatic aspirations, 37; Egypt, 352ff.; England, 1914, 121ff.; 1915, 169ff.; 1920, 268; 1924, 370ff.; 1936, 462ff.; father, *see* Michael

Hennessey Higgins; Federal indictment, 114-120, 180-190; Fourteenth Street apartment, 208, 266; France, 100-105; Geneva, 376-388; Germany, 1920, 280-290; 1927, 388ff.; Glasgow, 1913, 96ff.; 1920, 273f.; home, Corning, 12, Hastings, 61ff., Tucson, 459f., 491, Willow Lake, 357; Hong Kong, 349f., 490; India, 461-490; Japan, 316-336; Korea, 337f.; lecture tour, 1916, 192-208; Liverpool, 122ff.; marriage to William Sanger, 58ff.; marriage to J. N. H. Slee, 355ff.; mother, *see* Anne Purcell Higgins; Netherlands, 142-149; nurse, 46-57, 86-92; Post Avenue apartment, 107; prison term, 238-250; Provincetown, Mass., 95ff.; radicals, 68-85; religious training, 21; Russia, 433-459; Sachs case, 89-92; St. Moritz, 389; St. Nicholas Avenue apartment, 59; Saranac, 58ff.; school, 27f., 33ff.; Scotland, 1913, 96ff.; 1920, 273-276; sisters, *see* Mary and Nan Higgins and Ethel Byrne; Socialism, 75ff.; Spain, 153-168; Switzerland, 299, 376-391, 408ff.; teacher, 40f.; Town Hall raid, 301-315; trial for Brownsville clinic, 224-238; Truro, 264; tuberculosis, 58; *Woman Rebel*, 106-120; World Population Conference, 376-388; Yonkers, 60; Zurich, 408ff.
Sanger, Peggy, 65, 95, 97, 99, 103, 116, 175, 181f.
Sanger, Stuart, 59, 61, 63ff., 66, 75, 95, 97, 100, 116, 316, 402, 404, 431ff., 459, 492
Sanger, William, 56, 58, 60ff., 66, 68, 76, 104, 136, 176ff., 258
Sangster, Margaret E., 264
Sara, Henry, 136, 173
Saranac, N.Y., 58
Schmid, Dr. Julius, 54, 59
Schmid, Julius, manufacturer, 364
Schreiner, Olive, 11, 138ff.
Schroeder, Theodore, 112
Scotland, 96ff., 274ff.
Selincourt, Hugh de, 172f.
Seoul, 338
Shanghai, 343ff.
Shatoff, Bill, 117
Shaw, Bernard, 138, 371f., 411
Siegfried, André, 380
Silecchia, Vito, 250, 423

Simkhovitch, Mary, 225
Simonds, Herbert, 364
Sinclair, Upton, 69, 457
Singapore, 350ff.
Skidmore, Consul General at Tokyo, 320f.
Slee, J. Noah H., 355ff., 379
Smedley, Agnes, 252, 253, 351, 388, 456
Social agencies, criticism, 196f.
Socialism, 23, 68ff., 75f., 96, 109
Spain, 153-168
Spargo, John, 68
Spinney, Mabel, 260
Spinney, William, 245
Spermatoxin, 442
Stalin, 437, 439, 446
Stalingrad, 452
Steffens, Lincoln, 68
Stillman, Clara, 180
Stoddard, Lothrop, 302
Stokes, J. G. Phelps, 73
Stokes, Rose Pastor, 74, 188
Stone, Dr. Abraham, 434
Stone, Dr. Hannah M., 360, 363, 374, 399, 403f., 434
Stopes, Marie, 171, 186, 272
Strike, laundry workers, 78; Lawrence textile workers, 80; Paterson silk workers, 83
Stritt, Frau Maria, 112, 285
Strunsky, Anna, 74
Stuart, Amelia, 36, 54, 208
Sullivan, matron at penitentiary, 240, 244
Sullivan, Mrs. Mary, 403f., 406, 408
Sumners, Hatton W., 424
Sun, New York, 110, 186
Sundaram, Dr. Manjeri, 485, 488
Swann, Judge Thomas, 427
Swazey, George, 258, 259
Switzerland, 299, 376-391, 408ff.
Syndicalism, 101f.
Syracuse, 411

Tagore, Rabindranath, 471f.
Taj Mahal, 479
Tarver, Representative Malcolm C., 424
Thomas, Albert, 379
Tiflis, 454ff.
Tilton, Dr. Benjamin, 396
Times, New York, 305f.
Timme, Mrs. Walter, 395, 417
Todd, Helen, 232, 258, 259
Tokyo, 322ff.

INDEX

Toss, Irish setter, 15f.
Town Hall episode, 301ff., 306, 495
Trautman, William E., 80
Travancore, Maharani of, 481ff.
Tresca, Carlo, 80, 314
Trial, Ethel Byrne, 226ff.; Fania Mindell, 230; Margaret Sanger, 230ff.
Tribune, New York, 191, 306
Trivandrum, 481ff.
Trudeau, Dr., tuberculosis specialist, 58f.
Truro, Mass., 26ff.
Tucson, 460, 491

Ullrich, Dr. Mabel, 198
Untermyer, Samuel, 183ff.

Vanderlip, Frank, 295
Vandeveer, Mrs. J. B., 419
Vickery, Dr. Alice, 128, 169f., 172, 178, 273
Volga trip, 451ff.
Voluntary Parenthood League, 414f.
Vorse, Mary Heaton, 96, 188, 264

Wald, Lillian, 225
Wales, 123
Walling, William English, 74
Walton, Sidney, 464
Walworth Center, 296
Webster Hall, 82
Welch, Dr. William, 385
Wells, Catherine (Jane), 270ff.
Wells, H. G., 186, 268ff., 299, 316, 370, 380, 440
Westminster School, 432

What Every Girl Should Know, 77, 216, 219, 224, 230, 256
What Every Mother Should Know, 77
Whelan, Grover A., 405
Whitehurst, Margaret, 220, 310
White Plains Hospital, 45-57
White, Stanford, 56
Whitman, Governor Charles S., 232, 233, 255
Willet, Howard, 54
Williams, Dr. John Whitridge, 420
Williams, Dr. Linsley, 405
Williams, William E., 256
Willson, Dr. Prentiss, 425, 430
Wilson, Assistant District Attorney, 312
Wilson, Dr. C. I., 421
Wilson, President Woodrow, 186, 268
Winsor, Mary, 303f., 306, 313
Witcop, Rose, 136, 173, 280
Wobblies, *see* I.W.W.
Woman and the New Race, 266, 299, 362
Woman Rebel, 106-120, 170, 173, 184, 252
Woman suffrage, 17, 38, 190
Women's Co-operative Guild, England, 273
Woo, Dr. Arthur, 490
Wood, C. E. S., 204
Woodward, Dr. William C., 417
Workhouse, Blackwell's Island, 228, 240
World, New York, 227, 229, 299, 306, 384
World War, 131f., 143f., 148ff., 253f.

Yalta, 456
Yarros, Dr. Rachelle, 361
Yoshiwara, Tokyo, 332, 333

Zurich Conference, 408ff.

HQ
764
.S3
A3
,1938a